Phillips

The Bedford Bibliography for Teachers of Writing

The Bedford Bibliography for Teachers of Writing

Seventh Edition

Nedra Reynolds
University of Rhode Island

Jay Dolmage
University of Waterloo

Patricia Bizzell
College of the Holy Cross

Bruce Herzberg
Bentley College

Bedford / St. Martin's Boston ◆ New York

For Bedford/St. Martin's

Executive Editor: Leasa Burton
Developmental Editor: Alicia Young
Production Supervisor: Samuel Jones
Marketing Manager: Marjorie Adler
Project Management: Books By Design, Inc.
Cover Design: Donna Lee Dennison
Composition: Books By Design, Inc.
Printing and Binding: Haddon Craftsmen, Inc., an RR Donnelley & Sons Company

President: Joan E. Feinberg
Editorial Director: Denise B. Wydra
Editor in Chief: Karen S. Henry
Director of Marketing: Karen R. Soeltz
Director of Production: Susan W. Brown
Associate Director, Editorial Production: Elise S. Kaiser
Manager, Publishing Services: Andrea Cava

Library of Congress Control Number: 2011921719

Manufactured in the United States of America.

6 5 4 3 2 1
f e d c b a

For information, write: Bedford/St. Martin's, 75 Arlington Street, Boston, MA 02116 (617-399-4000)

ISBN: 978–0–312–64344-7

Publisher's Note

Bedford/St. Martin's is pleased to make available this reorganized and expanded seventh edition of *The Bedford Bibliography for Teachers of Writing*. We are gratified by the response to the first six editions. Not only have they proved useful additions to the professional libraries of thousands of individual instructors, but they have also found a place on the reading lists for many graduate courses on the teaching of writing.

Since first appearing in 1984, both the *Bibliography* and the list of books in the back have expanded — the *Bibliography* to reflect the growth in the body of literature in composition studies and the list to reflect the growth of our composition program. Bedford Books was founded in 1981 as an independent editorial arm of the St. Martin's Press college division. The two publishing programs were combined in 1998 under a single imprint — Bedford/St. Martin's. Today, we are the largest publisher of college composition texts in the country. We are immensely proud of the authors we have attracted to this list and of the books they have worked with us to produce. We continue to believe that any publisher ultimately must be judged by the quality of the books it publishes. As we celebrate our thirtieth anniversary, we continue to invite such judgment.

Joan E. Feinberg
President
Bedford/St. Martin's

Preface

The opening sentence of the preface to the first edition of *The Bedford Bibliography* in 1984 stated that "The study of composition is well established as a specialization in English, a serious discipline worthy of advanced graduate work." The former claim was based on the growing quantity and sophistication of scholarship in the field, on the rising numbers of composition specialists being hired and tenured, and on the appearance of more and more courses on composition theory and pedagogy in graduate school offerings. Still, the claim that the field was "well established" may have been just a little tendentious—a statement of confidence and hope rather than a clear fact. Today, though, the study of composition is unequivocally well established, as evidenced by the number of independent writing programs or departments, as well as new undergraduate writing majors, at dozens of institutions.

The result of such growth is more scholarship: Composition scholarship has expanded in ways that could not have been imagined in the early 1980s, when a need for this kind of bibliography first became apparent. Extraordinary growth in the discipline has been particularly evident to us in the time since the sixth edition of the *Bibliography* published in 2003. Most notable is the proliferation of books, both edited collections and monographs. Relatively few books appeared in the 1984 edition—a half dozen collections of previously published articles and a couple of pedagogical books by single authors. In subsequent editions of the *Bibliography*, those numbers increased, to be sure, but in preparing for the current edition we faced hundreds of books in history, theory, literacy, technology, administration, and every branch of pedagogy. In addition, new journals have arisen and established ones have flourished. As composition increasingly distinguishes its research from that of literary studies, developments in, for example, visual rhetorics and other new media have made possible a wealth of resources for those teaching at a variety of institutions. More writing teachers are becoming familiar with genre theory or post-process pedagogies; at the same time, teachers are moving beyond classrooms through outreach initiatives—civic engagement and community service projects—that challenge instructors and students alike to confront issues of race, gender, class, and abilities. In addition, first-year composition is no longer the raison d'être of many writing programs, which opens up countless opportunities for research and instruction. As composition becomes more specialized, new tools are needed, and bibliographies like this one increase in value: There is simply more material to sift through, and busy instructors need guidance on what to read or how to proceed. This seventh edition of *The Bedford Bibliography* responds to changing needs by revising, winnowing, combining, and otherwise altering the categories and entries to reflect a dynamic field on the march.

Reviewing and selecting from this mass of material would have been impossible for the four of us alone. While we have benefited from suggestions offered by many readers and reviewers, for the current edition we have also formally enlisted eighteen consultants (identified and thanked in the Acknowledgments that follow) to sift through the materials in particular categories and suggest which books and essays should be considered for inclusion in the *Bibliography*. Making selections was a difficult task for all of us.

For the most part, we have attempted to adhere to the same guidelines in the seventh edition that shaped the first: selecting materials that represent the theoretical and pedagogical concerns in composition studies today and those that will be useful to the working teacher of composition. We recognize, however, that the *Bibliography* has been used in graduate courses in composition and that there are now hundreds of teachers who are specialists in the field. Although we continue to believe that the job of the *Bibliography* is to introduce the wide range of valuable scholarship in the field to the many writing teachers who are not specialists, we have also included citations for works of history, theory, and research that are not, strictly speaking, "immediately applicable to classroom practice" but that engage pressing issues for the discipline. We have made decisions about what theoretical issues, scholarly disputes, and research findings might or might not be of interest to a diverse audience and about which of the older pedagogical materials included in past editions of the *Bibliography* have retained or lost their usefulness. Some pieces that should be on the reading lists of courses in composition theory or cited as milestones in the development of the field will not necessarily be found here.

In this seventh edition of the *Bibliography*, we have grouped the 862 entries under six major headings and thirty-two subheadings (see the table of contents).

First, under the heading "Resources" appears information on basic tools for research in the field, in sections on "Periodicals" and "General Bibliographies." (Bibliographies on specific topics appear in the appropriate sections.) Under the second major heading, "Histories and Theories," we have four subheads. "The Rhetorical Tradition" cites primary texts from classical to modern times. "History of Rhetoric and Education" selects secondary texts covering the same time period, but a new category, "History of Composition Teaching," provides a home for those texts specifically about composition teaching and which date to the early 1970s. "Rhetoric and Composition Theory" collects important works, including Kenneth Burke's major contributions, on discourse, language, argument, genre, ideology, approaches to composition pedagogy and research, and other theoretical concerns.

The third major heading, renamed for this edition, is "Composing and Literacy." It introduces "The Process Movement and Post-Process Approaches," which includes entries that range over a period of nearly forty years. The next three categories are all new to the seventh edition and replace "Electronic Writing Technologies": "Digital Writing," "Visual Rhetoric," and "New Media" mark an evolution in the last decade or two from "e-mail" to Web 2.0, wikis, and different notions of authorship. Finally, "Literacy Studies," the fifth section under this heading, includes works on literacy theory, cultural literacy, literacy programs, diversity, and teaching issues associated with these concerns.

The fourth major heading, "Rhetorics of Writing," collapses several earlier categories into four: "Invention," "Audience," "Revision," "Grammar and Style"—each of these fairly self-explanatory in their emphasis on canons of rhetoric or stages of composing.

The fifth major heading is "Writing Programs," a fairly large umbrella. Those familiar with earlier editions of *The Bedford Bibliography* will notice several changes here. "Writing Program Administration" addresses program design and evaluation, teacher training, and includes a variety of stories, reports, and survey results. "First-Year Composition," a category new to this edition, sees FYC as just one of many subspecialties in our field. "Response and Assessment" includes works on responding to student writing, conference teaching, grading, and portfolios. Of grave concern for most writing programs are issues of "Contingent Labor and Working Conditions," gathered here in a category that was formerly titled "Wyoming Resolution." The category "Writing Centers" now includes "and Supplemental Instruction" to indicate that the support for writers associated with the work of writing centers is now expanding into cyberspace, residence halls, classrooms, and coffee shops; this section cites theoretical and practical works on tutorial workshops and tutor training. "Writing across the Curriculum" now includes "and Writing in the Disciplines" to acknowledge the differences in those two movements and provides material on cross-disciplinary course design and on faculty development in interdisciplinary writing programs.

The sixth and final heading is "Curriculum Development," which also covers considerable territory. The first section, "Course Development," includes works on writing course design and teaching, and then addresses special topics. Retained from earlier editions, "Essay and Personal Writing" highlights works on the genre of the essay and on voice in writing while "Literature and Composition" includes works on the theoretical connections between the two and on the use of literature in composition classes. "Basic Writing" features works that help teachers to understand the circumstances of underprepared writers, the conditions of multicultural basic writing classrooms, the kinds of errors beginning college writers make, and the effects on their writing of cultural and political considerations. New to this edition, "Genre Studies" shares books and articles on genre theory as well as approaches to genre across the curriculum. In an expansion that reflects substantial activity in this area, "Service Learning" is now "Service Learning, Civic Engagement, and Public Writing"; this category cites resources for developing writing courses and programs that include a community-based component. The intersections of "Gender, Race, Class, and Abilities" are represented in a section that addresses the influence of socially constructed gender roles and sexual orientation on writing, techniques for feminist teaching, and newer work on disability studies. The implications for writing pedagogy of "Cultural Studies" appears next, followed by "Teaching English as a Second Language and Language Policy"; this category addresses linguistics, second-language writing research, the literacy experiences of L2 students, and the politics of language. Issues concerning writing in the workplace are divided into two sections, "Technical Communication" and "Business Communication," and both categories evince new interest in visual and intercultural communication.

In the annotations of articles and single-author books, we attempt to summarize the thesis and main points of the work. In annotations of edited collections, of which there are now a great many, we characterize the central theme of the collection and then list several of the authors and essays included, choosing titles that give a sense of the contents of the collection. In collections of previously published articles, we include cross-references if the article has been cited separately. For edited collections of new essays, however, we have as a matter of policy not cited articles separately when the entire collection is cited. We have been partial to edited collections whose themes are carefully articulated and whose contributors have adhered to the volumes' stated purposes.

The entries in *The Bedford Bibliography* are numbered consecutively. Numbers in brackets, used for citations in "A Brief History of Rhetoric and Composition" and for cross-references in the bibliographic listings, refer to these entry numbers and can also be used to locate items in the index.

In selecting works for *The Bedford Bibliography*, our chief concern has been to provide access to materials that would be helpful to practicing writing teachers. Even so, we have undoubtedly left out much that is important, despite our efforts—and the efforts of our consultants—to be fair if not exhaustive. We welcome, as always, suggestions for revision.

Acknowledgments

We are particularly indebted to our consultants, without whom completing this daunting task would have been inconceivable. Thanks to Linda Adler-Kassner, University of California, Santa Barbara; Anis Bawarshi, University of Washington, Seattle; Joseph Bizup, Boston University; Marc Bousquet, Santa Clara University; Melody A. Bowdon, University of Central Florida; Dànielle Nicole DeVoss, Michigan State University; Sue Doe, Colorado State University; Lisa Gerrard, University of California, Los Angeles Writing Programs; Harvey J. Graff, Ohio State University; Amy Kimme Hea, University of Arizona; Melissa Ianetta, University of Delaware; Susan C. Jarratt, University of California, Irvine; Paul Kei Matsuda, Arizona State University; Bruce McComiskey, University of Alabama at Birmingham; Mike Palmquist, Colorado State University; Matthew Parfitt, Boston University, College of General Studies; Kelly Ritter, University of North Carolina–Greensboro; and Christopher Thaiss, University of California, Davis.

Thanks also to Alicia Young and Leasa Burton at Bedford/St. Martin's, both of whom helped us bring this edition to fruition. We are also indebted to Patricia Weisenseel, an extraordinary research assistant who brought order to chaos and made countless contributions. Andrea Cava expertly guided the book through production, and Nancy Benjamin carefully copyedited the manuscript. We can never forget that *The Bedford Bibliography* was the brainchild of Chuck Christensen, the guiding force behind all of Bedford's work, and we are grateful to Joan Feinberg for her continued support of this resource. Finally, we warmly thank those who have used the *Bibliography* and told us that they found it helpful. They have made this project worthwhile.

Contents

The Bedford Bibliography for Teachers of Writing

A Brief History of Rhetoric and Composition

Classical Rhetoric: Stages of Composing, Functions of Discourse

The formal study of rhetoric in the West began in Greece in the fifth century BCE with the Sophists [76], followed by Isocrates [65], Plato [71], and Aristotle [45]. The main line of Greek rhetoric was extended by Roman rhetoricians, notably Cicero [55, 56] and Quintilian [69, 72]. Classical rhetoric, although concerned with oratory, still influences writing instruction. For example, by Roman times a five-stage model of the process of composing a speech had evolved. Three of these stages—invention, or discovering ideas; arrangement, or organizing ideas; and style, or putting ideas into words—have been modified into elements in modern models of writing processes. Memory and delivery, the last two classical stages, dwindled in postclassical times into mechanical techniques before being revived for serious study in modern departments of speech.

Scholars traditionally regarded classical rhetoric as a system with the built-in assumption that one first finds knowledge and then puts it into words. In our own day, in the context of a renewed interest in the Sophists, this view has been challenged by a number of historians of rhetoric, who argue that knowledge is actually created by words (see Jarratt [107] and Swearingen [137]). But the strongest influence on rhetoric has undoubtedly been the Aristotelian model. Aristotle described a number of *topoi*, or topics, for discovering ideas and arguments. These topics—ways of analyzing, evaluating, and extending virtually any subject—constitute a heuristic, or method of systematic inquiry.

Scholars have also emphasized classical rhetoric's sorting of discourse forms according to social function. Many classical rhetorics divide oratory into three categories. Deliberative speeches, primarily devoted to political purposes, aim to persuade hearers to choose or avoid some future course of action. Forensic speeches, used primarily in legal situations, aim to accuse or defend someone involved in a disputed past action. Epideictic speeches, produced in classical times on ceremonial occasions, aim to help hearers see some present event or person as worthy of praise or blame. Epideictic orations may make more use than others of literary ornaments and vocal pyrotechnics.

Although these classical categories for oral discourse have been reshaped by later rhetoricians, the premise that discourse can be classified according to social function has been persistently influential. In eighteenth-century American colleges, for example, discourse was classified according to its use by clergymen, lawyers, or politicians. Contemporary composition scholars have redirected the interest in social function to analyses of the ways in which audience or social context affects the interpretation of written text.

Medieval and Renaissance Rhetoric

We often think of the Middle Ages as a time when many classical sources were not accessible: Quintilian and much of Cicero, for example, were lost until the Renaissance. But it is more accurate to see medieval rhetoricians selecting and reshaping the classical heritage in light of Augustine's reinterpretation of rhetoric to suit Christian purposes [47]. One important emphasis in medieval rhetoric following Augustine was the redirection of deliberative discourse from political to religious ends. The goal became saving souls, not leading the state. Another important emphasis was the desire to codify authoritative classical precepts on good composition. Classical rhetoric texts had often been prescriptive, providing rules for achieving effective speeches. In the Middle Ages, this prescriptive impulse so intensified that many medieval rhetoric texts consist entirely of lists of rules and examples illustrating them.

Medieval university students studied grammar, rhetoric, and dialectic—the "trivium." As exemplified in the popular classical textbooks of Donatus, grammar means not simply the study of correct constructions but also the analysis of style. The study of grammar thereby shaded over into the medieval study of rhetoric, which emphasized style. Grammar and rhetoric merely prepared the beginning student for the serious business of the university, the study of dialectic, which offered practice in oral argumentation on historical, religious, or legal issues. Bishop Isidore of Seville wrote an important summary of the arts of grammar, rhetoric, and dialectic.

Dialectic was regarded as a preparation for logic, the oral arguments of which became opportunities for stylistic display, but the subject was still not considered closely allied with rhetoric. The study of rhetoric was manifested, however, in techniques for adult practitioners, for example, in ars dictaminis, the art of composing official letters through which church and state business was conducted, and ars praedicandi, the art of preaching. Medieval theorists of poetry also drew on rhetorical studies of style.

In the early Renaissance, major texts by Cicero and Quintilian were recovered. In the sixteenth century, a proliferation of rhetorics following classical models but written in the vernacular appeared, such as those in English by Leonard Cox, Richard Sherry, Thomas Wilson, and George Puttenham. Most of these rhetoricians emphasized the study of style, sometimes linking their practice explicitly with poetic. The generally acknowledged master of stylistic rhetoric in the Renaissance was Erasmus, whose *Copia* (1512) [60] was originally conceived as a textbook.

Another source of change for Renaissance rhetoric was the influential work of Peter Ramus (Pierre de la Ramée), whose ideas were recorded in *Institutiones Oratoriae* (1545) by his colleague Talaeus (Omer Talon). Ramus wished to reform the medieval trivium by reemphasizing the classical division of the stages of composing. Ramist rhetoric intensifies the separation between these stages and the importance of their sequence, at the same time divorcing invention and arrangement from rhetoric and assigning them to logic. Ramists hoped to define a logical, scientific discourse, untainted by nonlogical appeals, that would win assent from the rational audience by virtue of rationality alone. Ramus' fellow Puritans widely adopted this plain style for all serious matters.

Rhetoric under the Ramist scheme is left to deal only with style, memory, and delivery. Memory had figured importantly in some early Renaissance hermetic precursors of modern science, and delivery would give rise in the eighteenth century to elaborate elocutionary techniques for public speakers and actors. Still, memory and delivery tended to continue their decline in importance as the Renaissance dissemination of printing made written texts ever more important to academic, religious, and political life. Rhetoricians, then, came increasingly to focus on the study of language as the dress of ideas that were generated elsewhere. The goal of rhetorical study was to clothe one's ideas in the most elegant dress possible, and rhetoric thus came to be seen as the finishing refinement of an upper-class education.

Rhetoric in the Eighteenth Century: The Scottish Influence

Seeing rhetoric as the study of the dress of thought rather than the study of thought itself threatened to trivialize it. Rhetoricians from the University of Edinburgh sought to stop this trend by arguing that the study of correct and persuasive style produced not only competent public speakers but virtuous people. This was a strong defense, for the study of rhetoric in American colleges focused on oratory that would be useful to clergy, lawyers, and politicians. In addition, the Edinburgh rhetoricians connected the study of persuasion with the more prestigious scientific discipline of psychology. And these rhetoricians adapted ornamentation from Cicero to correct the emphasis on plain style that the Puritans had kept alive from Ramism.

Perhaps the most influential book to come from Edinburgh to America was Hugh Blair's *Lectures on Rhetoric and Belles-Lettres* [51], published in 1783 and adopted as the standard text at Yale in 1785 and Harvard in 1788. Blair's text was widely used in American colleges and secondary schools until the end of the nineteenth century. Americans found Blair's emphasis on the moral qualities of belletristic taste particularly important, since his approach justified the social leadership of the well-trained orator.

Less popular in the schools but perhaps more important for modern rhetoric was another Scottish rhetorician, George Campbell, whose *Philosophy of Rhetoric* (1776) [53] professes to validate its principles by relating them to the working of the human mind. More innovative than his contemporaries, Campbell extended the purpose of rhetoric beyond persuasion, defining eloquence as the "art or talent by which discourse is adapted to its end."

A later rhetorician in the Scottish tradition was Alexander Bain, who showed the importance of psychology for achieving goals of persuasion in *English Composition and Rhetoric: A Manual* (1866) [49]. Bain argued that persuasive discourse is organized by associating ideas in a way that produces the desired emotion in the audience. From Bain's work comes the now familiar taxonomy of essay structures, or modes of discourse: narration, description, exposition, and argumentation.

In America, the Scottish revision of classical rhetoric had special significance. A nascent democracy, so the argument went, needed people of refinement who could direct the vulgar taste into virtuous channels; the psychology of persuasion could help these leaders consolidate their control. Hence, the study of rhetoric both conferred and garnered prestige. Long before American colleges had English departments, they had distinguished professors of rhetoric.

Rhetoric in Nineteenth-Century America: The Harvard Influence

In 1806 Harvard College established the Boylston Professorship of Rhetoric and Oratory and became, thereafter, the dominant influence on the development of rhetoric at other American colleges. Edward T. Channing, who held the chair for thirty-two years (1819–1851), continued the Scottish emphasis on belletristic taste and the psychology of persuasion but shifted the emphasis in practice from speaking to writing and increased attention to literary exempla. From the literary models, Channing derived rules for correct grammar, style, and organization, which were taught more and more prescriptively as the century went on.

Francis J. Child, who held the Boylston Professorship after Channing (1851–1876), had studied philology at a German university before taking the chair and came to Harvard determined to turn the study of English from rhetoric to literature. Child bitterly resented the time he had to spend correcting student compositions. He delegated as much of this work as he could to faculty underlings and concentrated on enlarging Harvard's offerings in literature. In 1876, to keep Child from moving to Johns Hopkins (the first American university to be organized in departments on the German model), Harvard created the first Professorship of English for him, and Child spent the next twenty years developing the English literature curriculum. His successor in the Boylston Professorship, A. S. Hill, continued the rule-bound focus on written composition begun by Channing, but it was now clear that composition was a second-class subject and that rhetoric was hardly mentioned in the English department.

These changes are neatly encapsulated in Harvard's 1874 entrance requirement in English composition:

> Each candidate will be required to write a short English composition, correct in spelling, punctuation, grammar, and expression, the subject to be taken from such works of standard authors as shall be announced from time to time. The subject for 1874 will be taken from one of the following works: Shakespeare's *Tempest*, *Julius Caesar*, and *Merchant of Venice*; Goldsmith's *Vicar of Wakefield*; Scott's *Ivanhoe* and *Lay of the Last Minstrel*.

The Harvard model of freshman composition began to spread, particularly with the publication in 1890 of Harvard Professor Barrett Wendell's *English Composition: Eight Lectures*. Blair and Bain had used literary exempla to illustrate rhetorical principles. In the Harvard course, this belletristic tradition culminated in rules derived from the exempla and rigidly applied to student essays. Furthermore, the works of literature to be studied were strictly specified in lists of standard authors, such as the one given in the entrance requirements. These lists soon came to dictate secondary-school curricula, since one needed to know the listed works to perform well on admissions tests at prestigious colleges. And the prestige of those colleges that regulated their admissions according to the lists made it hard for other colleges to avoid similar requirements.

Progressive Education in Twentieth-Century America

In the early twentieth century, more and more secondary-school and college teachers came to oppose the domination of college admissions by the standard lists of works generated at Harvard and other elite eastern schools. The National Council of Teachers of English (NCTE) was formed in 1911 largely to consolidate resistance to the lists and to the conception of English studies they represented. To further this cause, the NCTE began to publish *English Journal* in 1912 [10]. The first president of the NCTE was Fred Newton Scott of the University of Michigan. A past president of the Modern Language Association (MLA), Scott possessed impeccable credentials in literary scholarship; nevertheless, he deplored the demotion of rhetoric and promoted an understanding of writing that reemphasized self-expression and the adaptation of prose to its social purposes.

At the same time, departments of speech were growing more numerous in American colleges, taking over the study of historical rhetoric and many of its traditional concerns, such as response to audience. Speech teachers broke away from the NCTE in 1914 to form their own professional organization, the National Association for Academic Teachers of Public Speaking—now the Speech Communication Association.

English teachers' dissatisfaction with the reading lists soon became caught up in the larger progressive reform movement, which directly challenged the idea that the goal of higher education in America should be to empower an elite. The progressives believed that the purpose of education is to integrate a diverse population into a community of productive citizens. Progressive education sought to equip students with intellectual and social skills they would need as adults and to give attention to the needs of each individual student. John Dewey was an important leader of this movement. He became chair in 1894 of the Department of Philosophy, Psychology, and Pedagogy at the University of Chicago, and his *School and Society* was published in 1899.

Progressive education sought to free writing instruction from the service of canonical literary study. Correctness remained a goal of writing instruction, justified not by some authoritative set of rules but by its usefulness in the world beyond school. While respectful of the diverse cultural backgrounds of a school population that included record numbers of immigrants, progressive education stressed the communicative function of writing to help draw diverse groups together and integrate them into the mainstream of American society. A class writing project, for example, might collect data about some local social problem and prepare a report to be sent to the appropriate public official.

The progressives were not very often successful, at least on the college level, in separating composition and literature. In progressive hands, however, writing about literature became a way to understand one's own responses to the text. Such an approach can be found in Louise Rosenblatt's *Literature as Exploration* (1938) and in early issues of *College English* (*CE*), which the NCTE began to publish in 1939 [4]. As progressive education moved into the 1930s and 1940s, its social agenda became more modest, but the main goal was still life adjustment—helping adolescents pass through their difficult developmental period and emerge as productive citizens.

Progressive education was also innovative in its interest in the social sciences as a source of information for English studies. Of course, progressives were not the first to look in this direction; rhetoric in the eighteenth and nineteenth centuries had incorporated some study of psychology. But with the demotion of rhetoric in the late nineteenth century, contacts between English and the social sciences were downplayed. Progressive education, in contrast, aimed to study students' abilities, needs, and achievements scientifically and to redesign curricula accordingly. These efforts had very little effect on college writing instruction, however.

Freshman English courses were rarely devoted only to writing instruction. Their main goal was to introduce students to literary study and in the process to correct the writing in students' literary essays according to long-established standards of grammatical, stylistic, and formal correctness. Where writing courses did exist, they usually patterned their syllabi after Bain's modes of discourse and justified their existence with arguments similar to Blair's for the good writer as a virtuous person. Widespread changes did not begin to occur until after World War II.

Beginnings of Modern Composition Studies: New Criticism

In the 1930s, New Criticism began to supplant biographical and philological criticism as the dominant mode of academic literary study. New Criticism put its emphasis on the close analysis of literary texts and appeared to have no common ground with the current forms of rhetorical study or composition pedagogy. By the 1940s, at any rate, the separation in English departments between literary study and the teaching of writing was so complete that academics committed to literary study could easily ignore the writing program.

New Criticism ultimately had a profound effect on writing instruction, however, because it approached literary texts as complex structures of meaning. In its view, changing a word in a poem changed the poem's meaning—it did not simply select an alternative dress for an idea that remained unchanged. New Criticism therefore made it possible to see the relation between thought and language as fundamental rather than superficial. The freshman English course patterned on a nineteenth-century model (the current-traditional model, as it is often called) treated the relation between thought and language too mechanically. What could be taken for granted in the writing class quickly became problematic.

Recognizing the need for serious reconsideration of the freshman writing course, the NCTE mandated the Conference on College Composition and Communication (CCCC) in 1949. The journal *College Composition and Communication* (CCC) appeared in 1950 [3]. In the 1950s, the CCCC did much to lay the foundations for the modern discipline of composition studies. On the practical side, the CCCC worked to improve conditions for the graduate assistants who taught almost all college writing courses and to exchange ideas among college writing program administrators. The conference also championed the cause of semanticists and linguists looking for a home in college English departments and urged that the PhD in English literature include coursework in linguistics as preparation for teaching writing.

Reinforcing these efforts pertaining to college composition was the post-Sputnik concern in the early 1960s to encourage excellence in all areas of American education. To make the college writing course more rigorous, ways were sought to expand its focus beyond socialization or linguistics to the full traditional range of rhetorical concerns. Distinguished literary critics such as Wayne Booth began to write on rhetoric. In 1963, the NCTE published a survey of research to date in composition, compiled by Richard Braddock, Richard Lloyd-Jones, and Lowell Schoer. Little valuable work was found, but the study itself encouraged high standards for new research in the field. To give such research an outlet, the NCTE began publishing the journal *Research in the Teaching of English* in 1967 [23].

The 1960s: Classical Rhetoric, Writing Processes, and Authentic Voice

With the encouragement of the CCCC in the early 1960s, composition specialists looked to the classical texts that had rarely been studied in English departments (although speech departments had preserved an interest in them) and to transformations of the classical heritage by later rhetoricians. Several important collections of premodern documents on rhetoric and discussions of classical rhetoric's value to the modern student were published. This renewed attention to classical sources helped to foster an increased interest in stages of the writing process and in style as an expression of personal ethos.

The classical model is a five-stage process, consisting of invention, arrangement, style, memory, and delivery. After the Ramists excluded invention and arrangement, and memory and delivery dwindled into elocution, American writing courses, in their focus on one stage—style—had lost a sense of writing as a process. Now writing as a process was reemphasized in the study of what Gordon Rohman called the prewriting stages, those that precede production of a finished piece of work. Invention and arrangement began to be reclaimed for composition studies as preliminary stages in the writing process. Style, too, was seen as a process of developing ideas by recasting sentences, not merely pouring ideas into preset sentence forms.

Interest in the writing process and in writing as self-expression prompted the MLA and the NCTE to sponsor the 1966 conference at Dartmouth College on the teaching of English (see John Dixon [568]). Attended by American and British educators from the elementary, secondary, and college levels, the conference helped spread the conviction that writing instruction should emphasize self-expressive uses of language and assist students in shaping their ideas through writing. Unlike the Harvard-model course, which imposed standards on passive students, the new Dartmouth-model writing course encouraged more interaction among teacher and students, more dramatic and collaborative activities. One influential process-oriented pedagogy appeared in James Moffett's *Teaching the Universe of Discourse* (1968) [576].

The Dartmouth conference called for writing instruction that takes more notice of students' needs for self-expression as opposed to their adjustment to social demands. Now composition studies searched for a pedagogy to help students find personal writing styles that were honest and unconstrained by conventions. Such a style came to be termed the writer's authentic voice—an important concept in the work of Ken Macrorie [609] and Peter Elbow [152, 601]. The need for such pedagogy seemed especially poignant in the late 1960s and early 1970s, when many writing teachers sought some critical response to the opaque, impersonal prose that dominates politics. Authentic-voice pedagogy contributed techniques, such as Elbow's free-writing, that became part of every writing teacher's repertoire.

The 1970s: Cognitive Processes, Basic Writing, and Writing across the Curriculum

In the 1970s, interest in the writing process prompted inquiry into what cognitive psychology and psycholinguistics might discover about it. Composition scholars began to refer not to the "writing" process but to the "composing" process, as in the pioneering work of Janet Emig [199, 261]. The significance of this shift in terminology was its emphasis on the cognitive activities involved in writing. "Composing," in other words, is what goes on in the writer's head and is then recorded in writing. This interest in composing processes first focused on what had been the initial stages in the classical process: invention and arrangement. Theorists developed structured invention techniques that would guide the student through an optimal composing process. The particle-wave-field heuristic devised by Richard E. Young, Alton L. Becker, and Kenneth L. Pike [386] was one influential modern invention technique.

Progressive educators before World War II had urged researchers to use social-scientific methods for investigating students' real needs. These urgings were rarely heeded in college English departments. Now empirical studies based on observations of working writers began, such as those of Nancy Sommers [400] and Sondra Perl [274]. The whole composing process came under study. Research indicated that there might be more than one successful composing process. Furthermore, the process no longer seemed to be neatly linear, as described in the classical model, but appeared recursive and hierarchical, as developed in the model of Linda Flower and cognitive psychologist John R. Hayes [265].

In comprehensive theoretical works, the philosophical and psychological bases for the study of composing were explored. Some authors argued that the forms of discourse are structurally similar to the forms of cognitive processes and perhaps even to the brain itself. To teach the forms of discourse, then, is not merely to teach conventional modes of arrangement but to provide students with models of actual cognitive processes. If the forms of discourse parallel cognitive processes, they should be equally accessible to every student, regardless of cultural background.

In the 1970s, the increasing number of college freshmen whose home language was not Standard English severely tested the applicability of cognitive theories of writing. The work of William Labov [648] and other sociolinguists on dialectal variation helped writing teachers see that this new classroom population, in need of so much help with the requirements of academic writing, was not cognitively deficient but, rather, linguistically and culturally diverse. One immediate result of this new understanding was a 1974 resolution by the CCCC on students' right to their own languages. This resolution argued that students would learn Standard English more easily if they were allowed to write some school assignments in their home languages, whether or not these were Standard. The document also called for teacher education to include work in dialectal variation.

Later in the decade, studies of basic writing explored the pedagogical problems posed by dialectal variation in the classroom. Mina P. Shaughnessy's important work, *Errors and Expectations: A Guide for the Teacher of Basic Writing* (1977) [660], argues for respect for students' home languages but also advises teachers on how to help these students become more comfortable with academic writing. Many student errors with Standard forms are actually regular, if not rule-governed, attempts to achieve academic correctness. A student whose home language is Black English, for example, might write her school papers in neither Black English nor Standard English but in an idiosyncratic blend of the two. Furthermore, socialization to school is a problem for many basic writers. If students' home cultures place little value on the intellectual abstractions of academic work, for example, a typical research paper assignment might seem pointless. The study of error, therefore, as Shaughnessy argues, must consider students' cultural background and how this may affect their relation to the social contexts of school as well as what appears on the page when they write.

With so many students seeming to need extra help in mastering college-level writing, many composition scholars came to feel that professors in all disciplines must be enlisted in the effort of teaching writing or, rather, helped to see that they were already contributing to students' introduction to academic discourse. They could learn to make this contribution in better ways, which would improve both students' writing and their learning of disciplinary content. To address these needs, cross-disciplinary writing programs, or programs in "writing across the curriculum," to use James Britton's phrase, began to develop. The first American writing-across-the-curriculum program was started at Carleton College in Minnesota in 1974, and Elaine Maimon directed an influential program at Beaver College in Pennsylvania [549, 550].

These programs typically attempt to educate students and faculty from all disciplines about the conventions of academic discourse and about the range of activities that constitute mature composing processes. Maimon argues that the literary training most composition scholars have received makes them uniquely suited to analyze the conventions of discourse for writers who are not aware of the conventions' function in the generation of knowledge [549]. Toby Fulwiler stresses the importance of journal keeping in the composing processes of all academic disciplines. Fulwiler finds that writing-across-the-curriculum programs encourage students and teachers alike to become more confident writers and eager collaborators in a literate community of scholars [543]. James L. Kinneavy suggests that a further outcome may be wider participation in a literate community beyond the academy, in which important public issues can be discussed [547].

The 1980s: Social and Historical Approaches to Rhetoric

In the 1980s, composition scholars focused on the social nature of writing, building upon previous work in both basic writing and writing across the curriculum. Research into the cognitive processes of writers continued, but it was informed by new interest in how these processes are conditioned by social circumstances. For example, Mike Rose shows that writer's block may be as much a result of bad writing instruction as of individual cognitive disabilities [276]. Moreover, ethnographic studies, such as that by Shirley Brice Heath [352], which focus on writers at various school levels and beyond school, became increasingly important.

James Kinneavy's early work on the modes of discourse (1971) [221] returned to Aristotle for a revitalized sense of the decisive role of social function in determining the form of discourse. Kinneavy classifies rhetorical situations according to their emphasis on the writer (expressive), audience (persuasive), subject matter (referential), or verbal medium (aesthetic). Kinneavy's theory allows for the literary analysis of a wide variety of texts, thus laying the groundwork for studies in writing across the curriculum. His work became more influential in the 1980s as these studies proliferated.

The search for a social theory of writing became broadly interdisciplinary. Composition scholars studied not only writing but all aspects of language use, which they regarded as actually creating knowledge, not merely disseminating it. These interests have been shared with scholars in history, literary criticism, philosophy, psychology, sociology, and speech communication. Scholars in all these fields sought an account of discourse—language in use—that acknowledges the power of rhetoric to help create a community's worldview, knowledge, and interpretive practices.

If rhetoric is epistemic, then there can be no language that does not require interpretation. As Richard Rorty shows, modern philosophers have failed to define a value-neutral language in which purely objective and rational arguments can be conducted (see Olsen and Gale [234]). Chaim Perelman describes the ways a community united by discourse establishes its interpretive practices [236, 237]. His "universal audience" is the audience that is presumed to adhere perfectly to a given community's interpretive practices and hence to serve as that community's standard of the purely objective and rational audience. Different communities can be expected to hold different conceptions of their universal audience.

Literary-critical theories of the role of the reader in making meaning also discuss the establishment of interpretive practices. Stanley Fish describes readers as participants in interpretive communities, which are defined by their agreement on the conventions of discourse. Fish's work suggests a method for analyzing the conventions a writer must learn to enter the academic discourse community. No taxonomy of such conventions has appeared, although studies of a number of fields have exposed much about disciplinary conventions. More recently, studies of writing in various disciplines have revealed and analyzed the social creation of disciplinary knowledge through discourse.

Historical studies of rhetoric have been another resource for a social theory of discourse. Andrea A. Lunsford and Lisa S. Ede drew on Aristotle for a theory of argument that legitimates ethical and pathetic as well as logical appeals. This theory supports the idea that cultural assumptions have more to do with persuasion than the "universal" rationality of a proposition [222]. S. Michael Halloran shows that when the classical emphasis on socially rooted appeals disappeared from nineteenth-century colleges, public debate on important national issues diminished [85, 97]. James A. Berlin describes the reduction of rhetoric to stylistic prescriptions [143]. He suggests that the roots of a more socially responsive rhetoric may be found in Emersonian romanticism.

The field of composition studies grew in professional respectability during the 1980s. By the end of the decade, graduate degrees in composition and rhetoric—not simply one introductory survey or teaching practicum—had come to be offered by departments of English in many prestigious universities. Under the auspices of the NCTE, the CCCC began publishing comprehensive bibliographies in the field [43]. The U.S. Department of Education funded an empirical research institute, the Center for the Study of Writing, at the University of California at Berkeley and Carnegie Mellon University. Series of bibliographic anthologies, collections, reprints, and monographs began to appear regularly from a number of research and university presses.

Part of the field's coming-of-age process was increased interest in the history of rhetoric and composition, now an extensive area of scholarly work and a regular curricular offering. Composition work was not to be seen as a temporary response to unusual gaps in college-bound students' preparation.

Rather, writing teachers and researchers came to view themselves as the most recent generation of serious thinkers about language in use, heirs of the rhetorical tradition. Many of our classroom practices were recast in light of historical traditions. For example, personal writing was connected with the genre of the personal essay stretching back at least to the Renaissance, as traced variously by William A. Covino [90] and Kurt Spellmeyer [616].

Although historical studies of rhetoric and poetic suggested theoretical bases for the location of composition studies in English departments, the relationship between composition studies and literary studies was (and is still to some extent) uneasy. Some composition scholars called for the formation of departments of composition and rhetoric, separate from departments of English. Some worked to redress the professional inequities that prompted the impulse to separate through, for example, the Wyoming Resolution and ensuing professional policy work by both the CCCC and the MLA [499]. Greatly increased self-consciousness about the institutional structures in which we work gave rise not only to more scholarship on writing-program administration but also to more ideologically sensitive criticism of our institutional functions, for example, in James Berlin's work on the history of twentieth-century writing [143, 173].

Analyses of the political problems within the profession extended to efforts to connect our profession with political problems in society at large, to a degree not seen, perhaps, since the late 1960s. An important intersection of personal work life and national political life emerged in the analyses of inequity and redress offered by feminist critics within composition studies. In 1988, Elizabeth A. Flynn [714] could lament that issues of feminism were rarely raised at our annual conventions, but this situation changed dramatically the very next year.

The late 1980s also saw a rise in awareness of the degree to which race and social class affect the situation of basic writers. Linda Brodkey analyzes teacher-student class differences in "The Literacy Letters" [637], and Mike Rose provides an autobiographical account of how such barriers may be negotiated in *Lives on the Boundary* [655]. "Politics" became a key concept for understanding the educational difficulties of all writers: witness Richard Bullock and John Trimbur's collection, *The Politics of Writing Instruction, Postsecondary* [742]. Composition scholars gave increased attention to pedagogical innovations with an explicitly liberatory political agenda, drawing once again on the work of Brazilian literacy educator Paulo Freire [344] (see Cooper and Holzman [566]) and learning from education theorists like Henry A. Giroux [210]. The desire to trace the influences of class, race, and gender to their roots also seemed to generate a great deal of attention among college-level writing teachers to work in the acquisition of literacy and its cognitive and cultural implications, as the works in the "Literacy" section of the Bibliography attest.

By the end of the 1980s, seeing writing in social and cultural contexts was the prevailing tendency in the field. Concern for writing in communal contexts appeared in the work of many theorists. Linda Flower, in a variation on the theme, argued for a sociocognitive theory of writing, according to which writer, text, and context are mutually constitutive [264]. Studying writing in context means more than assessing the immediate audience. Rather, as Marilyn M. Cooper argues, we must consider a complex "ecology of writing" that comprises not only immediate personal relationships and social purposes but also larger generic and cultural constraints on composing [260]. To study this rich network, we need to look not only at the individual writer but at the collaborative situation of his or her classroom, personal and institutional histories, and writers' and teachers' political hopes.

Rhetoric and Composition Studies in the 1990s: The Challenge of Diversity

The powerful themes of the 1980s—social construction, politics, literacy, and gender issues—extended in the 1990s to work that related composition to postmodernism and cultural studies. Social construction was widely accepted as a theoretical basis for understanding language use, as can be seen in the research directions of technical and business communication, English as a second language, and writing centers. The history of composition, too, received generous and fruitful attention in the 1990s, a time of stock-taking in the discipline, some of which was motivated by the challenge of diversity in all areas of the field.

A number of scholars explored the connections among social construction, postmodernism, politics, and cultural studies and their implications for composition. The contributors to Patricia Harkin and John Schilb's *Contending with Words: Composition and Rhetoric in a Postmodern Age* explored the sources of postmodern ideas in the works of influential theorists [214], and Lester Faigley analyzed the relationship of computer technologies and postmodern consciousness [202]. James Berlin drew upon cultural studies to argue for a reform of English studies [739], while others used these theories to complicate our notions of student subjectivity and to promote interdisciplinary research.

The impulse to write the field's history appeared in such collections as *Taking Stock: The Writing Process Movement in the 90s* [279] as well as in a series of landmark essays on the writing process [274], invention [387], voice [601], writing centers [450], and writing across the curriculum [539], published by Hermagoras Press. In addition, a number of scholars shone a light on the teaching of rhetoric in nineteenth-century American colleges, finding there the stories of how the field of composition was positioned—and in some ways compromised—for the next century and beyond. Revisionist histories of writing and rhetoric such as those written by Robert J. Connors [87], Thomas P. Miller [121], and Robin Varnum [168] situated the role of composition in the development of English studies, while books in the history of rhetoric focused very specifically on the rhetorical practices of women speakers and writers. Cheryl Glenn studied the rhetorical contributions of women from antiquity through the Renaissance [96], while Shirley Wilson Logan [117] and Carol Mattingly [120] documented the work of nineteenth-century women rhetors. Influenced by feminist theory, these histories attempted to recover lost or neglected voices in the rhetorical tradition, fill in disturbing gaps in our understanding of the history of rhetoric, and remind us of the wealth of archival research.

In response to the growing cultural diversity of student populations, composition welcomed its first longitudinal studies of college writers. Marilyn S. Sternglass' *Time to Know Them: A Longitudinal Study of Writing and Learning at the College Level* followed nine City College students through their academic careers [664], and Ruth Spack reported on a three-year study of a second-language student [789]. At the same time, composition also saw its first critique of process pedagogy; Lisa Delpit criticized the writing process movement for its tendency to restrict minority students' access to linguistic codes [711]. In 1991, Mary Louise Pratt called upon educators to think of the curriculum and the classroom as "contact zones" in which cultural groups of unequal power can interact under conditions that enable sharing and understanding [239]. Composition teachers and scholars were quick to respond to Pratt's challenge (see, e.g., Bizzell [181]) in ways that confirmed the richness of the contact zone metaphor and its potential for pedagogy; for example, while A. Suresh Canagarajah found the concept of "safe houses" important for his students [707], Joseph Harris found it problematic if those "houses" serve only as retreats where differences need not be negotiated [644].

The attraction of spatial metaphors to describe diverse classrooms continued with Gloria Anzaldúa's "borderlands" (*la frontera*), places of cultural, spiritual, geographical, and linguistic difference, where the reward for discomfort and conflict was a satisfying sense of shifting and multiple identities. Along with Pratt's contact zones, Anzaldúa's borderlands gave teachers and writers more ways to think about the space of the classroom and the curriculum, but more important, her "mestiza rhetoric" invited writers to blend genres, to occupy multiple identities, and to refuse to enclose discourses within well-defined parameters.

Such border crossing occurs in extracurricular studies of literacy. Beverly J. Moss' collection *Literacy across Communities* [360], and Brian V. Street's collection *Cross-Cultural Approaches to Literacy* [370] extended the work of Labov and Heath in sociolinguistic and anthropological studies of literacy outside the academy; these scholars helped composition teachers to understand the cultural histories and languages from which students increasingly came. With a growing recognition that literacy does not mean school literacy, Deborah Brandt [329, 330, 331] and Anne Ruggles Gere [346], among others, focused on extracurricular reading, writing, and communicative practices. Also interested in community literacy were those teachers beginning to pursue service learning, an effort to expand the awareness of cultural difference beyond classrooms and campuses and to introduce students to the rhetoric of citizenship.

With more understanding of the complexities of students' literacies and identities, composition continued to respond to issues of diversity in our classrooms, institutions, and communities. *Writing in Multicultural Settings*, edited by Carol Severino, Juan C. Guerra, and Johnnella E. Butler [734], attempted to describe, without prescribing answers, the conflicts, tensions, and struggles of both students and teachers in classrooms defined by difference. Mary Soliday described a program at City College designed to mainstream at-risk students—a program supported across the institution but also determined by the complex institutional politics of remediation [661]. And Vivian Zamel reminded us that ESL students' language use was too often equated with their intellectual ability [793]. Writing centers, similarly, began responding to the challenge of diversity. Anne DiPardo, for example, connected the difficulties of center clients from diverse cultures to campus tensions aroused by diversity and showed how tutors can help [640].

The late 1990s saw an emerging critical discourse on race in composition studies, a discourse that did not embrace multiculturalism, necessarily, but that tried to confront institutionalized racism through analyzing images, discourses, and practices. Keith Gilyard's edited collection, *Race, Rhetoric, and Composition* [718], as well as articles by Catherine Prendergast [731] and David L. Wallace and Annissa Bell [737], interrogated constructions of race in composition and in the academy. Feminist teaching and gender issues in the classroom continued to be important scholarly concerns in rhetoric and composition [720]. A variety of other women's concerns were reflected in studies of autobiographical writing [606], of academic women's sense of authority [722], and of the history of gender-coded texts [185]. At the same time, the typical categories of difference—race, class, and gender—began to be complicated by other, overlapping identities or subject positions. Harriet Malinowitz, for example, cast light on the writing problems of gay and lesbian students [728].

An important "contact zone" for composition scholars was electronic writing technologies. Still intrigued by the new frontiers of networking and hypertext and other online writing technologies, compositionists continued to explore these regions for their pedagogical implications. Their initial enthusiasm tempered by critical accounts of technology's exclusions, scholars approached computers armed with an awareness of, for example, how interfaces showed effects of domination and colonialism [291]. Theoretical interpretations of technology included Jay David Bolter's explanation of how electronic text radically changes the relationship between writer and reader and revives features of oral literature [280]. Studies of online writing were more likely to focus on the rhetoric and politics of exchanges [814] and to question the implications of adding technology to classrooms or writing centers [502].

As composition studies moved into a new century, there were many signs of its scholarly maturity. In 1999 the profession celebrated the fiftieth anniversary of the Conference on College Composition and Communication, and there were other signs, too, that composition had come of age. Expanding forums for publishing—print as well as electronic—enabled more voices and views to be heard while also encouraging the rise of specialized, focused studies.

Despite composition's maturity as a discipline and its rapid adoptions of new technologies, the inequities and injustices for low-status composition instructors, well-documented in books by Eileen Schell and Theresa Enos, remained, in part, Sharon Crowley argued, because composition remained a requirement [193]. Composition's characteristic commitment to exploring the relationship between theory and practice [203], however, would seem to indicate its continued productivity. While it remained to be seen if composition could construct new theories in a new century, the field continued to be defined by a blend of richly interdisciplinary interest in pedagogy, research, and theory.

Into the Twenty-First Century: Post-Process Perspectives and Concerns

Early in a new century, responses to diversity expanded to include more attention to disability studies [706, 721, 732], sexuality [701], and whiteness [241], all welcome complications to the category of gender, race, and class. As these categories have continued to blend and blur, greater consensus has emerged that attention to student identities must be accompanied by a full accounting of diverse histories, theories, and curricula. Thus, contemporary scholars and researchers are constantly engaged in efforts to rewrite composition history, formulate new theoretical perspectives, and analyze and adapt new media and technologies.

Historical scholarship abounds and has recently displayed a marked shift away from demonizing nineteenth-century current-traditional rhetoric; instead, historians are drawing a much fuller picture of the cultural issues and conditions that informed curricular histories, writing instruction, and conceptions of literacy. Until recently, composition's canonical histories and primary texts have made it difficult to see other patterns, namely the long-standing presence of African Americans in arenas of higher education and their successes as insiders (Royster and Williams [130]) or the role of cultural imperatives in shaping composition theory and practice (Paine [128]). But significant archival work has radically altered our understanding of current-traditional rhetorics and rhetorical education: activist rhetorical education, for example, was concerned more with language and ideology than correctness [110], and formal grammar instruction co-existed peaceably with progressive educational goals [155]. Women rhetorical educators prepared their students for civic engagement [95], while a classical curriculum in historically black colleges provided students with what Susan Jarratt calls "a sense of rhetorical enfranchisement" [106]. "Counter" histories reconsider periods as recent as the 1980s when new epistemological maps lumped vitalism with romanticism [217].

Accompanying these efforts to rewrite history are new theoretical perspectives that emphasize writing's materiality and a burgeoning interest in the ways in which writing and literacies are embodied [205, 249, 738] or how rhetorical training is a "bodily art" [100]. John Trimbur traces writing's materiality through circulation—a system of production and delivery [251], and Bruce McComiskey bases his social-process rhetorical inquiry on the cycle of production, distribution, and consumption [271]. The influence of materiality can also be seen in the proliferation of in-depth qualitative studies of everyday literacies—home, school, public, and multiple [325, 370, 371]—and in calls for materialist rhetorics to inform service learning [681]. The notion of literacy sponsors [331] has firmly taken hold and expanded into literacy sponsorships and multiple partnerships [544]. Challenges to the autonomous model of literacy continue to mount; for instance, Shannon Carter argues that taking vernacular literacies seriously depends on a notion of rhetorical dexterity [332].

The importance of self-reflection, learned in part from qualitative research, has also influenced scholarship in the areas of community service learning, civic engagement, and public writing, where recognition of community expertise, reciprocity, and sustainability are central concerns [684, 685, 695]. Indeed, many areas of rhetoric and composition studies now look beyond classrooms or academic discourses for the development of theories and practices. In the areas of multimodal composing or digital writing, for example, scholars are turning to new environments, spaces, media, and genres to reconsider plagiarism in a digital age [288, 813] or to adapt to visual literacies [306] or new media writing [313].

With widening contexts for understanding genres [672, 828], writing programs are also recognizing the importance of writing in the freshman year [454] and the difficulty of "transfer" [565, 572]. The aims and content of first-year courses are shifting in light of the recognition that there is no universal academic discourse [451]. At the same time, writing programs are acknowledging that we need to know more about such matters as the code-meshing of World Englishes [743] as well as the impact of "English Only" policies [767]. One of the central challenges facing program design is to imagine writing instruction and curriculum from an internationalist perspective, a challenge shared by business communication [843, 857] and technical communication [798].

Writing programs are also increasingly looking beyond the curriculum [589], beyond the academy, and toward community literacies [687]. Interest in community engagement, along with studying the rhetorics, tools, technologies, genres, and infrastructure for such engagement [689], is likely to hold composition's attention for many years to come. The size and scope of this seventh edition of *The Bedford Bibliography for Teachers of Writing* testify to the status of rhetoric and composition in the twenty-first century and indicate a continued development of subfields and secondary specializations.

Where going . . . . fertile ground –

Bibliography

Resources

Periodicals

1 *ADE Bulletin*. New York: Association of Departments of English. Three times a year, beginning 1964. Submissions and subscriptions: Annie Reiser, Modern Language Association, *ADE Bulletin*, 26 Broadway, 3rd Floor, New York, NY 10004-1789. Submit electronically at ade-bulletin@mla.org.

The journal of the Association of Departments of English. Articles on writing program and English department administration and the relationships between composition and literature. Ed. Stephen Olsen.

2 *The CEA Forum*. Chester, PA: The College English Association. Semiannually, beginning 1970. Now published exclusively online. Submissions, CEA members only: Janine Utell, Humanities Division, Widener University, One University Place, Chester, PA 19013. E-mail jmutell @mail.widener.edu.

The journal of the College English Association. Most articles concern the teaching of literature and composition. Ed. Janine Utell.

3 *College Composition and Communication*. Urbana, IL: NCTE/CCCC. Quarterly, beginning 1950. Subscriptions: 1111 Kenyon Rd., Urbana, IL 61801. Subscribe online at www.ncte.org/cccc/ccc/. Submissions: Kathleen Blake Yancey, Editor, *College Composition and Communication*, Dept. of English, 223 Williams Bldg., Florida State University, Tallahassee, FL 32306. E-mail cccedit@yahoo.com.

CCC The principal journal of the Conference on College Composition and Communication. Most articles explore pedagogical applications of composition theory and research. Ed. Kathleen Blake Yancey.

4 *College English*. Urbana, IL: NCTE College Section. Bimonthly, beginning 1939. Subscriptions: 1111 Kenyon Rd., Urbana, IL 61801. Subscribe online at www.ncte.org/journals/ce. Submissions: *College English*, Dept. of English, Indiana University, Ballantine Hall 442, 1020 E. Kirkwood Ave., Bloomington, IN 47405-7103. E-mail coleng@indiana.edu.

CE The principal journal of the NCTE College Section. Articles on teaching literature, literary theory, the history of the discipline, and teaching writing. Ed. John Schilb.

5 *Community Literacy Journal*. Biannually, beginning 2006. Subscriptions: John Warnock, *Community Literacy Journal*, English Department, University of Arizona, Tucson, AZ 85721. E-mail johnw@email.arizona.edu. Submissions: Michael R. Moore, Dept. of Writing, Rhetoric, and Discourse, 802 West Belden Ave., DePaul University, Chicago, IL 60614. E-mail mmoore46@depaul.edu. Submit electronically http://community literacy.org/index.php/clj.

Both scholarly articles and research agendas by literacy workers, practitioners, and community literacy program staff. Ed. Michael R. Moore.

6 *Composition Studies* (formerly *Freshman English News*). Three times a year, beginning 1972. Subscriptions and submissions: *Composition Studies*, University of Winnipeg, Dept. of Rhetoric, Writing, and Communications, 515 Portage Avenue, Winnipeg, Manitoba, Canada R2H 1K3. E-mail compositionstudies@uwinnipeg.ca.

Short articles on the theory and practice of teaching and writing and, occasionally, longer theoretical essays. Ed. Jennifer Clary-Lemon.

7 *Computers and Composition: An International Journal*. Norwood, NJ: Ablex Publishing Co. Three times a year, beginning 1984. Subscriptions: Elsevier Science Inc., 655 Avenue of the Americas, New York, NY 10010-5107. Submissions are accepted electronically at http://ees.elsevier.com/cocomp/.

Articles on the uses of computers in teaching writing. Ed. Cynthia Selfe and Gail Hawisher.

8 *Enculturation: A Journal of Rhetoric, Writing, and Culture*. One to two issues per year, beginning 1997. Online, open-access: http://enculturation.gmu.edu/. Submissions accepted electronically via the *Enculturation* Web site. E-mail byron.hawk@gmail.com with general queries.

Articles on contemporary theories of rhetoric, writing, and culture, including conventional articles, hypertexts, videos, and multimedia projects. Ed. Byron Hawk.

9 *English for Specific Purposes: An International Journal*. Oxford, England: Elsevier Science Ltd. Three times a year, beginning 1980. Subscriptions: Elsevier Science Ltd., Regional Sales Customer Support Dept., P.O. Box 945, New York, NY 10159-0945. Submissions are accepted electronically at http://ees.elsevier.com/esp/. E-mail s.starfield@unsw.edu.au or b.paltridge@usyd.edu.au.

Articles analyze the discourse conventions of writing in particular professions and disciplines. Ed. Brian Paltridge and Sue Starfield.

10 *English Journal*. Urbana, IL: NCTE Secondary Section. Bimonthly, beginning 1912. Subscriptions: 1111 Kenyon Rd., Urbana, IL 61801. Subscribe online at www.ncte.org/journals/ej. Submissions: Ken Lindblom, Editor, English Department, 2084 Humanities Bldg., Stony Brook University, Stony Brook, NY 11794-5350. E-mail English_Journal@notes.cc.sunysb.edu.

The principal journal of the NCTE Secondary Section. Articles on teaching literature and writing and on pedagogical research in the secondary schools. Ed. Ken Lindblom.

11 *JAC: A Journal of Composition Theory* (formerly *Journal of Advanced Composition*). Logan, UT: Council of Editors of Learned Journals, with support from the University of South Florida, Georgia State University, and Eckerd College. Annually, beginning 1980; twice a year, beginning 1990. Subscriptions and submissions: Lynn Worsham, Editor, *JAC*; English Department, Stevenson Hall, Illinois State University, Normal, IL 61790-4240. E-mail jac@ilstu.edu.

Articles on rhetorical theory, interviews with scholars, and pedagogical articles on expository, technical, creative, and other advanced writing courses. Ed. Lynn Worsham.

12 *Journal of Basic Writing*. New York: City University of New York Instructional Resource Center. Twice a year, beginning 1978. Subscriptions: P.O. Box 465, Hanover, PA 17331. Submissions: Rebecca Mlynarczyk, Co-Editor, *JBW*, Dept. of English, Kingsborough Community College, 2001 Oriental Blvd., Brooklyn, NY 11235. Electronic submissions preferred; e-mail Rebecca Mlynarczyk at rebecca.mlynarczyk@gmail.com or Hope Parisi at HopeKCC@aol.com.

From the Instructional Resource Center, previously directed by Mina Shaughnessy. Articles on literacy, teaching grammar and basic writing, English as a second language (ESL), and theoretical issues in basic writing. Ed. Rebecca Mlynarczyk and Hope Parisi.

13 *Journal of Business and Technical Communication*. Ames: Iowa State University. Four times a year, beginning 1987. Subscriptions: Sage Periodicals Press, 2455 Teller Rd., Thousand Oaks, CA 91320. Submissions are accepted electronically at http://mc.manuscriptcentral.com/jbtc.

Articles on business and technical writing practice and teaching. Ed. David R. Russell.

14 *Journal of Second Language Writing*. Norwood, NJ: Ablex Publishing Co. Quarterly, beginning 1992. Subscriptions: Elsevier Science, Regional Sales Office, Customer Support Department, P.O. Box 945, New York, NY 10159-0945. Submissions are accepted electronically at http://ees.elsevier.com/seclan/.

Full-length articles on theories of ESL composition. Selected bibliographies of recent scholarship. Ed. Ilona Leki and Rosa Manchón.

15 *Journal of Teaching Writing*. Indianapolis: Indiana Teachers of Writing. Twice a year, beginning 1981. Subscriptions and submissions: Indiana University, 425 University Blvd. CA 345, Indianapolis, IN 46202. E-mail jtw@iupui.edu.

Articles cover composition theory and the relation of composition to other fields, as well as pedagogical concerns. Ed. Kim Brian Lovejoy.

16 *Journal of Technical Writing and Communication*. Amityville, NY: Baywood Publications. Four times a year, beginning 1971. Subscriptions: Baywood Publishing Co., Inc., 26 Austin Ave., Box 337, Amityville, NY 11701. Submissions: Charles H. Sides, P.O. Box 546, Westminster, MA 01473. Electronic submissions encouraged; e-mail csides@fitchburg state.edu.

Articles on research and teaching in technical and professional writing. Ed. Charles H. Sides.

17 *Kairos: A Journal of Rhetoric, Technology, and Pedagogy*. One to four issues per year, beginning 1996. Online, open-access: http://kairos.techno rhetoric.net/. Submissions are accepted electronically via the *Kairos* Web site.

Articles written explicitly for online publication that explore the intersections of rhetoric, technology, and pedagogy. Ed. Cheryl Ball.

18 *Pedagogy: Critical Approaches to Teaching Literature, Language, Composition, and Culture*. Durham: Duke University Press. Three issues annually, beginning 2001. Submissions: *Pedagogy*, Dept. of English, Calvin College, 1795 Knollcrest Circle S.E., Grand Rapids, MI 49546. Electronic submissions preferred; e-mail pedagogy@calvin.edu.

Articles dealing with all areas of English studies, from literature and literary criticism to composition to cultural studies. Ed. Jennifer L. Holberg and Marcy Taylor.

19 *Philosophy and Rhetoric*. State College: Pennsylvania State University Press. Quarterly, beginning 1968. Subscriptions: Subscribe online at http://muse.jhu.edu/about/subscriptions/index.html. Submissions: Managing Editor, *Philosophy and Rhetoric*, University of Colorado–Boulder, Communication Department, 270 UCB, Boulder, CO 80309-0270. Electronic submissions preferred; e-mail pandr@colorado.edu.

Articles on classical rhetoric, rhetorical theory, and language theory from the perspectives of English, speech, and philosophy. Ed. Gerard A. Hauser.

20 *PRE/TEXT*. Arlington: University of Texas. Quarterly, beginning 1979. Subscriptions and submissions: Victor Vitanza, *PRE/TEXT*, 105 Riggs Dr., Clemson, SC 29631. E-mail pretext@earthlink.net.

Long essays on rhetorical theory and pedagogical philosophy. Ed. Victor J. Vitanza.

21 *Quarterly Journal of Speech*. Washington, DC: National Communication Association. Subscriptions: Subscribe online at www.informaworld.com /smpp/title~content=t713707519~tab=subscribe~db=all or contact NCA, 1765 N Street NW, Washington, DC 20036. Submissions are accepted electronically at http://mc.manuscriptcentral.com/rqjs. Questions can be addressed to the editor, Raymie E. McKerrow, at qjs@ohio.edu.

The principal theoretical journal of the National Communication Association. Articles on rhetorical theory and the history of rhetoric, and analyses of texts and speeches. Contributors from English and philosophy as well as speech. Ed. Raymie McKerrow.

22 *Radical Teacher*. Champaign, IL: Univ. of Illinois Press on behalf of the Center for Critical Education, Inc. Subscriptions: *Radical Teacher*, University of Illinois Press, Journals Division, 1325 S. Oak St., Champaign, IL 61820. Subscribe online at subscriptions@radicalteacher.org. Submissions are accepted electronically at manuscripts@radicalteacher.org.

Articles on the political concerns of teachers and students; perspectives on progressive pedagogy, feminism, and Marxism in teaching in all disciplines.

23 *Research in the Teaching of English*. Urbana, IL: NCTE. Four times a year, beginning 1967. Subscriptions: 1111 Kenyon Rd., Urbana, IL 61801. Subscribe online at www.ncte.org/journals/rte. Submissions: *RTE*, University of Illinois at Urbana–Champaign, College of Education, 236 Education Bldg. E-mail rte@education.illinois.edu.

Research reports on teaching English at all school levels, cognitive development and language skills, and the composing process. Ed. Mark Dressman, Sarah McCarthey, and Paul Prior.

24 *Rhetoric Review*. Tucson: Rhetoric Review Association of America. Quarterly, beginning 1982. Subscriptions and submissions: Theresa Jarnagin Enos, Dept. of English, University of Arizona, Tucson, AZ 85721. E-mail enos@email.arizona.edu.

Both theoretical and practical articles emphasizing the importance of rhetoric to composition instruction. Ed. Theresa Jarnagin Enos.

25 *Rhetoric Society Quarterly*. St. Cloud, MN: Rhetoric Society of America. Quarterly, beginning 1968. Subscriptions: Routledge Journals, Taylor & Francis Ltd., 325 Chestnut St., 8th Floor, Philadelphia, PA 19106. Submissions are accepted electronically at http://mc.manuscriptcentral.com/rrsq.

Articles on rhetorical theory, history, and professional concerns. Contributors from both English and speech. Ed. Carolyn R. Miller.

26 *Rhetorica*. Berkeley: University of California Press, International Society for the History of Rhetoric. Quarterly, beginning 1983. Subscriptions: University of California Press, Journals Division, 2000 Center St., Suite 303, Berkeley, CA 94720. Submissions: Mike Edwards, Institute of Classical Studies, University of London, Senate House North Block, Malet Street, London, WC1E 7HU, United Kingdom. E-mail mike.edwards@sas.ac.uk.

The journal of the International Society for the History of Rhetoric. Articles on premodern rhetoric by contributors from English, speech, philosophy, and history. Ed. Mike Edwards.

27 *Teaching English in the Two-Year College*. Urbana, IL: NCTE. Quarterly, beginning 1974. Subscriptions: 1111 Kenyon Rd., Urbana, IL 61801.

Subscribe online at www.ncte.org/journals/tetyc. Submissions: Jeff Sommers, Editor, *TETYC*, English Department, Main Hall, West Chester University, 700 S. High Street, West Chester, PA 19383. E-mail TETYC@wcupa.edu.

Summaries and reviews of composition theory, as well as teaching suggestions for teachers of freshman and sophomore writing courses. Ed. Jeff Sommers.

28 *Technical Communication Quarterly*. St. Paul: University of Minnesota for the Association of Teachers of Technical Writing. Four times a year, beginning 1991. Subscriptions: Routledge Journals, Taylor & Francis Ltd., 325 Chestnut Street, 8th Floor, Philadelphia, PA 19106. Subscribe online at www.informaworld.com/smpp/title~db=all~content=t775653704~tab=subscribe. Submissions are accepted electronically at http://mc.manuscriptcentral.com/tcq. Questions can be directed to Editor Amy Koerber at amy.koerber@ttu.edu.

Articles on pedagogy, research, theory, applications, software, and book reviews for teachers of technical communication. Ed. Amy Koerber.

29 *TESOL Quarterly*. Alexandria, VA: TESOL. Four times a year, beginning 1967. Subscriptions: *TESOL*, 700 South Washington St., Suite 200, Alexandria, VA 22314. Submissions are accepted electronically at www.editorialmanager.com/tq/.

Articles on teaching and research in English as a second language. Ed. Diane Belcher and Alan Hirvela.

30 *WPA: Writing Program Administration*. Normal: Illinois State University, Council of Writing Program Administrators. Twice a year, beginning 1979. Subscriptions: Keith Rhodes, Secretary, *WPA*, 312 Lake Ontario Hall, Grand Valley State University, Allendale, MI 49401. E-mail rhodekei@gvsu.edu. Submissions are accepted electronically at journal@wpacouncil.org.

Articles on writing-program administration and writing instruction; textbook bibliographies. Ed. Alice Horning.

31 *The Writing Center Journal*. Fairfield, CT: International Writing Centers Association. Twice a year, beginning 1980. Milwaukee, WI: International Writing Centers Association. Subscriptions and submissions: E-mail writingcenterjournal@english.udel.edu.

Full-length articles on writing-center administration and practices. Ed. Melissa Ianetta and Lauren Fitzgerald.

32 *The Writing Instructor*. San Marcos: California State University. Quarterly, beginning 1981. Subscriptions: *The Writing Instructor*, c/o Dawn Formo, Literature and Writing Studies Program, California State University, San Marcos, CA 92096-0001. E-mail dformo@csusm.edu. Submissions are accepted electronically; e-mail David Blakesley, *TWI* Co-Editor, at dblakes@clemson.edu.

A journal from the University of Southern California Freshman Writing Program. Articles on teaching college writing, writing program administration, and curriculum development. Ed. David Blakesley, Dawn Formo, and Jeremy Tirrell.

33 *Writing Lab Newsletter*. West Lafayette, IN: National Writing Centers Association of the NCTE. Monthly, beginning 1976. Subscriptions: Muriel Harris, Dept. of English, Purdue University, 1356 Heavilon Hall, West Lafayette, IN 47907-1356. Subscribe online at www.writinglab newsletter.org/new/subscribe.php. Submissions are accepted electronically at http://writinglabnewsletter.org/submission.php or by e-mailing submission@writinglabnewsletter.org.

Short articles by lab directors and tutors, including student tutors, on writing-lab theory, problems, and techniques. Ed. Muriel Harris.

34 *Writing on the Edge*. Campus Writing Center, University of California at Davis. Twice a year, beginning 1989. Subscriptions and submissions: John Boe, Campus Writing Center, One Shields Ave., University of California, Davis, CA 95616. Submit or subscribe electronically by e-mailing jdboe@ucdavis.edu.

Shorter articles on all facets of composition and rhetoric: history, theory, pedagogy, writing centers, and politics. Ed. John Boe.

35 *Written Communication*. Beverly Hills, CA: Sage Publications. Quarterly, beginning 1984. Subscriptions: Customer Service, Sage Publications, 2455 Teller Rd., Thousand Oaks, CA 91320. E-mail journals@sagepub.com. Submissions: Christina Haas, Editor, *Written Communication*; Department of Writing Studies, University of Minnesota; 180 Wesbrook Hall; 77 Pleasant St. SE, Minneapolis, MN 55455.

Research reports on social and cognitive factors in discourse production for young and adult writers. Ed. Christina Haas.

General Bibliographies

36 "Annotated Bibliography of Research in the Teaching of English." *Research in the Teaching of English* (Spring and Fall, 1967–present).

Items focusing on empirical work are divided into sections on literature, humanities, and media; written and oral communication; language and verbal learning; bilingual and dialectal programs; and general English curriculum. Subdivided by educational level. Items are annotated beginning Spring 1973.

37 Enos, Theresa, ed. *Encyclopedia of Rhetoric and Composition: Communication from Ancient Times to the Information Age*. New York: Garland, 1995.

Four hundred and sixty-seven entries by 288 scholars of rhetoric, composition, speech communication, and philosophy, covering the history, theory, concepts, and major figures in the field of rhetoric. Entries are arranged alphabetically and range from brief identifications of terms and minor figures to essays on major figures and topics. A selected bibliography follows each entry. Includes an index.

38 *ERIC: Educational Resources Information Center*. www.eric.ed.gov/. Operated by the National Institute of Education, U.S. Department of Education.

There are sixteen ERIC clearinghouses, each responsible for a particular area of education. ERIC/RCS, the Clearinghouse on Reading and Communication Skills, is sponsored by the NCTE. Abstracts of articles available through ERIC are published in *Resources in Education*. Microfiche and paper copies may be ordered through the ERIC Document Reproduction Service, Box 190, Arlington, VA 22210. ERIC materials since 1982 are available on CD-ROM; materials since 1966 are on OCLC.

39 Haswell, Richard. *CompPile*. http://comppile.org/.

An ongoing inventory of publications in postsecondary composition, rhetoric, ESL, and technical writing: 1939–present. Includes 306 journals, a list of major publishing houses, more than 3,400 volumes of edited collections, more than 50 edited series, and 6,231 dissertations from 1939–1993.

40 Heilker, Paul, and Peter Vandenberg, eds. *Keywords in Composition Studies*. Portsmouth, NH: Heinemann-Boynton/Cook, 1996.

Fifty-four brief essays by twenty-seven scholars in composition studies, arranged alphabetically and accompanied by brief bibliographies of important works, introduce the field of composition studies by identifying the issues that cluster around its key terms.

41 Kennedy, Mary Lynch, ed. *Theorizing Composition: A Critical Sourcebook of Theory and Scholarship in Contemporary Composition Studies*. Charlotte, NC: Information Age Publishing, 2006.

Sixty-six brief essays by seventy-three authors, arranged alphabetically, summarize various theoretical schools in composition studies, as well as those in literature, philosophy, and rhetoric that are relevant to composition studies. The theoretical school's main ideas are given and its significance to composition studies treated. Extensive bibliographies accompany the entries.

42 Lindemann, Erika. *Longman Bibliography of Composition and Rhetoric: 1984–1985* (1987) and *1986* (1988). New York: Longman.

The 1984–1985 volume contains 3,853 entries; the 1986 volume contains 2,724. Nearly all the entries have twenty-five- to fifty-word descriptive annotations. Includes journals, books, dissertations, textbooks, ERIC entries, and computer programs in the following categories: theory and research (in rhetoric, history of rhetoric, types of rhetoric, reading, linguistics, education, and psychology), teacher education and administration, curriculum (preschool through college, business and technical writing, adult education, and ESL), textbooks and instructional materials, and testing and evaluation.

43 Lindemann, Erika. CCCC *Bibliography of Composition and Rhetoric, 1987*. Carbondale: Southern Illinois University Press, 1990. Succeeding editions: *1988* (1991), *1989* (1992), *1990* (1993).

Hawisher, Gail E., and Cynthia L. Selfe. CCCC *Bibliography of Composition and Rhetoric, 1991*. Carbondale: Southern Illinois University Press, 1993. Succeeding editions: *1992* (1994), *1993* (1995).

Successor to the *Longman Bibliography of Composition and Rhetoric* [42], which covers elementary and secondary as well as college materials, the CCCC *Bibliography* focuses on work related to college and university teaching and research. Categories are Bibliographies and Checklists; Theory and Research (in fourteen subcategories); Teacher Education, Administration, and Social Roles (four subcategories); Curriculum (thirteen subcategories); and Testing, Measurement, and Evaluation (four subcategories). Each item is briefly annotated.

44 Tate, Gary, ed. *Teaching Composition: Twelve Bibliographic Essays*. Fort Worth: Texas Christian University Press, 1987.

A substantially revised and enlarged edition of the important *Teaching Composition: Ten Bibliographic Essays* (1976). Includes Richard E. Young on invention (supplements the 1976 essay); Richard L. Larson on non-narrative prose (summarizes and updates the 1976 essay); Edward P. J. Corbett on style (1976 essay reprinted with an update) [408]; Frank J. D'Angelo on the modes of discourse (substantially revised and updated); Richard Lloyd-Jones on testing (new essay); Mina P. Shaughnessy, "Basic Writing" [659]; Andrea A. Lunsford, "Basic Writing Update"; Jenefer M. Giannasi on language varieties (substantially revised); W. Ross Winterowd, "Literacy, Linguistics, and Rhetoric" (substantially revised and updated); Joseph Comprone, "Literary Theory and Composition" (new essay); Jim Corder, "Studying Rhetoric and Literature" (substantially revised); James L. Kinneavy on writing across the curriculum (new essay—surveys textbooks and programs as well as scholarship); and Hugh Burns on computers and composition (new essay). The first edition essays on media (by Comprone) and "Composition and Related Fields" (by James L. Kinneavy and C. Robert Kline) are not in the new edition.

Histories and Theories

The Rhetorical Tradition

45 Aristotle. *Aristotle on Rhetoric: A Theory of Civic Discourse*. ca. 333 BCE. Ed. and trans. George A. Kennedy. 2nd ed. New York: Oxford UP, 2007. Print.

46 Astell, Mary. *A Serious Proposal to the Ladies, Parts I and II*. 1694, 1697. Ed. Patricia Springborg. London: Pickering and Chatto, 1997. Print.

47 Augustine. *On Christian Doctrine*. 426 CE. Trans. D. W. Robertson. New York: Library of Liberal Arts, 1958. Print.

48 Baca, Damián, and Victor Villanueva, eds. *Rhetorics of the Americas, 3114 BCE to 2012 CE*. New York: Palgrave, 2010. Print.

49 Bain, Alexander. *English Composition and Rhetoric: A Manual*. 1866; American ed., rev. 1888. New York: Appleton, 1980. Print.

50 Bizzell, Patricia and Bruce Herzberg. *The Rhetorical Tradition: Readings from Classical Times to the Present*. 2nd ed. Boston: Bedford/St. Martin's, 2001. Print.

A new and enlarged edition focused on rhetorical theory. Substantial excerpts and some complete works from Classical Rhetoric (Gorgias, Aspasia, Isocrates, Plato, Aristotle, Cicero, Quintilian, *Rhetorica ad Herennium*, others); Medieval Rhetoric (Augustine, Boethius, Christine de Pizan, others); Renaissance Rhetoric (Erasmus, Ramus, Wilson, Bacon, Margaret Fell, others); Enlightenment Rhetoric (Mary Astell, Vico, Sheridan, Campbell, Blair); Nineteenth-Century Rhetoric (Whately, Maria W. Stewart, Sarah Grimké, Frederick Douglass, Frances Willard, Bain and Hill, Nietzsche, others); Modern and Postmodern Rhetoric (Bakhtin, Virginia Woolf, Richards, Burke, Weaver, Perelman, Toulmin, Foucault, Cixous, Gates, Anzaldúa, others). Includes a general introduction, period and author introductions, and annotated bibliographies.

51 Blair, Hugh. *Lectures on Rhetoric and Belles-Lettres*. 1783. Ed. Harold Harding. Carbondale: Southern Illinois UP, 1966. Print.

52 Burke, Edmund. *A Philosophical Enquiry into the Origin of Our Ideas of the Sublime and the Beautiful*. 1757. Ed. James T. Boulton. Notre Dame: U of Notre Dame P, 1968. Print.

53 Campbell, George. *The Philosophy of Rhetoric*. 1776. Ed. Lloyd Bitzer. Carbondale: Southern Illinois UP, 1963. Print.

54 Castiglione, Baldesar. *The Book of the Courtier*. 1527. Trans. Charles Singleton. New York: Scribner's, 1959. Print.

55 Cicero. *De Inventione*. ca. 88 BCE. Trans. H. M. Hubbell. Cambridge: Harvard UP, 1949. Print.

56 Cicero. *De Oratore*. 55 BCE. *Books I–II*. Trans. E. W. Sutton and H. Rackham. Cambridge: Harvard UP, 1942. *Book III*. Trans. H. Rackham. Cambridge: Harvard UP, 1942. Print.

57 *Contrasting Arguments: An Edition of the* Dissoi Logoi. ca. 400 BCE. Ed. and trans. R. M. Robinson. New York: Arno, 1979. Print.

58 de la Cruz, Sor Juana. *The Answer/La Respuesta, Including a Selection of Poems*. 1691. Eds. and trans. Electa Arenal and Amanda Powell. New York: Feminist, 1994. Print.

59 de Pisan, Christine. *The Treasure of the City of Ladies, or the Book of the Three Virtues*. 1405. Ed. and trans. Sarah Lawson. New York: Viking Penguin, 1985. Print.

60 Erasmus, Desiderius. *Copia: Foundations of the Abundant Style*. 1512. Trans. Betty I. Knott. *Collected Works of Erasmus*. Ed. Craig R. Thompson. 42 vols. Toronto: U of Toronto P, 1978. Print.

61 Erasmus, Desiderius. *On the Writing of Letters/De conscribendis epistolis. Collected Works of Erasmus, Volumes 25–26*. 1522. Ed. and trans. Charles Fantozzi. Toronto: U of Toronto P, 1985. Print.

62 Fell, Margaret. *Women's Speaking Justified by the Scriptures*. 1666. Ed. David J. Latt. Los Angeles: William Andrews Clark Memorial Library, Augustan Rept. Soc. Publication #194, 1979. Print.

63 Golden, James L., and Edward P. J. Corbett, eds. *The Rhetoric of Blair, Campbell, and Whately*. 1968. New York: Holt, 1980. Print.

64 Grimké, Sarah. *Letters on the Equality of the Sexes and Other Essays*. 1838. Ed. Elizabeth Ann Bartlett. New Haven: Yale UP, 1988. Print.

65 Isocrates. *Against the Sophists and Antidosis*. ca. 390 BCE, 353 BCE. *Isocrates*, II. Ed. and trans. George Norlin. Loeb Classical Library. Cambridge: Harvard UP, 1982. Print.

66 Kennedy, George A. *A New History of Classical Rhetoric*. Princeton: Princeton UP, 1994. Print.

67 Longinus. *On the Sublime*. ca. 40 CE. *Aristotle, The Poetics, and Longinus, On the Sublime*. Trans. W. Hamilton Fyfe. Includes *Demetrius, On Style*. Trans. W. Rhys Roberts. Cambridge: Harvard UP, 1932. Print.

68 Murphy, James J. *Three Medieval Rhetorical Arts*. Berkeley: U of California P, 1971. Print.

Contains medieval manuals on letter writing and on preaching, excerpts from textbooks on Aristotelian dialectic, and Geoffrey of Vinsauf's *Poetria Nova*.

69 Murphy, James J., ed. *Quintilian on the Teaching of Speaking and Writing: Translations from Books One, Two and Ten of the Institutio Oratoria*. Trans. J. S. Watson; rev. by J. J. Murphy. Carbondale: Southern Illinois UP, 1987. Print.

These selections from the *Institutio* concern Quintilian's ideas about child development and the relationships among reading, writing, and speaking. Murphy's helpful introduction sets Quintilian's life and work in the context of Roman times and traces the reception of his ideas through the Renaissance and to the present.

70 Pernot, Laurent. *Rhetoric in Antiquity*. Trans. W. E. Higgins. Washington: Catholic U of America P, 2005. Print.

71 Plato. *Apology, Menexenus, Gorgias, Protagoras, Phaedrus, Symposium, Republic*. ca. 370 BCE. *The Collected Dialogues of Plato*. Ed. Edith Hamilton and Huntington Cairns. Princeton: Princeton UP, 1961. Print.

72 Quintilian. *Institutio Oratoria*. ca. 88 CE. Trans. H. E. Butler. 4 vols. Cambridge: Harvard UP, 1922. Print.

73 Ramus, Peter. *Arguments in Rhetoric against Quintilian*. 1549. Trans. Carole Newlands and James J. Murphy. De Kalb: U of Northern Illinois P, 1983. Print.

74 Ramus, Peter. *Peter Ramus's Attack on Cicero: Text and Translation of Ramus's Brutinae Quaestiones*. 1547. Ed. and intro. James J. Murphy. Trans. Carole Newlands. Davis: Hermagoras, 1992. Print.

75 *Rhetorica ad Herennium*. ca. 86 BCE. Trans. Harry Caplan. Cambridge: Harvard UP, 1954. Print.

76 Sprague, Rosamond Kent. *The Older Sophists*. Columbia: U of South Carolina P, 1972, 1990. Print.

77 Toulmin, Stephen, Richard Rieke, and Allan Janik. *An Introduction to Reasoning*. 2nd ed. New York: Macmillan, 1984. Print.

78 Toulmin, Stephen. *The Uses of Argument*. 1958. Updated ed. Cambridge: Cambridge UP, 2003. Print.

79 Waterfield, Robin, Trans. *The First Philosophers: The Presocratics and the Sophists*. New York: Oxford UP, 2000. Print.

80 Whately, Richard. *Elements of Rhetoric*. 1828. Ed. Douglas Ehninger. Carbondale: Southern Illinois UP, 1963. Print.

81 Willard, Frances E. *Woman in the Pulpit*. Boston: Lothrop, 1888 (other 1888 editions published regionally). Print.

82 Witherspoon, John. *The Selected Writings of John Witherspoon*. 1810. Ed. Thomas Miller. Carbondale: Southern Illinois UP, 1990. Print.

History of Rhetoric and Education

83 Adams, Katherine H. *Progressive Politics and the Training of America's Persuaders*. Mahwah: Erlbaum, 1999. Print.

Toward the end of the nineteenth century, as rhetoric shrank to freshman composition, a number of forces combined to create advanced composition courses. In traditional universities like Harvard, advanced writing courses were designed to improve sophistication and fluency. The Progressive movement, though focused educationally on lower schools, influenced the creation of journalism courses and programs at the turn of the twentieth century through its emphasis on citizenship. Advanced courses in journalism spawned imitators in engineering schools, which began to offer business and technical writing. At the same time, the creation of land grant colleges with their agricultural, commercial, and technical specialization led naturally to advanced courses in business and technical writing, business journalism, and advertising. During this period and since, instruction in persuasive writing—despite the importance of persuasion in American public and business life—remained absent from the general curriculum, even while advanced writing courses developed a wide range of persuasive skills.

84 Campbell, Karlyn Kohrs. *Man Cannot Speak for Her, Volume I: A Critical Study of Early Feminist Rhetoric*. Westport: Praeger/Greenwood, 1989. Print.

Nineteenth-century women had to struggle for their very right to speak in public against age-old prohibitions, largely religiously based. They argued for one moral law governing both men and women, a law that compelled their activism on behalf of abolition and African American rights, women's suffrage, temperance, and more. They learned how to address male audiences, emphasizing either that men and women were essentially morally and intellectually equal or that women possessed superior spiritual insight that required they benefit society with their political participation. In the latter part of the century, women's efforts concentrated on winning the vote—not without increasing tensions between white and black activists. Among the women rhetors with whom Campbell illustrates this groundbreaking study are Sarah and Angelina Grimké, Elizabeth Cady Stanton, Susan B. Anthony, Frances Willard, Ida B. Wells, and Mary Church Terrell. Volume II of Campbell's study collects representative speeches by these and other nineteenth-century women rhetors.

85 Clark, Gregory, and S. Michael Halloran, eds. *Oratorical Culture in Nineteenth-Century America: Transformations in the Theory and Practice of Rhetoric*. Carbondale: Southern Illinois UP, 1993. Print.

Eleven original essays trace and analyze the development of American rhetoric from neoclassical oratorical forms that focused on civic matters to rhetorics that reflected a growing individualism and professionalism. Essays include an introduction by Clark and Halloran; Ronald F. Reid on Edward Everett and neoclassical oratory; Gregory Clark on Timothy Dwight; P. Joy Rouse on Margaret Fuller; Nan Johnson on elocution and the private learner; Nicole Tonkovich on *Godey's Lady's Book*; and Catherine Peaden on Jane Addams.

86 Conley, Thomas M. *Rhetoric in the European Tradition*. Chicago: U of Chicago P, 1990. Print.

Rhetoric has been defined somewhat differently in different ages, reflecting the needs—and particularly the crises—of the times. Greek notions of rhetoric reflect several different views of nature and beliefs about the ends of rhetoric. The four basic Greek models, which see rhetoric as variously manipulative or consensus seeking (the Sophistic versions) or dialectical (in Plato) or problematic (in Aristotle) persist throughout the history of rhetoric, one or another dominating at different times. Conley traces the dominant theories from Greek to modern times, focusing on schools and individual rhetorical theorists, giving most attention to those who exerted the greatest influence on their own contemporaries and on later thinkers, and setting each in the historical and political context that seems to account for the nature of the rhetorical model. Conley's purpose is to provide the background material needed to comprehend the major texts themselves, as well as to reorder our idea of which texts and figures are truly the major ones.

87 Connors, Robert J. *Composition-Rhetoric: Backgrounds, Theory, and Pedagogy*. Pittsburgh: U of Pittsburgh P, 1997. Print.

The period from about 1760 to 1960 was significant in the history of rhetoric for the growth of theory and pedagogy that focused on written rhetoric to be used by newly expanding professional and managerial classes, a kind of rhetoric once called "current-traditional." Before the Civil War, it tended to combine instruction in oral and written rhetoric and to be taught in small classes or by tutorial. After the Civil War, as new state universities and new opportunities for higher education for women greatly enlarged and diversified the school population, class size grew and textbooks became increasingly important in defining the curriculum. By the early twentieth century, instruction in composition-rhetoric was largely institutionalized in the required multisection first-year programs known today and dominated by textbooks that inculcated formal and mechanical correctness. Composition-rhetoric had lost status as a discipline, courses were taught by academic underlings, and research on writing had virtually ceased. Connors organizes his analysis of these developments thematically, focusing on the influences of changing gender roles and increasing coeducation; textbooks and the emphasis on mechanical correctness; new standards of professionalism and licensure; and the teaching of discourse taxonomies, theories of style, types of assignments, and invention procedures.

88 Connors, Robert J., Lisa S. Ede, and Andrea A. Lunsford, eds. *Essays on Classical Rhetoric and Modern Discourse*. Carbondale: Southern Illinois UP, 1984. Print.

In this festschrift for Edward P. J. Corbett, seventeen contributors discuss the importance of classical rhetoric to modern composition studies.

Essays include Robert J. Connors, Lisa S. Ede, and Andrea A. Lunsford, "The Revival of Rhetoric in America"; James L. Golden, "Plato Revisited: A Theory of Discourse for All Seasons"; James L. Kinneavy, "Translating Theory into Practice in Teaching Composition: A Historical View and a Contemporary View"; James C. Raymond, "Enthymemes, Examples, and Rhetorical Method"; John T. Gage, "An Adequate Epistemology for Composition: Classical and Modern Perspectives"; and S. Michael Halloran and Annette Norris Bradford, "Figures of Speech in the Rhetoric of Science and Technology." Also includes a bibliography of works by Corbett. Mina P. Shaughnessy Prize cowinner.

89 Corbett, Edward P. J., and Robert J. Connors. *Classical Rhetoric for the Modern Student*. 4th ed. New York: Oxford UP, 1999. Print.

Training in classical rhetoric can help modern students understand public persuasive discourse while they discover the educational tradition that has shaped Western culture for two thousand years. Chapters on discovery of arguments, arrangement of material, and style explain logic, the types of appeal, the topics, resources for invention, types of refutation, schemes, and tropes, illustrated by modern essays and speeches. The final chapter is a brief history of rhetoric. A comprehensive introduction to classical rhetorical theory and practice. For the fourth edition, Corbett is joined by Connors, who expands and updates the chapter on the history of rhetoric and contributes a new chapter on the progymnasmata, the sequence of prose composition exercises employed in classical Greek rhetorical education.

90 Covino, William A. *The Art of Wondering: A Revisionist Return to the History of Rhetoric*. Portsmouth: Heinemann-Boynton/Cook, 1988. Print.

Conventional histories of rhetoric depict its major texts as sets of prescriptions for constructing sentences, organizing speeches, and (amorally) manipulating audiences. In contrast, a revisionist history could see Plato, Aristotle, and Cicero as describing and performing a rhetoric that explores ambiguities. From this perspective, an alternative tradition might be traced through Montaigne, Vico, Hume, Byron, and De Quincey, a tradition of rhetoric used to inquire into uncertain questions from multiple viewpoints while remaining open to any stylistic innovations that facilitate such explorations. This rhetoric, an "art of wondering," is particularly appropriate to the postmodern, epistemological orientation of Burke, Derrida, Feyerabend, and Geertz. It fosters tolerance and interdependence by keeping the exploratory conversation going.

91 Covino, William A. "Defining Advanced Composition: Contributions from the History of Rhetoric." *JAC: A Journal of Composition Theory* 8 (1988): 113–22. Print.

In their demand for rigor in managing broad and difficult topics and reducing their complexity, advanced composition courses reflect a post-Cartesian notion of advanced knowledge as schematized and well-ordered.

Advanced writing students must demonstrate mastery of the conventions of closure, both in composition and, often, in an academic discipline as well. But the post-Cartesian model can be challenged by the older classical definition of advanced rhetors as more tolerant of ambiguity. Poor rhetors must rely on formulae, whereas better ones probe and search freely. Plato and Cicero depict questioning dialogists as superior to those who seek simple answers or summaries. Montaigne, Vico, and De Quincey criticize Descartes and support the dialogic-dialectical approach to the lost art of rhetoric. As a model for advanced composition, the dialogic approach suggests that research and writing be used to defer judgment, to explore a variety of perspectives on an issue, and to set aside conviction in order to practice rhetoric.

92 Covino, William A., and David A. Jolliffe. *Rhetoric: Concepts, Definitions, Boundaries*. Boston: Allyn, 1995. Print.

An anthology offering information and selections in nearly every area of rhetoric. Part I: An Introduction to Rhetoric defines the field in a few brief chapters. Part II: Glossary of Major Concepts, Historical Periods, and Rhetors is a small encyclopedia with sixty-eight one-page entries. Part III: Perspectives on the History and Theory of Rhetoric is an anthology of fifteen essays by well-known scholars chiefly on major themes in the history of the field. Part IV: The Contents of Rhetoric is an anthology of essays by authors in a wide range of fields, with three to five essays in each of the following categories: Rhetoric and Cultural Studies; Rhetoric and Non-Western Culture; Rhetoric, Feminism, and Gender Studies; Rhetoric and Philosophy; Rhetoric and the Arts; Rhetoric and Literary Criticism; Rhetoric and Science; Rhetoric and Linguistics; Rhetoric and Education; Rhetoric and Literacy; Rhetoric and Composition; Rhetoric and Technology; and Rhetoric and Oratory. Includes an index.

93 de Romilly, Jacqueline. *Great Sophists in Periclean Athens*. 1988. Trans. Janet Lloyd. Oxford: Clarendon, 1992. Print.

The greatest Sophists were Protagoras, Gorgias, Prodicus, Hippias, and Thrasymachus. Before their advent in the fifth century BCE, Athenian education focused on athletics and music, and aimed to cultivate only the well-born. The Sophists became famous as teachers of public speaking who would impart successful techniques to anyone who could pay their fees, and they emphasized intellectual development. Under their influence, the scientific study of nature began, and philosophy turned its attention from cosmogony to human action, which likewise became the focus of history, drama, and art. The gods, oracles, and the supernatural generally diminished in importance. The Sophists promoted cultural toleration and Panhellenism. They argued that human societies were held together by man-made laws that people could choose to break, rather than by divine decrees of justice that compelled obedience. Although this view could lead (as in Protagoras) to a sort of social contract theory of human society, the Sophists were attacked for encouraging impiety and lawless behavior. Nevertheless, their ideas formed the foundation of Western philosophy and education.

94 Donawerth, Jane. "Conversation and the Boundaries of Public Discourse in Rhetorical Theory by Renaissance Women." *Rhetorica* 16.2 (Spring 1998): 181–99. Print.

Madeleine de Scudéry, Margaret Cavendish, Margaret Fell, and Mary Astell appropriated classical rhetorical theory for their own purposes. Barred by their gender from the public practice of rhetoric and from exercising verbal power openly, each in her own way developed the supposedly private genre of conversation as a women's rhetorical venue, where influence on public events could be exercised indirectly. Donawerth argues that although recommending conversation to women as an appropriate rhetorical sphere paid lip service to existing restrictions on women's public action, it did not relegate women to a realm of powerlessness. They had the opportunity to influence public events, however indirectly—indeed, these women were so influential that their conversation, with its public implications, can hardly be considered a "private" genre. De Scudéry, Cavendish, and Astell were well connected among the ruling nobility of France (de Scudéry) and England—Cavendish herself was a duchess—and Fell was a noted Protestant reformer, one of the founders of the Society of Friends (Quakers).

95 Enoch, Jessica. *Refiguring Rhetorical Education: Women Teaching African American, Native American, and Chicano/a Students, 1865–1911*. Carbondale: Southern Illinois UP, 2008. Print.

Five women refigure rhetorical education through their resistance to the professional and cultural construction of the female teacher and to forms of schooling that disenfranchised their students. Lydia Maria Child, Zitkala-Ša, Jovita Idar, Marta Peña, and Leonor Villegas de Magnón taught black, Indian, and Mexican students at the turn of the twentieth century and invented unique forms of rhetorical education that built on students' languages, cultural practices, and histories to position them to participate in communal life. Primary and archival research contributes to interrogating how issues of race, culture, language, power, and access meet whenever discussions of rhetorical education arise: Child offers her readers of *The Freedmen's Book*, a multivocal text, and invites them to create their own arguments or to recognize when the rules of decorum, for example, might be productively broken; Zitkala-Ša's essays in *Atlantic Monthly* establish her rhetorical sovereignty and her resistance to the "script" of the Carlisle Indian School; Idar, Peña, and Villegas, through their pedagogical contributions to *La Cronica*, create a rhetorical education specific to their Mexican community in Texas and thereby enable students to contribute to and participate in a cultural citizenship. Although they were marginalized members of their own communities, these five teachers belong inside the history of rhetorical education because they prepared students for civic engagement.

96 Glenn, Cheryl. *Rhetoric Retold: Regendering the Tradition from Antiquity through the Renaissance*. Carbondale: Southern Illinois UP, 1997. Print.

The traditional image of rhetorical practice depicts men speaking in public while women remain silent at home. Recent feminist scholarship has disrupted this traditional image by arguing that it does not represent all possible instances of rhetoric in use. Thus traditional historiography has been undermined, while female rhetorical figures have been recovered for study and new venues of rhetorical practice, where women participate actively, have been explored. Efforts to understand why and how women have been excluded from the rhetorical tradition must proceed in tandem with work that studies their rhetorical contributions. This scholarly process defines Glenn's project here. Areas of study include Sappho, Aspasia, and Diotima of classical Greece; ancient Roman women such as Cornelia; medieval mystics Julian of Norwich and Margery Kempe; and Renaissance women including Elizabeth I, Protestant intellectual Margaret More Roper, and Protestant martyr Anne Askew. Glenn situates these women in the political and cultural climate of their times, and critically analyzes previous scholarship that has highlighted or, more likely, neglected their rhetorical contributions.

See: David Gold, *Rhetoric at the Margins: Revising the History of Writing Instruction in American Colleges, 1873–1947* [155].

97 Halloran, S. Michael. "Rhetoric in the American College Curriculum: The Decline of Public Discourse." *PRE/TEXT* 3.3 (Fall 1982): 245–69. Print. Rpt. in Vitanza [254].

Classical rhetoric emphasizes effective communication about public problems. Seventeenth-century theories of rhetoric in American colleges led away from such public discourse by assigning argument to the realm of logic and retaining only "pleasing expression" in rhetoric, as well as by ignoring vernacular English in favor of Greek and Latin. In the eighteenth century, a more "classical" conception of rhetoric recovered invention, arrangement, and audience, and English became the language of formal academic disputation, which dealt more often with public concerns. In the nineteenth century, emphasis shifted to written products, to the "modes" of discourse, and to correctness, and away from invention and public discourse. These changes were closely related to the dominance of belletristic aesthetics, to the specialization of the curriculum that presented knowledge in small course-units, and to a shift in the function of education from preparation for public service to preparation for personal advancement. Many aspects of classical rhetoric are being revived, but public discourse has not yet reemerged.

98 Hauser, Gerard A. "Aristotle on Epideictic: The Formation of Public Morality." *Rhetoric Society Quarterly* 29.1 (Winter 1999): 5–23. Print.

Democracy is plagued by tension between the majority of people, who may not have a clear grasp of moral issues, and the privileged minority, who see themselves as the guardians of virtue. When no strong, experienced leader can mediate this tension, the merely clever who can manipulate people's emotions may gain political influence while the community fragments. This is what happened in Athens with the rise of Demosthenes, after the rule of Pericles. Aristotle wished to rectify the situation by creating an art of rhetoric that the good person can learn so as to use it in teaching the majority what good values are, thus mitigating tension and creating political consensus. Aristotle saw, according to Hauser, that while deliberative and forensic rhetoric may teach values incidentally, by implying them as the bases for judgment, epideictic rhetoric is the most important means of teaching values. In the epideictic speech, the rhetor does not merely tell about the values that he (or she) deems most central to the community, but attempts to demonstrate them in his (or her) performance. Audiences thus witness the very possibility of virtue enacted before their eyes. Hauser closes with brief discussions of a few contemporary examples of speeches that serve this epideictic function.

99 Havelock, Eric A. *The Literate Revolution in Greece and Its Cultural Consequences*. Princeton: Princeton UP, 1982. Print.

A revolutionary development in human thought was the Greek alphabet, around 700 BCE. It was the first to assign symbols to individual sounds rather than to whole words or syllables, thus greatly reducing the number of symbols to memorize, which democratized the new technology and helped it spread. Literacy, in turn, encouraged dramatic changes in human thought processes. In the earlier world of orality, both verbal style and thought processes are characterized by parataxis, the simple juxtaposition of ideas; by concrete imagery that appeals to the senses and the emotions; by ritualized references to authority—for example, in proverbs; and by an agonistic posture in disputation. In contrast, literate verbal style and thought processes are marked by hypotaxis, the subordination of one idea to another in logical hierarchies; by generalizations that appeal to reason and text-assisted memory for validation; and by a questioning attitude toward authority that encourages the disinterested criticism of ideas. These literate modes, treating language as an artifact that can be examined and molded, enabled philosophical discourse.

100 Hawhee, Debra. *Bodily Arts: Rhetoric and Athletics in Ancient Greece*. Austin: U of Texas P, 2004. Print.

Several concepts and practices bind athletics and rhetoric together, including *mētis*, *kairos*, *phusiopoiesis*, and the space of the gymnasium. Agonism, in its sense as "gathering" or "assembly," was central to the production of *aretê*, a quest related to training and performance. These two concepts join together in the production of a discursive art. Sophistic rhetoric in particular involved the arts of cunning and flexibility akin to wrestling and "required a particular modality of knowledge production—knowledge held and made by bodies." Facilitated by the gymnasium and performed for festivals, both rhetorical and athletic training were grounded in bodies, methods, and habits; the sophistic method of rhetorical training emphasized rhythm, repetition, and response. Two dozen illustrations provide historical and cultural evidence; for example, a sculpture of Kairos rendered as an athlete helps to make a case for *kairos* as embodied awareness.

101 Hobbs, Catherine, ed. *Nineteenth-Century Women Learn to Write*. Charlottesville: UP of Virginia, 1995. Print.

The thirteen essays in this collection focus on women's education: the contexts in which women acquired advanced literacy in the nineteenth century and the practices they developed as they put their literacy to use. Essays include Jane E. Rose, "Conduct Books for Women, 1830–1860: A Rationale for Women's Conduct and Domestic Role in America"; Devon A. Mihesuah, "'Let Us Strive Earnestly to Value Education Aright': Cherokee Female Seminarians as Leaders of a Changing Culture"; June Hadden Hobbs, "His Religion and Hers in Nineteenth-Century Hymnody"; Nicole Tonkovich, "Writing in Circles: Harriet Beecher Stowe, the Semi-Colon Club, and the Construction of Women's Authorship"; Shirley Wilson Logan, "Literacy as a Tool for Social Action among Nineteenth-Century African American Women"; P. Joy Rouse, "Cultural Models of Womanhood and Female Education: Practices of Colonization and Resistance"; and Sue Carter Simmons, "Radcliffe Responses to Harvard Rhetoric: 'An Absurdly Stiff Way of Thinking.'"

102 Horner, Winifred Bryan, ed. *Historical Rhetoric: An Annotated Bibliography of Selected Sources in English*. Boston: Hall, 1980. Print.

Selected primary and secondary sources, divided into five areas: the classical period, the Middle Ages, the Renaissance, the eighteenth century, and the nineteenth century. Each chapter has an introduction, primary sources listed chronologically, and secondary sources listed alphabetically. Most entries are annotated.

103 Horner, Winifred Bryan, ed. *The Present State of Scholarship in Historical and Contemporary Rhetoric*. Rev. ed. Columbia: U of Missouri P, 1990. Print.

An indispensable collection of six bibliographic essays by eminent scholars in each period: Richard Leo Enos and Ann M. Blakeslee, "The Classical Period"; James J. Murphy and Martin Camargo, "The Middle Ages"; Don Paul Abbott, "The Renaissance"; Winifred Bryan Horner and Kerri Morris Barton, "The Eighteenth Century"; Donald C. Stewart, "The Nineteenth Century"; and James L. Kinneavy, "Contemporary Rhetoric." The authors also identify areas where further study is needed.

104 Howell, Wilbur Samuel. *Eighteenth-Century British Logic and Rhetoric*. Princeton: Princeton UP, 1971. Print.

Classical rhetoric and logic remained influential throughout the eighteenth century, though challenged by the new rhetoric and logic of science. Classical logic, which came from Aristotle, aimed to deduce new truths from those already known and to communicate them to a learned audience. Classical rhetoric was of three kinds: Ciceronian rhetoric aimed to communicate truths to a popular audience; stylistic rhetoric analyzed orations and literary works; and elocutionary rhetoric, a new form, prescribed methods of delivery for public speaking, stage acting, and polite conversation. In contrast, the new logic propounded by Francis Bacon and John Locke worked inductively, testing ideas against perceived reality. The new rhetoric claimed to be a general theory of communication, learned as well as popular, advocating inductive reasoning and plain style. Adam Smith and George Campbell were its chief proponents.

105 Howell, Wilbur Samuel. *Logic and Rhetoric in England, 1500–1700*. Princeton: Princeton UP, 1956. Print.

In Renaissance England, a persistent metaphor likened logic, the discourse of science, to a closed fist (tight and rigorous) and rhetoric, the discourse of popularized knowledge, to an open hand (loose and popular). In the early sixteenth century, rhetorical study had three patterns: the Ciceronian pattern focused on the five rhetorical arts; the stylistic pattern concerned the study of tropes and figures; and the formulary pattern studied models for imitation. Later in the sixteenth century, Ramism reformed dialectic and rhetoric (see "A Brief History of Rhetoric and Composition"). At the end of the seventeenth century, the *Port-Royal Logic* popularized Cartesian logic. Bacon's logic and rhetoric paralleled this development and led to the Royal Society's project for language reform. Howell's work is the standard history of this important period in the history of rhetoric.

106 Jarratt, Susan C. "Classics and Counterpublics in Nineteenth-Century Historically Black Colleges." *CE* 72.2 (Nov. 2009): 134–59. Print.

The founding of Historically Black Colleges and Universities (HBCUs) in the decades following the Civil War contributed to a thriving black counterpublic, one that emerged in part from debates about curricula, particularly the worth of the classics. Student-produced periodicals in the archives of Fisk, Atlanta, and Howard universities provide a record of curricular histories and enlarge our understanding of rhetorical education. From the archived magazines, where students took considerable risks in publishing their views, student perspectives suggest that a classical curriculum gave southern black students "a sense of rhetorical enfranchisement." Their engagement with the classics, as well as their rhetorical participation, functioned as assertions of personhood, established relationships across differences, and invoked versions of "Ethiopianism." Throughout this analysis, the writings of W. E. B. Du Bois offer context and commentary—passages, for example, on classical learning and on the continuity of historical knowledge.

107 Jarratt, Susan C. *Rereading the Sophists: Classical Rhetoric Refigured.* Carbondale: Southern Illinois UP, 1991. Print.

The Greek Sophists of the fifth century BCE developed a theory and practice of socially constructed discourse, focused on the historical contingency and democratic usefulness of strategies of persuasion, and delighted in the play of language. Recovered from its denigration by Plato and Aristotle, sophism provides a good model for understanding the political effects and goals of feminist discourse and critical-education discourse today.

108 Johnson, Nan. *Gender and Rhetorical Space in American Life, 1866–1910.* Carbondale: Southern Illinois UP, 2002. Print.

Thousands of readers in postbellum America had the opportunity to study rhetoric only through the parlor curriculum: conduct literature, advice and etiquette manuals, and (parlor) encyclopedias, all designed to offer instruction in elocution, oratory, and composition. The influence of the parlor-rhetoric movement appears in a range of nineteenth-century texts and artifacts — newspaper advertisements, letters, biographies, and autobiographies. The nineteenth-century middle-class parlor was a rhetorical space devoted to improving and enlarging the discourse practices and possibilities of middle-class women, yet successfully marketed parlor instruction, including a common "separate-desks" motif, served to keep women in the home and to restrict their access to public rhetorical activities. Cultural interests combined to silence women in spite of their access to prestige discourses: Parlor rhetorics performed ideological work in a culture desperate to restrict public rhetorical space. Women orators were judged in an era defined by cultural anxiety about women's increasing appearances at the podium. Performing gender, then, was an explicit criterion by which women orators were judged; they had to be persuasive that they had not really left the parlor at all.

109 Johnson, Nan. *Nineteenth-Century Rhetoric in North America.* Carbondale: Southern Illinois UP, 1991. Print.

Nineteenth-century rhetoric was a synthesis of classical elements (the canons of invention, arrangement, and style), belletrism (focusing on criticism and literary taste), and epistemological ideas about the relation of language and persuasion to the mental "faculties" (will, imagination, understanding, and passions). All three of these approaches developed in the eighteenth century and found a solid place in the discipline of rhetoric, in theoretical treatises as well as textbooks. The civic and cultural status of rhetoric was as yet secure in the nineteenth century: It was still seen as a significant factor in maintaining social and political order, as well as in formulating the conventions for scientific and philosophical communication. Both oratory and composition were firmly within its purview. "Nineteenth-century rhetoricians claimed for rhetoric the status of science, practical art, and civil servant. In laying this claim, they addressed and confirmed the dominant intellectual and cultural values of their era."

See: James L. Kastely, *Rethinking the Rhetorical Tradition: From Plato to Postmodernism* [219].

110 Kates, Susan. *Activist Rhetorics and American Higher Education, 1885–1937*. Carbondale: Southern Illinois UP, 2001. Print.

Rhetoric curricula designed for specific student constituencies served the needs of disenfranchised students by making their marginalization in the larger culture a focus of course content. Educators Mary Augusta Jordan of Smith College; Hallie Quinn Brown of Wilberforce University; and Josephine Colby, Helen Norton, and Louis Budenz of Brookwood Labor College were concerned more with language and ideology than with correctness. A variety of archival materials and pedagogical artifacts distinguish activist rhetorical education from more traditional forms and demonstrate the ways in which activist rhetoric instruction has a long history in the United States—characterized by an emphasis on writing and speaking, language and identity, and service and social responsibility. Because the prospect of confronting difference in the rhetoric classroom is a more complex endeavor than most educational theorists realize, the pedagogical legacies of these activist educators should inform current controversies in composition studies.

111 Kennedy, George A. *The Art of Persuasion in Greece*. Princeton: Princeton UP, 1963. Print.

Volume 1 of Kennedy's history of classical rhetoric (see [112]), the standard work on the period, treats individual rhetoricians and their works and supplies historical background. Kennedy emphasizes that Greek rhetoric was overwhelmingly an art of oral discourse. He discusses the conflict between rhetoric and philosophy, and traces the development of the great central theory of rhetoric to which all classical rhetoricians contributed, foreshadowing Greek influence on the Romans.

112 Kennedy, George A. *The Art of Rhetoric in the Roman World 300* BC–AD *300*. Princeton: Princeton UP, 1972. Print.

This is volume 2 of Kennedy's history of classical rhetoric (see [111]), the standard work on the period. It treats individual rhetoricians and their works in detail, supplies much historical background, and traces the fall and rise of persuasion as the main focus of rhetoric under Roman influence. Kennedy has two chapters on Cicero, two on Augustan rhetoric, one on Quintilian, and two on later Greek rhetoric.

113 Kennedy, George A. *Classical Rhetoric and Its Christian and Secular Tradition from Ancient to Modern Times*. Chapel Hill: U of North Carolina P, 1980. Print.

Originally formulated in ancient Greece as an art, rhetoric later developed into three types. Technical rhetoric prescribed the correct forms for invention, organization of speeches, and style. Sophistic rhetoric, taught by imitation, emphasized the speaker's ethos and the magical powers of stylistic display, whereas philosophical rhetoric sought to discover truth and convey it to audiences for their good. Kennedy traces these lines of rhetorical study up to the 1700s, chiefly through summaries of the contributions of important rhetoricians.

114 Kimball, Bruce A. *Orators and Philosophers: A History of the Idea of Liberal Education*. New York: Teachers College, 1986. Print.

The history of liberal education from the Middle Ages to the present can be seen as a struggle between two kinds of teacher-scholars. *Orators* stressed citizenship education, emphasized commonly held ("liberal") notions of the good, and valued rhetoric as a method of creating consensus on public issues. *Philosophers* stressed education for the pursuit of pure truth, supported education for the elite by defining "liberal" as liberation from worldly cares (hence, freedom to pursue the truth), and denigrated rhetoric in their search for a language transparent to the truth. Philosophers have come to dominate Western education through the force of science and technology, but the influence of the Orators ought to be restored.

115 Levin, Carole, and Patricia A. Sullivan, eds. *Political Rhetoric, Power, and Renaissance Women*. Albany: State U of New York P, 1995. Print.

The Renaissance was a time of powerful queens and also of violent invective against women in political life, much of it religiously motivated. This collection examines the political rhetoric of powerful Renaissance women, men's rhetoric directed against them, literature by male and female authors of the time that considers women as political agents, and historical evaluations of powerful Renaissance women from their own time to the present. Fifteen essays include Carole Levin and Patricia A. Sullivan, "Politics, Women's Voices, and the Renaissance: Questions and Context"; Daniel Kempton, "Christine de Pisan's *Cité des Dames* and *Trésor de la Cité*: Toward a Feminist Scriptural Practice"; Ilona Bell, "Elizabeth I—Always Her Own Free Woman"; Elizabeth Mazzola, "Expert Witnesses and Secret Subjects: Anne Askew's *Examinations* and Renaissance Self-Incrimination"; Arlen Feldwick, "Wits, Whigs, and Women: Domestic Politics as Anti-Whig Rhetoric in Aphra Behn's Town Comedies"; and Jane Donawerth, "The Politics of Renaissance Rhetorical Theory by Women."

116 Logan, Shirley Wilson. *"We Are Coming": The Persuasive Discourse of Nineteenth-Century Black Women*. Carbondale: Southern Illinois UP, 1999. Print.

Although the public discourse of prominent black women was not always recorded or preserved, much was produced in the last two decades of the nineteenth century—in the nadir—when club women, church women, and educators addressed concerns of all classes. Largely trained in speaking skills in the black church and despite resistance to their activities, black women chose to participate in public discourse in ways grounded in African origins but adapted to multiple audiences and multilayered exigencies, arguing for, for example, common communities of interest. The speeches of Maria Stewart, Frances Harper, Ida B. Wells, Fannie Barrier Williams, Anna Julia Cooper, Victoria Earle Matthews, and others, analyzed through the new rhetorics of Perelman and Olbrechts-Tyteca, Burke, and Bitzer, reveal strategic shifts, audience adaptations, and tactics of arrangement that achieved particular communicative aims, molded and constrained by prevailing conventions and traditions. The discourse of racial uplift, in particular, induced social action by representing it as work, and black women created, organized, and publicized a large number of public forums, firmly establishing a tradition of political activism among black women.

117 Logan, Shirley Wilson. *With Pen and Voice: A Critical Anthology of Nineteenth-Century African-American Women.* Carbondale: Southern Illinois UP, 1995. Print.

In unprecedented numbers, African American women entered public rhetorical fora in the nineteenth century to agitate for African American rights, women's rights, higher education for African Americans of both sexes, temperance, and more. They developed distinctive rhetorical strategies that responded to traditional prohibitions against their public activism on grounds of race and gender. Logan collects representative works by seven women: Maria W. Stewart, Sojourner Truth, Frances Ellen Watkins Harper, Anna Julia Haywood Cooper, Ida B. Wells, Fannie Barrier Williams, and Victoria Earle Matthews. Logan provides a critical summary of each woman's career, and introduces the volume with an essay that sets these rhetors in their political and cultural contexts.

118 Lunsford, Andrea A., ed. *Reclaiming Rhetorica: Women in the Rhetorical Tradition.* Pittsburgh: U of Pittsburgh P, 1995. Print.

Sixteen original essays examine the contribution to rhetorical theory of women such as Aspasia (Susan Jarratt and Rory Ong), Diotima (C. Jan Swearingen), Christine de Pisan (Jenny Refern), Mary Astell (Christine Mason Sutherland), Margaret Fuller (Annette Kolodny), Ida B. Wells (Jacqueline Jones Royster), Sojourner Truth (Drema R. Lipscomb), Suzanne K. Langer (Arabella Lyon), and Louise Rosenblatt (Annika Hallin).

See: Andrea A. Lunsford and Lisa S. Ede, "Classical Rhetoric, Modern Rhetoric, and Contemporary Discourse Studies" [222].

119 Marrou, H. I. *A History of Education in Antiquity*. Trans. George Lamb. New York: Sheed, 1956. Print.

The standard introduction to the subject. Marrou describes the origins of classical education from Homer to Isocrates and traces primary, secondary, and postsecondary education from Greek and Roman times to early Christian schooling and Byzantine and monastic education.

120 Mattingly, Carol. *Well-Tempered Women: Nineteenth-Century Temperance Rhetoric*. Carbondale: Southern Illinois UP, 1998. Print.

The temperance movement was the largest political movement of women in the nineteenth century. It began as a struggle against the sale of alcohol, which was heavily implicated in the impoverishment and physical abuse of women and children by addicted men. Under the leadership of Frances Willard, president of the Women's Christian Temperance Union (WCTU) in the latter part of the century, temperance activism enlarged to embrace other social reform issues, such as improved treatment of prostitutes and women criminals, improved availability of day care for working mothers, unionized labor contracts for both women and men, and women's suffrage. In this mass movement, women took the speaker's platform and published their opinions in unprecedented numbers, in part due to the WCTU's deliberate policy of encouraging women to find their public voices. Mattingly argues that the temperance movement did more than any other force to educate nineteenth-century women in rhetorical practices. She provides richly detailed documentation of women's temperance rhetoric, studies temperance fiction, and explores racial tensions within the movement.

121 Miller, Thomas P. *The Formation of College English: Rhetoric and Belles Lettres in the British Cultural Provinces*. Pittsburgh: U of Pittsburgh P, 1997. Print.

In the middle of the eighteenth century, the first professorships to teach composition, rhetoric, and literature in English were founded in British universities, primarily in schools in the cultural provinces of Scotland and Ireland and in Dissenters' academies in England. The whole discipline of English studies has developed from these professorships, which were originally established to focus on a new kind of instruction in rhetoric. While Ciceronian rhetoric, deductive logic, and prescriptive grammar—essentially a classicist approach—persisted at Oxford and Cambridge, a utilitarian plain style of rhetoric was taught at these schools, along with inductive logic and grammar based in usage. The new approaches emerged where they did because these were the schools in which previously excluded groups were entering the academy and seeking language training that would facilitate their upward mobility. Parallel to this trend was an unprecedented effort to codify the English that they would learn, through the publication of record numbers of dictionaries and grammar books. Instruction in rhetoric and in moral philosophy were linked by the aim of both to direct people's actions. The new professors of rhetoric sought to make moral philosophy more empirical by developing the social sciences, such as economics and political science; they sought to make rhetoric similarly scientific with an emphasis on psychology. Eventually, the curriculum of higher education was divided between the arts and the sciences. Rhetoric was still too engaged in the contingencies of persuasion to become either fully scientific or aesthetically focused. Hence it tended to fall out of the new curriculum, while English studies was reduced to the aesthetic appreciation of nonutilitarian texts, or what is now called "literature."

See: Roxanne Mountford, "On Gender and Rhetorical Space" [228].

122 Murphy, James J., ed. *Renaissance Eloquence: Studies in the Theory and Practice of Renaissance Rhetoric*. Berkeley: U of California P, 1983. Print.

Many leading scholars in Renaissance rhetoric are represented in this collection of twenty-three essays that survey the field, including Paul Oskar Kristeller, "Rhetoric in Medieval and Renaissance Culture"; James J. Murphy, "One Thousand Neglected Authors: The Scope and Importance of Renaissance Rhetoric"; John Monfasani, "The Byzantine Rhetorical Tradition and the Renaissance"; Nancy Struever, "Lorenzo Valla: Humanist Rhetoric and the Critique of the Classical Languages of Morality"; John W. O'Malley, "Content and Rhetorical Forms in Sixteenth-Century Treatises on Preaching"; Richard J. Schoeck, "Lawyers and Rhetoric in Sixteenth-Century England"; Judith Rice Henderson, "Erasmus on the Art of Letter-Writing"; Thomas O. Sloane, "Reading Milton Rhetorically"; and Brian Vickers, "'The Power of Persuasion': Images of the Orator, Elyot to Shakespeare."

123 Murphy, James J. *Rhetoric in the Middle Ages*. Berkeley: U of California P, 1974. Print.

Saint Augustine turned the prescriptive Aristotelian and Ciceronian rhetorics to Christian use by arguing that rhetoric is neither empty nor merely ornamental if it is filled with religious truth and dedicated to saving souls. Medieval rhetoricians, following Augustine, made the art of preaching one of the three chief rhetorical genres. The others were letter writing, devoted to political ends, and prescriptive grammar, which was studied by writing and analyzing poetry. Prescriptive rhetoric, based on fragmentary knowledge of classical texts, declined after the rediscovery in the 1400s of complete copies of Quintilian's *Institutio* and Cicero's *De Oratore*.

124 Murphy, James J., ed. *The Rhetorical Tradition and Modern Writing*. New York: MLA, 1982. Print.

Twelve essays treat the place of classical, eighteenth-century, and nineteenth-century rhetoric in the modern curriculum and analyze the work of Cicero, John Locke, Alexander Bain, and other premodern rhetoricians. Essays include James J. Murphy, "Rhetorical History as a Guide to the Salvation of American Reading and Writing: A Plea for Curricular Courage"; James L. Kinneavy, "Restoring the Humanities: The Return of Rhetoric from Exile"; Susan Miller, "Classical Practice and Contemporary Basics"; S. Michael Halloran and Merrill D. Whitburn, "Ciceronian Rhetoric and the Rise of Science: The Plain Style

Reconsidered"; Winifred Bryan Horner, "Rhetoric in the Liberal Arts: Nineteenth-Century Scottish Universities"; and Donald C. Stewart, "Two Model Teachers and the Harvardization of English Departments."

125 Murphy, James J., ed. *A Short History of Writing Instruction: From Ancient Greece to Twentieth-Century America*. Davis: Hermagoras, 1990. Print.

Seven essays focus on the contributions of rhetoricians to writing instruction: Kathleen Welch, "Writing Instruction in Ancient Athens after 450 BC"; James J. Murphy, "Roman Writing Instruction as Described in Quintilian"; Marjorie Woods, "The Teaching of Writing in Medieval Europe"; Don Paul Abbott, "Rhetoric and Writing in Renaissance Europe and England"; Winifred Bryan Horner, "Writing Instruction in Great Britain: Eighteenth and Nineteenth Centuries"; S. Michael Halloran, "From Rhetoric to Composition: The Teaching of Writing in America to 1900"; and James A. Berlin, "Writing Instruction in School and College English, 1890–1985." Includes a glossary and a bibliography.

126 Murphy, James J., ed. *A Synoptic History of Classical Rhetoric*. Davis: Hermagoras, 1983. Print.

Six essays provide an introductory overview of rhetoric in Greek and Roman culture and include summaries of major works: James J. Murphy, "The Origins and Early Development of Rhetoric"; Forbes I. Hill, "The *Rhetoric* of Aristotle"; James J. Murphy, "The Age of Codification: Hermagoras and the Pseudo-Ciceronian *Rhetorica ad Herennium*"; Donovan J. Ochs, "Cicero's Rhetorical Theory"; Prentice A. Meador Jr., "Quintilian and the *Institutio Oratoria*"; James J. Murphy, "The End of the Ancient World: The Second Sophistic and Saint Augustine." Also includes a basic bibliography on classical rhetoric compiled by Michael C. Leff.

See: Jasper Neel, *Plato, Derrida, and Writing* [229].

127 Ong, Walter J., S.J. *Ramus, Method, and the Decay of Dialogue*. 1958. Rpt. New York: Farrar, 1974. Print.

Although the works of Peter Ramus decisively changed rhetoric, he was heavily influenced by his scholastic predecessors. Like them, he attempted to describe a universal method for systematizing knowledge into academic disciplines that could be easily taught to the young boys who attended the university. Unlike them, Ramus lived in a world in which printed texts were increasingly available. He came to conceive of knowledge as broken up into "fields" (like the visual field of the printed page), composed of discrete bits of information (like printed letters), and hence susceptible to quantification. Ramus "reformed" classical rhetoric by moving invention and arrangement to the realm of dialectic and by treating dialectic as the arranging of bits of information in dichotomies, which presumably convince by virtue of their logical structure alone. Ramus dropped memory and delivery because they are not necessary for print communication. Rhetoric itself has to do only with style, and, because the dichotomies of Ramist dialectic convey rational truth, rhetoric need be used only when a recalcitrant audience required ornamentation of the truth to induce belief. Ramus's view of the quantifiable nature of knowledge contributed to the development of empirical scientific method, and his plain style seemed the appropriately neutral medium for scientific study. Ong argues that Ramus himself cared little about advancing knowledge of the external world or rescuing language from the "distortions" of rhetorical ornamentation.

128 Paine, Charles. *The Resistant Writer: Rhetoric as Immunity, 1850 to the Present.* Albany: State U of New York P, 1999. Print.

An inoculation and resistance model of education, particularly strong in the nineteenth century and today, serves to maintain individuality and the status quo. While most composition histories have focused on villainous forebears and our inheritance of current traditional practices, reading composition history through competing cultural institutions complicates historiography and questions the dominant portrayal of nineteenth-century composition instruction as being in league with capitalism and business. Rather than demonstrating that connections exist between composition instruction and larger cultural issues, work must be done to investigate how larger cultural issues have actually *transformed* composition theory and practice. The rhetorical theories of Edward T. Channing and Adams Sherman Hill responded to cultural imperatives similar to those today. Channing tried to help students distance themselves from mainstream culture while indoctrinating them into the university. Hill produced his rhetorical theory during an era of intense animosity between intellectuals and the powerful rise of mass culture, particularly the newspaper industry. Hill's easy-to-manage rhetorical assignments allowed the construction of a stable self—critical and aloof and able to resist cultural norms. Rather than designing writing courses to shore up students' defenses, composition instructors should teach students to live *in* conflict, not overcome it.

129 Peterson, Carla. *"Doers of the Word": African-American Women Speakers and Writers in the North (1830–1880).* New York: Oxford UP, 1995. Print.

The cultural work of nineteenth-century black women activists was produced from social, psychological, and geographical positions of marginality that shifted as these women diversified their rhetorical approaches. They had to contend with silencing and exploitation of the body that emerged not only from the dominant white culture but also from their home communities. Often fortified by a sense of divine mission, they persevered and accomplished much for racial uplift. Among the speakers and writers Peterson studies are Sojourner Truth, Maria Stewart, Jarena Lee, Harriet A. Jacobs, and Frances Ellen Watkins Harper.

See: Krista Ratcliffe, *Anglo-American Feminist Challenges to the Rhetorical Traditions: Virginia Woolf, Mary Daly, Adrienne Rich* [240].

See: Kelly Ritter, *Before Shaughnessy: Basic Writing at Yale and Harvard, 1920–1960* [654].

130 Royster, Jacqueline Jones and Jean C. Williams. "History in the Spaces Left: African American Presence and Narratives of Composition Studies." CCC 50.4 (June 1999): 563–84. Print.

Several historical accounts of composition studies have established national parameters for the field but none accounts for the seventeen historically African American colleges and universities established in the 1890s. Historians have not typically been pushed to specify their own ideological locations and the resulting limitations to their gaze; their reliance on primary texts can block their perception of the simultaneous existence of multiple viewpoints. Student-centered narratives of composition often ignore the long-standing presence of African Americans in arenas of higher education and their successes as insiders, resulting in a conflation of ethnicity, otherness, and basic writing, and making race a rare focal point for scholars' analyses. Setting the gaze toward the nineteenth century allows for a fuller understanding of African American students as active participants in higher education. Several historical moments, such as the establishment of Howard University in 1867, created academic spaces for intellectual work in the African American community; recovering the contributions of African American teachers and scholars begins by acknowledging the achievements of Alain Locke, Hallie Quinn Brown, and Hugh M. Gloster. As official narratives take on social, political, and cultural consequences, resisting these narratives invites a search for better interpretive frames and different methodologies that will account more richly for the participation of historically suppressed groups.

131 Royster, Jacqueline Jones. *Traces of a Stream: Literacy and Social Change Among African American Women.* Pittsburgh: U of Pittsburgh P, 2000. Print.

Acts of literacy are rhetorical events that embody an individual vision and voice but are also culturally produced and often enacted in the interest of social change, as illustrated by the essaying practices of African American women writers. Tracing the development of rhetorical prowess in public domains and analyzing essays of social change begins at the intersections of context, ethos formation, and rhetorical action—and requires the tools of advocacy and activism. Although they are not monolithic in personhood or in literate practices, African American women use language and literacy as a tool to authorize, entitle, and empower themselves and others, with characteristic reliance on cooperative practices and commitment to social responsibility. Separated from their original homelands, these women brought a sense of ancestral connection, one that translated into their uses of written language. Best analyzed in a kaleidoscopic view of the rhetorical process, the literate forms of African American women show evidence of a blurring of literacy and orality, with features that are inclusive, healing, and generative. Despite a litany of obstacles, these women persevered to achieve higher education at such institutions as Oberlin College, where they received formal rhetorical training, participated in literary clubs, and went on to organize cooperative community activities or reform movements. African American women wrote for the periodical press, critical mechanisms for participating in public discourse, and spoke before varied audiences; they operated in *both* religious and secular contexts. Organized by three views—rhetorical, historical, and ideological—Royster outlines a paradigm for Afrafeminist scholarship and argues, in part, "people who do intellectual work need to understand their intellectual ancestry." Includes a photographic essay and a thematic bibliography.

132 Rudolph, Frederick. *Curriculum: A History of the American Undergraduate Course of Study since 1636*. San Francisco: Jossey-Bass, 1977. Print.

An invaluable history of the establishment and development of colleges in the United States, their curricula, student populations, purposes for education and certification, and the rationale in each period and at key colleges for determining what counts as knowledge.

133 Salvatori, Mariolina Rizzi, ed. *Pedagogy: Disturbing History, 1819–1929*. Pittsburgh: U of Pittsburgh P, 1996. Print.

"Pedagogy" was a disputed term throughout the nineteenth century in Europe and the United States. Its meaning moved along a spectrum defining it, at one extreme, as useless pedantry and, at the other, as the crucial knowledge required of responsible teachers. But often, as the concept of pedagogy was rehabilitated, it also had to be renamed "education." Often at issue was whether pedagogy was an art, proceeding primarily by inspiration, or a science, subject to empirical investigation and codification in rules. Important sites of this struggle were the new normal schools for teachers that emerged in the 1840s and the university departments of education that came of age in the 1880s and 1890s. Among the disputants of these contested meanings were the authors of dictionaries and encyclopedias, women's conduct book writers, philosophers of education, professors of education, and teachers. In this volume, Salvatori collects primary documents from all these sources and provides historical analysis of the nuances of their arguments. Ultimately, she aims to show that pedagogy does have a history and that it does not deserve the lack of respect it often incurs in the academy today.

134 Schultz, Lucille M. *The Young Composers: Composition's Beginnings in Nineteenth-Century Schools*. Studies in Writing and Rhetoric Series. Carbondale: Southern Illinois UP, 1999. Print.

Composition historians have overlooked the importance of nineteenth-century first books, or those written for children in the primary grades, and the pedagogical innovation that these books suggest. As the concept of childhood changed, so did the role of writing in a child's education; most significantly, students practiced writing from lived experience. Major changes in school-based language instruction can be traced to reform educator Johann Pestalozzi, whose object-centered teaching influenced Frost's *Easy Exercises*. Illustrations in these first books served both as writing prompts and as moral lessons. Evidence of extracurricular writing, such as letters and memoirs, suggests that current-traditional pedagogy did not rule all literacy instruction in the mid and late century. Schultz considers the experience-based essay as the most significant innovation of these nineteenth-century writing classrooms.

135 Sloane, Thomas O. *On the Contrary: The Protocol of Traditional Rhetoric*. Washington: Catholic U of America P, 1997. Print.

Practice in arguing both sides of a question, traced here to recommendations in Cicero's *De oratore*, has been a mainstay of traditional rhetorical education in the West since classical times. It has been the basic method of rhetorical invention, the process whereby one finds ideas for one's discourse. Familiarity with this pedagogy aids in understanding two great Renaissance texts, the *De copia* of Desiderius Erasmus and the *Discourse on Usury* of Thomas Wilson. Sloane argues that what he calls a "contrarian" pedagogy would also assist modern students to learn critical thinking and rhetorical invention. He urges that this method not be dismissed as too agonistic and masculine in orientation. While the process does require putting ideas into opposition with each other, Sloane argues that it is in fact "maieutic," a sort of mental midwifery that assists at the birth of well-examined ideas in the minds of one's readers or hearers. Sloane announces that his scholarly method here is "antiquarian," devoted to digging up details from the past that are entertaining as well as relevant to his argument but that have as their ultimate purpose the revelation of the intellectual poverty and lack of humanity in education today, when compared with traditional instruction in rhetoric.

136 Sutherland, Christine Mason, and Rebecca Sutcliffe, eds. *The Changing Tradition: Women in the History of Rhetoric*. Calgary: U of Calgary P, 1999. Print.

Seventeen essays (one printed in French with a translation) by scholars from seven countries who attended the 1997 annual conference of the International Society for the History of Rhetoric expand traditional definitions of rhetoric by considering the rhetorical activities of women who have been excluded from the tradition or who have developed practices parallel to it. The essays look at images of rhetorical women in myth and fiction as well as historical figures, treat women's reception as well as production of rhetoric, and more. They include Christine Mason Sutherland, "Women in the History of Rhetoric: The Past and the Future"; C. Jan Swearingen, "Plato's Women: Alternative Embodiments of Rhetoric"; Vicki Collins, "Account of the Experience of Hester Ann Rogers: Rhetorical Functions of a Methodist Mystic's Journal"; John Ward, "Women and Latin Rhetoric from Hrotsvit to Hildegard"; Erin Herberg, "Mary Astell's Rhetorical Theory: A Woman's Viewpoint"; Suzanne Bordelon, "Resisting Decline Stories: Gertrude Buck's Democratic Theory of Rhetoric"; and Lynette Hunter, "Feminist Thoughts on Rhetoric."

137 Swearingen, C. Jan. *Rhetoric and Irony: Western Literacy and Western Lies*. New York: Oxford UP, 1991. Print.

Is language a lie, a fiction capable of creating only fictive meanings and identities? Preplatonic philosophers resisted the idea that language was deceptive and began to develop a writing-based technical rhetoric to anatomize arguments and cast them in forms reflecting truth. Plato tried to scuttle this movement, proposing instead that only honest dialogue could attain truth. Plato condemned the self-consciously manipulative rhetor as an "eiron," regarding the manipulator as a liar. Technical rhetoric nevertheless triumphed with Aristotle, progenitor of the "linear-monological-grammatical-logical systems" that have dominated rhetoric in the West. Cicero tried, too, to combat technical rhetoric in favor of dialogue, an effort blocked and obscured by the loss of his mature works. Augustine criticized mendacity in language, also connected, for him, to the deceptive techniques of rhetoric, which were to be corrected by sermonic teaching and inner dialogues between self and soul. The dialogic rhetorics of Plato, Cicero, and Augustine are pertinent to our own age, when textual literacy is being challenged by new technologies and linear-logical argument forms are regarded as too restrictive and abstract.

138 Tuana, Nancy, ed. *Feminist Interpretations of Plato*. University Park: Pennsylvania State UP, 1994. Print.

In this collection of work by philosophers and classicists, six essays look at Plato's explicit views on women, and six consider Plato's use of feminine imagery in his philosophy. The first group includes Gregory Vlastos, "Was Plato a Feminist?"; Elizabeth V. Spelman, "Hairy Cobblers and Philosopher-Queens"; and Natalie Harris Bluestone, "Why Women Cannot Rule: Sexism in Plato Scholarship." Among the second group are Page duBois, "The Platonic Appropriation of Reproduction"; Andrea Nye, "Irigaray and Diotima at Plato's Symposium"; and Nancy Tuana and William Cowling, "The Presence and Absence of the Feminine in Plato's Philosophy."

139 Wertheimer, Molly Meijer, ed. *Listening to Their Voices: The Rhetorical Activities of Historical Women*. Columbia: U of South Carolina P, 1997. Print.

Nineteen essays both analyze and exemplify feminist rhetorical scholarship on topics ranging from classical times to the present, including Cheryl Glenn, "Locating Aspasia on the Rhetorical Map"; Barbara Warnick, "Lucie Olbrechts-Tyteca's Contribution to *The New Rhetoric*"; Robert W. Cape Jr., "Roman Women in the History of Rhetoric and Oratory"; Shirley Wilson Logan, "Black Women on the Speaker's Platform (1832–1899)"; Julia Dietrich, "The Visionary Rhetoric of Hildegard of Bingen"; Vicki Tolar Collins, "Women's Voices and Women's Silence in the Tradition of Early Methodism"; and Jane Donawerth, "'As Becomes a Rational Woman to Speak': Madeleine de Scudéry's Rhetoric of Conversation" and "Textbooks for New Audiences: Women's Revisions of Rhetorical Theory at the Turn of the Century."

140 Woodward, William Harrison. *Studies in Education during the Age of the Renaissance, 1400–1600*. Cambridge: Cambridge UP, 1906. Print.

In what is still an authoritative source for the period, Woodward describes the Quattrocento beginnings of humanist education, traces its influence in Europe by examining the careers of important educators (including Guarino, Agricola, Erasmus, Vives, and Melanchthon), examines Italian and English doctrines of courtesy, and reviews the humanist education of Elizabethan aristocrats.

History of Composition Teaching

141 Adams, Katherine H. *A History of Professional Writing Instruction in American Colleges*. Dallas: Southern Methodist UP, 1993. Print.

Professional writing courses began around 1900 as attempts to meet the need for instruction beyond freshman composition and to respond to vocational and professional pressures on the university. At first, instructors were literature faculty, but soon professional writers were brought in. These professionals taught genres and formats particular to their fields—poetry, journalism, business, technology. This training expanded to the study of actual rhetorical situations in the field. Soon, as such courses seemed increasingly anomalous in English departments, journalism became a separate program. Creative writing, linked to literature, remained in English. Technical and business writing never gained sufficient support from business and technical departments to become independent programs and so remained peripheral parts of English departments. After World War II, more advanced writing courses and programs appeared, typically following public events: Scientific writing grew during the space race, journalism following Watergate. Professional writing courses have always been dogged by the question of whether they are necessary: could practical writing be learned better out in the field? Were theory-based courses worthwhile? Were they good uses of curricular time? Despite such questions, many schools now offer professional-writing minors and majors, a trend that appears likely to continue.

142 Applebee, Arthur N. *Tradition and Reform in the Teaching of English: A History*. Urbana: NCTE, 1974. Print.

Since the 1600s, English curriculum design in America has reflected a struggle between traditional goals of preserving high literary culture and a standard language and progressive goals of democratic social reform. European cultural and institutional models dominated the curriculum until the late 1800s, when the first English departments appeared in American colleges. Applebee discusses English studies, in both literature and language arts, at the elementary, high school, and college levels. He also discusses the work of professional organizations in shaping curriculum. An excellent short history of American English education.

143 Berlin, James A. *Rhetoric and Reality: Writing Instruction in American Colleges, 1900–1985*. Carbondale: Southern Illinois UP, 1987. Print.

Discussions of writing pedagogy in textbooks and essays during the twentieth century can be divided into three groups, based on their theoretical assumptions about the nature of reality and the purpose of rhetoric. Objective theories regard external reality as empirically knowable and treat rhetoric as the medium (ideally transparent) for conveying this knowledge. Subjective theories regard truth as attainable only through inner vision and value a rhetoric that uses emotionally charged language to stimulate subjective knowing as well as to communicate one's vision to others. Transactional theories see truth as at least partly provisional, arrived at by argument and interpretation. Transactional theories, then, see rhetoric as a means of persuasion and of negotiating different interpretations of reality. Objective theories dominated writing instruction in the early years of the century, challenged only by progressive education and the communications movement. In recent years, though, subjective and transactional theories have increased in importance. See Berlin [144].

144 Berlin, James A. *Writing Instruction in Nineteenth-Century American Colleges*. Carbondale: Southern Illinois UP, 1984. Print.

Three rhetorics shaped nineteenth-century writing instruction. The first, classical rhetoric, was concerned with conveying universal truths to rational beings with the aid of emotional and ethical appeals. Early in the nineteenth century, classical rhetoric was replaced by the rhetoric of the eighteenth-century Scottish Common Sense philosophers, which emphasized conveying facts derived from sensory experience to beings possessing normal faculties of perception, with the aid of forms of discourse suited to divergent kinds of experience. This rhetoric dominated nineteenth-century writing instruction and remains influential in the form of so-called current-traditional rhetoric. A third rhetoric, derived from Emersonian romanticism, emphasized the individual writer's vision, which creates knowledge of reality by an interpretive insight into its underlying ideal structure, and which evokes a similarly holistic response from the audience. Romantic rhetoric did not challenge eighteenth-century rhetoric's dominance until the end of the nineteenth century, but it has recently inspired some of the most cogent critiques of current-traditional rhetoric.

145 Bloom, Lynn Z., Donald A. Daiker, and Edward M. White. *Composition in the Twenty-First Century: Crisis and Change*. Carbondale: Southern Illinois UP, 1995. Print.

Sixteen paired essays and a response to each pair, on issues that face the profession in this century. Originally papers presented at the Conference on Composition in the 21st Century, most offer challenges and warnings. Selections include David Bartholomae, "What Is Composition and (if you know what that is) Why Do We Teach It?"; Sylvia Holladay, "Order Out of Chaos: Voices from the Community College"; Robert J. Connors, "The Abolition Debate in Composition: A Short History"; Peter Elbow, "Writing Assessment in the 21st Century: A Utopian View"; Anne Ruggles Gere, "The Long Revolution in Composition"; John Trimbur, "Writing Instruction and the Politics of Professionalization"; Stephen M. North, "The Death of Paradigm Hope, the End of Paradigm Guilt, and the Future of (Research in) Composition"; James A. Berlin, "English Studies, Work, and Politics in the New Economy"; Shirley Brice Heath, "Work, Class, and Categories: Dilemmas of Identity"; Linda Flower, "Literate Action"; and Andrea Lunsford, "Intellectual Property in an Age of Information: What Is at Stake for Composition Studies?"

146 Brereton, John C., ed. *The Origins of Composition Studies in the American College, 1875–1925: A Documentary History*. Pittsburgh: U of Pittsburgh P, 1995. Print.

A number of histories of composition have focused on the formative years of the discipline, around the turn of the twentieth century. The major original documents from this critical period have, however, been difficult to access. Having many of them together in this volume makes it possible to see their self-consciousness about theoretical choices, their rhetorical sophistication, and their diversity. The documents are in five sets: Harvard's program from 1870–1900, with course descriptions, reports from the composition committee, and reflections by Adams Sherman Hill and Barrett Wendell; the new writing curriculum from 1895–1915, with essays by John Genung, program descriptions from a dozen representative institutions, and reports from the MLA's pedagogical section; the attack on Harvard, with essays on teaching composition by Gertrude Buck, Lane Cooper, Thomas Lounsbury, and others; textbooks, with excerpts from sixteen texts by Hill, Genung, Wendell, Scott, Cooper, Strunk, and others; and essay writing, with a wide selection of articles, textbook extracts, sample admission essays, and course materials. Includes a substantial introductory history by Brereton and, as a concluding chapter, Warner Taylor's *National Survey of Conditions in Freshman English* of 1929.

147 Brereton, John, ed. *Traditions of Inquiry*. New York: Oxford UP, 1985. Print.

Eight essays assess the contributions of important teachers of writing: Wallace Douglas, "Barrett Wendell"; Donald C. Stewart, "Fred Newton Scott"; Ann E. Berthoff, "I. A. Richards"; John Brereton, "Sterling Andrus Leonard"; William F. Irmscher, "Kenneth Burke"; Walker Gibson, "Theodore Baird"; Richard Lloyd-Jones, "Richard Braddock"; and Robert Lyons, "Mina Shaughnessy."

148 Connors, Robert J. "The Erasure of the Sentence." CCC 52.1 (Sept. 2001): 96–128. Print.

Sentence-based pedagogies of the 1960s and 1970s have been completely elided within contemporary composition studies despite the evidence that they did work to improve student writing. Three sentence-based rhetorics of the New Rhetoric were the generative rhetoric of Francis Christensen, imitation exercises, and sentence-combining. The first full-scale empirical study of the Christensen system did demonstrate statistically significant classroom results; imitation was also tested and determined successful in helping writers to internalize sentence structures and design. Kellogg Hunt's work on syntactic maturity and his concept of the T-unit paved the way for important experiments on sentence-combining, with confident results that sentence-combining exercises improved both syntactic maturity as well as perceived quality of writing in general. Reasons for the erasure of the sentence and the devaluation of sentence rhetorics can be linked to anti-formalism, anti-behaviorism, and anti-empiricism, and to the changing demographics of composition studies as it became a subfield of English.

149 Connors, Robert J. "The Rise and Fall of the Modes of Discourse." CCC 32.4 (Dec. 1981): 444–55. Print.

This survey of the most popular rhetoric textbooks used in American colleges since the early 1800s shows that, until the 1950s, the dominant method of writing instruction was imitation of models of the modes of discourse — narration, description, exposition, and argument. In the 1950s, self-expression and audience models challenged the older method. Connors traces the influence of Bain, Hill, Scott, Genung, the CCCC, and others. Braddock Award winner.

150 Corbett, Edward P. J., Nancy Myers, and Gary Tate. *The Writing Teacher's Sourcebook*. 4th ed. New York: Oxford UP, 2000. Print.

Thirty-six previously published essays (twenty-five of which appeared in the third edition) on immediate pedagogical concerns of writing teachers, divided into ten sections: Perspectives, Teachers, Students, Locations, Approaches, Assigning, Responding and Assessing, Composing and Revising, Audiences, and Styles. Essays include Richard Fulkerson, "Four Philosophies of Composition"; James Berlin, "Contemporary Composition: The Major Pedagogical Theories"; Peter Elbow, "Embracing Contraries in the Teaching Process"; Dan Morgan, "Ethical Issues Raised by Students' Personal Writing" [610]; Vivian Zamel, "Strangers in Academia: The Experiences of Faculty and ESL Students across the Curriculum" [793]; Gary Tate, "A Place for Literature in Freshman Composition"; Hephzibah Roskelly, "The Risky Business of Group Work"; Sondra Perl, "Understanding Composing"; Nancy Sommers, "Between the Drafts"; Jeanne Fahnestock and Marie Secor, "Teaching Argument: A Theory of Types"; Brooke Horvath, "The Components of Written Response: A Practical Synthesis of Current Views" [476]; Douglas Park, "The Meanings of 'Audience'" [393]; Lisa Ede and Andrea Lunsford, "Audience Addressed/Audience Invoked: The Role of Audience in Composition Theory and Pedagogy" [388]; Peter Elbow,

"Closing My Eyes as I Speak: An Argument for Ignoring Audience" [389]; Richard Ohmann, "Use Definite, Specific, Concrete Language" [423]; Winston Weathers, "Teaching Style: A Possible Anatomy" [424]; David Bartholomae, "The Study of Error" [634]; and Mike Rose, "Remedial Writing Courses: A Critique and a Proposal" [657].

151 Donahue, Patricia, and Gretchen Flesher Moon, eds. *Local Histories: Reading the Archives of Composition*. Pittsburgh: U of Pittsburgh P, 2007. Print.

In an effort to undo the common historical understanding of the development of composition studies, which is often attributed to the elite colleges in the mid to late nineteenth century, this collection makes visible the smaller private and public universities as well as the junior and liberal arts colleges and works to include them in the historical discourse of the discipline by asserting that composition "developed in many locales concurrently." Foreword by Mariolina Rizzi Salvatori and afterword by Jean Ferguson Carr. Included are Gretchen Flesher Moon, "Locating Composition Theory"; Kathleen A. Welsch, "Thinking like *That*: The Ideal Nineteenth-Century Student Writer"; Patricia Donahue and Bianca Falbo, "(The Teaching of) Reading and Writing at Lafayette College"; Heidemarie Z. Weidner, "A Chair 'Perpetually Filled by a Female Professor': Rhetoric and Composition Instruction at Nineteenth-Century Butler University"; Julie Garbus, "Vida Scudder in the Classroom and in the Archives"; Kenneth Lindblom, William Banks, and Risë Quay, "Mid-Nineteenth-Century Writing Instruction at Illinois State Normal University: Credentials, Correctness, and the Rise of a Teaching Class"; Kathryn Fitzgerald, "The Platteville Papers Revisited: Gender and Genre in a Normal School Writing Assignment"; Beth Ann Rothermel, "'Our Life's Work': Rhetorical Preparation and Teacher Training at a Massachusetts State Normal School, 1839–1929"; Patrice K. Gray, "Life in the Margins: Student Writing and Curricular Change at Fitchburg Normal, 1895–1910"; William DeGenaro, "William Rainey Harper and the Ideology of Service at Junior Colleges"; Jeffrey L. Hoogeveen, "The Progressive Faculty/Student Discourse of 1969–1970 and the Emergence of Lincoln University's Writing Program"; and Patricia Donahue, "Disciplinary Histories: A Meditation on Beginnings."

152 Elbow, Peter. *Writing without Teachers*. New York: Oxford UP, 1973. Print.

Many writers have been trained to think that good writing proceeds from an organized outline through a near-perfect rough draft to an error-free final draft. This view is wrong for many writers, for it assumes that writers know exactly what they want to say before they begin writing. For those who don't (most of us), a better way to begin is "free-writing," deliberately unfocused but sustained written brainstorming from which a "center of gravity" for an organized essay can emerge. Working on drafts is then a process of "growing," or allowing the organization to remain flexible at first while you generate as many ideas as possible on your subject, and "cooking," or submitting your draft to constructive critical interaction with the demands of fellow writers, literary genres, or your own expectations. A group of people committed to working on their writing in this way can form a teacherless class. They can work on academic writing, too, if they understand that academic work is carried on by the interplay of the "doubting game"—radical skepticism about another's work—and the "believing game"—fully entering another's worldview.

153 Fahnestock, Jeanne, and Marie Secor. "Teaching Argument: A Theory of Types." CCC 34.1 (Feb. 1983): 20–30. Print. Rpt. in Corbett, Myers, and Tate [150].

Argument can be taught by the logical/analytic, content/problem-solving, or rhetorical/generative approaches. The first does not work because formal logic is not the logic of discourse, as shown by Perelman and Olbrechts-Tyteca [237]. The second approach works better because students infer argumentative techniques by taking stands on controversial issues, but the issues tend to take over the course. The rhetorical/generative approach is best because it teaches forms of argument that are transferable to a wide variety of situations. Most arguments take one of four forms: categorical propositions, causal statements, evaluations, and proposals. Students should learn to write an argument of each kind, in this sequence, on their own topics.

154 Fulkerson, Richard. "Composition at the Turn of the Twenty-First Century." CCC 56.4 (June 2005): 654–87. Print.

As illustrated by two collections targeted to new teachers published twenty years apart, composition has become a less unified and more contentious discipline. Indirect evidence indicates that three axiologies drive the major approaches to the teaching of composition: critical/cultural studies, expressivism, and procedural rhetoric. All approaches necessarily include views of process. As contemporary mimeticism, cultural studies courses resemble literature-based composition courses and make the role of writing teachers "deeply problematic," while expressivist composition courses foster personal development—with or without an emphasis on improving written communication or critical thinking. Rhetorical approaches emphasize argumentation, the direct study of genre, and/or attention to discourse communities. In short, there is genuine controversy within the field and little agreement about what our courses are supposed to achieve or what an effective classroom looks like.

155 Gold, David. *Rhetoric at the Margins: Revising the History of Writing Instruction in American Colleges, 1873–1947*. Carbondale: Southern Illinois UP, 2008. Print.

A wide variety of archival sources about three educational institutions in Texas serve to challenge prior histories of rhetorical education. Oratorical training, for example, was an essential part of the curriculum and campus culture at Wiley College in Marshall, Texas, well into the 1930s, where Melvin Tolson, whose teaching practices ranged across epistemologies usually regarded as contradictory, upheld the ethos of the black liberal arts college. At Texas Woman's University, founded as a public women's college by activist women's club members, a gender-centered, vocational curriculum included a wide variety of rhetorical practices, many of them displayed in the pages of a student-published magazine titled the *Daedalian*, founded in 1905. East Texas Normal College, an independent teacher-training institution, served rural students with curricula tailored to their needs. Its founder, William Leonadis Mayo, emphasized public speaking, daily chapel exercises, experiential learning, strict classroom discipline, and the mechanics and structure of English. Wiley, TWU, and East Texas illustrate the practical value of the traditional goals of rhetoric and the liberal arts and were sites where current-traditional rhetorical practices, like formal grammar instruction, co-existed peaceably alongside progressive educational goals—complicating master narratives of rhetoric and composition history.

156 Hawhee, Debra. "Composition History and the *Harbrace College Handbook*." CCC 50.3 (Feb. 1999): 504–23. Print.

First published in 1941 and in its twelfth edition, *The Harbrace College Handbook* has helped to "write" the discipline of composition and has shaped teacher and student subjectivities. Other than a few minor changes, the *Harbrace* has functioned as a stable force in an otherwise unstable field. The original goal of John C. Hodges' handbook was to make paper marking an easier task, determined by what errors students made in an extensive study at the University of Tennessee in the late 1920s and early 1930s. An analysis of 20,000 essays determined a need for thirty-five rules, in a volume small enough to fit into a coat pocket but systematic enough to liberate instructors. The student subject is defined in terms of lack or deficiency, with overt instances of infantilization and no room for experimentation. Current editions of the *Harbrace* continue to illustrate the disciplinary function of current-traditional rhetoric.

157 Kirsch, Gesa E., and Liz Rohan, eds. *Beyond the Archives: Research as Lived Process*. Carbondale: Southern Illinois UP, 2008. Print.

Archives are no longer static sources, but rather subjective, interested perspectives meant to mark a cultural memory and excite or ignite passionate researchers on their searches for knowledge. The contributors to this seventeen-chapter collection divulge their research methodologies in an attempt to pinpoint how they pursued the process of historical archival research, from start to finish, and how such an endeavor influenced their own lives and future research plans. Includes a foreword by Lucille M. Schultz and an introduction by the editors titled "The Role of Serendipity, Family Connections, and Cultural Memory in Historical Research." Essays in Part I, When Serendipity, Creativity, and Place Come into Play, include David Gold, "The Accidental

Archivist: Embracing Chance and Confusion in Historical Scholarship"; and Gesa E. Kirsch, "Being on Location: Serendipity, Place, and Archival Research." Part II, When Personal Experience, Family History, and Research Subjects Intersect, includes Wendy B. Sharer, "Traces of the Familiar: Family Archives as Primary Source Material"; Ronald R. Stockton, "The Biography of a Graveyard"; and Kathleen Wider, "In a Treeless Landscape: A Research Narrative." Part III, When Personal, Cultural, and Historical Memory Shape Politics of the Archives, includes Victor Villanueva, "Colonial Memory, Colonial Research: A Preamble to a Case Study"; Malea Powell, "Dreaming Charles Eastman: Cultural Memory, Autobiography, and Geography in Indigenous Rhetorical Histories"; and Kate Davy, "Cultural Memory and the Lesbian Archive." Part IV, When the Lives of Our Research Subjects Parallel Our Own, includes Liz Rohan, "Stitching and Writing a Life"; Anca Vlasopolos, "When Two Stories Collide, They Catch Fire"; and Lisa Mastrangelo and Barbara L'Eplattenier, "Stumbling in the Archives: A Tale of Two Novices."

158 Kneupper, Charles W. "Teaching Argument: An Introduction to the Toulmin Model." CCC 29.3 (Oct. 1978): 237–41. Print.

Stephen Toulmin's model of argumentation has three parts: the claim or issue, which concludes the argument; the data, or evidence for the claim; and the warrant, which is the general principle that links data and claim. In simple arguments, the warrant may be assumed. If the warrant is specified, then three more elements enter the model: the qualifier, an acknowledgment that the claim is probably but not certainly true; the reservation, which spells out constraints on the warrant; and the backing, which supports the warrant. Teaching students to analyze essays according to this model will improve their ability to write coherently and argue reasonably.

See: Neal Lerner, "Rejecting the Remedial Brand: The Rise and Fall of the Dartmouth Writing Clinic" [520].

159 Lunsford, Andrea, and Lisa Ede. *Singular Texts/Plural Authors: Perspectives on Collaborative Writing*. Carbondale: Southern Illinois UP, 1990. Print.

Despite the dominant trope of writing as a solitary act, the results of two surveys and follow-up interviews demonstrate that collaborative writing is a fact of life for many professionals, as it is for the authors. Descriptions of several writers and scenes of writing act as snapshots of "everyday, commonsense collaboration" and provide insights into the social process and contexts for collaborative writing for members of several academic disciplines. A history of the concept of authorship illustrates the complex role of the author in our culture; for example, destabilized by contemporary theories, concepts of individual authorship have nevertheless persisted in composition studies, alongside a developing pedagogy of collaboration. Because hierarchical modes of collaboration are dominant, dialogical modes often serve a subversive purpose by including a plurality of voices. Further studies of authorship and collaboration need to acknowledge material changes in technology and copyright laws in order to interrogate both theory and practice for social writing processes. Appendices include copies of the questionnaires, summaries of responses, and collaborative writing assignments.

160 Marshall, Margaret J. *Response to Reform: Composition and the Professionalization of Teaching.* Carbondale: Southern Illinois UP, 2004. Print.

The professional status of teaching in the United States has been undermined, for at least one hundred years, by discourses that attempt to expand and improve education by finding fault with teachers. Riddled with contradictions, rhetorical constructions of teaching compete with economic or logistical realities. Training female teachers as professionals in the nineteenth century, for example, clashed with traditional expectations for women. Despite efforts to professionalize teaching, the cultural structures in place that devalue teaching and teachers are unbending. Reform efforts such as the report from the Boyer Commission (1998) still fall short by failing to distinguish between material conditions and professional education. Examples from a wide range of documents illustrate the "inherited discourse" that has shaped the public's conception of teaching—that it is *not* intellectual work—and has fueled a public criticism of education. Composition programs, therefore, have an important task of preparing teachers to be professionals and not merely laborers.

161 Masters, Thomas M. *Practicing Writing: The Postwar Discourse of Freshman English.* Pittsburgh: U of Pittsburgh P, 2004. Print.

Freshman English in the postwar era was a distinct discursive practice stemming from six paradoxical presumptions: instrumentality, priority, efficiency, individuality, transmission, and correspondence. Evidence of these formative beliefs emerges from archival documents of four different colleges and universities in Illinois. Despite their differences, the University of Illinois at Urbana, the University of Illinois at Chicago, Wheaton College, and Northwestern University had remarkably similar freshman English programs. The belief in transmission, for example, led each program to emphasize the reading and discussion of canonical literature. A practice-based history—constructed from syllabi, memos, meeting minutes, committee records, interviews, and more—illustrates the "durable ideological apparatus" that structures freshman English and suggests that "the primary reality of freshman English lies not in rhetorical theory but in concrete practices."

162 North, Stephen M. *The Making of Knowledge in Composition: Portrait of an Emerging Field.* Upper Montclair: Boynton/Cook, 1987. Print.

Composition is an interdisciplinary field comprising three methodological communities: first, the practitioners, who generate lore about writing instruction through classroom experience; second, the scholars, whose research produces histories and philosophical works; and third, the researchers, whose empirical methods include protocol analysis and ethnography. At present, scholars and researchers are battling for control of the field and for the allegiance of the practitioners—whose status has been downgraded by the implication that they should adopt one or the other of these ways of making knowledge. North summarizes and critiques examples of work in each of the communities.

163 Odell, Lee, and Dixie Goswami, eds. *Writing in Nonacademic Settings*. New York: Guilford, 1985. Print.

Fourteen essays describe how to conduct research on writing in the workplace; what such research has found concerning the structure of professional discourse, the use of electronic media, and the social/institutional influences on nonacademic writing; and how such research can influence academic and nonacademic writing instruction. Essays include Stephen Doheny-Farina and Lee Odell, "Ethnographic Research on Writing: Assumptions and Methodology"; Carolyn R. Miller and Jack Selzer, "Special Topics of Argument in Engineering Reports"; Lester Faigley, "Nonacademic Writing: The Social Perspective"; David A. Lauerman, Melvin W. Schroeder, Kenneth Sroka, and E. Roger Stephenson, "Workplace and Classroom: Principles for Designing Writing Courses."

164 Roen, Duane, ed. *Views from the Center: The CCCC Chairs' Addresses, 1977–2005*. Boston: Bedford/St. Martin's, 2006. Print.

A complete collection of reprinted CCCC chairs' addresses, followed by an afterword by the still living chair or close colleagues and friends of the deceased chair, makes every address from 1977 to 2005 available to members of the discipline. Roen's introduction is a history of CCCC and includes a breakdown of the features of the addresses; a detailed chart of past CCCC chairs and their respective universities, conference locations, themes, and the chairs' speech titles; and CCCC members' memories of chairs' addresses. Past chairs in chronological order include Richard Lloyd-Jones, Vivian I. Davis, William F. Irmscher, Frank D'Angelo, Lynn Quitman Troyka, James Lee Hill, Donald C. Stewart, Rosentene B. Purnell, Maxine Hairston, Lee Odell, Miriam T. Chaplin, David Bartholomae, Andrea A. Lunsford, Jane E. Peterson, Donald McQuade, William W. Cook, Anne Ruggles Gere, Lillian Bridwell-Bowles, Jacqueline Jones Royster, Lester Faigley, Nell Ann Pickett, Cynthia L. Selfe, Victor Villanueva, Keith Gilyard, Wendy Bishop, John C. Lovas, Shirley Wilson Logan, Kathleen Blake Yancey, and Douglas Hesse.

165 Russell, David R. "Romantics on Writing: Liberal Culture and the Abolition of Composition Courses." *Rhetoric Review* 6.2 (Spring 1988): 132–48. Print.

The required composition course has, during its hundred-year history, frequently been attacked by proponents of Arnoldian "liberal culture," who advocate an elitist view of education and oppose the democratic, professional, and scientific character of the modern university. In the view of Thomas Lounsbury, Oscar James Campbell, and others, writing is a creative act that cannot be taught; the required composition course is stultifying to students, instructors, and the English department as a whole; and writing ability should therefore be regarded as an admission criterion, not a college course. The combination of composition with an introduction to literature in many programs reflects the influence of the liberal-culture argument. In recent times, the assumptions underlying calls for abolition of the composition course persist in conflicts over the status of composition in English departments, in expressivist composition theories, and in policy decisions about admissions standards.

166 Russell, David R. *Writing in the Academic Disciplines: A Curricular History*. 2nd ed. Carbondale: Southern Illinois UP, 2002. Print.

In a long flirtation with writing instruction in the disciplines, universities began hundreds of programs to teach writing across the curriculum in the twentieth century, all of which became marginalized. Writing was not integrated in content learning, and professors continued to resist teaching writing and reading papers. These failures continue to reflect the persistent attitude that writing is a skill, a form of recorded speech, that writing instruction is remediation, and that the academy is a single discourse community. They also reflect the myth of transcience, the belief that students' inability to write is a problem that will soon, or eventually, be solved. The structure of the university makes cross-disciplinary conversation unproductive; to acknowledge the diversity of discourse conventions would require more attention to one's own conventions and present a clear necessity to teach them. This denial results in a fantasy that the academy is a single discourse community. General education reforms reinforced this delusion, as well as the myth of transcience, by calling for a unified society and explicitly remedial writing courses. Writing in the disciplines is much more difficult to learn under these conditions, which contributes to the perceived high status of the disciplines, but also opposes social equity by creating a hurdle that many students cannot vault. Writing across the curriculum has been more influential since 1970, but the same forces of resistance are still at work. The new edition includes a foreword by Elaine P. Maimon.

167 Santa, Tracy. *Dead Letters: Error in Composition, 1873–2004*. Cresskill: Hampton, 2007. Print.

Understanding how composition has theorized error also illuminates how it has constructed student writers. Examining the phenomenon of error over 130 years, particularly the rhetorical impact of error on readers, reveals patterns and milestones. For example, Charles Fries' *American English Grammar* (1940) "marked a significant departure in how error was viewed" while another critical shift occurred with the revision of error within the context of reader-response theory (dated 2000–2002). In addition to correcting themes with a controlling gaze and deconstructing basic writing via critical pedagogy, composition instructors have also explored "The Frontier of Error," opened by Mina Shaughnessy. While Shaughnessy's work "punctured the dominant perceptions of error," it did little to address the stigma of error or loosen the demands on students to follow the rules. Despite historical shifts, composition teachers persist in reading student texts as if conducting an autopsy. Central to a contemporary reading of error is an understanding of how "error is populated by the intentions of others."

See: Mina P. Shaughnessy, *Errors and Expectations: A Guide for the Teacher of Basic Writing* [660].

See: David W. Smit, *The End of Composition Studies* [250].

168 Varnum, Robin. *Fencing with Words: A History of Writing Instruction at Amherst College during the Era of Theodore Baird, 1938–1966*. Urbana: NCTE, 1996. Print.

In Theodore Baird's two-semester first-year writing course, he and the instructors together designed a common sequence of assignments that called on students to write from experience and to bring their work to class for discussion. Students and instructors found themselves engaged in stiff competition for the cachet of intellectual excellence, a dynamic that was intended to make students independent and reliant on only their own imaginative resources. Varnum sees this course as reflecting American ideologies of masculinity, particularly a combat-oriented ideal valorized by World War II. Although Baird never attempted to promote his approach in the profession, it has been widely influential through the teachers he trained, among them Walker Gibson, Roger Sale, and William Coles.

169 Wozniak, John Michael. *English Composition in Eastern Colleges, 1850–1940*. Washington: UP of America, 1978. Print.

A detailed history of composition courses, textbooks, methods, rationales, and instructors, interwoven with an analysis of theories and purposes and a general history of institutional development.

Rhetoric and Composition Theory

170 Bartholomae, David. "Inventing the University." *When a Writer Can't Write: Studies in Writer's Block and Other Composing Process Problems*. Ed. Mike Rose [276]. New York: Guilford 1985. 143–65. Print.

Students must learn to sound like experts when they write, and they thus adopt personae that seem to them authoritative and academic. The errors of inexperienced writers should be seen as the result of this effort to approximate and finally to control a complex and alien discourse.

Students "extend themselves, by successive approximations, into the commonplaces, set phrases, rituals and gestures, habits of mind, tricks of persuasion, obligatory conclusions and necessary connections" that constitute knowledge in academic communities. Writer, audience, and subject are all located in discourses that exist outside the individual, and it requires an act of courage to penetrate such discourses and earn the right to speak in them.

171 Bartholomae, David. "Writing with Teachers: A Conversation with Peter Elbow." CCC 46.1 (Feb. 1995): 62–71. Print. Rpt. in Villanueva [253].

Academic writing—writing done in the shadow of others—is the real work of the academy and therefore the key term for teaching writing. To pretend otherwise is to withhold from students knowledge of the politics of discursive practice. Student writing is situated in a heavily populated textual space in an institution where power is unequally distributed. The image of a free space for expression, found in Peter Elbow's work, reflects a desire to be outside of history and culture; a desire for a common language, free of jargon and full of presence; a desire for an autonomous author and a democratic classroom. If we wish to help students become aware of the forces at work in producing knowledge, we need, rather, to invoke the reality of the classroom as a substation in the cultural network, not disguise it as a utopian space. Critical knowledge requires working with texts, understanding the possibilities beyond quotation, and not pretending that writing is purely one's own. Composition should not foster the genre of sentimental realism and pretend it is transcendent, but preside over critical writing, academic writing. See Elbow [197].

172 Bazerman, Charles. "What Written Knowledge Does: Three Examples of Academic Discourse." *Philosophy of the Social Sciences* 11 (Sept. 1981): 361–87. Rpt. in Bazerman, *Shaping Written Knowledge*. Madison: U of Wisconsin P, 1988. Print.

We can study the way written knowledge contributes to a discipline by analyzing how writers in different disciplines use specialized lexicons, citations, tacit knowledge, and personae. Examples from biochemistry, sociology of science, and literary criticism illustrate the ways in which discourse constitutes knowledge in each field.

173 Berlin, James A. "Rhetoric and Ideology in the Writing Class." *CE* 50.5 (Sept. 1988): 477–94. Print.

Rhetoric has generally been seen as the arbiter of ideological claims, but rhetorical theories are themselves ideological constructs. Three rhetorics that have had significant influence in composition classrooms—cognitive psychology, expressionism, and the social-epistemic—have distinctive ideological bases. Cognitive psychology claims to be scientific and ideologically neutral. Moreover, it offers no critique of epistemology, the formation of values, or the arrangements of power. In this way, it accepts and therefore advances the current hegemonic political and social order.

Its rationalization of the writing process is an extension of rationalized economic activity. Expressionism begins with a critique of oppressive social and political constraints, positing that writing is liberating for the individual. But its critical position is vitiated by the romantic and individualistic approach that fends off collective opposition to oppression. If individualism modulates into entrepreneurship, expressivism becomes a capitalist tool. The social-epistemic approach attempts to keep ideological analysis at its center, to recognize that the self, the community, and the material conditions of existence are in dialectical tension. In this view, rhetoric is the study of how knowledge comes into existence: it asks how the perception of reality is structured, how values are formed, and how change is constrained or enabled.

See: James A. Berlin, *Rhetorics, Poetics, and Cultures: Refiguring English Studies* [741].

174 Berthoff, Ann E. "Is Teaching Still Possible? Writing, Meaning, and Higher Order Reasoning." *CE* 46.8 (Dec. 1984): 743–55. Print. Rpt. in Berthoff [176].

The human capacity for thinking about thinking is "the ground of hope in the enterprise of teaching reading and writing." A positivist view of language as a medium cannot account for meaning and leads to models of cognitive stages and composing processes that misapply psychology, overestimate empirical research, and rely on shaky analogies. Positivist research leads to teaching by exhortation and away from the consciousness of consciousness that allows us to make meaning. A pedagogy of knowing, on the other hand, works from the premise that language can both name (hypostatize) the world and allow us to reflect on it in discourse: to abstract and then to generalize. Teaching can develop this ability when it does not run aground on spurious developmental concepts. See also Berthoff [175, 377].

175 Berthoff, Ann E. *The Making of Meaning: Metaphors, Models and Maxims for Writing Teachers*. Upper Montclair: Boynton/Cook, 1981. Print.

Teachers should see composing as the active formation of understanding by the imagination, an act of sorting and selecting experiences according to our needs and purposes. To study composing is to study how we use language to interpret and know the world. In this collection of essays, Berthoff connects the theories of Richards [243], Vygotsky, and Tolstoy and the pedagogies of Paulo Freire [344], Sylvia Ashton-Warner, Jane Addams, and others. A useful book for teachers at all levels.

176 Berthoff, Ann E. *The Sense of Learning*. Portsmouth: Heinemann-Boynton/Cook, 1990. Print.

"The sense of learning" is an innate human ability to make sense of experience with the aid of signs. It is variously explored in the eleven essays in this volume, including "Is Teaching Still Possible?" [174]; "Is Reading Still Possible?"; "'Reading the World . . . Reading the Word': Paulo Freire's Pedagogy of Knowing"; "Democratic Practice, Pragmatic

Vistas: Louise Rosenblatt and the Reader's Response"; and "I. A. Richards and the Concept of Literacy." An epilogue imagines that "Ramus Meets Schleiermacher and They Go Off for a Triadic Lunch with Peirce; Vico Drops By."

177 Bitzer, Lloyd F. "The Rhetorical Situation." *Philosophy and Rhetoric* 1 (Winter 1968): 1–14. Print.

Rhetorical discourse is determined by its situation, which has three constituent elements: exigence, the complex of people, events, and objects that create a need that rhetorical discourse attempts to satisfy; audience, the people who, if persuaded, will act on the exigence; and constraints, the audience's beliefs, traditions, and interests and the rhetor's ethos, style, and logic, all of which bear on the persuasive power of the discourse. Some discourse, such as scientific and poetic discourse, is not rhetorical.

178 Bitzer, Lloyd F., and Edwin Black, eds. *The Prospect of Rhetoric*. Englewood Cliffs: Prentice, 1971. Print.

Proceedings of the Wingspread Conference, at which leading figures from speech communication and English addressed common theoretical concerns about rhetoric. Fourteen essays include Richard McKeon, "The Uses of Rhetoric in a Technological Age: Architectonic Productive Arts"; Henry W. Johnstone Jr., "Some Trends in Rhetorical Theory"; Wayne C. Booth, "The Scope of Rhetoric Today: A Polemical Excursion"; Chaim Perelman, "The New Rhetoric"; and Wayne E. Brockriede, "Trends in the Study of Rhetoric: Toward a Blending of Criticism and Science."

179 Bizzell, Patricia. *Academic Discourse and Critical Consciousness*. Pittsburgh: U of Pittsburgh P, 1992. Print.

Bizzell traces the development of her thought about discourse communities, basic writers, and education for critical consciousness in this collection of eleven previously published and two new essays, with a lengthy introduction. Includes "The Ethos of Academic Discourse," "Thomas Kuhn, Scientism, and English Studies" [182], "Cognition, Convention, and Certainty: What We Need to Know about Writing" [180], "Academic Discourse and Critical Consciousness: An Application of Paulo Freire," "What Happens When Basic Writers Come to College?" [636], "Composing Processes: An Overview," "Foundationalism and Anti-Foundationalism in Composition Studies," "What Is a Discourse Community?" and "Beyond Anti-Foundationalism to Rhetorical Authority: Problems Defining 'Cultural Literacy.'"

180 Bizzell, Patricia. "Cognition, Convention, and Certainty: What We Need to Know about Writing." *PRE/TEXT* 3.3 (Fall 1982): 213–43. Rpt. in Bizzell [179] and in Vitanza [254]. Print.

Composition research has proceeded along two theoretical lines: inner-directed research that looks at the writer's cognitive processes, and outer-directed research that looks at the social context of language use. Inner-directed researchers look for innate processes and mental structures, but they regard these processes as teachable. Linda Flower and John Hayes, for example, claim to have described a set of thought processes that produce writing. They assert that the process followed by good writers should be taught to students. Their model separates thought ("planning") from writing ("translating") and fails to account for the writer's knowledge or sense of context. Outer-directed research examines the dialectical relationship between thought and language by describing the intentions, genres, communal expectations, and knowledge that shape language use. In the Flower and Hayes model, basic writers are cognitively deficient, whereas in the sociolinguistic model, they are simply alien to the community in which they are being judged. Inner-directed models seek scientific certainty, while outer-directed models examine political, ethical, and social dynamics. What we need to know about writing will emerge from the debate between these two camps.

181 Bizzell, Patricia. "Contact Zones and English Studies." *CE* 56.2 (Feb. 1994): 163–69. Print.

Multiculturalism is stalled by the outdated national and chronological structure of English studies. Adding new materials to the old categories will not suffice. New categories like feminism continue to essentialize and separate. But the contact-zone notion conceptualized by Mary Louise Pratt provides a way of seeing how diverse literatures may come into productive dialogue with each other. A contact zone is an historical time and space in which a cultural struggle occurs. Instead of seeing literature as a monolingual exchange, the contact zone casts it as a negotiation among people with different languages attempting to represent themselves each to the others. America has always been a congeries of overlapping contact zones, and the growing diversity of our classrooms brings this out. Contact-zone categories release us from evaluating the literary goodness of a text: Instead, we look at the rhetorical effectiveness of a writer in dealing with the matter at hand. This approach reconnects literature with composition and rhetoric, not only through rhetorical criticism but also by casting student writing as contending in contact zones and engaging in the arts of cultural mediation.

182 Bizzell, Patricia. "Thomas Kuhn, Scientism, and English Studies." *CE* 40.7 (Mar. 1979): 764–71. Rpt. in Bizzell [179].

Kuhn's description of paradigms and paradigm shifts in the sciences has led to speculation about an impending paradigm shift in the field of composition. Presumably, this shift, based on empirical research, will put composition studies on a scientific basis. But such speculations betray a desire to escape into scientific "certainty" and fundamentally misread Kuhn's thesis that knowledge in all disciplines develops by a rhetorical process of debate. Thus, Kuhn teaches us to study the ways in which rhetoric constitutes knowledge. Cf. Bazerman [172].

See: Doug Brent, *Reading as Rhetorical Invention: Knowledge, Persuasion, and the Teaching of Research-Based Writing*. [378].

183 Brodkey, Linda. "Modernism and the Scene(s) of Writing." Rpt. in Brodkey [184]. Print.

Scholars in English studies usually picture the scene of writing as "a solitary writer alone in a cold garret" working late at night by the light of one candle. This is a modernist image, akin to themes of alienation in modern art and atomism in modern science. The image presents the act of transcribing as a synecdoche for the entire composing process. The image removes all responsibility for what is written from the writer, since it does not suggest that there will be consequences when the text being written in the garret is read. The image also allows readers to treat the text as an autonomous entity, ignoring not only these consequences but also the text's provenance—the author's personality, cultural background, and historical circumstances. Thus the prevailing image of a writer becomes one of a person who is ignored, isolated, a victim or prisoner of writing. Also, this writer is always male—as can be inferred from the struggle chronicled in Virginia Woolf's work for women to find (a) room in which to write. Perhaps because they are aware of this struggle, Woolf and other women writers generally reject the modernist alienated victim position and take a more pragmatic view of the world and how to change it. Brodkey critiques the modernist imagery at length because she fears its influence on writing teachers, most of whom have much more professional training in modernist-influenced literary study than in composition. Ironically, too, if these teachers do know recent cognitive research on writing, they only see again the solitary writer—in this case, artificially isolated by the research situation. To effectively teach a richly collaborative and recursive writing process, teachers must experience their own writing this way, as well as encounter the composition research that explores writing's social contexts.

184 Brodkey, Linda. *Writing Permitted in Designated Areas Only*. Minneapolis: U of Minnesota P, 1996. Print.

This volume collects seventeen of Brodkey's previously published and unpublished works on literacy, ethnography, cultural studies, and composition pedagogy, including "Modernism and the Scene(s) of Writing" [183], "On the Subjects of Class and Gender in 'The Literacy Letters'" [637], "On the Intersection of Feminism and Cultural Studies," and "Writing about Difference: 'Hard Cases' for Cultural Studies," coauthored with Richard Penticoff. Several essays discuss the innovative composition curriculum that Brodkey designed for the University of Texas and the controversy that engulfed it. A concluding section presents five essays by students in a graduate seminar of Brodkey's, demonstrating her pedagogy by way of its results. Brodkey provides introductions to the volume and to each of the four sections in which the pieces are organized.

185 Brody, Miriam. *Manly Writing: Gender, Rhetoric, and the Rise of Composition*. Carbondale: Southern Illinois UP, 1993. Print.

In the Western rhetorical tradition, good writing has typically been described in terms of masculine virtues: it is coherent, clear, forceful, trustworthy, and true. Bad writing has been characterized in terms of vices usually associated with women: it is confused, overly ornamented, timid, and obscure or deliberately deceitful. Good writing has often openly been called "manly," while bad writing has been labeled "effeminate." Yet scholarship has left this gendering of evaluative terms largely unexamined. Brody traces its origins to Quintilian and argues that its status was assured by the condemnation of elaborate rhetoric promulgated by the British Royal Society in the late 1600s. Eighteenth-century theorists of rhetoric such as Adam Smith and Hugh Blair made these gendered distinctions into pedagogical commonplaces. Brody tracks them into nineteenth-century American composition texts and finally into the work of twentieth-century composition scholar Peter Elbow.

186 Bruffee, Kenneth A. "Collaborative Learning and the 'Conversation of Mankind.'" *CE* 46.7 (Nov. 1984): 635–52. Print.

Psychologists contend that the ability to think is not innate but is developed socially. As children converse with those around them, they learn how to think in ways the community sanctions. Children internalize this conversation, which becomes reflective thought, and finally, when learning to write, externalize their thought in a social medium. Thus both thought and writing are transformations of oral conversation. William Perry, Stanley Fish, and Richard Rorty argue that knowledge, like thought, is socially generated and authorized. They describe a process of "conversation," spoken and written, which constitutes knowledge for participants in a discourse community. If students are to think and write according to academic standards, they must have opportunities for academic talk, as they have in collaborative learning—in a writing workshop, for example, with peer tutors. If students lack academic knowledge, teachers can structure collaborative tasks to generate this knowledge. Teachers should emphasize that academic discourse is not intended to stifle creativity: It is only one of many available discourses the student can choose. Mastery of any community's discourse, however, should be understood as acculturation, which may change the student profoundly. See also Olson [530].

187 Bruffee, Kenneth A. *Collaborative Learning: Higher Education, Interdependence, and the Authority of Knowledge*. Baltimore: Johns Hopkins UP, 1993. Print.

Collaborative learning embodies a nonfoundational conception of knowledge as communal consensus achieved by conversation. A foundational or cognitive conception that knowledge is a transferable entity now dominates university teaching. This view maintains the authority of knowledge and the authority of the teacher, challenged by collaboration and its assumption that knowledge is socially constructed. In college, students must enter new communities and cultures. Collaborative learning is the most effective way to gain such acculturation because it works as cultures really do, through social interaction. Conversation allows people to cross boundaries, to become more like others and learn a new discourse. Not only is collaboration more effective than top-down learning, it creates more critical acuity as well. Collaborative teachers use different teaching procedures: setting group tasks, managing the groups, and keeping time. The process teaches interdependence, vital in our interdependent world, while helping students understand the nature of knowledge and its creation.

188 Burke, Kenneth. *A Grammar of Motives*. Englewood Cliffs: Prentice, 1945. Print.

The "basic forms of thought . . . are exemplified in the attributing of motives." Thought and language are modes of action, and all action can be regarded as dramatic. The dramatistic method analyzes motives by dividing motivated action into a dramatic pentad: act, scene, agent, agency, and purpose. Composition specialists have extracted Burke's pentad from this rich book of philosophy and literary criticism and have used it as a heuristic (see Comprone [380]). For Burke's comments on this use of the pentad, see "Questions and Answers about the Pentad," CCC 29 (Dec. 1978): 330–35.

189 Burke, Kenneth. *A Rhetoric of Motives*. Englewood Cliffs: Prentice, 1950. Print.

The persuasive power of rhetoric lies in "identification": The persuader convinces the audience that they share traditions, experiences, and values, all embodied in their shared language. The use of identification for persuasion need not be deliberate, nor acquiescence to identification conscious, except for the desire to identify. Thus, rhetoric is an instrument of socialization, and all social interactions are rhetorical.

190 Cintron, Ralph. *Angels' Town: Chero Ways, Gang Life, and Rhetorics of the Everyday*. Boston: Beacon, 1997. Print.

An ethnography of a Latino/a community called Angelstown studies rhetorics of everyday life through the *tekhne* of making and the *topos* of order. A variety of scenarios and participants contribute to the theme of distinct semiotic systems and the tension of order versus disorder. First, maps and texts are used as practical tools that help to fix a place—in this case, the field site bordered by a railroad levee. A ward map of the town serves to reflect on the discourses of measurement—the city grid a synecdoche for social controls. Other dominant social controls occur in the form of paperwork and official documents: Mexican immigrants refer to *arreglar sus papeles*, to fix your papers, and Don Angel's false documents "parodied and manipulated bureaucratic discourse," allowing him to hide behind the representations. Similarly, Valerio's bedroom walls demonstrate the effort to create respect under conditions of little or no respect. The ideology and guiding ethos that circulate through Angelstown become embodied as felt truths, evidenced in part by the language of violence. Graffiti and the use of gang colors illustrate the possibilities for appropriating mainstream symbols and recontextualizing them into new meanings. Cintron reflects on writing as the making of an order, raises questions about the ordered worlds that texts give rise to, and critiques the making of ethnographic texts.

191 Clark, Gregory. *Dialogue, Dialectic, and Conversation: A Social Perspective on the Function of Writing*. Carbondale: Southern Illinois UP, 1990. Print.

Through collaborative textual exchange, readers and writers construct their collectivity, negotiating beliefs, values, and actions. Dialogue, as defined by Bakhtin and others, is the conscious, cooperative exchange of discourse in this process of social construction. Dialectic, in both classical and modern definitions, is the process of constructing knowledge collaboratively. Conversation, as social science research confirms, is the actual experience of persuading and compromising through which dialogue and dialectic are enacted. Many disciplines today share and develop this perspective on the creation of knowledge in communities, suggesting that social life is essentially a rhetorical process. The social theory of discourse entails an ethics of reading that places the responsibility for a text's social force and function on its readers, whose criticism should be public. We should teach composition students to read and write as a democratic practice, as an exercise in public discourse that collaboratively constructs and sustains the community.

192 Clifford, John, and John Schilb, eds. *Writing Theory and Critical Theory*. New York: MLA, 1994. Print.

Historiography, cultural studies, rhetoric, social construction, politics, discourse communities, social construction, narrative, postmodernism, and the move to theory itself—the dominant concerns of composition theory today—are analyzed and criticized in these essays. Fourteen essays comprise the three main sections of the book. Essays include Susan Miller, "Composition as a Cultural Artifact: Rethinking History as Theory"; James Slevin, "Reading and Writing in the Classroom and the Profession"; Kurt Spellmeyer, "On Conventions and Collaboration: The Open Road and the Iron Cage"; Suzanne Clark, "Rhetoric, Social Construction, and Gender: Is It Bad to Be Sentimental?"; Susan Wells, "The Doubleness of Writing and Permission to Lie"; Beth Daniell, "Theory, Theory Talk, and Composition"; Joseph Harris, "The Rhetoric of Theory"; Judith Summerfield, "Is There a Life in This Text? Reimagining Narrative"; Lester Faigley, "Street Fights over the Impossibility of Theory: A Report of a Seminar"; and Linda Brodkey, "Making a Federal Case Out of Difference: The Politics of Pedagogy, Publicity, and Postponement." These are followed by three responses to Brodkey and a symposium, "Looking Backward and Forward," with Louise Rosenblatt,

Robert Scholes, W. Ross Winterowd, Elizabeth Flynn, Sharon Crowley, and Victor Villanueva.

See: Marilyn M. Cooper, "The Ecology of Writing" [260].

193 Crowley, Sharon. *Composition in the University: Historical and Polemical Essays*. Pittsburgh: U of Pittsburgh P, 1998. Print.

The first-year composition requirement is motivated by institutional and disciplinary functions, leaving the course with no rhetorical purpose and questionable reasons for its persistence. As rhetorical education shifted toward the bourgeois project of self-improvement, civic virtue was replaced by a pedagogy of taste, signaling the end of rhetorical instruction and ushering in the study of literature and the belief that correctness constitutes character. Using literature to replace rhetoric in freshman English courses enabled the creation of English studies and made composition from its inception a service course, taught by those with low status. Various movements—basic skills, communication skills, process pedagogy—have not changed the policing mechanism of the first-year requirement or the focus on students' identities, and the staying power of the requirement results from composition specialists' middle-class affiliations and the reluctance to tamper with hard-won prestige. Marshaling historical and ideological evidence, Crowley argues that English departments have colonized composition and that writing in the university need not depend upon freshman English.

See: Ellen Cushman, "The Rhetorician as an Agent of Social Change" [683].

194 Dillon, George L. *Constructing Texts*. Bloomington: Indiana UP, 1981. Print.

Psycholinguists, deconstructionists, and reader-response critics agree that to read is to create meaning, not merely to decode what the text encodes. The reader is enabled to create meaning by prior knowledge of the conventions governing text formation in a given discourse community and of patterns of concepts, or schemata, familiar within the discourse community. Conventions and schemata are cognitive in function, but they are not cognitively determined according to fixed, innate rules: They change gradually as the community itself changes. Writing instruction should reflect this flexible definition of conventions and schemata rather than persist in treating writing as encoding information. Dillon criticizes Hirsch's Philosophy of Composition for such cognitive determinism.

195 Donawerth, Jane, ed. *Rhetorical Theory by Women before 1900: An Anthology*. Lanham: Rowman & Littlefield, 2002. Print.

Presents a broad selection of women rhetorical theorists before 1900. Following an introduction that outlines a history of rhetorical theory by women, chapters offer biographical information and excerpts from women who wrote conduct books, composition and rhetoric textbooks, or about a variety of communication arts: conversation, letter writing, elocution, public speaking, or the Delsarte method. Included are Aspasia, Pan Chao, Sei Shonagon, Bathsua Makin, Mary Astell, Maria Edgeworth, Lydia Sigourney, Hallie Quinn Brown, Genevieve Stebbins, Jennie Willing, Sara Lockwood, Anna Morgan, Mary Augusta Jordan, and ten others.

196 Edbauer, Jenny. "Unframing Models of Public Distribution: From Rhetorical Situation to Rhetorical Ecologies." *Rhetoric Society Quarterly* 35.4 (Fall 2005): 5–24. Print.

Conceptual frameworks of rhetorical situation (Bitzer's and others') depend on *elements* rather than on *flux*. Adding dimensions of movement creates theories of communication that turn fixed sites or containers into networks, interactions, and ecologies. Such an affective rhetorical model (dependent upon structures of feeling) is illustrated through the circulation of a popular slogan, "Keep Austin Weird," and the fluidity of its distribution: "the (neo)Bitzerian models cannot account for the amalgamations and transformations—the *viral* spread—of this rhetoric within its wider ecology." Putting the dimension of movement back into discussions of rhetoric means more than decoding a text's properties; it suggests an emphasis on production, generative research, processes, and encounters.

197 Elbow, Peter. "Being a Writer vs. Being an Academic: A Conflict in Goals." CCC 46.1 (Feb. 1995): 72–83. Print. Rpt. in Villanueva [253].

Although it would be best if students could be comfortable in both the role of the writer and of the academic, freshman composition cannot aim at both. The role of the writer is preferable. Writing should be the predominant course activity, with reading secondary. Academics are chiefly readers and their courses privilege reading—input—over writing. Academic readers exercise control over the text by nullifying the author, while writers seek a reader who believes in them. Similarly, academics get to be readers of student texts and decide what they mean. Writers must be free to insist that readers cannot ignore intentions and searches for meaning; they must be free to ignore readers. Writing teachers who wish to foster the writer's role should primarily *understand* what writers are saying and only secondarily point out where that understanding is difficult to attain. The writing course need not situate writers in the ongoing intellectual conversation, but cannot pretend that no authorities have written on students' topics before. Students should see themselves at the center, not the periphery, of discourse. See Bartholomae [171].

198 Elbow, Peter. *Embracing Contraries: Explorations in Learning and Teaching.* New York: Oxford UP, 1986. Print.

Twelve essays trace Elbow's thinking since the late 1960s about the complexity—even messiness—of the learning process, the conflicts raised by assumptions about teaching and its goals, the authority of teachers, the mystifications of evaluating students, and the philosophical basis for embracing contraries through dialectical thinking. Includes "Cooking" (from *Writing without Teachers* [152]), "The Pedagogy of the Bamboozled" (on American attempts to use Freire [344]), "Trying to Teach while Thinking about the End" (on competency-based teaching), "Evaluating Students More Accurately," "The Value of Dialectic," and "Methodological Doubting and Believing." Also includes a bibliography of Elbow's works on writing and teaching.

199 Emig, Janet. *The Web of Meaning: Essays on Writing, Teaching, Learning, and Thinking*. Ed. Dixie Goswami and Maureen Butler. Upper Montclair: Boynton/Cook, 1983. Print.

Eleven selections trace the development of Emig's thought from 1963 to 1982, including Chapters 4, 6, and 7 from *The Composing Processes of Twelfth Graders* [261]; "Hand, Eye, Brain: Some 'Basics' in the Writing Process"; "Writing as a Mode of Learning" [382]; and "Non-Magical Thinking: Presenting Writing Developmentally in Schools." Mina P. Shaughnessy Prize winner.

200 Enos, Theresa, and Stuart C. Brown. *Defining the New Rhetorics*. Newbury Park: Sage, 1993. Print.

This collection of fifteen essays characterizes twentieth-century rhetoric as pluralistic. Essays include Richard Leo Enos, "Viewing the Dawns of Our Past Days Again: Classical Rhetoric as Reconstructive Literacy"; Carolyn Miller, "Rhetoric and Community: The Problem of the One and the Many"; S. Michael Halloran, "Further Thoughts on the End of Rhetoric"; Robert Scott, "Rhetoric Is Epistemic: What Difference Does That Make?"; James Berlin, "Poststructuralism, Semiotics, and Social-Epistemic Rhetoric: Convergence Agendas"; Christopher Burnham, "Expressive Rhetoric: A Source Study"; Linda Flower, "Cognitive Rhetoric: Inquiry into the Art of Inquiry"; and James Porter, "Developing a Postmodern Ethics of Rhetoric and Composition."

201 Enos, Theresa, and Stuart C. Brown. *Professing the New Rhetorics*. Englewood Cliffs: Blair, 1994. Print.

Fourteen selections from major figures in the development of twentieth-century rhetorical theories, followed by thirteen essays of "commentary and application" by scholars in composition and speech communication. Theorists represented are Ferdinand de Saussure, I. A. Richards, Kenneth Burke, Mikhail Bakhtin, Richard Weaver, Ernesto Grassi, Stephen Toulmin, Richard McKeon, Chaim Perelman, Michel Foucault, Michael Polanyi, Jürgen Habermas, Roland Barthes, and Wayne Booth. Scholars are Donald Bryant, Richard Ohmann, Robert Scott, Douglas Ehninger, S. Michael Halloran, Terry Eagleton, E. D. Hirsch Jr., Walter Fisher, Andrea Lunsford and Lisa Ede, Jim Corder, Paulo Freire and Donaldo Macedo, Patricia Bizzell, and James Berlin.

202 Faigley, Lester. *Fragments of Rationality*. Pittsburgh: U of Pittsburgh P, 1992. Print.

The postmodern era is characterized by randomness of experience, unopposed by any transcendent terms, a randomness that terrifies with the prospect of total dissolution while exhilarating with the possibility of free play of identities and social locations—that is, of subject positions. Composition pedagogy is often unresponsive to postmodernity, continuing to assume that unitary selves compose purposeful, linearly structured, generically recognizable texts. While this focus is often promoted by academic institutions as serving the practical ends of efficient communication, composition scholars increasingly resist it as oppressive to diverse students. A more postmodern composition study entails looking at how discourses, and the unequal power relations among them, are historically produced. Yet the field is still reluctant to abandon a unitary notion of students' subjectivities. The field needs the kind of destabilized, decentered view that characterizes the networked classroom, where online discussion allows free play with different personae and even "forbidden" discourses (e.g., homophobic, racist, sexist). The problem that remains is how to establish an ethics of engagement for social action against the oppressive economic and discursive structures that postmodern analysis purports to reveal. Winner of CCCC Outstanding Book Award for 1994.

203 Farris, Christine, and Chris M. Anson, eds. *Under Construction: Working at the Intersections of Composition Theory, Research, and Practice*. Logan: Utah State UP, 1998. Print.

The authors of eighteen chapters seek to complicate composition by reconsidering the relationship among theory, research, and practice—an issue that largely defines our discipline. Essays include Peter Vandenberg, "Composing Composition Studies: Scholarly Publication and the Practice of Discipline"; James Zebroski, "Toward a Theory of Theory for Composition Studies"; David Seitz, "Keeping Honest: Working-Class Students, Difference, and Rethinking the Critical Agenda in Composition"; Susan Peck MacDonald, "Voices of Research: Methodological Choices of a Disciplinary Community"; Yuet-Sum Chiang, "Insider/Outsider/Other?: Confronting the Centeredness of Race, Class, Color, and Ethnicity in Composition Research"; Ruth Ray and Ellen Barton, "Farther Afield: Rethinking the Contributions of Research"; and Gail Y. Okawa, "Coming (in)to Consciousness: One Asian American Teacher's Journey into Activist Teaching and Research."

204 Fishman, Stephen M., and Lucille McCarthy. *John Dewey and the Challenge of Classroom Practice*. New York: Teachers College, 1998. Print.

A key theme in John Dewey's philosophy is to refuse either-or choices and to attempt to integrate dualisms. Dewey sees a person's growth as involving not only formal education, in which oppositions between student and curriculum must be reconciled, but also morality, requiring individual and group to be mutually dependent; art, where creativity and appreciation must balance; and day-to-day practice, in which action should induce reflection that conditions further action. In general, Dewey urges uncovering the conflicting forces at work in any problem and attempting to integrate them. Learning occurs when problems are engaged, which is why Dewey favors curricula that involve students in interesting problems and show them how to use academic knowledge to address these problems. Dewey emphasizes that emotional and moral engagement in problem-solving is essential to learning. Fishman details the nested dualisms underlying student-curriculum integration and how this integration should work to develop students' moral character. In the second half of the book, McCarthy reports on her research in Fishman's classroom where he experimented with Deweyan methods of collaborative learning. Deweyan approaches are especially needed now, Fishman and McCarthy argue, to replace destructive classroom competition with a new sense of community.

205 Fleckenstein, Kristie S. *Embodied Literacies: Imageword and a Poetics of Teaching*. Carbondale: Southern Illinois UP, 2003.

Destabilizing the binary between image and word reframes imagery as a *process* by which we create and respond to artifacts. Texts, in addition, are reframed as image. *Imageword* emphasizes "the inextricability of language and imagery in any literate act" and can transform our concept of meaning into "an ecology of mutually transacting relationships." As an ecological system, imageword dissolves boundaries and makes them porous. Bodies, culture, places, and times are four permeable sites where literacies are enacted. A poetics of teaching begins, then, with embodied literacies—somatic, polyscopic, lateral—that highlight reciprocity and loop through cycles of immersion, emergence, and transformation. In this ecology, texts that are "slippery" in topic, genre, and media lead to slippery learning: fluid, kaleidoscopic, performative. Teaching through the alternative imagery of imageword and through embodied literacies suggests an approach of doublemapping, "a process by which we deliberately juxtapose the corporeal logic of image and the discursive logic of word so that at some level they are always contending with each other."

206 Foss, Sonja K., Karen A. Foss, and Robert Trapp. *Contemporary Perspectives on Rhetoric*. 3rd ed. Prospect Heights: Waveland, 2002. Print.

The diversity of contemporary rhetoric and the continual expansion of rhetorical theory are demonstrated through the work of eleven rhetorical theorists, arranged by the breadth of their theories about rhetoric: I. A. Richards, Ernesto Grassi, Chaim Perelman and Lucie Olbrechts-Tyteca, Stephen Toulmin, Richard M. Weaver, Kenneth Burke, Jürgen Habermas, bell hooks, Jean Baudrillard, Michel Foucault. Following an introduction to rhetoric in Chapter 1, each chapter features a theorist by presenting biographical information, an overview of their ideas, analysis of their contributions to rhetoric, and commentary on their theories. Extensive bibliographies complete each chapter.

207 Gallagher, Chris W. *Radical Departures: Composition and Progressive Pedagogy*. Urbana: NCTE, 2002. Print.

Composition and Rhetoric is uniquely positioned to participate in a reclamation of pedagogical progressivism, if pedagogy is cast as shared knowledge-building rather than as the binary opposite of theory. Pedagogy, a form of collective action and reflexive inquiry, is necessarily a collaboration between teachers and learners. Two distinct groups of progressives—pedagogical and administrative—developed in the same years as the new NCTE. Administrative progressivism became more dominant, as evidenced by current educational reforms. A new strand of progressivism, now the mainstream discourse of critical pedagogy, has, ironically, drawn composition away from pedagogical progressivism; critical pedagogy positions students and teachers in disempowering ways. Placing pedagogy at the center of our work in the academy works against disciplinary and administrative constraints, both historical and contemporary. Rather than debating abolitionism, composition needs to rethink disciplinarity altogether, particularly replacing "service" with outreach. Six intraludes offer narrative representations of the issues.

208 Gere, Anne Ruggles. *Into the Field*. New York: MLA, 1993. Print.

Twelve essays explore the connections between composition and other disciplines as forms of *restructuring*—the idea that interaction between fields is not simply borrowing but reconceptualizing, repositioning on disappearing, contested, or negotiated boundaries. Essays include Kurt Spellmeyer, "Being Philosophical about Composition: Hermeneutics and the Teaching of Writing"; Brenda Deen Schildgen, "Reconnecting Rhetoric and Philosophy in the Composition Class"; George Disson, "Argumentation and Critique: College Composition and Enlightenment Ideals"; James Berlin, "Composition Studies and Cultural Studies: Collapsing Boundaries"; John Trimbur, "Composition Studies: Postmodern or Popular"; Irene Papoulis, "Subjectivity and Its Role in 'Constructed' Knowledge: Composition, Feminist Theory, and Psychoanalysis"; and David Bleich, "Ethnography and the Study of Literacy: Prospects for Socially Generous Research."

209 Gere, Anne Ruggles. *Writing Groups: History, Theory, and Implications*. Carbondale: Southern Illinois UP, 1987. Print.

Since the eighteenth century, American college students have formed literary clubs—essentially writing groups—to coach one another on writing and speaking. Literary clubs that featured formal presentation and critique of papers were also popular among adults, at least until the twentieth century, and offered intellectual opportunities that were especially important to women. Writing groups work against alienation and the solo-performer view of the author. Vygotsky's theory that language development is socially conditioned, along with recent revisionist work on literacy as a communal phenomenon, partly explains why group work helps students write better. Groups work best when all members have agreed on clearly defined tasks and on ways to evaluate their performance on these tasks. Includes an extensive annotated bibliography.

210 Giroux, Henry A. *Schooling and the Struggle for Public Life: Critical Pedagogy in the Modern Age*. Minneapolis: U of Minnesota P, 1988. Print.

The discourse of democracy and citizenship must be reclaimed by progressive educators to counteract the historical amnesia promoted by the New Right. A critical theory of citizenship reveals the ideological conflicts in American history, opposes chauvinism (especially in media images), and envisions a public philosophy that truly honors equality, liberty, and human life. Questions about the student's voice, literacy, and teacher authority are central to this project.

211 Glenn, Cheryl. *Unspoken: A Rhetoric of Silence*. Carbondale: Southern Illinois UP, 2004. Print.

Too often interpreted as passivity or perceived as emptiness, silence has rhetorical powers that have been ignored for too long. Silence and silencing denote purposeful uses of language structured by power and control; at the same time, speech and silence are reciprocal, not opposed. Uses of silence are often gendered, tribal, or cultural; Southwest Indians, for example, shared with the author how they use silence to "nourish themselves or protect their culture." Testimonies, narratives, transcribed interviews, and research from linguistic anthropology, among other resources, illustrate that the unspoken is a rhetorical art.

212 Hairston, Maxine. "Diversity, Ideology, and Teaching Writing." CCC 43.2 (May 1992): 179–93. Print. Rpt. in Corbett, Myers, and Tate [150].

Making ideology and social goals the center of a writing course or program, as many theorists have advocated, threatens the low-risk, student-centered classroom in which writing is not about anything other than itself. The leftward political move is the result of critical theories in English departments trickling down to the freshman English floors below. Composition theorists who are part of English departments naturally seek approval from the power structure, which favors political theories. But writing classes should focus on student writing, and writing teachers are not qualified to teach complex issues such as racial discrimination and class or gender inequities. Moreover, no classroom should be the forum for the professor's political agenda. Students learn to write by writing about what they care about, not by conforming to a political position and stifling their creative impulses. A diverse student body writing about and sharing their own experiences will produce real cultural diversity. (Responses appear in CCC 44.2 [May 1993].)

213 Halasek, Kay. *A Pedagogy of Possibility: Bakhtinian Perspectives on Composition Studies*. Carbondale: Southern Illinois UP, 1999. Print.

The complexity of dialogue as Bakhtin characterizes it is often overlooked in composition practices. A dialogic paradigm serves as a model for a conversation among competing pedagogies, their points of contact and conflict. Recognizing the inherent dialogism within the word and among utterances demands that students and teachers *enact* the intertextual nature of discourse. Bakhtinian discourse theory reimagines the rhetorical situation as a site where centripetal and centrifugal discourses battle; the writer, audience, and subject must all be reimagined, by analyzing the implications of metaphors for describing writing and writers and by characterizing both the audience and subject as coauthors and coparticipants in the discourse—the subject as hero. Understanding essays as utterances rather than as organic wholes situates students in a process of ideological becoming. A pedagogy of possibility engages with critical literacy, authoritative and internally persuasive discourses, and, for example, the politics of reported speech. Halasek readily takes on all of the tensions between Bakhtinian theories and their application in the classroom and provides a model of scholarship that strives to maintain a dialogic balance between practice and theory. Winner of 2001 CCCC Outstanding Book Award.

214 Harkin, Patricia, and John Schilb, eds. *Contending with Words: Composition and Rhetoric in a Postmodern Age*. New York: MLA, 1991. Print.

"A collection of essays for college and university teachers of English who believe that the study of composition and rhetoric is not merely the service component of the English department, but also an inquiry into cultural values." Twelve essays on the general theme of the discursive formation of knowledge contend with the many current attempts to formulate the aims of composition programs and courses: Don Bialostosky, "Liberal Education, Writing, and the Dialogic Self"; William A. Covino, "Magic, Literacy, and the *National Enquirer*"; John Clifford, "The Subject in Discourse"; Patricia Bizzell, "Marxist Ideas in Composition Studies"; Bruce Herzberg, "Michel Foucault's Rhetorical Theory"; Lynn Worsham, "Writing against Writing: The Predicament of *Ecriture Feminine* in Composition Studies"; Susan Jarratt, "Feminism and Composition: The Case for Conflict"; Patricia Harkin, "The Postdisciplinary Politics of Lore"; Victor Vitanza, "Three Countertheses: Or, A Critical In(ter) vention into Composition Theories and Pedagogies"; John Schilb, "Cultural Studies, Postmodernism, and Composition"; and two reflections on the collection itself by Sharon Crowley and James Sosnoski.

215 Harris, Joseph. *A Teaching Subject: Composition since 1966*. Upper Saddle River: Prentice, 1997. Print.

The 1966 Dartmouth conference serves as a starting point for this account of the conflicts and tensions that continue to shape the teaching of writing. Five key words—growth, voice, process, error, and community—have served to make composition an academic enterprise but not an intellectual endeavor. The process movement, for example, sacrifices content to method and asks teachers to be composing coaches rather than *readers*. Even seemingly revolutionary views of error completely ignore revision and position students as academics-in-training rather than as critics and intellectuals. Harris offers the key word *public* as a counter to the metaphor of the contact zone and as an invitation to "wrangle" with the ways in which differences get negotiated.

216 Harris, Joseph. "The Idea of Community in the Study of Writing." CCC 40.1 (Feb. 1989): 11–22. Print.

The concept of discourse community has helped reveal the ways that writers' intentions emerge not from within but through interaction with communal projects. The image of "community," notably, is entirely positive and unified. Thus, David Bartholomae [170, 562, 634] and Patricia Bizzell [180, 181, 182] suggest that students must completely abandon other discourse communities in order to fully enter the academic community. The idea of community should instead acknowledge the normal presence of internal conflict and competing voices. Braddock Award winner.

217 Hawk, Byron. *A Counter-History of Composition: Toward Methodologies of Complexity*. Pittsburgh: U of Pittsburgh P, 2007. Print.

In its zeal to establish disciplinarity, composition's epistemological maps of the 1980s reduced vitalism to genius and lumped it with romanticism, expressivism, or mysticism, closing off vitalism's relationships to art, method, and situation. A new paradigm is needed, beyond expressivism and social-epistemic rhetoric, to allow for postdialectical ecological complexity and for a posthuman model of subjectivity. A counter-history of vitalism acknowledges its roots in Aristotle and provides a new narrative for understanding Coleridge's contributions to rhetoric and invention. In the modern period, vitalism developed into three modes: oppositional, investigative, and complex. Complex vitalisms, framed through Deleuze, situate rhetoric, humans, technê, and heuristics within a larger complex ecology. Pushing the concept of ecology to its limits cannot happen within the dialectic of social-epistemic rhetoric; Berlin's epistemological map for composition, for example, excludes "critical elements of knowledge production." In twenty-first-century digital culture, the pedagogical methods of Kameen and Ulmer "situate student bodies in complex ecological environments as an epistemological basis for invention." To get there, it is important to distinguish process from method. A complex vitalist paradigm needs new methods that utilize rhetorical ecologies.

218 Jung, Julie. *Revisionary Rhetoric, Feminist Pedagogy, and Multigenre Texts*. Carbondale: Southern Illinois UP, 2005. Print.

A disruptive theory/practice of revision sees it as a "process of *delaying* clarification of meaning so that differences can be heard, explored, and understood." A relational rhetoric advocates for delayed consensus and more attention to conflicts or disconnections. This revisionary rhetoric is founded on concepts of silence and listening, margins and borders, and reading and responsibility. Feminism and revision combine to question the idea of progression—that texts, for example, will get "better" rather than merely change—and to suggest multigenre texts as one possibility for "writing that listens" and/or triggers "productive discomfort." Jung's multigenre approach invites readers into her classrooms, her childhood diaries, her responses to texts, and shares with them the development of her pedagogical identity.

See: Julie Jung, "Textual Mainstreaming and Rhetorics of Accommodation" [721].

219 Kastely, James L. *Rethinking the Rhetorical Tradition: From Plato to Postmodernism*. New Haven: Yale UP, 1997. Print.

Using language requires that one betray one's morality because it provides an inevitably partial view of the world—that is, both incomplete and biased, conditions under which morality cannot be consistently applied. Thus, using language inevitably implicates one in injustice: the most serious problem with language use, for the ancient Greeks. Rhetoric is designed to deal with this human condition, in which people must make decisions based on limited knowledge, which cannot be fair to everyone. Rhetoric's chief method for dealing with this condition is a kind of skepticism that requires one to doubt and question every assertion. By doubting—that is, by attempting to ensure that all possible views will be considered—rhetoric provides the best chance of arriving at admittedly provisional but collective agreements. This was Plato's view of rhetoric. But this function of rhetoric was destroyed by Aristotle when he schematized rhetoric so that it could make assertions. Postmodern theorists are either too concerned with the limitations on human knowledge or not concerned enough with the problem of injustice. Plato's view of rhetoric, then, is needed now more than ever, to restore public discourse. Kastely illustrates the evolution of these ideas through analyzing Plato, Greek tragedy, Jane Austen, Jean-Paul Sartre, Paul de Man, Richard Rorty, and other thinkers.

220 Kent, Thomas. *Paralogic Rhetoric: A Theory of Communicative Interaction*. Lewisburg: Bucknell UP, 1993. Print.

Expressivism, cognitivism, and social constructionism all construe the mind and external reality as completely separate, with contact mediated by transcendent mental forms, cognitive processes, or discourse conventions, respectively. The mind is thus unable to get in touch with other minds—the mediating structure is always in the way. The mind is also unable to verify the structure it must use. Relativism is the inescapable conclusion of such views. Philosopher Donald Davidson suggests a better model of communication as a triangulated process in which two people compare their impressions of a shared sensory stimulus, each guessing what the other has in mind. To the extent that they are able to communicate, they may ascertain whether these guesses are correct. This process is paralogical, not logical, because it is not reducible to rules. It follows that the communication process cannot be taught, as there are no rules to teach. Communication can only be practiced, collaboratively. Winner of CCCC Outstanding Book Award for 1995.

221 Kinneavy, James L. A *Theory of Discourse*. 1971. New York: Norton, 1980. Print.

Discourse can be divided into four main types: reference, persuasive, literary, and expressive, each emphasizing a particular element in the exchange between writer and audience about the subject of the discourse. Reference discourse emphasizes the subject, which it presents with as little interference as possible from writer, reader, or language itself. In persuasive discourse, the aim is to move the reader, and the other elements—writer, subject, and language—are subordinated to that end. Literary discourse focuses on language itself: Writer, reader, and subject are incidental. Expressive discourse emphasizes the writer, suiting subject and language to the writer's need for self-expression. A complex and influential work in the study of discourse. See also James L. Kinneavy, "The Basic Aims of Discourse," CCC 20 (Dec. 1969): 297–304. Rpt. in Corbett, Myers, and Tate [150].

See: Andrea A. Lunsford, "Toward a Mestiza Rhetoric: Gloria Anzaldúa on Composition and Postcoloniality" [750].

222 Lunsford, Andrea A., and Lisa S. Ede. "Classical Rhetoric, Modern Rhetoric, and Contemporary Discourse Studies." *Written Communication* 1 (Jan. 1984): 78–100. Print.

Some proponents of the "new rhetoric" claim that in classical rhetoric humans are regarded as rational beings moved chiefly by logic but subject to the coercion of rhetors. Grimaldi shows, however, that for Aristotle, both inductive argument (by example) and deductive argument (by enthymeme) rely on all three appeals (logos, pathos, and ethos) in order to discover contingent truths. Thus, classical rhetoric is similar to modern rhetoric as a cross-disciplinary enterprise. But unlike modern rhetoric, classical rhetoric relied on oral language and searched for stable truths in the world.

223 Mailloux, Steven. *Reception Histories: Rhetoric, Pragmatism, and American Cultural Politics*. Ithaca: Cornell UP, 1998. Print.

Rhetoric is the study of how textual effects are produced and received. Thus, rhetoric has affinities with hermeneutics and is particularly helpful to interpretation in cross-cultural situations. This view of rhetoric is found in the work of the Greek Sophists, and its connection to contemporary pragmatism can be traced through the history of the Sophist Protagoras' reception by founding pragmatists William James, John Dewey, and F. C. S. Schiller. Mailloux illustrates his concept of "rhetorical hermeneutics" by analyzing three reception histories: Margaret Fuller's review of Frederick Douglass' *Narrative*; 1970s reader-response critics' readings of John Bunyan's *Pilgrim's Progress*; and the function of the metaphor of reading as eating in nineteenth-century debates over adolescent education and juvenile delinquency. Mailloux concludes by calling for increased attention to rhetoric in English studies and by describing what happened when he attempted to persuade his colleagues to structure the major around his approach at Syracuse University.

See: Paula Mathieu, *Tactics of Hope: The Public Turn in English Composition* [695].

224 Micciche, Laura R. *Doing Emotion: Rhetoric, Writing, Teaching.* Portsmouth: Heinemann-Boynton/Cook, 2007. Print.

Emotion plays a legitimate role in analyzing meaning and rhetorical action. It is not simply the focus of textual analysis or a tool for persuasion; emotion is performative, enacted and produced during "collisions of contact." The emotional appeal needs to be reconsidered not as *emoting* but as *producing* something, including institutional conditions. Disappointment in WPA work, for example, shows how emotions have political effects as they accumulate and adhere to work locations, a view that detaches emotions from "the personal" and sees them as something embodied. Such strategies, utilized as deep embodiment pedagogy, widen the selection of choices available to rhetors and foreground emotions as things we *do* rather than feelings we *have*.

225 Miller, Richard E. "Fault Lines in the Contact Zone." *CE* 56.4 (Apr. 1994): 389–408. Print.

How should teachers handle student work that attacks the institution of schooling or that expresses virulently prejudiced views? This question was posed dramatically by a student paper submitted to openly gay teacher Scott Lankford, which he first shared at an MLA workshop in 1991. The writer describes an evening out with drunken friends during which they harass gay men on the street and severely beat a homeless man. Should such a student writer be reported to the police or referred for psychological counseling? That response risks treating as fact an account that may be fictional. On the other hand, responding to the paper solely as a work of fiction and commenting only on its structural and stylistic features, as Lankford did, ignores content that the student may have meant to be provocative and thus silences this kind of resistance to the classroom agenda. A third approach might ask Lankford's student to write another version of the evening from the perspective of one of the victims, but this risks eliciting work that insincerely reproduces the teacher's views. Needed, instead, is a pedagogy that responds to the kinds of parodic, oppositional, and/or inflammatory texts that are likely to be produced in a course that emphasizes addressing cultural differences, as often recommended in work that builds on Mary Louise Pratt's concept of the "contact zone" [see 239]. A pedagogy is needed that examines the cultural forces that produce papers like Lankford's, and that encourages students to evaluate a range of written responses to situations of cultural conflict, including some that may be hateful to the teacher or to some class members.

226 Miller, Susan. *Rescuing the Subject: A Critical Introduction to Rhetoric and the Writer.* Carbondale: Southern Illinois UP, 1989. Print.

The story of instruction in language use must be liberated from the traditional major-texts approach. Premodern rhetoric cannot provide an adequate theoretical base for modern composition studies, first, because it focuses on oratory and neglects intertextuality, and second, because it focuses on officially sanctioned forms of language use and neglects adventitious and popular uses. We need a textual rhetoric that highlights intertextuality while avoiding the social and historical decontextualization of writing that besets contemporary literary studies. This approach includes a complex view of the writing subject that avoids both the naive classical definition of the rhetor as a "good man speaking well" and the postmodern reduction of the person to a discursive position.

227 Miller, Susan. *Textual Carnivals: The Politics of Composition*. Carbondale: Southern Illinois UP, 1991. Print.

Composition teachers submit to the continuing subordination of composition to literature and even unwittingly reinforce the perception of composition as a merely practical art without disciplinary status or intellectual rigor. Like other groups marginalized by race, gender, or class, composition teachers have created self-images of sacrifice and rebellion that actually maintain their inequality, reproduce the received history of composition's inferiority, and hide the institutional agendas that stigmatize it. To change the story told about composition requires a close examination of the connections between it and literature, a critique of received history, and an effort to "endow agency and dignity" on the protagonists of the story: students, teachers (like the "sad women in the basement"), and program administrators. Includes an appendix, "The Status of Composition: A Survey of How Its Professionals See It." Winner of the CCCC Outstanding Book Award for 1992.

228 Mountford, Roxanne. "On Gender and Rhetorical Space." *Rhetoric Society Quarterly* 31.1 (Winter 2001): 41–71. Print.

Rhetorical space becomes a useful concept if it accounts for the effect of physical spaces on a communicative event, including the cultural and material arrangement of space. The pulpit, an embodiment of clerical authority, is a gendered location so constructed as to make women's presence "metonymically problematic." Literary images of the pulpit have located women preachers in natural settings (meadows or front porches), where the sermons develop from the setting, and women preachers must continually reimagine the space of the traditional pulpit because, as architecture, pulpits participate in the "social imaginary" or the cultural dimension of space. Gender hierarchies, persistently associated with geography, emphasize that status in the social imaginary must be marked by geographical exclusions, sometimes resulting in symbolic trespasses upon sacred ground. Rhetorical spaces carry the residue of history and the physical representation of relationships and ideas; thus, the complex relationship of gender and rhetorical space in the art of preaching can be traced through the history of church architecture and its functions in producing meaning.

229 Neel, Jasper. *Plato, Derrida, and Writing*. Carbondale: Southern Illinois UP, 1988. Print.

Plato and Derrida launch much the same attack on writing, denying that the process of writing can generate transcendent truth. Plato argued that the rhetor must find truth by philosophical means before attempting to convey it and should convey it by speech rather than writing, because interlocutors cannot interrogate a text about its method. Derrida denies Plato's contentions that philosophy can attain transcendent truth and that dialogue gives access to the philosophical method. Instead, says Derrida, we have only the fictions constructed by writing, a web of texts accumulating over time, allusively linked. Derrida argues correctly that transcendent truth does not exist (or at least that such truth is unknowable), but he is mistaken when he concludes that no *usable* truth exists. There is sufficient truth to serve as a basis for decisions about social action in the "strong discourse" of Sophists—be they Isocrates and Gorgias or the leaders of modern democracies. The strong discourse of probabilistic rhetoric is not mere propaganda, as Plato argued, if only because such discourse tends to generate competing discourses that test its claims. Composition studies can work to free rhetoric from the strictures of philosophy so that it can fulfill its political mission.

230 Ohmann, Richard. *English in America.* New York: Oxford UP, 1976. Print.

The professional, institutional, and economic structures within which we teach severely constrain the efficacy of liberalizing curricular reforms. Universities continue to serve the needs of government and industry for efficient, docile communicators, while teachers resist acknowledging the political implications of their control of knowledge. This book includes a chapter by Wallace Douglas on English education in America in the 1800s, focusing on the influence of Channing of Harvard.

231 Olson, Gary A., ed. *Philosophy, Rhetoric, Literary Criticism: (Inter)views.* Carbondale: Southern Illinois UP, 1994. Print.

Six interviews with scholars outside of composition—philosopher Donald Davidson, literary theorists Stanley Fish, bell hooks, J. Hillis Miller, and Jane Tompkins, and philosopher Stephen Toulmin—are each followed by two response essays by composition scholars. The responses explore the applications of "outside" theories to composition and sometimes react contentiously to them. Response essays are by Susan Wells, Reed Way Dasenbrock, Patricia Bizzell, John Trimbur, Joyce Irene Middleton, Tom Fox, Patricia Harkin, Jasper Neel, Susan Jarratt, Elizabeth Flynn, Arabella Lyon, and C. Jan Swearingen. Includes a foreword by Clifford Geertz, introduction by Patricia Bizzell, and commentary by David Bleich.

232 Olson, Gary A., ed. *Rhetoric and Composition as Intellectual Work.* Carbondale: Southern Illinois UP, 2002. Print.

Rhetoric and composition is engaged in an ongoing disciplinary debate about whether it should be an intellectual as well as a service discipline. Organized in five parts (Disciplinary Concerns, Historical Inquiry, Ideological Inquiry, Philosophical Inquiry, and New Directions), nineteen chapters include Jasper Neel, "Reclaiming Our Theoretical Heritage: A Big Fish Tale"; Charles Bazerman, "The Case for Writing Studies as an Intellectual Discipline"; Susan Wells, "Claiming the Archive for Rhetoric and Composition"; Gary A. Olson, "Ideological Critique in Rhetoric and Composition"; Keith Gilyard, "Holdin It Down: Students' Right and the Struggle over Language Diversity"; Steven Mailloux, "From Segregated Schools to Dimpled Chads: Rhetorical Hermeneutics and the Suasive Work of Theory"; Victor J. Vitanza, "Seeing in Third Sophistic Ways"; Sharon Crowley, "Body Studies in Rhetoric and Composition"; John Trimbur, "Delivering the Message: Typography and the Materiality of Writing"; Cynthia L. Selfe and Richard J. Selfe, "The Intellectual Work of Computers and Composition Studies."

233 Olson, Gary A., and Sidney I. Dobrin, eds. *Composition Theory for the Postmodern Classroom*. Albany: State U of New York P, 1995. Print.

Twenty-two essays originally published in *JAC* [12], including James Kinneavy, "The Process of Writing: A Philosophical Base in Hermeneutics"; Jasper Neel, "Dichotomy, Consubstantiality, Technical Writing, Literary Theory: The Double Orthodox Curse"; Patricia Sullivan, "Writing in the Graduate Curriculum: Literary Criticism as Composition"; David Smit, "Some Difficulties with Collaborative Writing"; Thomas Fox, "Repositioning the Profession: Teaching Writing to African American Students"; W. Ross Winterowd, "Rediscovering the Essay"; Robert Wood, "The Dialectic Suppression of Feminist Thought in Radical Pedagogy"; Henry Giroux, "Paulo Freire and the Politics of Postcolonialism"; Joseph Harris, "The Other Reader"; John Trimbur, "Articulation Theory and the Problem of Determination: A Reading of *Lives on the Boundary*"; J. Hillis Miller, "Nietzsche in Basel: Writing Reading"; and Richard Coe, "Defining Rhetoric—and Us: A Meditation on Burke's Definitions."

234 Olson, Gary A., and Irene Gale, eds. *(Inter)views: Cross-Disciplinary Perspectives on Rhetoric and Literacy*. Carbondale: Southern Illinois UP, 1991. Print.

Seven interviews with scholars outside of composition—Mary Field Belenky, Noam Chomsky, Jacques Derrida, Paulo Freire, Clifford Geertz, Richard Rorty, and Gayatri Spivak—each followed by two response essays by composition scholars. The responses explore and criticize the applications of their theories to composition. Response essays are by Elizabeth Flynn, Marilyn Cooper, James Sledd, Sharon Crowley, Jasper Neel, James Berlin, C. H. Knoblauch, Linda Brodkey, Kenneth Bruffee, and Thomas Kent. Includes a foreword by David Bleich and an afterword by Andrea Lunsford.

235 Owens, Derek. *Resisting Writings (and the Boundaries of Composition)*. Dallas: Southern Methodist UP, 1994. Print.

Composition courses that teach only academic discourse or the personal essay are ethnocentric. Rather, the introductory course should survey kinds of writing produced in different cultures, in feminist work, and in experimental writing inspired by electronic media in which fiction and nonfiction are often blurred. Upper-division courses could be devoted to each of these kinds of writing. Additionally, academics should push for a wider variety of writing to be acceptable in all undergraduate and graduate courses and in scholarly publications. Only in this way will American education's "process of rigid mechanization and self-effacement" be resisted creatively by students and teachers alike, with healthy results for social justice.

236 Perelman, Chaim. *The Realm of Rhetoric*. Trans. William Kluback. Notre Dame: U of Notre Dame P, 1982. Trans. of *L'Empire Rhetorique*. 1977. Print.

A summary of *The New Rhetoric* [237].

237 Perelman, Chaim, and L. Olbrechts-Tyteca. *The New Rhetoric: A Treatise on Argumentation*. Trans. John Wilkinson and Purcell Weaver. 1958. Rpt. Notre Dame: U of Notre Dame P, 1969. Print. Excerpted in Bizzell and Herzberg [50].

Rhetoric is the art of gaining adherents to propositions that cannot be verified through calculations. All rhetorical discourse, then, is argumentation. Some arguments aim to convince only a particular audience, whereas others try to persuade all rational people—the imagined "universal audience." Arguments can be evaluated rationally and good reasons given for or against adherence to them, both for particular and for "universal" audiences. Such evaluations, though rational, are conditioned by the culture of the evaluator's discourse community—its traditions, language-using conventions, and beliefs. This book exhaustively catalogs the kinds of arguments that can be used in most Western discourse communities, with numerous examples from canonical works in philosophy, literature, history, and other fields. A seminal work in discourse theory.

238 Petraglia, Joseph, ed. *Reconceiving Writing, Rethinking Writing Instruction*. Mahwah: Erlbaum, 1995. Print.

Should general-skills first-year writing programs be abolished? Most programs claim to inculcate a set of abilities that can be transferred to any other writing situation. The idea that such skills could be taught, however, flies in the face of much current research on writing. Yet the profession has ignored this contradiction and diverted scholarly attention to areas not directly relevant to the classroom. The thirteen essays included here address the "abolition" question: by looking at the history of attempts to abolish first-year general-skills courses (e.g., Robert Connors, "The New Abolitionism: Toward a Historical Background," and Maureen Daly Goggin, "The Disciplinary Instability of Composition"); by exploring the mismatches between pedagogical practices in such courses and current theories of composing (e.g., Joseph Petraglia, "Writing as an Unnatural Act," and Cheryl Geisler, "Writing and Learning at Cross Purposes in the Academy"); and by analyzing the theoretical inadequacies undergirding such courses (e.g., David Jolliffe, "Discourse, Interdiscursivity, and Composition Instruction").

239 Pratt, Mary Louise. "Arts of the Contact Zone." *Profession* 91 (1991): 33–40. Print.

Contact zones are social spaces where cultures meet and clash, often in contexts of highly asymmetrical power relations, such as colonialism or its aftermath. In such situations we find examples of texts that subordinate groups produce to describe themselves to the dominant group and engage with representations others have made of them. Such texts selectively use the forms and idioms of the other group (a part of the process of transculturation) and may, as in the case of Inca Guaman Poma's Andean text addressed to the king of Spain, be a marginalized group's entry into literacy. Such texts seem chaotic unless read as expressions of those who live in a contact zone. The utopian image of a unified speech community with shared norms is challenged by such texts. What are we to do when the classroom community, another imagined utopia, is challenged by unsolicited oppositional discourse, as is happening more frequently? Multicultural curricula can and should create contact zones in which all interests are represented, where multiple cultural histories intersect, where there are ground rules for communication across lines of difference and hierarchy, and where there is a systematic approach to cultural mediation.

240 Ratcliffe, Krista. *Anglo-American Feminist Challenges to the Rhetorical Traditions: Virginia Woolf, Mary Daly, Adrienne Rich*. Carbondale: Southern Illinois UP, 1996. Print.

Because of different material and cultural circumstances, women relate to language differently from men. Because these circumstances have usually been oppressive, women need to find ways to liberate their potential for creative language use. Woolf is especially alert to how women's limiting material circumstances are conditioned by social class as well as gender. She advocates both borrowing freely from male traditions of language use, when these can be adapted for women's purposes, and creating new ways of using language that are expressly feminine. She looks for a "woman's sentence" in literature. Daly rejects completely patriarchal ways of using language. Even more aggressively than Woolf, she indicts traditional ways of using language as designed to silence women. She devises her own argumentative forms and polemically punning vocabulary to advance her radical theology and, more, the possibilities of a whole new women's culture. Rich struggles in her poetry to escape the stifling hand of the male tradition and to find ways of using language that speak to and for women's, and especially lesbians', experiences. She advocates a "politics of location" in which the literary artist attempts to account for the complexity of her material and cultural circumstances and to take a stand for social reform in the interests of white women and of people of color. Ratcliffe critically juxtaposes these writers' ideas about language with themes in traditional rhetorical theory, showing both resonances and redefinitions.

241 Ratcliffe, Krista. *Rhetorical Listening: Identification, Gender, Whiteness.* Carbondale: Southern Illinois UP, 2005. Print.

Rhetorical listening is a trope for interpretive invention and can facilitate cross-cultural communication by directly confronting a number of troubled identifications with gender and whiteness. It supplements Kenneth Burke's rhetorical theory by making more room, within the concept of identification, for differences. Listening to autoethnography, academic research, and the stories of others illustrates how, for example, rhetorical listening turns *hearing* into *invention.* Three tactics of rhetorical listening address its potential: listening metonymically replaces the dysfunctional silence that characterizes public debates of gender and race in the United States; eavesdropping helps to resist the invisibility of gendered whiteness in scholarly discourses within rhetoric and composition studies; and listening pedagogically addresses classroom resistance and proposes redefining race and gender not as problems but as differences to be negotiated and celebrated.

242 Reynolds, Nedra. "Composition's Imagined Geographies: The Politics of Space in the Frontier, City, and Cyberspace." CCC 50.1 (Sept. 1998): 12–35. Print.

A geographic study of composition asks us to confront many of our assumptions about place and space as they influence our conceptions of classrooms, those who occupy them, and ways to control textual space. Socially produced through discourse, the politics of space are often enacted through spatial metaphors, and the most powerful of these metaphors tend to mask material conditions or deny material reality. Geographers and spatial theorists demonstrate the impact of time-space compression and transparent space; both concepts are a result of changing conceptions of space in a late-capitalist economy and both are problematic. Three imagined geographies in the discourses of composition—the frontier, city, and cyberspace—have given composition vision and a sense of mission but also leave unexamined the consequences of the politics of space; in giving composition a sense of disciplinary identity, imagined geographies ignore worn urban classrooms or the increased workloads from electronic technologies. A spatial politics of writing instruction calls for a paradoxical sense of space, resists notions of transparent space, and examines the impact of time-space compression on composition's workers.

243 Richards, I. A. *The Philosophy of Rhetoric.* New York: Oxford UP, 1936. Print. Excerpted in Bizzell and Herzberg [50].

All discourse allows multiple meanings, but most interpretations of discourse are based on cultural conventions and the widespread idea that words have single determinate meanings. Rhetoric is the study of the misunderstandings that arise from such interpretations. Rhetoric looks at the "context" of disputed passages—the surrounding text, which constrains the meaning of the passage. Because meaning is determined by context, usage must be based on appropriateness to context rather than on fixed standards. Rhetoric must rely on Coleridge's idea that all language is metaphor and that we understand the world through the resemblances offered by language. See also Berthoff [175].

244 Rose, Mike. "The Language of Exclusion: Writing Instruction at the University." *CE* 47.4 (Apr. 1985): 341–59. Print.

The language used to describe and defend writing programs contributes to the attitude that writing is a secondary part of the university curriculum. "Error" was a convenient object of study for behaviorists, who then recommended drilling as a remedy. Their positivistic defense of writing instruction lingers on, despite its limitations and its degrading connotations. The once-effective defense of writing as a "skill" now relegates it to second-class intellectual status. "Remediation" suggests medical deficiency, or that material should have been learned before and is therefore inappropriate to the college curriculum. "Illiteracy" oversimplifies a complex problem and stigmatizes both students and teachers. Finally, the myth that remediation leads to a final cure persists, despite historical evidence, and further marginalizes writing programs and their students as merely temporary phenomena. We must contest the assumptions of such language and offer instead a more cognitively, historically, and culturally accurate description of writing.

245 Roskelly, Hephzibah, and Kate Ronald. *Reason to Believe: Romanticism, Pragmatism, and the Teaching of Writing.* Albany: State U of New York P, 1998. Print.

The "social turn" in composition and the influence of postmodern theory in literary studies have undercut teachers' belief in students' abilities to produce powerful language, without which belief teaching is hardly possible. Composition studies must recover "romantic/pragmatic rhetoric," rather than treating "romantic" and "pragmatic" as opposites. American romanticism, best exemplified in the work of Emerson, develops a sustaining vision of human possibility. American pragmatism applies romanticism to action in the world. C. S. Pierce, William James, and others encourage a pragmatic method that inquires into human experience by testing hypotheses, using as varied a range of inquirers and sites of inquiry as possible, and tending to show the relations between opposing ideas and to arrive at contingent truths. Major proponents of a pedagogy devised from romantic/pragmatic thinking are John Dewey and Paulo Freire. Roskelly and Ronald trace the development of romantic/pragmatic ideas from Puritan times, analyze how these ideas became occulted in current theory, and provide accounts of classrooms in which romantic/pragmatic pedagogy functions successfully.

See: Thomas Rosteck, ed., *At the Intersection: Cultural Studies and Rhetorical Studies* [753].

246 Schilb, John. *Between the Lines: Relating Composition Theory and Literary Theory*. Portsmouth: Heinemann-Boynton/Cook, 1996. Print.

Literary theory defines rhetoric as irony, while composition theory defines rhetoric as persuasion. Theoretical differences were clear at two seminal conferences. The 1963 CCCC, site of the birth of modern composition studies, was marked by great interest in classical rhetoric, with its stable, unitary subject who could make rational choices about language use. In contrast, the 1966 Johns Hopkins conference, "The Languages of Criticism and the Sciences of Man," introduced Jacques Derrida, Roland Barthes, and Jacques Lacan to American academics and featured a poststructuralist view of the subject as unstable, fragmented, and determined by texts. Composition studies remained firmly subordinate in English departments of the 1960s so as to protect the elite status of the cultural capital regulated by the literature faculty. Yet both composition studies and literary studies wrongly neglected to attempt to form politically active citizens. Postmodernism has debilitated both fields. Its epistemology can help students understand power relations but oversimplifies politics. Its artistic strategies are not adequate for civic action. Its global cultural trends may be studied usefully, but only if connected to students' everyday lives. Composition studies and literary studies have recently converged in their interest in personal writing, which helps students learn the way self-identities are constructed but which can degenerate into self-indulgence, as practiced, for example, by Jane Tompkins. The fields have also converged in their attention to collaboration, which literary studies should learn from composition studies to value. At the same time, composition studies need to learn from literary studies to be suspicious of the ethical problems posed by collaboration. The fields have also converged in their questioning of the efficacy of theory, but as a critique of the work of Stanley Fish shows, theories that are tested by pedagogy, as those of composition studies are and those of literary studies should be, do not present the totalizing threats against which Fish inveighs.

247 Schroeder, Christopher. "Knowledge and Power, Logic and Rhetoric, and Other Reflections in the Toulminian Mirror: A Critical Consideration of Stephen Toulmin's Contributions to Composition." *JAC: A Journal of Composition Theory* 17.1 (Winter 1997): 95–107. Print.

Philosopher Stephen Toulmin's model of practical reasoning has proved tremendously useful in composition classes. However, writing teachers should be aware of a number of problems with it. Toulmin's model does not distinguish between logically valid and merely probable arguments. It does not require consideration of all available data; on the contrary, it encourages selecting data, perhaps misleadingly, to fit the claim and warrant. The model tends toward relativism in that warrants are presumed not to be universally applicable but to require backing, which depends for acceptance on audience belief. It ignores ethos and pathos as argumentative strategies. It can be used to structure not an entire essay but only individual arguments within the larger text. The most serious problem with the Toulmin model, however, is that it depoliticizes argument, drawing attention away from the social and political power issues that generate claims and legitimate warrants. The function of ideology is obscured. For example, the model itself, fundamentally hierarchical, could be analyzed as an example of masculine thinking, but nothing in the Toulmin approach suggests subjecting it to such analysis.

248 Selzer, Jack, ed. *Understanding Scientific Prose*. Madison: U of Wisconsin P, 1993. Print.

Thirteen essays analyze a single scientific essay, "The Spandrels of San Marco," by Stephen Jay Gould and R. C. Lewontin. Each analysis uses a different critical method in order to "domesticate new methods of practical criticism," to show their usefulness when applied to scientific discourse, and to reveal the complexities of scientific prose. Essays include Charles Bazerman, "Intertextual Self-Fashioning: Gould and Lewontin's Representations of the Literature"; Susan Wells, "'Spandrels,' Narration, and Modernity"; Carl G. Herndl, "Cultural Studies and Critical Science"; Mary Rosner and Georgia Rhoades, "Science, Gender, and 'The Spandrels of San Marco'"; Carolyn Miller and S. Michael Halloran, "Reading Darwin, Reading Nature; or, On the Ethos of Historical Science"; John Lyne, "Angels in the Architecture: A Burkean Inventional Perspective on 'Spandrels'"; Gay Gragson and Jack Selzer, "The Reader in the Text of 'The Spandrels of San Marco'"; Debra Journet, "Deconstructing 'The Spandrels of San Marco'"; Greg Myers, "Making Enemies: How Gould and Lewontin Criticize"; and Stephen Jay Gould, "Fulfilling the Spandrels of World and Mind." Includes the original article by Gould and Lewontin.

249 Selzer, Jack, and Sharon Crowley, eds. *Rhetorical Bodies*. Madison: U of Wisconsin P, 1999. Print.

A product of the Fifteenth Penn. State Conference on Rhetoric and Composition in 1997, this book includes sixteen essays on material rhetoric or rhetoric's materiality. Chapters include Jack Selzer, "Habeas Corpus: An Introduction"; Carole Blair, "Contemporary U.S. Memorial Sites as Exemplars of Rhetoric's Materiality"; Karyn Hollis, "Material of Desire: Bodily Rhetoric in Working Women's Poetry at the Bryn Mawr Summer School, 1921–1938"; Peter Mortensen, "Figuring Illiteracy: Rustic Bodies and Unlettered Minds in Rural America"; Lester Faigley, "Material Literacy and Visual Design"; Christina Haas, "Materializing Public and Private: The Spatialization of Conceptual Categories in Discourses of Abortion"; J. Blake Scott, "Rhetoric and Technoscience: The Case of Confide"; Yameng Liu, "Dick Morris, Ideology, and Regulating the Flow of Rhetorical Resources"; Celeste Condit, "The Materiality of Coding: Rhetoric, Genetics, and the Matter of Life"; and Sharon Crowley, "Afterword: The Material of Rhetoric."

250 Smit, David W. *The End of Composition Studies*. Carbondale: Southern Illinois UP, 2004. Print.

Composition studies has reached the end—its conceptual limits—of what it can accomplish through research and scholarship. As a set of related subfields, composition functions from "underconceptualized" notions of what writing is, what writing ability is, how we learn to write, or how people compose. What *exactly*, for example, do expert writers know that novices do not? Concepts that have been accepted widely, such as writing as a social practice, prove to be limited; the value of a concept like discourse community is "largely hermeneutic." In addition, overwhelming evidence suggests that kinds of knowledge or skills do not necessarily transfer to new situations. Thus, generic writing courses are inadequate because they cannot immerse learners in particular discourses, where they get extensive practice and can develop fluency, critical frameworks, and a metacognitive sense of how writing functions for a specific group. Understanding that "you get what you teach for" can guide reform efforts to make transfer a major feature. Smit provides an overview of what an undergraduate writing curriculum, "justified by current research," would look like.

251 Trimbur, John. "Composition and the Circulation of Writing." CCC 52.2 (Dec. 2000): 188–219. Print.

College students' writing does not often circulate beyond "trade papers with a partner," yet the circulation of writing, the complex delivery systems through which writing circulates, should figure more prominently in writing instruction. Composition's tendency to figure classroom life as a middle-class family drama foreshortens the delivery system by linking production directly to consumption within the intimate space of the classroom/home. In addition, cultural studies' approaches to teaching writing, by their focus on critique and interpretation, also neglect other moments in the circulation of cultural forms and products while encoding and decoding restrict analysis to production and consumption. Marx's the *Grundrisse* offers a conceptual model that challenges a linear model of circulation by insisting that the *use* value of cultural products should not be separated from their *exchange* value. When exchange value and use value are united dialectially, as they are in Marx's notion of the commodity, we avoid the fallacy that by changing the manner of writing (the style) one can solve the problem of circulation. Delivery is inseparable from the circulation of writing and the widening diffusion of socially useful knowledge. Thus, assignments should problematize expertise from within the process of production and circulation, not erase the materiality of writing or isolate an education in writing from the means of production and delivery.

252 Trimbur, John. "Consensus and Difference in Collaborative Learning." *CE* 51.6 (Oct. 1989): 602–16. Print. Rpt. in Villanueva [253].

The purpose of collaborative learning as described by Bruffee [507] and Wiener [489] is to help students experience the process of negotiating and reaching consensus. This goal has been attacked on the ground that it subjects individual students to leveling peer pressure. But since individuals must face peer pressure as part of living in society, collaborative learning can help them learn how to deal with it. Moreover, the collaborative approach can teach students how to deflect control by authorities to which they might be subject as isolated individuals. Some critics of collaborative learning caution that consensus may actually be acquiescence to prevailing social attitudes; consensus would thus reproduce the oppressions of a nonegalitarian social structure. Richard Rorty, whose views are called upon to support collaborative learning, seems to exacerbate that danger by presenting consensus as a seamless conversational web that can be ruptured only occasionally by individuals. But, contrary to Rorty's thinking, most people participate in a variety of overlapping discourses that often come into conflict. Thus, a collaborative classroom would treat "dissensus," however muted, as the normal state of affairs in most discourse communities and would teach students to think of genuine consensus, following Habermas, not as something achievable but as a commitment to engage in polyvocal conversations as free from relations of domination as possible.

253 Villanueva, Victor, Jr., ed. *Cross-Talk in Comp Theory: A Reader*. Urbana: NCTE, 1997. Print.

Forty-one previously published essays have been chosen to demonstrate generative debates over basic issues in the contemporary field of composition studies. Section I addresses the writing process and includes Janet Emig, "Writing as a Mode of Learning" [382]; Nancy Sommers, "Revision Strategies of Student Writers and Experienced Adult Writers" [400]; Walter J. Ong, "The Writer's Audience Is Always a Fiction" [392]; and Lisa Ede and Andrea Lunsford, "Audience Addressed/Audience Invoked: The Role of Audience in Composition Theory and Pedagogy" [388]. Section II proposes definitions of discourse and advice on its teaching, including James Kinneavy, "The Basic Aims of Discourse" [221]; Patrick Hartwell, "Grammar, Grammars, and the Teaching of Grammar" [415]; and Stephen P. Witte and Lester Faigley, "Coherence, Cohesion, and Writing Quality" [427]. Section III presents work on developmental schemes and writing instruction, including Linda Flower and John R. Hayes, "A Cognitive Process Theory of Writing" [265], and Patricia Bizzell, "Cognition, Convention, and Certainty: What We Need to Know about Writing" [180]. Writing in society is addressed in Section IV, including Kenneth A. Bruffee, "Collaborative Learning and the 'Conversation of Mankind'" [186], and John Trimbur, "Consensus and Difference in Collaborative Learning" [252]. Section V looks at controversies over voice, including David Bartholomae, "Writing with Teachers: A Conversation with Peter Elbow" [171]; Peter Elbow, "Being a Writer vs. Being an Academic: A Conflict in Goals" [197]; Elizabeth A. Flynn, "Composing as a Woman" [714]; and Lisa D. Delpit, "The Silenced Dialogue: Power and Pedagogy in Educating

Other People's Children." Section VI looks briefly at developing issues, including James A. Berlin, "Rhetoric and Ideology in the Writing Class" [173], and Patricia Bizzell, "Contact Zones and English Studies" [181].

254 Vitanza, Victor, ed. *PRE/TEXT: The First Decade*. Pittsburgh: U of Pittsburgh P, 1993. Print.

Ten essays from the journal: Paul Kameen, "Rewording the Rhetoric of Composition"; Louise Wetherbee Phelps, "The Dance of Discourse"; Patricia Bizzell, "Cognition, Convention, and Certainty: What We Need to Know about Writing" [180]; S. Michael Halloran, "Rhetoric in the American College Curriculum: The Decline of Public Discourse" [97]; C. Jan Swearingen, "The Rhetor as Eiron"; William Covino, "Thomas De Quincey in a Revisionist Rhetoric"; Charles Bazerman, "The Writing of Scientific Non-Fiction"; Sharon Crowley, "Neo-Romanticism and the History of Rhetoric"; John Schilb, "The History of Rhetoric and the Rhetoric of History"; and Susan Jarratt, "Toward a Holistic Historiography." Includes a history of the journal by Vitanza, a comment by James Berlin, and afterwords by David Bartholomae and Steven Mailloux.

255 Warnick, Barbara. "Rhetorical Criticism of Public Discourse on the Internet: Theoretical Implications." *Rhetoric Society Quarterly* 28.4 (Fall 1998): 73–84. Print.

Humanists have avoided analyzing computer-mediated communication (CMC), perhaps because it disrupts traditional notions of author and audience, all of whom may be anonymous, and text, which is destabilized by hypertext links. Nevertheless, cyberspace communicators are still trying to persuade, and rhetoricians can analyze their practices. Especially important will be to discern how these practices connect with moral judgments. Rhetorical criticism of hypertext can look for patterns among a large number of texts, whose boundaries are usually blurred. Rhetorical criticism of audience can look at how different groups are characterized or characterize themselves, policing their own online ethos. Ethical questions include whether computer-simulated political activities affect participation in the real-world public sphere; whether CMC promotes hyperconformity and suppresses dissenting opinions, thus truncating deliberation; and whether access is improved the more technical expertise one claims to possess—often a form of sexist elitism.

256 Weaver, Richard M. "Language Is Sermonic." *Dimensions of Rhetorical Scholarship*. Ed. Robert E. Nebergall. Norman: U of Oklahoma Dept. of Speech, 1963. 49–64. Print. Rpt. in Bizzell and Herzberg [50].

Rhetoric should be restored to its once prominent place in the curriculum, for it is "the most humanistic of the humanities," concerned with the intimate details of human feelings, needs, and historical pressures in its attempt to find ways to persuade people to right action. Rhetoric is therefore incompatible with science—the search for universals. To study rhetoric is to evaluate the force of appeals to action—an "existential, not hypothetical" concern. Finally, all speech is rhetorical—intended to persuade, never neutral—and all language is value-laden, a system for making predications and propositions: "We are all of us preachers."

257 Yancey, Kathleen Blake, ed. *Delivering College Composition: The Fifth Canon*. Portsmouth: Heinemann-Boynton/Cook, 2006. Print.

Often paired with the art of speaking, the study of the rhetorical canon of delivery in writing classes has dwindled. However, this collection of essays optimistically explores how the canon of delivery presently shifts, shapes, and defines college composition and composing spaces, and how delivery will continue to do so in the future. Fifteen essays include Kathleen Blake Yancey, "Delivering College Composition: A Vocabulary for Discussion"; Martin Jacobi, "The Canon of Delivery in Rhetorical Theory: Selections, Commentary, and Advice"; Irwin Weiser, "Faculties, Students, Sites, Technologies: Multiple Deliveries of Composition at a Research University"; Joyce Magnotto Neff, "Getting Our Money's Worth: Delivering Composition at a Comprehensive State University"; Carol Rutz, "Delivering Composition at a Liberal Arts College: Making the Implicit Explicit"; Teresa Redd, "Keepin' It Real: Delivering College Composition at an HBCU"; David A. Jolliffe and Bernard Phelan, "Advanced Placement, Not Advanced Exception: Challenges for High Schools, Colleges, and Universities"; Christine Farris, "The Space Between: Dual-Credit Programs as Brokering, Community Building, and Professionalization"; Paul Bodmer, "Is It Pedagogical or Administrative? Administering Distance Delivery to High Schools"; Todd Taylor, "Design, Delivery, and Narcolepsy"; Marvin Diogenes and Andrea A. Lunsford, "Toward Delivering New Definitions of Writing"; Joseph Harris, "Undisciplined Writing"; Richard Courage, "Asynchronicity: Delivering Composition and Literature in the Cyberclassroom"; Rebecca Rickly, "Distributed Teaching, Distributed Learning: Integrating Technology and Criteria-Driven Assessment into the Delivery of First-Year Composition"; and Kathleen Blake Yancey, "Delivering College Composition into the Future."

Composing and Literacy

The Process Movement and Post-Process Approaches

258 Breuch, Lee-Ann M. Kastman. "Post-Process 'Pedagogy': A Philosophical Exercise." *JAC: A Journal of Composition Theory* 22.1 (Winter 2002): 119–50. Print.

Composition's "pedagogical imperative" has categorized post-process theory as (only) a critique of process with no pedagogical application. Instead, post-process assumptions, while opposed to the concept of mastery or universal models, see writing as an activity—public, interpretive, and situated. Post-process theory *does* object to system-based explanations of writing, but it also embraces indeterminacy in the writing act; however, the belief that writing is indeterminate does not mean pedagogy is ignored. "The real thrust of post-process theory has to do not with content or subject matter, but rather with *what we do with content*." The strongest application of post-process theory is in practices of mentoring, one-to-one instruction, and writing center work.

259 Britton, James, et al. *The Development of Writing Abilities (11–18)*. London: Macmillan, 1975. Print.

A study of about two thousand papers written by British schoolchildren between the ages of eleven and eighteen suggests that their writing falls into three categories: transactional (communicating information); poetic (creating beautiful verbal objects); and expressive (exploring ideas and relating them to feelings, intentions, and other knowledge). Most school writing is transactional, but this emphasis is wrong because children use expressive writing as a mode of learning. Transactional writing, with its complex sense of audience, can develop only from expressive facility. Transactional writing puts the writer in a passive, spectator role, whereas expressive writing encourages an active, participant role.

260 Cooper, Marilyn M. "The Ecology of Writing." *CE* 48.4 (Apr. 1986): 364–75. Print. Rpt. in Cooper and Holzman [566].

Cognitive-process models of composing rely too heavily on the image of a solitary author. A better, ecological model would situate the writer and the writer's immediate context in larger social systems, of which there are several. The system of ideas integrates private experience with public knowledge. The system of purposes links the actions of many different writers. The system of interpersonal relations connects writers in terms of social and linguistic conventions. The system of cultural norms reflects the attitudes of social groups to which writers belong. The system of textual forms marks generic conventions and innovations. These systems make up the material circumstances that constrain writers and are in turn subject to the writer's power to shape and change them through interpretation.

261 Emig, Janet. *The Composing Processes of Twelfth Graders*. Urbana: NCTE, 1971. Print.

Eight twelfth graders were asked to "compose aloud" while writing three essays. Extensive interviews with one of the students form a case study showing that twelfth graders compose in two modes: reflexive and extensive. Reflexive writing concerns the writer's feelings and personal experience. The style is informal, and several kinds of exploratory writing accompany drafts. The student usually initiates reflexive writing and is its primary audience. Extensive writing focuses on information to be conveyed to a reader. The style is more formal, and much less time is spent on planning and drafting than in the reflexive mode. The directive to write usually comes from the teacher, who is the primary audience. Twelfth graders write much more often, though less well, in the extensive than in the reflexive mode. They should have more opportunities to write reflexively in school. This study has been influential because of its conception of composing as a process, its suggestion that the composing process should be taught and studied, and its method of composing aloud.

262 Faigley, Lester. "Competing Theories of Process: A Critique and a Proposal." *CE* 48.6 (Oct. 1986): 527–42. Print. Rpt. in Graves [571] and in Perl [274].

Three theories of the composing process—expressive, cognitive, and social—characterize the discipline of composition. The expressive theory embodies a neo-romantic view of process that invokes the ideas of integrity, spontaneity, and originality. Integrity—or sincerity—becomes an evaluative category; spontaneity suggests the organic unfolding of writing; and originality changes from genius to self-actualization. The cognitive theory uses notions of cognitive development to explain how writing is learned, while using a cybernetic model (feedback, memory, processing) of the individual composing process. Cognitive theory created a science consciousness in composition researchers. Several lines of research—poststructuralism, sociology of science, ethnography, and Marxism—combine to form the social theory, which explains writing as a function of the activities of the writer in a discourse community. These process methods are superior to previous methods; they validate student writing, examine writing behavior, and investigate the social systems that stand in relation to the act of writing.

263 Flower, Linda. *The Construction of Negotiated Meaning: A Social Cognitive Theory of Writing*. Carbondale: Southern Illinois UP, 1994. Print.

Literacy is a constructive process, an attempt to create meaning as part of social action. Literacy is shaped by literate, social, and cultural practices of a community, but, at the same time, it is a personal attempt to communicate. The issues of positioning within a community, communicative intent, and mediating social practices overshadow the mechanical concerns usually associated with literacy. A social-cognitive view of literacy, which situates the individual within a social context, explains more of the diversity and complexity of literate action. Such action occurs between the poles of thought (interpreting, problem-solving, reflecting) and culture (the texts, voices, and knowledge out of which interpretations are built). To examine an individual's thinking within the context of literate action can reveal the underlying logic of literate performance. Other metaphors for meaning-making, such as reproduction and conversation, are too limited to account for the individual's engagement in the process. Negotiation better describes the individual's agency within social constraints. Writers can articulate their strategic knowledge (goals, strategies, and awareness) to reveal their processes of meaning-construction in social settings.

264 Flower, Linda. "The Construction of Purpose in Writing and Reading." *CE* 50.5 (Sept. 1988): 528–50. Print.

Purpose emerges from the interactions of individual language users with social and cultural contexts. A cognitive view of a writer's purpose would see it not as a unitary, conscious intention but rather as a web of intertwined goals and plans, not all of which are fully conscious or rationally attributable to immediate context and text content. The writer deals with this web through a constructive planning process in which goals are prioritized to help guide the composing process even as the goal hierarchy may be revised during composing. Good planners are opportunistic. A reader constructs a similar web or scenario made up of goals and plans (again, not necessarily fully conscious) for using or responding to the reading. The reader's web also includes estimates of the author's purposes, forecasts of what may be coming next in a difficult or lengthy text, and so on. Framing such scenarios helps a reader group information and responses drawn from a text and isolate trouble spots that need more interpretation. Expert writers and readers generate more complex webs than do novices.

265 Flower, Linda, and John R. Hayes. "A Cognitive Process Theory of Writing." *CCC* 32.4 (Dec. 1981): 365–87. Print.

The structure of the composing process is revealed by "protocol analysis"—asking writers to think aloud while writing and then analyzing the writers' narratives. The three elements of the composing process are the task environment, which includes such external constraints as the rhetorical problem and text produced so far; the writer's long-term memory, which includes knowledge of the subject and knowledge of how to write; and the writing processes that go on inside the writer's head. This last category comprises a planning process, subdivided into generating, organizing, and goal setting; a translating process, in which thoughts are put into words; and a reviewing process, subdivided into evaluating and revising. The whole process is regulated by a monitor that switches from one stage to another. The process is hierarchical and recursive. All writers exhibit this process, but poor writers carry it out ineffectively.

266 Flower, Linda, David L. Wallace, Linda Norris, and Rebecca E. Burnett, eds. *Making Thinking Visible: Writing, Collaborative Planning, and Classroom Inquiry*. Urbana: NCTE, 1994. Print.

A report on Carnegie Mellon's Making Thinking Visible project, a four-year collaboration among thirty-three high school and college teachers, in which students and teachers attempted to document the processes of thinking about writing and teaching writing. Some of the twenty-seven chapters are brief accounts of classroom and teaching discoveries. Others are full essays, including Linda Flower, "Teachers as Theory Builders"; Linda Flower, "Writers Planning: Snapshots from Research"; David Wallace, "Teaching Collaborative Planning: Creating a Social Context for Writing"; Leslie Byrd Evans, "Transcripts as a Compass to Discovery"; James Brozick, "Using the Writing Attitude Survey"; David Wallace, "Supporting Students' Intentions for Writing"; and Wayne Peck, "The Community Literacy Center: Bridging Community- and School-Based Literate Practices."

267 Foster, Helen. *Networked Process: Dissolving Boundaries of Process and Post-Process*. West Lafayette: Parlor, 2007. Print.

Profiling process and post-process helps to determine a point of stasis between them, and then allows that space, named *networked process*, to be mapped, particularly the "conundrum" of subjectivity and the possibilities for disciplinary identity. Thomas Kent's theory of paralogic hermeneutics precedes the use of post-process by others in rhetoric and composition to describe an emerging frustration with the limits of process paradigm. Different strands of post-process—a heterogeneous group best characterized as a sensibility rather than a position—are positioned variously in relation to the social-cultural turn and to process. Networked process can be traced through the cognitive maps of James Berlin, which lay the groundwork for networked subjectivity, a theory of the subject who writes "in an imbricated relationship with discourse, others, and the world." The heuristic of networked subjectivity encourages the critique of disciplinary artifacts and sites (textbooks, writing programs). The metaphor of networked process, as both disciplinary metaphor and heuristic, can inform "the long revolution" in our field.

268 Fox, Tom. *The Social Uses of Writing: Politics and Pedagogy*. Norwood: Ablex, 1990. Print.

Case studies show how freshmen use writing to negotiate conflicts between academic values and values they hold as a consequence of race, gender, and class. Teachers' responses to the students' writing are affected, in turn, by their own culturally constructed values. These tensions between culture-based values can be the topic of study in an interactive pedagogy that helps students see how such socially constructed values as beauty, objectivity, and upward mobility affect their writing. Interactive pedagogy, moreover, seeks to replace evaluation with interpretation and to bring student and academic discourse together instead of seeking to move students to a univocal academic discourse.

269 Greene, Stuart. "Making Sense of My Own Ideas: The Problems of Authorship in a Beginning Writing Classroom." *Written Communication* 12.2 (Apr. 1995): 186–218. Print.

A detailed study of two students composing research papers shows that Vuong, a Hmong immigrant, relied heavily on what he thought was the teacher's definition of the task, namely, to summarize the ideas in the source texts. He structured his paper as a comparison of different authors. Writing about cultural literacy, Vuong had strong opinions about the topic based in his own experience, but he did not want to bring these opinions into his paper. He avoided acting as arbiter among the texts he summarized. On the other hand, Jesus initially defined his task as permitting the use of his own experience as well as source texts. He structured his paper as a set of topics addressing aspects of a problem he identified in a central source text. Unlike Vuong's paper, Jesus' paper expressed a strong point of view throughout, clearly distinguished from the ideas of the authors he discussed. Greene urges writing teachers to realize that different cultural and educational backgrounds may prompt students to choose different composing strategies. Explicit classroom discussion of the authorial roles students might adopt in their writing would be helpful.

See: John Hagge, "The Process Religion and Business Communication" [845].

270 Kent, Thomas, ed. *Post-Process Theory: Beyond the Writing-Process Paradigm*. Carbondale: Southern Illinois UP, 1999. Print.

Most post-process theorists assume that writing is public, interpretive, and situated. Thirteen chapters define post-process theory, its pedagogical ramifications, and its possibilities for reforming practices. Essays include Gary Olson, "Toward a Post-Process Composition: Abandoning the Rhetoric of Assertion"; Barbara Couture, "Modeling and Emulating: Rethinking Agency in the Writing Process"; Nancy Blyler, "Research in Professional Communication: A Post-Process Perspective"; David Russell, "Activity Theory and Process Approaches: Writing (Power) in School and Society"; John Clifford and Elizabeth Ervin, "The Ethics of Process"; and John Schilb, "Reprocessing the Essay."

271 McComiskey, Bruce. *Teaching Composition as a Social Process*. Logan: Utah State UP, 2000. Print.

"Social-content" composition courses treat cultural theory as content to be mastered while "social-process" writing instruction situates composing within particular sociopolitical contexts. A balanced approach to the three levels of composing—textual, rhetorical, and discursive—leads students to the fullest understanding of their writing processes. The post-process movement in composition studies, characterized here as social-process rhetorical inquiry, extends rather than rejects the writing process movement. Informed by cultural studies methodologies, social-process rhetorical inquiry is a set of heuristic questions, intended to guide student inquiry and instructional practice, based on the cycle of production, distribution, and composition. Rather than focusing on a single moment or text to analyze, social-process rhetorical inquiry focuses on both the processes and products of discourse. Students are asked to produce both critical essays and practical documents that reconcile competing discourses. Through assignments in critical-discourse analysis, students are prepared for participation in postmodern communal democracies.

272 Nelson, Jennie. "Reading Classrooms as Text: Exploring Student Writers' Interpretive Practices." CCC 46.3 (Oct. 1995): 411–29. Print.

Students enter college classrooms with many strategies for responding to writing assignments that have been successful for them in past schooling. These strategies typically include "reading" the entire classroom experience for clues to the teacher's expectations. Interviews with several student writers reveal, for example, that professors' grades and written comments on papers influence how students define and pursue writing tasks much more than professors' statements about such tasks. Also, while overly vague assignments can confuse students, overly explicit ones can also do damage when they are interpreted as a "blueprint for the final product," thus short-circuiting students' creative thinking. Students write better when assignments and the entire classroom atmosphere encourage them to participate in defining their intellectual tasks.

273 Penrose, Ann M., and Barbara M. Sitko, eds. *Hearing Ourselves Think: Cognitive Research in the College Writing Classroom*. New York: Oxford UP, 1993. Print.

Cognitive research, investigating the relationship between how writers think about the writing process and the way they engage in the process, reveals much about the factors that determine how easy and successful writing will be. Process research in the classroom—methods for critical reflection on ways of learning and writing—can lead to an understanding by students and teachers of the ways that writers choose and can improve their writing strategies. Ten essays explain cognitive classroom research and its application to teaching: Ann Penrose and Barbara Sitko, "Introduction: Studying Cognitive Processes in the Classroom"; Christina Haas, "Beyond 'Just the Facts': Reading as Rhetorical Action"; Stuart Greene, "Exploring the Relationship between Authorship and Reading"; Ann Penrose, "Writing and Learning: Exploring the Consequences of Task Interpretation"; Lorraine Higgins, "Reading to Argue: Helping Students Transform Source Texts"; Jennie Nelson, "The Library Revisited: Exploring Students' Research Processes"; Rebecca Burnet, "Decision-making during the Collaborative Planning of Coauthors"; Karen Schriver, "Revising for Readers: Audience Awareness in the Writing Classroom"; Barbara Sitko, "Exploring Feedback: Writers Meet Readers"; and Betsy Bowen, "Using Conferences to Support the Writing Process."

274 Perl, Sondra, ed. *Landmark Essays on Writing Process.* Davis: Hermagoras, 1994. Print.

Eighteen essays, arranged chronologically, beginning with Janet Emig's "The Composing Process: Review of the Literature" (1971). Essays include: Sondra Perl, "The Composing Processes of Unskilled College Writers"; Linda Flower and John Hayes, "The Cognition of Discovery: Defining a Rhetorical Problem"; Nancy Sommers, "Revision Strategies of Student Writers and Experienced Adult Writers" [400]; Mike Rose, "Rigid Rules, Inflexible Plans, and the Stifling of Language: A Cognitivist Analysis of Writer's Block"; Sondra Perl, "Understanding Composing"; Ann Berthoff, "The Intelligent Eye and the Thinking Hand"; James Reither, "Writing and Knowing: Toward Redefining the Writing Process"; Lester Faigley, "Competing Theories of Process: A Critique and a Proposal" [262]; Min-Zhan Lu, "From Silence to Words: Writing as Struggle" [650]; Elizabeth A. Flynn, "Composing as a Woman" [714]; and Nancy Sommers, "Between the Drafts."

275 Ponsot, Marie, and Rosemary Deen. *Beat Not the Poor Desk.* Upper Montclair: Boynton/Cook, 1982. Print.

Writing teachers can facilitate student writing, even under the constraints of time and circumstance, by eliminating class activities that are not writing and by providing opportunities for error-free practice of the elemental skill of writing. Writing should be prolific and guided by the whole structure of the essay. Teachers trained in literature can provide images of the shape of essays: the fable offers a structure for a story with a conclusion, and the parable creates a need for a thesis and clear point of view. Such shapes can be developed inductively and can help make the transition to a sense of other shapes for exposition. The authors describe intermediate steps, many possible shapes for essays, class activities, sample essays, syllabi, ways of teaching grammar, writing about literature, and organizing collaboration. Mina P. Shaughnessy Prize winner.

276 Rose, Mike, ed. *When a Writer Can't Write: Studies in Writer's Block and Other Composing Process Problems.* New York: Guilford, 1985. Print.

Eleven essays address the social and psychological constraints that contribute to serious hesitations and false starts in writing. They include Donald H. Graves, "Blocking and the Young Writer"; Stan Jones, "Problems with Monitor Use in Second Language Composing"; David Bartholomae, "Inventing the University" [170]; and Mike Rose, "Complexity, Rigor, Evolving Method, and the Puzzle of Writer's Block: Thoughts on Composing Process Research."

277 Rose, Mike. *Writer's Block: The Cognitive Dimension.* Carbondale: Southern Illinois UP, 1984. Print.

A number of case studies of students who frequently experienced writer's block and some who seldom blocked show that writers who block frequently may rely on context-independent rules for good writing, edit individual sentences as they are being written, plan only after beginning to write, or interpret writing assignments too narrowly in light of their limited knowledge of discourse modes. Writers who seldom block are "opportunists" who treat what they know about writing as strategies, not rules, which can be varied in different writing situations. The capacities to write well and to enjoy writing are not related to blocking. This study suggests that no composing method should be taught as if applicable to all writing situations.

278 Schreiner, Steven. "A Portrait of the Student as a Young Writer: Reevaluating Emig and the Process Movement." CCC 48.1 (Feb. 1997): 86–104. Print.

In *The Composing Processes of Twelfth Graders*, Janet Emig compares her research subject Lynn unfavorably with established literary writers. Emig suggests that Lynn writes too easily because she relies on stale academic strategies and avoids personally painful topics. Hence Emig advocates a pedagogy that would encourage Lynn to work over her writing more and to delve into self-expressive topics—an early and influential version of writing-process pedagogy. But this pedagogy, following Emig, ignores how Lynn's (and other students') strengths as a writer emerge not just from natural talent but also from sophisticated schooling and conditions of race and class privilege that equip her (but perhaps not other students) to be considered as a potential literary writer. Thus, process pedagogy risks neglecting important educational and cultural differences among students.

279 Tobin, Lad, and Thomas Newkirk, eds. *Taking Stock: The Writing Process Movement in the '90s*. Portsmouth: Heinemann-Boynton/Cook, 1994. Print.

Sixteen essays examine the history, theory, successes, problems, and prospects of writing-process pedagogy. Essays include James Moffett, "Coming Out Right"; Lisa Ede, "Reading the Writing Process"; Donald Murray, "Knowing Not Knowing"; Ken Macrorie, "Process, Product, and Quality"; Mary Minock, "The Bad Marriage: A Revisionist View of James Britton's Expressive Writing Hypothesis in American Practice"; Peter Elbow, "The Uses of Binary Thinking: Exploring Seven Productive Oppositions"; Thomas Recchio, "On the Critical Necessity of 'Essaying'"; and James Britton, "There Is One Story Worth Telling."

Digital Writing

280 Bolter, Jay David. *Writing Space: The Computer, Hypertext, and the History of Writing*. Hillside: Erlbaum, 1991. Print.

Writing is a technology inseparable from the materials and techniques of writing. Forms of text—scroll, codex book, electronic text—determine the organization and presentation of knowledge. Print books make text seem permanent and widen the gap between text and author. Electronic text does the opposite: the reader organizes, shapes, and adds to text, calls up other texts from databases, and creates a unique text in the process of reading. Print text must impose a hierarchy on ideas, reducing the typically associative writing process to linear form. Hypertext restores associative composing and requires associative reading through the layering of text. It comprises a network of verbal ideas. Electronic text recalls older forms of literacy, using picture writing in its icons, and restoring the formulaic, associative, and dynamic qualities of oral literature. Electronic texts dissolve into parts to be recombined and merge into larger textual structures, disrupting the traditional notion of authorship. Electronic fiction takes advantage of these qualities, offering a multitude of paths for the reader to travel. The plurality of the text and the disappearance of the author, imagined by innovative authors and critical theorists, are realized in electronic texts.

281 Handa, Carolyn, ed. "Digital Rhetoric, Digital Literacy, Computers, and Composition." Special issues of *Computers and Composition* 18.1 (May 2001) and 18.2 (June 2001). Print.

The use of new multimodal digital elements in writing requires sophisticated rhetorical knowledge, not just the ability to compose HTML or use video software. Therefore, many of the things that we already understand about rhetoric must be applied to new texts and tasks. Literacy is being redefined, with increased emphasis on design issues, visuality, aurality, and the space of the Web. Yet, the value we place on critical thinking and rhetorical knowledge, and our expertise in teaching these things, is indispensible to understanding and creating digital texts. For instance, students can understand digital genres, their persuasive possibilities, and their delivery and audience reception (or use) through rhetorical frameworks. The articles in these two special issues advance multidisciplinary but distinctly rhetorical schemes for reading and composing digital texts. Authors include Geoffrey Sirc, Clay Spinnuzi, Patricia A. Sullivan, Ann Wysocki, and others. The second issue also contains a large bibliography of books, articles, and Web sites about digital rhetoric.

282 Hawisher, Gail E., Paul LeBlanc, Charles Moran, and Cynthia L. Selfe. *Computers and the Teaching of Writing in American Higher Education, 1979–1994: A History*. Norwood: Ablex, 1996. Print.

Computers and composition has become a coherent subfield within composition studies, growing from early experimental beginnings. Its development is chronicled in five chapters: 1979–1982, focusing on how personal computers were integrated into writing instruction; 1983–1985, described as the period of greatest enthusiasm for computer use; 1986–1988, when computers and composition emerged as a field; 1989–1991, when revisionist critiques of computer use began to appear; and

1992–1994, exploring the sudden impact of the Internet and commercially viable multimedia. Each chapter situates the field of computers and composition within a time period's developments in both composition studies and computer technology; notes then-current trends in the field; and links the field's issues with contemporary social and political developments. All but the first chapter also include interviews with key figures, both pioneers and emerging leaders.

283 Johnson-Eilola, Johndan. "Living on the Surface: Learning in the Age of Global Communication Networks." *Page to Screen: Taking Literacy into the Electronic Era.* Ed. Ilana Snyder. New York: Routledge, 1998. 185–210. Print.

Watching a child or teenager playing video games reveals the complex interaction between users and interfaces; the presence and immediacy of global networks transports this interaction across a range of communicative mediums. Several common binaries disintegrate: history vs. simultaneity, depth vs. surface, modernism vs. postmodernism. The expansion of global communication networks troubles the division of these poles and challenges the functional and intellectual superiority of "traditional" mediums. Many adults may have trouble with the "everything-all-the-time" feeling of digital environments and distrust these mediums or view them only in terms of their functionality, not as cultures in and of themselves. Yet teachers must look more deeply for the complex possibilities for organization, agency, connection, and play in digital environments.

284 Johnson-Eilola, Johndan, and Stuart A. Selber. "Plagiarism, Originality, Assemblage." *Computers and Composition* 24.4 (Oct. 2007): 375–403. Print.

Students work and live in a "remix culture," borrowing and re-ordering or revising texts and ideas across genres and mediums. Thus, teachers need to recognize that traditional notions of originality and authorship can and should change. Ideally, the remix can aid invention, allow students to access and utilize new resources, and recognize the social dimensions of composing. These practices also challenge the notion of the single isolated author, disrupt rules for plagiarism that create a hierarchy with "original" texts on top and student content on the bottom, and operationalize new composing techniques. Seeing remixing as assemblage rather than "stealing" means understanding that it isn't possible to simply take a digital template and replace its content. Selection requires rhetorical sophistication in the same way that creation does, and through assemblage we must make complex design decisions. Assemblages develop from existing texts to solve writing or communication problems in new settings: they are critical answers to the new questions raised within networked and mediated cultures.

285 McKee, Heidi A., and Dànielle Nicole DeVoss, eds. *Digital Writing Research: Technologies, Methodologies, and Ethical Issues.* Cresskill: Hampton, 2007. Print.

Digital writing technologies can and will reshape research. At the same time, to research digital writing itself, ethical guidelines must be developed. Because digital writing shifts conceptions of agency, authorship, and identity, and even shifts or confuses traditional conceptions of the times, spaces, and contexts of writing, researchers must develop new strategies. Further, because of the increasing digitization of *all* forms of research, teachers and researchers must be receptive to the introduction of new technologies for collecting, analyzing, and disseminating data. The focus in this collection is on describing and developing research methodologies, rather than presenting new research, though most essays offer examples of research applications. Contents include Kevin DePew, "Through the Eyes of Researchers, Rhetors and Audiences: Triangulating Data from the Digital Writing Situation"; Michelle Sidler, "Playing Scavenger and Gazer with Scientific Discourse: Opportunities and Ethics for Online Research"; Stuart Blythe, "Coding Digital Texts and Multimedia"; Amy Kimme Hea, "Riding the Wave: Articulating a Critical Methodology for Web Research Practices"; Colleen Reilly and Doug Eyman, "Whose Research Is It, Anyway? The Multifaceted Methods for Multimodal Texts: Alternate Approaches to Citation Analysis for Electronic Sources"; and Rebecca Rickly, "Messy Contexts: Research as a Rhetorical Situation."

286 Moore Howard, Rebecca. "Understanding Internet Plagiarism." *Computers and Composition* 24.1 (Mar. 2007): 3–15. Print.

Through contemporary panic about Internet plagiarism, teachers position the Internet as the cause of evil and temptation and suggest top-down surveillance and discipline as the only solution. Instead, we should see the Internet as a rich source of intertextuality and as a cultural space that values this intertextuality. In opposition to these values, plagiarism detection software fails to recognize the communal and democratic character of the Internet, ignores the new textual activities that arise online or refuses to acknowledge their possible virtues, precludes teachers from genuinely connecting with students, and thus undermines the development of critical literacies and academic values.

287 Porter, James. "Why Technology Matters to Writing: A Cyberwriter's Tale." *Computers and Composition* 20.4 (Dec. 2003): 375–94. Print.

The computer (or any other technology of writing) is not a tool or instrument. Instead, technology should be seen *as use*: existing through the interface and interaction of human and machine. As such, technology shapes the writer (and vice versa) and interacts with a larger social "conglomerate" interconnected by the technology. Thus, the technologies that we use and have used significantly impact us, our cultures and ideologies, and will continue to do so. How we compose and what we compose with, composes us.

288 Ridolfo, Jim, and Dànielle Nicole DeVoss. "Composing for Recomposition: Rhetorical Velocity and Delivery." *Kairos* 13.2 (2009): n. pag. Web. 14 July 2010.

Writers in a digital age need to consider not just who will read their work, and how, but also "how might the text be rewritten?" and "why, where, and for whom might this text be rewritten?" Third parties, because of the ease of Web searching, the availability of so much information, and the ubiquity of copy-and-paste, might "plagiarize" texts. But writers can strategically produce texts for which this "plagiarism" is actually the desired end. "Rhetorical velocity" is the term used to measure or describe the speedy dissemination and broad travel of texts, leading to multiple possible recompositions or remixes. In the remix and redelivery of texts, certain elements may be amplified while others are discarded, and writers need to be aware of how their chosen medium and genre delimits or enables reuse. In the sphere of recomposition, then, delivery takes on increased importance as we write for others to reuse.

289 Selber, Stuart A. *Multiliteracies for a Digital Age*. Carbondale: Southern Illinois UP, 2004. Print.

Writing teachers will not all have uniform access to technology in or out of the classroom. This said, all writing teachers need to be invested in developing computer literacy among students. Currently, "the stakes could not be higher" for addressing the failures of technological literacy and developing multiliterate students. It is important to understand the specific literacies and rhetorical skills that a "multiliterate" student will develop and should possess. These skills and literacies should be taught in English departments by composition teachers. Compositionists are uniquely prepared to do this teaching and can structure systems, environments, curriculum, and classroom interactions to facilitate this learning. Winner of *Computers and Composition*'s Distinguished Book Award (2005) and the NCTE Award for Best Book in Technical and Scientific Communication (2005).

290 Selfe, Cynthia L. *Technology and Literacy in the Twenty-First Century: The Importance of Paying Attention*. Carbondale: Southern Illinois UP, 1999. Print.

The national project to expand technological literacy supports and exacerbates inequities within our culture and the public education system. The Technology Literacy Challenge, a federal literacy project begun in 1996, provides a case study of the failure of such an initiative when it does not address the uneven distribution of technologies along the lines of race and socioeconomic status and the continuing reproduction of both illiteracy and poverty. Government initiatives, educators, businesses, parents, and ideology all play a role in creating a potent configuration for technological literacy that feeds Americans' belief that science + technology = progress, and that disguises the fact that technology is not available to everyone. Discounting the importance of multiple literacies and presenting either/or versions of technology, the dominant brand of technological literacy is defined as "competence with computers" rather than as a complex set of values, practices, and skills. The tendency to construct computers as either bane or boon encourages people to ignore the complicated relationships between technology and literacy, or to assume that the social and financial costs of technological literacy are inevitable. Humanist educators and literacy professionals should work on the local level to construct a larger vision of these issues; then intervene in the national project of expansion; and finally advocate critical technological literacy, which analyzes the technology–literacy link at fundamental levels of both conception and social practice.

291 Selfe, Cynthia L., and Richard J. Selfe Jr. "The Politics of the Interface: Power and Its Exercise in Electronic Contact Zones." CCC 45.4 (Dec. 1994): 480–504. Print.

Limited access is the most obvious political issue related to computers; more serious are the ways in which computer interfaces reproduce racist, sexist, and colonialist attitudes. Mapping computer interfaces illustrates their representation of knowledge as hierarchical, rational, and logical, including the dominance of American corporate culture in the languages and icons. A critically reflective stance toward computers will highlight the effects of domination and colonialism and will require educators and computer specialists to locate themselves on the map of interfaces. One tactic is to teach students to be technology critics, not just technology users; another is to redesign interfaces around different metaphors of work and production.

292 Sibyelle, Gruber. "Technology and Tenure: Creating Oppositional Discourse in an Offline and Online World." *Computers and Composition* 17.1 (Apr. 2000): 41–56. Print.

Specialists in computers and composition may be positioned as outsiders to the traditional promotion and tenure process, but simple dichotomies don't do justice to the contradictions and multiplicity that characterize the status of technorhetoricians, who can take advantage of the complexity of their status to enact change. Sandoval's idea of differential movement creates an oppositional consciousness that can help to form coalitions. Those faculty working with instructional uses of technology should see their work as an oppositional form of praxis, where current value systems can be used to promote transformation within the academy. Technology-enhanced work does not simply follow accepted norms nor does it undermine those norms. Those who become chimeras, cyborgs, or boundary crossers employ theories of opposition to renegotiate what is marginal.

293 Sidler, Michelle, Richard Morris, and Elizabeth Overman Smith, eds. *Computers in the Composition Classroom: A Critical Sourcebook*. Boston: Bedford/St. Martins, 2008. Print.

Writing has always been a technology of literacy, and like any technology, writing is a product of culture as it also shapes culture. Thus, digital writing reflects and influences important cultural shifts. This "shifting" may mean that teachers are underprepared to teach new forms of digital writing to students who are themselves immersed in new media. This collection seeks to provide teachers with the histories, theories, tools, and teaching ideas to fully recognize the potential of computers in the composition classroom and to map the impact of computers on literacy in general. The editors begin the collection with landmark works and end with issues that are still (as of 2008) "on the horizon." The book is divided into six parts: "foundations of computers and composition," "literacy and access," "writers and identity," "writers and composing," "institutional programs," and "the rhetoric of new media writing." Includes current entries (or excerpts from entries) from [290] and [291].

294 Sullivan, Patricia, and James E. Porter. *Opening Spaces: Writing Technologies and Critical Research Practices*. Greenwich: Ablex, 1997. Print.

Critical research practices in computers and composition, key to the development of knowledge, require a revision of methodology that calls attention to its rhetorical nature as well as to the rhetorical situation of participants, writing technologies, and technology design. Methodology has theoretical dimensions and should be seen as a heuristic rather than as a set of rules; "announcing" a method, for example, does not ground a study in site-specific, situated ways. Postmodern researchers can develop a critical praxis to combat traditional methodological rules or guidelines; methodology in a postmodern sense is local, contingent, malleable, and heuristic, and research becomes a form of political and ethical action. Postmodern mapping serves as an analytic tool for critical framing; mapping relationships and positions visually and spatially helps to achieve methodological reflectiveness and epistemological vigilance in examining issues in the study of computers in the classroom and in the workplace. Critical postmodern theory helps to articulate criteria for determining uses of computers for studying writing with a focus on the politics and ethics of research in terms of both participants and aims. Enacting critical research practices requires a doubling action: an interplay of tensions and tactics not only at the level of overarching concerns but also in terms of specific critical moves. Tactics such as advocacy charting are offered for exploring the tensions between researchers and participants; an early chapter serves as a glossary.

295 Writing in Digital Environments (WIDE) Research Center Collective. "Why Teach Digital Writing?" *Kairos* 10.1 (2005): n. pag. Web. 14 July 2010.

Computers are not just writing tools. Students have many new multimodal avenues and many new digital spaces in which to deliver their ideas. Thus, rhetorical theories need to be dramatically repurposed for digital writing theory because technology has changed writing practice. It follows that writing should no longer be taught in traditional classrooms. Simply, most everyday writing takes place online—so should writing instruction. This may place new pressures on programs and institutions, but this shift is necessary. When we move to the appropriate networked spaces for writing, then, we need to change our thinking about writing theory and pedagogy. Students must be given technological choices, teachers must be up to speed on these choices, encourage collaboration and critical thinking, and encourage students to "learn how to learn" so that they may gain more than technical skills. The result will be powerful new compositions, and powerful writers, enabled by the applications, spaces, and theories that emerge from digital environments.

296 Zappen, James P. "Digital Rhetoric: Toward an Integrated Theory." *Technical Communication Quarterly* 14.3 (July 2005): 319–25. Print.

We need an integrated theory of digital rhetoric that recognizes the transformation of traditional rhetoric within digital spaces. Key foci of this new theory would be an exploration of the formation of identity or *ethos* through online interaction, a reduced emphasis on traditional forms of persuasion, and inversions and reorganizations of traditional reader-writer relationships.

Visual Rhetoric

297 Allen, Nancy, ed. *Working with Words and Images: New Steps in an Old Dance*. Westport: Ablex, 2002. Print.

To become better writers and better teachers of writing in the twenty-first century, we need a deeper understanding of the complex relationship between words and images. Part I examines theories of perception, interpretation, and learning. Part II applies these theories of word-and-image interaction to specific sites, mediums, and genres, from the graphic novel to the theater. Part III focuses on word-and-image in digital spaces. Contents include James Kalmbach, "The Ransom Note Fallacy and Acquisition of Typographic Emphasis"; Richard Johnson-Sheehan, "Being Visual, Visual Beings"; Nancy Allen, "Telling Our Stories in Pictures: Case History of a Photo Essay"; Barry Pegg, "Two-Dimensional Features in Text: How Print Technology Has Preserved Linearity"; Amy Kimme Hea, "Articulating (Re)Visions of the Web: Exploring Links among Corporate and Academic Web Sites"; and Neil Kleinman, "Exercises and Experiments for the Workbench."

298 George, Diana. "From Analysis to Design: Visual Communication in the Teaching of Writing." CCC 54.1 (Sept. 2002): 11–39. Print.

We have generally limited our use and discussion of visual rhetoric in the classroom to analysis of visual texts, not their design. The visual has historically been linked to low culture, and thus discounted. Visual design has also been seen by many writing teachers as unteachable or, at the very least, as outside of the domain of composition. The lack of (or uneven) access to technology has also made it difficult for teachers to expand their pedagogy. Yet, despite this, students continue to create visual texts in whatever ways they can, and often outside the classroom. They will do so because the visual is increasingly connected to the verbal and saturates the world around them. Teaching visual design can allow teachers to access new rhetorical knowledge and activate existing rhetorical concepts. Seeing and designing lead to better writing. Visual communication also allows students to connect with and understand culture.

299 Handa, Carolyn, ed. *Visual Rhetoric in a Digital World: A Critical Sourcebook*. Boston: Bedford/St. Martin's, 2004. Print.

New visual and digital literacies will have a huge impact on the future of education. Culture shapes visual rhetoric. Currently, visual communication and understanding is being markedly shaped by multimedia networks, artifacts, and interfaces. Thus, to effectively teach argument, design, critical thinking, and writing, teachers must understand visual rhetorics within digital contexts. Contents include Gunther Kress, "Multimodality, Multimedia, and Genre"; Charles A. Hill, "Reading the Visual in College Writing Classes"; Roland Barthes, "Rhetoric of the Image"; Scott McCloud, "From the Vocabulary of Comics"; Barbara Stafford, "Visual Pragmatism for a Virtual World"; James E. Porter and Patricia A. Sullivan, "Repetition and the Rhetoric of Visual Design"; and Richard A. Lanham, "The Implications of Electronic Information for the Sociology of Knowledge." Handa concludes with "Selected Readings for Further Study."

300 Hill, Charles A., and Marguerite Helmers, eds. *Defining Visual Rhetorics*. Mahwah: Erlbaum, 2004. Print.

There is little consensus among composition scholars and teachers on what exactly the definitions, topics, methodologies, and applications of visual rhetoric are or should be. Yet the last few decades have seen a shift among teachers and scholars toward an emphasis on the visual nature of the rhetorical process. Hill and Helmers advocate for maintaining openness to visual rhetorical approaches, and the essays in this collection reflect this variety, as they also reflect this "visual turn." Along axes of the rhetorical and the visual, topics range from advertising to campaign films to statistical maps to architecture; methodologies range from semiotic to aesthetic to historical to psychological, with emphases on gender, class, ethnicity; authors offer a wide variety of taxonomies, vocabularies, and tools for visual rhetorical analysis. The collection provides a framing of existing approaches and a map for future study. Notable essays include David Blakesley, "Defining Film Rhetoric: The Case of Hitchcock's *Vertigo*"; Charles Kostelnick, "Melting-Pot Ideology, Modernist Aesthetics, and the Emergence of Graphical Conventions: The Statistical Atlases of the United States, 1874–1925"; Cara A. Finnegan, "Doing Rhetorical History of the Visual: The Photograph and the Archive"; Diane S. Hope, "Gendered Environments: Gender and the Natural World in the Rhetoric of Advertising"; and Sonja K. Foss' epilogue, "Framing the Study of Visual Rhetoric: Toward a Transformation of Rhetorical Theory."

301 Hocks, Mary E., "Understanding Visual Rhetoric in Digital Writing Environments." CCC 54.4 (June 2003): 629–56. Print.

Visual rhetoric is a transformative process of design. Thus, to teach visual rhetoric, we need to teach writing as and alongside design. Students can and should both critique and produce visual rhetorical artifacts in digital environments. Teachers can assist students in recognizing rhetorical principles such as audience stance and agency, the interactivity of elements, transparency, and "messiness" or hybridity in these texts and through their creation. Students might begin by mapping the visual elements of existing Web texts, as Hocks does in her analysis of two academic hypertexts. Then, students can storyboard their own texts and enter a speculative design process that incorporates their new rhetorical knowledge, revising and receiving peer feedback before they begin to compose an actual text. The final product might then be a permanent Web site, such as the student work Hocks includes in this essay.

302 Hocks, Mary E., and Michelle R. Kendrick, eds. *Eloquent Images: Word and Image in the Age of New Media.* Cambridge: MIT P, 2003. Print.

There is a complex and changing relationship between word and image, and this complexity and mutability surfaces and shifts remarkably through new digital media. Following an opening section with essays focusing on emerging technologies, Section Two of the book offers a historical shift, examining ancient Egyptian, Classical, Old English, and Romantic "media" merging word and image. Section Three offers perspectives from cognitive science and cultural studies. Section Four focuses on issues of identity. Contents include Jay David Bolter, "Critical Theory and the Challenge of New Media"; Anne Frances Wysocki, "Seriously Visible"; Matthew G. Kirschenbaum, "The Word as Image in an Age of Digital Reproduction"; Gail E. Hawisher and Patricia Sullivan, "Feminist Cyborgs Live on the World Wide Web: International and Not So International Contexts"; Alice Crawford, "Unheimlich Maneuver: Self-Image and Identificatory Practice in Virtual Reality Environments"; and Josephine Anstey, "Writing a Story in Virtual Reality."

303 Kress, Gunther, and Theo van Leeuwen. *Reading Images: The Grammar of Visual Design.* 2nd ed. New York: Routledge, 2006. Print.

Images have a "grammar" of visual design that can and should be examined systematically and semiotically. There are "regularities" in the ways that images are used to convey meaning, and thus there can be a common language for visual design. For instance, elements within an image can be placed, angled, or sized in order to position the viewer. The use of color, the interaction of visual and verbal elements, and the narrative character of images can be similarly studied. Throughout the book, exemplary images are placed at the front of chapters or sections, the authors provide systematic readings of these images, and they then develop models that explain their modes of interpretation.

304 Nakamura, Lisa. *Digitizing Race: Visual Cultures of the Internet.* Minneapolis: U of Minnesota P, 2008. Print.

Race is both seen and produced online. The Internet has become not just an important site for writing, but also offers (or mandates) important means of displaying and visualizing identity. Internet users collaboratively create images of the body for specific purposes. The Internet may pose as "blind" to race, but is anything but. Nakamura examines the distillation of identity in AIM buddies, the small icons attached to instant messages; she critiques online racial profiling and forms of physiognomy; she looks at the role of interactive digital interfaces in film, in particular the ways such interfaces frame race; she examines the use of avatars on a pregnant woman's message board; and she interrogates the racial digital divide.

305 Prelli, Lawrence J., ed. *Rhetorics of Display*. Columbia: U of South Carolina P, 2006. Print.

Display refers to how things look and appear—how they are demonstrated and shown. Display refers not just to visual images, but also to verbal images, exhibits, the presentation of information, the packaging of goods, and so on. Displays operate persuasively and rhetorically and should be analyzed accordingly. Further, rhetorics themselves enact display, and thus display should be recognized as one of the ways that we rhetorically construct realities. Rhetorical displays are everywhere in contemporary communication and life, and thus deserve our attention and analysis. Prelli's introduction traces a 2,500-year history of rhetorics of display, touching upon nearly all facets of the rhetorical canon. But the articles in this collection are focused almost exclusively on contemporary contexts of display. The collection comprises seventeen articles, each representing a case study of a contemporary display, from museum exhibitions to monuments, to iconic photographs, to public demonstrations, to tattoos and piercings. The first major section of the book focuses on the "verbal depiction of the visual and the visual depiction of the verbal"; Part II looks at the "disposition of place and the placing of disposition"; Part III focuses on "demonstrations as rhetorical display and rhetorical displays as demonstrative"; and Part IV examines "epideictic identifications and divisions."

306 Selfe, Cynthia L. "Toward New Media Texts: Taking Up the Challenges of Visual Literacy." *Writing New Media: Theory and Applications for Expanding the Teaching of Composition*. Ed. Anne Frances Wysocki, Johndan Johnson-Eilola, Cynthia L. Selfe, and Geoffrey Sirc. Logan: Utah State UP, 2004. 67–110. Print.

In teaching new media texts, we need to shift attention to nonalphabetic—specifically visual—literacies. Visual literacy is, in part, "the ability to read, understand, value, and learn from visual materials . . . especially as these are combined to create a text." Instead of the traditional author writing, the composer/designer of new media texts is involved in a complex set of activities to argue and to "order and make sense of the world." To illustrate and encourage these complex activities, this chapter includes a set of unique assignments designed to advance visual literacy through the composition of a visual essay, a visual argument, a traveling photo exhibit, and a text redesign and revision. Selfe comments on the goals of each assignment—both basic and advanced—as she provides all of the necessary material to teach these assignments.

See: Cynthia L. Selfe and Richard J. Selfe Jr., "The Politics of the Interface: Power and Its Exercise in Electronic Contact Zones" [291].

307 Westbrook, Steve. "Visual Rhetoric in a Culture of Fear: Impediments to Multimedia Production." *CE* 68.5 (May 2006): 457–80. Print.

Students have been positioned as consumers of visual texts or located outside of the sphere of visual discourse altogether. Student work, which has rarely been visual, multimedia, or multigenre, has been positioned only within the academy. Students should be producers of multimedia and visual texts. These texts should be seen as having the potential to shape public culture, and thus should be disseminated outside of the academy. Particularly in a post-9/11 culture of fear, copyright and censorship suppress dissent, and education is disconnected from the public sphere. For writing to be relevant to students, and for student writing to reach and persuade public audiences, we need to protect students' rights as producers of visual rhetorical texts.

308 Wysocki, Anne Frances. "With Eyes that Think, and Compose, and Think: On Visual Rhetoric." *Teaching Writing with Computers: An Introduction*. Ed. Pamela Takayoshi and Brian Huot. Boston: Houghton, 2002. 182–201. Print.

To understand visual rhetoric, one must "work with (or sometimes against) the expectations and assumptions and values of one's audience concerning ALL the visual aspects of a text." It is not enough to simply recognize visual strategies, but rather we must see how these strategies fit within larger visual contexts and technologies. Wysocki plays with visual elements in this text to reinforce her own arguments and explorations and to further exemplify the issues discussed. She shows that even this essay itself is placed within the visual context of the book: when Wysocki plays with the book's conventions, she draws our attention to them. Wysocki offers several examples of student visual arguments and considers each student's visual strategies, and the context in which they are made, as well as the range of choices available to them. The essay ends with a series of provocative suggestions about how we can go about teaching visual rhetoric. We need to concurrently teach students to recognize the physiology of seeing; understand design and architecture; recognize larger visual contexts, such as technologies or the built environment; view *all* visual aspects of texts as rhetorical; develop wide repertoires of visual persuasion; and experiment with new strategies that change how we see.

New Media

309 Alexander, Jonathan, ed. "Media Convergence: Creating Content, Questioning Relationships." Special issue of *Computers and Composition* 25.1 (Mar. 2008). Print.

Thanks to advances in technology, students can now easily access and create media-convergent texts—texts that use multiple media to create meaning. These new avenues of access and production allow students to "talk back" to texts, reworking, extending, remixing, and subverting meanings. In these ways, students' relationship to texts changes, and questions of authority, agency, ownership, and collaboration arise and gain prominence, alongside more "traditional" rhetorical considerations for writers and teachers of writing. Media convergence challenges traditional notions of literacy, and considering these changes offers a chance to take stock of other overlaps and disconnects: between classroom writing and students' other literate worlds, between generations, between "high" and "low" culture, between the goals of the corporate university and the goals of progressive pedagogy, between "real" and "virtual" life, and so on. The essays in this collection engage with these new and evolving convergences and include Jonathan Alexander, "Media Convergence: Creating Content, Questioning Relationships"; Bronwyn T. Williams, "'What South Park Character Are You?': Popular Culture, Literacy, and Online Performances of Identity"; Suzanne Webb and Dànielle Nicole DeVoss, "Grand Theft Audio: Negotiating Copyright as Composers"; and Heidi McKee, "Ethical and Legal Issues for Writing Researchers in an Age of Media Convergence."

310 Anderson, Daniel. "Prosumer Approaches to New Media Composition: Consumption and Production in Continuum." *Kairos* 8.1 (2003): n. pag. Web. 14 July 2010.

While in the past only experts produced digital texts, new digital tools now blur the boundary between producers and consumers. Many entry-level technologies allow students to produce mutimodal texts without expert knowledge. Students can also repurpose existing texts in critical ways, using these technologies—for instance, cutting together video clips using free or inexpensive film-editing software. As producers and consumers, or "prosumers," students are better able to analyze digital texts because they have also produced forms of them. Students are then better able to produce texts because they understand their consumption, reception, and/or repurposing in sophisticated ways as well. Anderson's webtext is highly multimodal itself, with many links, videos, as well as text and audio overlapping. The essay showcases video examples of student collaboration, as well as the texts that students create and their explication of their own work as "prosumers."

311 Ball, Cheryl E., and Ryan M. Moeller. "Reinventing the Possibilities: Academic Literacy and New Media." *Fibreculture Journal* 10 (Nov. 2007): n. pag. Web. 14 July 2010.

Authors and audiences for new media texts enter into a space of negotiated meaning-making unlike the transfer between writers and readers of traditional print texts. The authors explore two key concepts for new media literacy: commonplaces and topoi. Topoi are the available means, the strategies that designers/writers use to make meaning and can range from software to texts that already exist on the Web but that might be reused. In other words, topoi are the materials and forms of a digital text. Commonplaces are the spaces and also the experiences in which readers and writers can come together to negotiate meaning. These might be message boards or chat sites. This webtext itself models these two concepts. Readers progress through the text by clicking on different letters of the alphabet and thus viewing a range of arguments written by the authors, examinations of relevant rhetorical theories, descriptions of curriculum, examples created by their students, and so on—topoi. Readers are encouraged to progress through the text in their own way, yet they are given links, charts, downloads, student voices, maps, and citations that orient—commonplaces.

312 Bolter, Jay David, and Richard Grusin. *Remediation: Understanding New Media*. Cambridge: MIT P, 1999. Print.

Two seemingly contradictory logics—immediacy and hypermediacy—are mutually dependent; both old and new media invoke these twin logics to remake themselves and each other. New digital media oscillate between immediacy and hypermediacy, between transparency and opacity, with a social dimension as important as their formal and technical dimensions. A double logic of remediation, which can function explicitly or implicitly, began with the introduction of digital media and borrows from film, television, and photography. However, no medium today does its cultural work in isolation from other media; all new media emerge from within cultural contexts and refashion other media, and a particular medium is always understood in relation to other past and present media. The kind of borrowing extremely common in popular culture today is very old, but unlike paintings, the digital medium can be more aggressive in its remediation. Such contemporary media as computer games, digital photography, film, virtual reality, and the Web illustrate the process of remediation. Users or viewers enter into a twofold relationship with the medium; the reflexive relationship between user and medium results in consequences for our culture's definitions of the self, defined by the perspectives that the subject occupies in the virtual space. New media are fully involved in the struggle to define the self as both embodied and mediated by the body. The remediated self, the virtual self, and the networked self illustrate that whenever identity is mediated, it is also remediated.

313 DeVoss, Dànielle Nicole, Ellen Cushman, and Jeff Grabill. "Infrastructure and Composing: The *When* of New-Media Writing." CCC 57.1 (Sept. 2005): 14–44. Print.

Instead of paying attention to the what and why of new media compositions like student video texts, teachers and researchers should pay greater attention to the *when* of new media composing. Usually invisible institutional and political arrangements condition the emergence of new media texts, creating both possibilities and limitations, valuing some forms of work and not others. Understanding the *when* of composing allows us to better view the processes of invention, production, revision, and reflection, but it also might allow us to strategically renegotiate some of the infrastructure and networks that can limit access to new media tools or devalue some forms of new media work.

314 Hawisher, Gail E., and Cynthia L. Selfe, eds. *Passions, Pedagogies, and 21st Century Technologies*. Logan: Utah State UP and NCTE, 1999. Print.

This substantial collection addresses issues of information technologies and the technocultural contexts facing those in the English profession. Each of the four parts contains a response essay. Essays include Doug Hesse, "Saving a Place for Essayistic Literacy"; Gunther Kress, "'English' at the Crossroads: Rethinking Curricula of Communication in the Context of the Turn to the Visual"; Lester Faigley, "Beyond Imagination: The Internet and Global Digital Literacy"; Marilyn Cooper, "Postmodern Pedagogy in Electronic Conversations"; Charles Moran, "Access: The A Word in Technology Studies"; James Porter, "Liberal Individualism and Internet Policy: A Communitarian Critique"; Gail E. Hawisher and Patricia A. Sullivan, "Fleeting Images: Women Visually Writing the Web"; Cynthia L. Selfe, "Lest We Think the Revolution Is a Revolution: Images of Technology and the Nature of Change"; Anne Frances Wysocki and Johndan Johnson-Eilola, "Blinded by the Letter: Why Are We Using Literacy as a Metaphor for Everything Else?"; and Janet Carey Eldred, "Technology's Strange, Familiar Voices."

315 Hawk, Byron, David M. Rieder, and Ollie Oviedo, eds. *Small Tech: The Culture of Digital Tools*. Minneapolis: U of Minnesota P, 2008. Print.

Some examples of "small tech" include iPods, cell phones, digital cameras, Personal Digital Assistants, and Global Positioning Systems (and the evolving convergences between these technologies). While much attention has been paid to the Internet and the personal computer, these "smaller" technologies also hold (increasing) rhetorical, artistic, and educational importance and potential. Essays in this collection cover a very wide array of issues that are commonly quite theoretical and specialized. Several of the selections offer important (re)definitions of mediums that composition instructors might use in the classroom, from digital photography to the podcast, and many selections are explicitly pedagogical. Essays in this collection include Lev Manovich, "Data Visualization as New Abstraction and as Anti-Sublime"; Karla Saari Kitalong, "Remembering Dinosaurs: Toward an Archeological Understanding of Digital Photo Manipulation"; Collin Gifford Brooke, "Revisiting the Matter and Manner of Linking in New Media"; Jenny Edbauer Rice, "Overhearing: The Intimate Life of Cell Phones"; Paul Cesarini, "I Am a DJ, I Am What I Say: The Rise of Podcasting"; Johndan Johnson-Eilola, "Communication Breakdown: The Postmodern Space of Google"; James J.

Sosnoski, "Virtual Reality as a Teaching Tool: Learning by Configuring"; and Jason Nolan, Steve Mann, and Barry Wellman, "Sousveillance: Wearable and Digital Tools in Surveilled Environments."

316 Pagnucci, Gian S., and Nicholas Mauriello, eds. *Re-Mapping Narrative: Technology's Impact on the Way We Write*. Cresskill: Hampton, 2008. Print.

The Internet has introduced an increased multivocality that should change how we view literacy and narrative. Linear, authoritative narrative has been replaced by fluid discourse, a sea of voices in constant dialogue online. Identity is socially constructed; power is negotiated relationally but nonhierarchically; writers and writing evolve and transform continuously. The authors in this collection explore the impact of new technologies on our conceptions of literacy and narrative and how they are taught. Some highlights include Lisa Gerrard, "'Diets Suck!' and Other Tales of Women's Bodies on the Web"; Ellen Barton, "The Presence of Interlocuters vs. the Sites of the Internet: The Restricted Range of Disability Narratives"; and Jennifer Cohen, Paula Mathieu, Eric Smith, James Sosnoski, Bridget Harris Tsemo, and Vershawn Ashanti Young, "Culture Wise: Narrative as Research, Research as Narrative."

317 Rice, Jeffrey. *The Rhetoric of Cool: Composition Studies and New Media*. Carbondale: Southern Illinois UP, 2007. Print.

Cool is a rhetorical act. Teaching cool as writing and writing as cool entails the development of an electronic rhetoric. In this rhetoric, both writer and writing are "media beings"—beings that engage with media but are also constructed through media, never separate from digital culture. What makes this rhetoric cool is its refusal to choose one definition or even one avenue of communication. That said, cool has characteristics: it values chora, appropriation, juxtaposition, commutation, nonlinearity, and imagery. Cool is choral: fluid, moving, interlinking, multivocal, and performative. A rhetoric of cool encourages appropriation, but appropriation that transcends the limits of academic discourse, valuing all of the composing we do as media beings. When we compose, we do more than write. We also appropriate, we creatively sample and juxtapose, and this is another facet of cool: creating new connections and commutations through our own writing and other voices and images. The "products" of cool are not just nonlinear texts with multiple points of entry, but also new articulations and uses of digital media and technology. It is easy to dismiss "cool" as an expression. Yet, to see cool as a rhetoric allows us to better understand the subtly formative and ongoing impact of new media on writing and writers—foregrounding chora, appropriation, juxtaposition, commutation, nonlinearity, and imagery.

318 Rife, Martine. "The Fair Use Doctrine: History, Application, and Implications for (New Media) Writing Teachers." *Computers and Composition* 24.2 (Apr. 2007): 154–78. Print.

With the ubiquity of digital technologies and networked environments, the doctrine of "fair use" has come to the center of discussions in composition, joining and complicating traditional discussions of plagiarism. As a result, writing teachers need to understand fair use, its legal and ethical entailments and ramifications, and the manner in which discourse around fair use can inform students' analyses and creation of digital texts. Fair use is a legal framework that promises to shape writing and the teaching of writing. We have always used outside sources and materials as writers; now these uses are changing and so are the rules. In short, copyrighted work can be "fairly used" for teaching, scholarship, research, or reporting, so long as this use stands up to the "four factor test": a series of considerations used to ensure that a copyrighted work is used properly, for nonprofit educational purposes, in ways that do not negatively impact the rights of the author of the work. To help implement fair use, digital writing teachers need to help students properly situate materials that they intend to use according to copyright and fair use regulations. Teachers also need to concentrate on information literacy with a focus on ethical research and citation. Finally, teachers should model fair use in their own teaching.

319 Selfe, Cynthia L. "The Movement of Air, the Breath of Meaning: Aurality and Multimodal Composing." CCC 60.4 (June 2009): 616–63. Print.

Historically, an emphasis on alphabetic writing led to the undervaluing of aurality and sound. But teaching only alphabetic writing limits and constrains students who rely on other modalities and learning styles. Teachers and scholars of composition need to recognize and respect a wider range of literacies and modalities and the role they play in composing. Looking at digital audio texts as case studies, Selfe suggests that students who use sound as a composing modality come to understand written language better (and the inverse is true as well). She also shows that sound is the preferred modality of some students and argues that delimiting their available means of expression is unjust.

320 Selfe, Cynthia L., ed. *Multimodal Composition: Resources for Teachers*. Cresskill: Hampton, 2007. Print.

Composition teachers must expand their expertise beyond alphabetic literacies. In this resource book, sample worksheets, rubrics, assignments, student essays, a glossary, and information about hardware, software, and digital tools are offered in order to make this pedagogical expansion easier. While the audience for the book is teachers, much of the information could also be used with students—the entire appendix gathers handouts and forms for teachers to utilize directly in their classes. The collection features Pamela Takayoshi and Cynthia L. Selfe, "Thinking about Multimodality"; Iswari Pandey, "Saving, Sharing, Citing, and Publishing Multimodal Texts"; Sonya C. Borton and Brian Huot, "Responding and Assessing"; Sylvia Church and Elizabeth Powell, "When Things Go Wrong"; Richard J. Selfe, "Sustaining Multimodal Composition"; Marilyn M. Cooper, "Learning and Teaching Digital Technologies"; and an afterword by Deborah Journet.

321 Stroupe, Craig. "Hacking the Cool: The Shape of Writing Culture in the Space of New Media." *Computers and Composition* 24.4 (Oct. 2007): 421–42. Print.

The shape of the writing environment and economy in new media writing is significantly different from the shape of traditional print. For instance, networks have an "exteriority" that contrasts with the intimacy of verbal communication. The attention span and the distribution of our attention online also contrasts with the more stringent narrative and/or linear demands of print.

322 Wysocki, Anne Frances, Johndan Johnson-Eilola, Cynthia L. Selfe, and Geoffrey Sirc, eds. *Writing New Media: Theory and Applications for Expanding the Teaching of Composition*. Logan: Utah State UP, 2004. Print.

A collection of six essays by four authors, offering several unique approaches to writing new media, framed as both a primer and a resource book. In addition to the essays, there are nineteen assignments and/or classroom activities included in the book—three to five practical classroom applications for each of the six essays. The assignments are accompanied by teacher's notes and other useful information, such as evaluation scales or handouts for students. Wysocki's opening essay argues for a "generous" rather than expert and exacting approach to unconventional new media texts, assuming that authors have made rhetorical choices, not errors. Selfe then offers a case study of a student new media composer, arguing that students will show us how literacy is changing and lead us in new directions. Selfe's second essay focuses on the challenges of visual literacy, offering strategies for the recognition of rhetorical complexity in visual texts and advocating for the usefulness and sophistication of visual literacies that have been traditionally subordinated to alphabetic print literacy. Geoffrey Sirc explores the value of searching, acquiring, associating, annotating, arranging, and reflecting in new media composition, connecting the role of the composer to that of the artist and curator. Wysocki's second essay explores how visual texts can be created for specific rhetorical circumstances, not limited to reproduction. Visual texts can reshape values and relations—challenging held notions of beauty, for instance. The final essay, by Johnson-Eilola, explores new media texts through theories of postmodern authorship, arguing that acts of selection and connection are rhetorically significant, active, and creative.

323 Yancey, Kathleen Blake. "Made Not Only in Words: Composition in a New Key." CCC 56.2 (Dec. 2004): 297–328. Print.

Today we face huge structural educational change, change that calls for a "new composition." This composition will include print, but also a new key for composing: a key tuned to the composing that happens outside of school, largely online, in new social contexts, genres, and through a steady procession of new technologies. Oral and print literacy will be joined by screen literacy. The curriculum and content of composition will change, as will the circulation of our ideas, hopefully toward a new "writing public." This "writing public" would better understand the ways that texts and genres and technologies interrelate; would incorporate multiple modes and media; would situate the student as maker of knowledge; would anticipate, envision, and welcome change; and would advocate for democracy and a commitment to humanity.

Literacy Studies

See: Linda Adler-Kassner and Susanmarie Harrington, *Basic Writing as a Political Act: Public Conversations about Writing and Literacies* [632].

324 Barton, David. *Literacy: An Introduction to the Ecology of Written Language*. Malden: Blackwell, 1994. Print.

An ecological metaphor for literacy ("a set of social practices associated with particular symbol systems and their related technologies") allows social, psychological, and historical approaches to literacy studies to be brought together. In an ecological model, literacy is practices and events, rather than formal learning, and develops from a constructivist theory of language. Readers are introduced to key terms and definitions, to important research (Scribner and Cole, Heath, Street), to the relation of spoken and written language, and to writing systems and other notations. Other chapters cover the development of printing, emergent literacy, the literary view of literacy, school practices, issues in adult literacy, and global literacy.

325 Barton, David, and Mary Hamilton. *Local Literacies: Reading and Writing in One Community*. New York: Routledge, 1998. Print.

A description and investigation of literacy in one local community of Lancaster, England, presented as a microcosm of change and continuity in literacy practices. Sixty-five people in the neighborhood of Springside were interviewed, with twelve selected for the case studies; data collection included a collaborative ethnography stage. Four people are profiled in-depth in terms of their literacy life and history with such topics as education, getting things done in the community, living a local life, and leisure and pleasure. As a set of social practices inferred from events that are mediated by written texts, literacy may serve multiple functions in any given activity; for example, literacy acts as evidence, display, threat, and/or ritual, and people can be incorporated into the literacy practices of others without reading or writing a single word. Despite wide diversity of literacies in the home, there was also coherence in the diversity. Broad patternings included the gendering of home practices, the intertwining of literacy and numeracy practices, and the significance of multilingual experience of literacy. Literacies are used for collective goals but also to make sense of events in individuals' lives. More than fifty "asides" illustrate cooking literacy, learning at work, family traditions of reading, dealing with dyslexia, doing the accounts, helping with the homework, computers in the home, and others.

326 Bernstein, Basil. *Class, Codes, and Control*. New York: Schocken, 1975. Print.

School writing and speaking tasks call for the use of the elaborated code—a formal way of using language that explicitly identifies context and carefully fills in transitions and details for an anonymous reader. Most everyday speech, however, calls only for the restricted code, which is highly context-dependent. Socioeconomic class tends to determine whether children learn how to use the elaborated code at home, hence whether they can readily perform the kind of linguistic tasks assigned and expected at school. Working-class children experience social relations in which elaborated code use is rare, unlike middle-class children, who can distinguish the codes and when to use them. Thus, working-class children are often judged to be stupid when they only lack access to school-like linguistic forms.

327 Bleich, David. *The Double Perspective: Language, Literacy and Social Relations*. New York: Oxford UP, 1988. Print.

We learn how to communicate by internalizing the double perspective of speaker and interlocutor first experienced as small children in dialogue with our parents. Effective adult communication is never an assertion of will but part of an oscillation between socially constructed pairs of opposing concepts. In teaching, a productive oscillation is needed between the classroom, in which subjective expression and collaboration are encouraged, and the academy, which valorizes "objective" scholarship produced by "independent" thought. In this as in other pairs of perspectives, one term must not be privileged: A double perspective is to be maintained. Bleich gives many examples of assignments and student work to illustrate his pedagogy.

328 Bloome, David, ed. *Classrooms and Literacy*. Norwood: Ablex, 1989. Print.

Eleven essays explore the idea that literacy education is a function of the curriculum as a whole and the school as a social institution. Essays include David Bloome, "Beyond Access: An Ethnographic Study of Reading and Writing in a Seventh Grade Classroom"; Catherine Snow et al., "Giving Formal Definitions: An Oral Language Correlate of School Literacy"; Thomas Eisemon and Theresa Rogers, "The Acquisition of Literacy in Religious and Secular Schools"; Jay Lemke, "Social Semiotics: A New Model for Literacy Education"; and Patricia Stock and Jay Robinson, "Literacy as Conversation: Classroom Talk as Text Building."

329 Brandt, Deborah. "Accumulating Literacy: Writing and Learning to Write in the Twentieth Century." *CE* 57.6 (Oct. 1995): 649–68. Print.

Literacy practices in the twentieth century expanded both vertically and horizontally—as a result of rising levels of formal schooling, and "residual" materials and practices that get passed on, transformed, or assimilated. Interview participants from across four generations relate their early childhood experiences with literacy, schooling or training, and their uses and inheritances of language as adult writers. Two extended examples illustrate how individuals transform or adapt "residual literacy"—that is, practices and materials from earlier times "that linger at the scenes of contemporary literacy learning." As technologies and documentary practices evolve, old forms don't disappear but are transformed: a son gives his mother his used computer, and she passes on her manual typewriter to her grandchildren to play with, or a son draws upon his father's sermons in a C.M.E. church to write his own administrative and professional texts. Literacy needs to be defined in light of the "piling up" of artifacts and the ubiquity of print.

330 Brandt, Deborah. *Literacy as Involvement: The Acts of Writers, Readers, and Texts*. Carbondale: Southern Illinois UP, 1990. Print.

The oral-literate dichotomy and the accompanying assumption that text literacy requires the ability to manage decontextualized language are in error. Rather, all forms of literacy are deeply context-bound, and reading and writing are forms of social interaction and intersubjectivity.

331 Brandt, Deborah. *Literacy in American Lives*. New York: Cambridge UP, 2001. Print.

Eighty in-depth interviews with a diverse group of Americans born between the 1890s and the 1980s focus on literacy learning and characterize literacy contextually, "as it has been lived." Treating literacy as a resource, as a form of raw material for an economic engine, leads to a different conceptual approach, one of importance to *literacy sponsors*, agents, or "underwriters" of literacy learning and use, who lend resources or credibility but also stand to gain the same in return. One chapter profiles four generations of a single family—how each learned to write—and illustrates increased stratification around literacy as well as its accumulation and inflationary cycle. Another chapter documents the importance of the church and other sponsors of literacy in African American lives. For every generation, learning to read and write has taken place for different reasons and under different circumstances, and patterns of literacy sponsorship change markedly in only one generation.

332 Carter, Shannon. *The Way Literacy Lives: Rhetorical Dexterity and Basic Writing Instruction*. Albany: State U of New York P, 2008. Print.

Challenging the pervasive autonomous model of literacy (Brian V. Street) begins by taking vernacular literacies seriously. Created from the position that (almost) no one is illiterate, a basic writing curriculum should deconstruct the meaning of literacy, acknowledging the dominant status of academic literacy but also supporting a "situated perspective of literacy as it functions in the real lives of our students."

Out-of-school literacies have much to teach us about academic ones, but the conflict between home and school is likely to be more profound for those students labeled basic writers. When students bring into writing classes their expertise from particular communities of practice—for example, online gaming—their ability to transfer those skills depends on rhetorical dexterity: "the ultimate goal of rhetorical dexterity is to develop the ability to effectively read, understand, manipulate, and negotiate the cultural and linguistic codes of a new community of practice based on a relatively accurate assessment of another, more familiar one." Curricular decisions and assignments are shared in appendices.

333 Chiseri-Strater, Elizabeth. *Academic Literacies: The Public and Private Discourse of University Students*. Portsmouth: Heinemann-Boynton/Cook, 1991. Print.

Detailed case studies of two college writers reveal linguistic resources that are not always recognized by the university. The academy favors lecture-recitation and combative debate formats that suited one of the students, while the other found less agonistic ways of communicating and learning. Both students used nonverbal expression, like visual images and dance, as aids to learning, even though these media were rarely valued in coursework. The development of multiple literacies can be fostered by adopting collaborative learning strategies and writing assignments that breach the traditional separation between public knowledge and private life.

334 Cook-Gumperz, Jenny. *The Social Construction of Literacy*. Cambridge: Cambridge UP, 1986. Print.

Ten essays investigate the settings in which and means by which literacy is acquired. Includes: Jenny Cook-Gumperz, "Literacy and Schooling: An Unchanging Equation?"; John Gumperz, "Interactional Sociolinguistics in the Study of Schooling"; Gordon Wells, "The Language Experience of Five-Year-Old Children at Home and at School"; James Collins, "Differential Instruction in Reading Groups"; and Herbert Simons and Sandra Murphy, "Spoken Language Strategies and Reading Acquisition."

335 Cushman, Ellen. *The Struggle and the Tools: Oral and Literate Strategies in an Inner City Community*. Albany: State U of New York P, 1998. Print.

In daily struggles with public service agencies, inner-city residents demonstrate sophisticated linguistic strategizing and draw upon a wide variety of literacy tools. Faced with eviction, for example, residents collaborated on ways to find housing, including rehearsing conversations and sharing years of experiences with racism and bureaucracy. Through a cyclic process of learning, deploying, and assessing their oral and literate strategies for interactions with gatekeepers, the subjects of this study practiced language transfer, code-switching, and metadiscourse. Based on more than three years of fieldwork, these findings challenge the notion of "illiteracy" as well as the concept of false consciousness.

Cushman advocates an activist methodology and more studies of extracurricular literacies.

336 Daniell, Beth. "Against the Great Leap Theory of Literacy." *PRE/TEXT* 7.3-4 (Fall–Winter 1986): 181–93. Print.

Literacy scholarship is divided into two camps, those who embrace and those who oppose the Great Leap theory. This theory holds that literacy shifts a culture's perception from holistic to analytic. It is advanced by Eric Havelock [350], Walter J. Ong, S.J. [361, 362], and Thomas Farrell [342]. But the conflation of thought itself with the qualities of formal discourse prejudices the characterization of oral communities, equating Western forms of academic thinking with human intelligence. The theory also permits broad generalization about language competence and cognitive ability from small language samples. Many researchers oppose this theory, having found that a continuum from oral to literate or a complex intermixing of these forms of discourse more accurately describes the language use of particular societies.

337 Daniell, Beth. "Narratives of Literacy: Connecting Composition to Culture." CCC 50.3 (Feb. 1999): 393–410. Print.

Lyotard's theory of grand narratives and little narratives helps to illustrate a number of issues in the relationship of literacy and composition. The "Literacy for Liberation Narrative," for example, largely informed by Freire, attempts to refute the "Great Leap Narrative," but in our tendency to buy into the narrative of literacy heroism, composition scholars have largely misunderstood Freire's Catholic and spiritual vision of education. Recent studies tend to be little narratives of literacy, most of which argue that literacy cannot be neatly linked to either freedom or oppression. The little narratives connect composition to culture by studying writing in everyday life and by representing the ideological contradictions of literacy.

338 DeStigter, Todd. "The *Tesoros* Literacy Project: An Experiment in Democratic Communities." *Research in the Teaching of English* 32.1 (Feb. 1998): 10–42. Print.

A ten-week collaboration between ESL (Latino) students and at-risk Anglo students put into practice John Dewey's ideas about the importance of relationships to democratic communities. This project attempts to resolve, not just to critique, the inequities in the educational environment of Addison High, where students collaborated weekly on reading and writing projects and, in the process, established affective relationships and illustrated the importance of valuing difference.

339 Donehower, Kim, Charlotte Hogg, and Eileen E. Schell. *Rural Literacies*. Carbondale: Southern Illinois UP, 2007. Print.

Not nearly enough literacy research has been done in rural or small-town communities, and past representations of rural literacies have reinforced stereotypes and stigmatization, sometimes reinforced by literacy sponsors. At the same time, literacy sponsorships may also be crucial to challenging stereotypes and to arguing for "a notion of rural literacy based on a concept of sustainability." Farm Aid, for example, operates as a literacy sponsor invested in establishing the mutual interests of sustainable family farms. Interviews conducted in one Appalachian community illustrate the role of reading and writing to maintaining social networks, while a qualitative study with older white women in Paxton, Nebraska, shows that "literate acts abound" in such forms as the Rural Womyn Zone, a technological network. In short, rural settings present opportunities for educators that have been too often overlooked. Each of the three authors contributes to the final chapter on citizenship and pedagogy.

340 Duffy, John M. *Writing from These Roots: Literacy in a Hmong-American Community*. Honolulu: U of Hawaii P, 2007. Print.

Hmong immigration to Wausau, Wisconsin, provides an "opportunity to study the forces that influence the development of reading and writing abilities in cultures in which writing is not widespread." Narratives of writing shaped Hmong culture long before the arrival of missionaries' alphabets and scripts. The literacy experiences of the Hmong challenge a deficit theory of "preliteracy," as Lao schooling, military bureaucracy, and missionary Christianity offered "a distinctive identity and position within a larger institutional framework." Informed by and contributing to New Literacy Studies, fifty life-history interviews conducted over a two-year period offer an account of literacy development as rhetorical. Diverse, self-sponsored literacy practices among the Hmong included the writing of letters, editorials, grant proposals, essays, and memoirs. Rhetorics constructed through these writings include the rhetoric of testimony, the rhetoric of new gender relations, and the rhetoric of the Fair City.

341 Eldred, Janet Carey, and Peter Mortensen. "Reading Literacy Narratives." *CE* 54.5 (Sept. 1992): 512–39. Print.

Sociolinguistic scholarship on literacy provides critical insights into literary works that feature narratives of literacy acquisition. This scholarship has exploded the myth that increased literacy brings social progress and individual advancement, a myth that can be found in literature. Literacy scholarship also calls attention to the ways that literacy acquisition affects the formation of new identities, seen in narratives of socialization. In literature of the contact zone (see Pratt [239]), people struggle with literacy imposed by colonizers. A number of literary works, like Shaw's *Pygmalion*, focus on literacy narratives.

342 Farrell, Thomas J. "I.Q. and Standard English." *CCC* 34.4 (Dec. 1983): 470–84. Print.

There is no genetic cause for black children's persistently lower scores on I.Q. tests. Black English communities, however, exhibit many patterns of oral, rather than literate, language use. If I.Q. tests measure cognitive abilities valued by society, and if the acquisition of literacy confers these abilities, the low I.Q. scores of African American children can be attributed to their orality—their ignorance of Standard English, which is shaped by literacy. Thus, their cognitive abilities may be enhanced by teaching them to speak and write Standard English. See also "Responses to Thomas J. Farrell, 'I.Q. and Standard English,'" CCC 35.4 (Dec. 1984): 455–77.

See: Kristie S. Fleckenstein, *Embodied Literacies: Imageword and a Poetics of Teaching* [205].

343 Fox, Tom. *Defending Access: A Critique of Standards in Higher Education.* Portsmouth: Heinemann-Boynton/Cook, 1999. Print.

Lack of access remains the most crucial problem in higher education—not a crisis of standards—and we must, accordingly, abandon the notion that skills alone provide access. A brief account of literacy learning among African Americans provides a dramatic contrast to the institutional history of composition and illuminates the ideologies of access and exclusion. John Ogbu's theory of oppositional culture explains, in part, why initiation doesn't work as a curricular strategy. What is needed are constant critiques of the ideologies that reduce writing courses to service and skills. Efforts to transform the structures that work against access can begin by imagining writing program administration as a set of coordinated actions. Similarly, standards for teaching writing are part of coordinated political action, where standards are in a critical relationship with social and political change.

344 Freire, Paulo. *Pedagogy of the Oppressed.* Trans. Myra Bergman Ramos. New York: Seabury, 1968. Print.

Pedagogy can be liberating if it truly enables the oppressed to name the world for themselves rather than merely imposing the knowledge of the dominant group. The banking approach to education, in which the teacher knows, thinks, speaks, and disciplines, treats people as adaptable and manipulable rather than as agents in the world with the power to create and transform. Liberating education consists of acts of cognition, not transfers of information. Teaching from generative themes drawn from the lives of the students can lead to critical consciousness as the students come to understand the situation in which they live, gain the power to name it, and see the possibility of changing it themselves.

345 Freire, Paulo, and Donaldo Macedo. *Literacy: Reading the Word and the World.* South Hadley: Bergin & Garvey, 1987. Print.

Literacy is a form of cultural politics, in the United States as elsewhere. It may reproduce the existing social formation or promote emancipatory change. Critical literacy encourages cultural production rather than reproduction, enabling people to tell their own stories about their individual and collective experience.

346 Gere, Anne Ruggles. "Kitchen Table and Rented Rooms: The Extracurriculum of Composition." CCC 45.1 (Feb. 1994): 75–92. Print.

In urban centers and small farming communities, countless writers gather regularly in self-sponsored workshops to share their writing. Participants gain confidence, hone their craft, contribute positive criticism, and create opportunities for performance and publication. These writing groups and the writing development they encourage are not accounted for in histories of composition studies, characteristically neglectful of extracurricular literary clubs and other literacy practices outside of formal education. Gere identifies self-help guides for writers, many used by groups that developed across gender, class, and racial lines: there were clubs for white women, African American women, and working-class women—all of which contributed to and sustained composition's extracurriculum. Motivated by desire, writers who participate in these groups remind composition teachers that "an unswerving concentration on professionalism" blinds us to the cultural work that writing accomplishes. Writers often write for the love of it, to enact power, and to perform.

347 Gilyard, Keith. *Voices of the Self: A Study of Language Competence*. Detroit: Wayne State UP, 1991. Print.

Native Black English speakers in an urban public school environment can acquire Standard English language skills and "sociolinguistic competence" if they are encouraged to see their experience according to a transactional model that emphasizes their ability to negotiate and manipulate school language expectations in response to their own belief systems and personal traits. Gilyard surveys research on code-switching, bidialectalism, and the sociopolitical dimensions of schooling, interspersing these scholarly discussions with narratives of his own experience as one such urban Black English speaker making his way through school.

348 Graff, Harvey J. *The Labyrinths of Literacy: Reflections on Literacy Past and Present*. Pittsburgh: U of Pittsburgh P, 1995. Print.

Sixteen previously published essays by Graff explore the history of literacy and the implications of that history. Present-day conceptions of literacy are historically grounded, reflecting the oversimple view of literacy as the key to civilization (dominant until quite recently) yet serving as the basis of a more complex understanding of literacy at present. The connection between literacy and social development was based on untested assumptions and ideological predispositions: Literacy was mistaken for a neutral technology; alphabetic literacy was extolled, to the exclusion of other significant literacies; a false dichotomy was discerned between literacy and orality; and a hierarchy that irrevocably harmed individuals and societies perceived as illiterate was erected. Critical theory and social history have worked to test and correct these conceptions, revealing a far more complex understanding of the nature and types of literacy, the ways that literacies are learned and used, the functions of literacy in communities, and the policies that have been employed to foster—or impede—literacy.

349 Graff, Harvey J. *The Legacies of Literacy: Continuities and Contradictions in Western Culture and Society*. Bloomington: Indiana UP, 1987. Print.

Graff reviews classical and medieval education but concentrates on the advent of print literacy in the Renaissance, exploring its consequences for popular schooling in eighteenth- and nineteenth-century Europe and America. He examines literacy in the social context to determine who achieves literacy, what kind of literacy is achieved, and what purposes literacy serves.

350 Havelock, Eric. *Preface to Plato*. Cambridge: Belknap–Harvard UP, 1963. Print.

Plato's attack on poetry was in fact an attack on the use of oral poetry as the archive of Greek culture and the means of cultural instruction. Poetry distorts truth, Plato charges, making it entirely inappropriate for this task. Behind this attack is a rejection of oral forms of cultural preservation and transmission. In nonliterate societies, oral literature is the only means of preserving and handing on collective knowledge. Oral literature is didactic, teaching accepted beliefs and practices. Poetic form is an aid to memorization. Writing, which developed between the time of Homer and Plato, changes all of this by allowing cultural information to be stored more permanently and transmitted more reliably. Poetic form is no longer necessary, as a result of which propositional forms, including logic, developed. The effect was a cognitive revolution based on alphabetic literacy, changing fundamentally the way that people thought.

351 Hawisher, Gail E., and Cynthia L. Selfe, with Yi-Huey Guo and Lu Liu. "Globalization and Agency: Designing and Redesigning the Literacies of Cyberspace." *CE* 68.6 (July 2006): 619–36. Print.

Literacy narratives of two women, both graduate students in the United States and originally from China and Taiwan, illustrate the importance of such concepts as the Chinese term *guanxi* (relationships, "something akin to a complex set of social networks operating through personal connections") in shaping a cultural ecology of literacy. In Lu Liu's case, learning English went hand in hand with access to computer technologies. Yi-Huey Guo took private computer lessons in Taiwan and used both Chinese and English in working with computers. Their stories demonstrate how deeply literacy practices are situated within complicated constellations of income, education, access, support systems, and other factors. Similar to Brandt's notion of literacy sponsorship, *guanxi* provides "a more complex, concrete, and global perspective on how such relationships function in an increasingly networked world."

352 Heath, Shirley Brice. *Ways with Words: Language, Life, and Work in Communities and Classrooms*. New York: Cambridge UP, 1983. Print.

Research in three Carolina communities reveals socially conditioned patterns of oral and written language use, but no clear distinctions between literate and oral or preliterate groups.

353 Holzman, Michael. "A Post-Freirean Model for Adult Literacy Education." *CE* 50.2 (Feb. 1988): 177–89. Print. Rpt. in Cooper and Holzman [566].

In economically underdeveloped countries, many literacy educators use Paulo Freire's [345] methods with adult students. Here, an "animator" helps students develop literacy materials from their experience that foster insight into the politically oppressive conditions of their lives and the determination to change these conditions. In being so ideologically directive, though, Freirean pedagogy risks appropriating learners' responsibility for their own literacy goals. A post-Freirean model urges the teacher to wait for local initiative and to help student groups organize for whatever educational purposes—including literacy—they feel necessary.

354 Horsman, Jennifer. *Something in My Mind Besides the Everyday: Women and Literacy*. Toronto: Women's Press, 1990. Print.

Literacy programs often assume that their clients are completely illiterate and even unintelligent, that traditional school literacy is what they need, and that any failure to complete the program is owing to the individual's lack of motivation. Interviews with twenty-three women enrolled in literacy programs and ten workers in the programs suggest, to the contrary, that learners have varied abilities and a variety of personal and career goals related to literacy. They want to end their dependence on social service agencies. They are often hampered in their efforts by the complex demands of life in disadvantaged socioeconomic settings and by the debilitating links between many literacy programs and the very social agencies the students wish to escape. Literacy programs need to listen more to learners' self-definitions of their needs and to encourage the use of literacy for social criticism.

355 Kintgen, Eugene R., Barry M. Kroll, and Mike Rose, eds. *Perspectives on Literacy*. Carbondale: Southern Illinois UP, 1988. Print.

Twenty-eight major essays on the theory, history, and pedagogical and social implications of literacy. Essays include Jack Goody and Ian Watt, "The Consequences of Literacy"; Walter J. Ong, S.J., "Some Psychodynamics of Orality"; Sylvia Scribner and Michael Cole, "Unpackaging Literacy"; Harvey J. Graff, "The Legacies of Literacy"; Eric A. Havelock, "The Coming of Literate Communication to Western Culture"; David R. Olson, "From Utterance to Text"; John U. Ogbu, "Literacy and Schooling in Subordinate Cultures"; Yetta Goodman, "The Development of Initial Literacy"; Shirley Brice Heath, "Protean Shapes in Literacy Events"; Paulo Freire, "The Adult Literacy Process as Cultural Action for Freedom"; Carl Kaestle, "The History of Literacy and the History of Readers"; Jay Robinson, "The Social Context of Literacy"; David Bartholomae, "Inventing the University" [170]; Kyle Fiore and Nan Elsasser, "'Strangers No More': A Liberatory Literacy Curriculum"; and William Diehl and Larry Mikulecky, "The Nature of Reading at Work."

356 Knoblauch, C. H., and Lil Brannon. *Critical Teaching and the Idea of Literacy*. Portsmouth: Heinemann-Boynton/Cook, 1993. Print.

Critical teaching aims to prepare students to live comfortably with cultural diversity and to work actively for social and economic justice. These goals have been hampered by the scare tactics of those who, like Dinesh D'Souza, deride political correctness but have much more power than those they warn against. Critical teaching is also thwarted by limiting models of literacy: the functionalist model, emphasizing supposedly practical skills; the cultural-literacy model, inculcating Western culture; and the expressivist model, celebrating personal growth while disguising political realities. A preferable model is critical literacy, which, as Paulo Freire argues, empowers students to name the inequities in their world and work to change them.

357 Lee, Carol D., and Peter Smagorinsky, eds. *Vygotskian Perspectives on Literacy Research: Constructing Meaning through Collaborative Inquiry*. New York: Cambridge UP, 2000. Print.

Central tenets of Vygotsky's theory have influenced current debates in literacy research and in activity theory; the centrality of language and the inherently social nature of literacy learning and practice have provided the basis for modern analysis, and Vygotsky's ideas have also been modified through the studies that draw on them. Eleven chapters, following an introduction by the editors, include the following: James V. Wertsch, "Vygotsky's Two Minds on the Nature of Meaning"; LeeAnn G. Putney, et al., "Consequential Progressions: Exploring Collective-Individual Development in a Bilingual Classroom"; Kris D. Gutierrez and Lynda D. Stone, "Synchronic and Diachronic Dimensions of Social Practice: An Emerging Methodology for Cultural-Historical Perspectives on Literacy Learning"; Carol D. Lee, "Signifying in the Zone of Proximal Development"; Arnetha F. Ball, "Teachers' Developing Philosophies on Literacy and Their Use in Urban Schools: A Vygotskian Perspective on Internal Activity and Teacher Change"; and Luis C. Moll, "Inspired by Vygotsky: Ethnographic Experiments in Education."

358 Lunsford, Andrea A., Helene Moglen, and James Slevin, eds. *The Right to Literacy*. New York: MLA, 1990. Print.

Twenty-nine compact essays address the public and professional issue of literacy, the literacy problems of particular social groups, and political and pedagogical concerns. Essays include Theodore Sizer, "Public Literacy: Puzzlements of a High School Watcher"; Jacqueline Jones Royster, "Perspectives on the Intellectual Tradition of Black Women Writers"; James Moffett, "Censorship and Spiritual Education"; Deborah Brandt, "Literacy and Knowledge"; Glynda Hull and Mike Rose, "Toward a Social-Cognitive Understanding of Problematic Reading and Writing"; and Shirley Brice Heath, "The Fourth Vision: Literate Language at Work."

359 Macedo, Donaldo. *Literacies of Power: What Americans Are Not Allowed to Know*. Boulder: Westview, 1994. Print.

Drills in discrete skills give people sufficient literacy to decode but not to demystify government propaganda. Adding a cultural-literacy component to education perpetuates cultural genocide on those who do not belong to the majority culture, if the model favors Western culture, as does E. D. Hirsch's. Following Paulo Freire, we should encourage multilingual, multicultural literacy education in order to effect change toward social justice. Macedo testifies to the value of such education from personal experience.

360 Moss, Beverly J., ed. *Literacy across Communities*. Cresskill: Hampton, 1994. Print.

Five of the six essays in this collection study nonacademic literacy practices in mainstream communities: Marcia Farr, "En Los Dos Idiomas: Literacy Practices among Chicano Mexicanos"; Gail Weinstein-Shr, "From Mountaintops to City Streets: Literacy in Philadelphia's Hmong Community"; Daniel McLaughlin, "Toward a Dialogical Understanding of Literacy: The Case of Navajo Print"; Jabari Mahiri, "Reading Rites and Sports: Motivation for Adaptive Literacy of Young African-American Males"; and Beverly Moss, "Creating a Community: Literacy Events in African-American Churches." In the final essay, "World Travelling: Enlarging Our Understanding of Nonmainstream Literacies," Elizabeth Chiseri-Strater comments on the preceding studies and recommends, following them, that teachers should function as coaches, not authority figures; that classrooms should be collaborative learning communities; and that school-home communication should become bidirectional.

361 Ong, Walter J., S.J. "Literacy and Orality in Our Times." *ADE Bulletin* 58 (Sept. 1978): 1–7. Print. Rpt. in Enos [641] and in Young and Liu [387].

Writing is essential for analytic, linear, and sequential thought, in contrast to speech, which is "rhapsodic"—loosely constructed of clichés, proverbs, and other "loci" (topoi). Students, particularly those from highly oral cultural communities, must move from the oral to the written form of thought; their writing often has the loose structure of conversation. It can be helpful to teach students about the contrast between oral and written thought, but it is essential for writing teachers to know about the differences. See also Ong [362].

362 Ong, Walter J., S.J. *Orality and Literacy: The Technologizing of the Word*. New York: Methuen, 1982. Print.

Ong applies Eric Havelock's theory of cognitive differences between oral and literate cultures to modern society. See also Ong [361] and Daniell [336].

See: Steve Parks and Eli Goldblatt, "Writing beyond the Curriculum: Fostering New Collaborations in Literacy" [555].

363 Pattison, Robert. *On Literacy: The Politics of the Word from Homer to the Age of Rock*. New York: Oxford UP, 1982. Print.

Historical and cross-cultural study focusing on ideological implications of different definitions and forms of literacy. Literacy, finally, cannot be defined as a mechanical skill, a touchstone of civility, or a prerequisite for economic advancement but as consciousness of the problems raised by language.

364 Powell, Katrina M. *The Anguish of Displacement: The Politics of Literacy in the Letters of Mountain Families in Shenandoah National Park*. Charlottesville: U of Virginia P, 2007. Print.

In the 1930s, five hundred families were displaced in order to create a national park. Housed in a park archive, three hundred letters written by the displaced to government officials offer a counter-narrative about the region and its people, illustrate competing literacies, and mark significant acts of social participation. Some letters requested materials from razed buildings or asked politely for permission, assistance, or reimbursement; others challenged the authority of the government and demanded action. Those reading the letters made erroneous assumptions about class and education and treated many of the residents' concerns as petty. Despite a lack of formal education, mountain residents indicated their understanding of socially accepted codes and of the rhetorical situation; as they grew to understand the park's regulations, their requests altered accordingly. Increasingly, armed with knowledge of how the system worked, residents began to resist park authority. These letters, a direct result of the park's establishment, broaden our understanding of a community's literacy history.

365 Roberts, Peter. *Education, Literacy, and Humanization: Exploring the Work of Paulo Freire*. Westport: Bergin & Garvey, 2000. Print.

If educators from the First World are to avoid the danger of domestication, Freire's writings and pedagogical practice must be properly contextualized and studied in a holistic and critical manner. Reading Freire's entire pedagogical history as a narrative of hope, and the process of reinventing Freire's ideas, begins with acknowledging the particular social circumstances under which his pedagogy was forged. When we engage in critical, dialogical praxis, we pursue the idea of humanization, which is a continuous, unfinished process and makes problematic the tendency among Western educators to reduce Freirean theory to a set of methods. Freire's works contain a number of binary oppositions, but his later writings suggest that there is no single antithesis to liberating education. In Freirean programs of adult literacy education, dialogue is pivotal, and to become literate in the sense Freire intends requires not merely a mastery of signs and symbols, but also a willingness to participate in the process of building and rebuilding one's society. Despite accepting a number of insights from postmodernists, Freire remained essentially a modernist, resulting in strong criticism such as charges of antidialogue and criticisms of universalist thought. The "stages" model of conscientization and an individualist view of critical consciousness should be rejected in order to concentrate on the link between conscientization and praxis; Freire's ideal can be reassessed in light of postmodernist notions of multiple subjectivities.

See: Jacqueline Jones Royster, *Traces of a Stream: Literacy and Social Change Among African American Women* [131].

366 Scribner, Sylvia, and Michael Cole. *The Psychology of Literacy*. Cambridge: Harvard UP, 1981. Print.

Research among the African Vai, a people with widely varying degrees of literacy, reveals no pattern of cognitive gains associated with literacy.

367 Sheridan, Dorothy, Brian V. Street, and David Bloome. *Writing Ourselves: Mass-Observation and Literacy Practices*. Cresskill: Hampton, 2000. Print.

Because the everyday literacy practices of ordinary people are made nearly invisible, the Mass-Observation Project at the University of Sussex offers a unique institutional context for writing and the means of understanding the nature of writing in Britain in the late twentieth century, illustrating the intimate relationships between literacy practices and social life. Begun in 1937 as an effort to establish an "anthropology of our own people," Mass-Observation asked "ordinary people" to record their lives and submit their writings to the Archive. Relaunched in 1981, the Project today sends volunteer observers or correspondents directives three times a year (e.g., "keep a diary for the day of the 1981 Royal Wedding"). The Archive places recently received material directly in the public domain. Mass-Observation is closely linked with the intellectual history of the discipline of social anthropology in Britain; more importantly, Mass-Observation material provides a way of exploring cross-cultural literacy practices, the social uses and meanings of reading and/or writing. Mass-Observers' commentaries on their own writing practices, in particular, adopt an ethnographic perspective on literacy. The dialogues of nine Mass-Observation correspondents are constructed to illustrate how writing is implicated in the exercise of power, definitions of personhood, and the creation and transformation of social space.

368 Smitherman, Geneva. *Talkin' and Testifyin'*. Boston: Houghton, 1977. Print.

Black English takes many grammar rules and pronunciation patterns from West African languages. In the United States, the use of Black English is associated with a culture that values several forms of oral display, such as church oratory, and that holds a worldview different from that associated with Standard English, for example, in its preference for logical structures that are hierarchical or cyclical rather than linear. This book focuses less on Black English than on black culture, which it describes in detail. Smitherman strongly opposes requiring Standard English forms and culture for Black English speakers. For her comments on a court case mandating bilingual instruction for Black English speakers, see "'What Go Round Come Round': *King* in Perspective," *Harvard Education Review* 51.1 (Feb. 1981), rpt. in Brooks [638].

369 Sohn, Katherine Kelleher. *Whistlin' and Crowin' Women of Appalachia: Literacy Practices since College*. Carbondale: Southern Illinois UP, 2006. Print.

Case studies of three women, and interviews with five others, illustrate how college influenced "the literacy habits of [these] former non-traditional, working-class women" and how members of underrepresented groups use literacy in the workplace, home, and community. All Appalachian-born, these women sought education to better their lives and those of their families, and their stories establish the relationships among place, silence, voice, and identity. The post-college literacy practices of Lucy, Jean, and Sarah ranged from reading monthly newsletters and self-help books to writing nursing assessment forms and annual reports for foster care agencies. They built upon layers of literacy (e.g., biblical literacy) in choosing practical majors and in building confidence and overcoming odds.

370 Street, Brian V., ed. *Cross-Cultural Approaches to Literacy*. New York: Cambridge UP, 1993. Print.

Opposing a psycholinguistic focus on discrete reading and writing skills, this collection illustrates approaches to literacy informed by anthropology and focused on social contexts and practices. Twelve essays study literacies around the world, many in nonacademic settings. Includes Kathleen Rockhill, "Gender, Language, and the Politics of Literacy"; Miriam Camitta, "Vernacular Writing: Varieties of Literacy among Philadelphia High School Students"; Amy Shuman, "Collaborative Writing: Appropriating Power or Reproducing Authority?"; Gail Weinstein-Shr, "Literacy and Social Process: A Community in Transition"; and an introduction by Street.

371 Street, Brian V., ed. *Literacy and Development: Ethnographic Perspectives*. New York: Routledge, 2001. Print.

The contributors to this volume are ethnographers of literacy projects who have spent many years conducting in-depth qualitative studies of everyday literacies in different parts of the world. Essays address educational interventions, the broader contexts of development interventions, and the specific aspects of development agendas. Included is an introduction by the editor, an afterword, and ten chapters, including Caroline Dyer and Archana Choksi, "Literacy, Schooling and Development: Views of Rabari Nomads, India"; Martha Wagar Wright, "More Than Just Chanting: Multilingual Literacies, Ideology and Teaching Methodologies in Rural Eritrea"; Priti Chopra, "Betrayal and Solidarity in Ethnography on Literacy: Revisiting Research Homework in a North Indian Village"; Pat Herbert and Clinton Robinson, "Another Language, Another Literacy? Practices in Northern Ghana"; Anna Robinson-Pant, "Women's Literacy and Health: Can an Ethnographic Researcher Find the Links?"; and Shirin Zubair, "Literacies, Gender and Power in Rural Pakistan."

372 Stubbs, Michael. *Language and Literacy: The Sociolinguistics of Reading and Writing*. London: Routledge, 1980. Print.

A functional or sociolinguistic theory of literacy accounts for the relationship between spoken and written language and delineates the "communicative functions served by different types of language in different social settings." Although spoken language is usually learned before written language, speech is much more variable than writing, the orthography of which often does not reflect pronunciation. Written language is thus semiautonomous from and often higher in prestige than spoken language. These differences make writing difficult to learn for children whose spoken language varies widely from the written form dominant in school. Psychological theories of verbal deprivation that purport to explain these difficulties are reductive. All languages are equally effective media of communication. Language-learning difficulties must be understood in terms both of children's varied social experiences with language and of their teachers' attitudes toward their preferred language forms.

373 Taylor, Denny, and Catherine Dorsey-Gaines. *Growing Up Literate: Learning from Inner-City Families*. Portsmouth: Heinemann-Boynton/Cook, 1988. Print.

Detailed ethnographic study of poor, urban black families, depicting them as creating productive environments for literacy learning.

374 Tuman, Myron C. *A Preface to Literacy: An Inquiry into Pedagogy, Practice, and Progress*. Tuscaloosa: U of Alabama P, 1987. Print.

Discussions of literacy present conflicting definitions of the term, from transcription of speech and minimal reading ability (the unproblematic model) to sophisticated interpretive skills that require inferring a context to find meaning in a message (the problematic model). These definitions have supported particular ideological agendas that affect our understanding of literacy education.

375 Villanueva, Victor, Jr. *Bootstraps: From an American Academic of Color*. Urbana: NCTE, 1993. Print.

Linguistic deficit theories are grossly inadequate to explain the school difficulties of students from minority social groups, who are stigmatized by color and social class, unlike immigrant students, even if their native language is English. Particularly disadvantaged are students of castelike minorities that have been economically and culturally colonized by dominant U.S. culture. The dominant culture requires racelessness and abandonment of the home culture as conditions of acceptance, making biculturalism a difficult option. These students need to develop a critical consciousness of the historically generated social conditions that block their freedom and to become conscious intellectuals who can lead progressive social change. Educators should hold minority students to high standards while teaching forms of literacy that foster cultural and linguistic diversity, and political analyses that address the economic decline and individualistic fragmentation of postmodern life.

376 Yagelski, Robert P. *Literacy Matters: Writing and Reading the Social Self.* New York: Teachers College P, 2000. Print.

Exploring the nature of literacy and its ambiguous role in our lives begins by defining literacy as a local act of self-construction within discourse. Outmoded beliefs about literacy that continue to drive conventional English curriculum in American schools do not help us to understand the specific acts of reading and writing that students engage in or the complexities and contradictions involved in literate acts. Children receive mixed messages about literacy, in part because school-based literacy instruction is centered mostly on individual abilities and achievements and ignores the fact that official literacies can marginalize as well as empower. The task of the literacy educator is to enable learners to understand how literacy functions as a means of participation in ever-shifting discourses that shape our lives. Exploring how individual texts come to be and what they mean to individual writers and readers working within complex, inherently social contexts and discourses can illuminate the local nature of literacy in the context of its basic social functions. An adequate understanding of literacy requires accounting for tension between individual writer and social context and should take into account the ways in which new literacy technologies might be redefining the value of literacy in an increasingly technological and multicultural world.

Rhetorics of Writing

Invention

See: Anis Bawarshi, *Genre and the Invention of the Writer: Reconsidering the Place of Invention in Composition* [668].

377 Berthoff, Ann E. *Forming/Thinking/Writing: The Composing Imagination.* Rochelle Park: Hayden, 1978. Print.

Writing is a process of making meaning, of discovering how we think and feel about the world as we try to shape our thoughts in language. This textbook offers a series of "assisted invitations" to explore the composing process, from simple observation to forming concepts and writing critically about one's own knowledge.

378 Brent, Doug. *Reading as Rhetorical Invention: Knowledge, Persuasion, and the Teaching of Research-Based Writing.* Urbana: NCTE, 1992. Print.

A rhetoric of discourse consumption explains how people come to be persuaded by the texts they read and how they decide among texts' competing claims. Assuming that texts can convey shareable good reasons for belief, readers adjudicate among them, granting or withholding assent on the basis of the text's match with what the reader already knows and believes. The richer the reader's repertoire of knowledge and examined belief, the more readily she can learn from reading. This ability to learn from texts is the fundamental academic research skill. It can be taught, even to beginners, by emphasizing that the purpose of research is not to retrieve data but to converse about it, that all texts are biased, that gut feelings of commitment to one text over another can be trusted, and that research is recursive.

379 Coe, Richard M. "If Not to Narrow, Then How to Focus: Two Techniques for Focusing." CCC 32.3 (Oct. 1981): 272–77. Print.

The typical advice of textbooks to narrow a topic to one of its parts or to focus on one aspect of a topic may limit students to trivial topics or choke off development of ideas. Instead, students should shape a topic by looking for a contradiction in it and resolving the contradiction as the thesis of the essay.

380 Comprone, Joseph. "Kenneth Burke and the Teaching of Writing." CCC 29.4 (Dec. 1978): 336–40. Print.

Burke's theory of language as symbolic action is applicable to writing as an active process. The pentad can be used as a heuristic in the invention stage by focusing on agent and scene as a way to interpret experience and, later, in the drafting stage by focusing on agency and purpose as a way to move the audience. Burke's concept of "terministic screens" can help writers understand the need to translate their worldviews for an audience, and the concept of "identification" can point to persuasive techniques. Comprone restates the pentad as a set of questions for the writer. Cf. Burke [188, 189].

381 Crowley, Sharon. *The Methodical Memory: Invention in Current-Traditional Rhetoric*. Carbondale: Southern Illinois UP, 1990. Print.

Current-traditional rhetoric, until recently the dominant approach in American schools, developed in the late eighteenth and nineteenth centuries when rhetoricians like George Campbell and Richard Whately rejected classical rhetoric's invention schemes. To discover arguments, they claimed, the writer had merely to investigate the workings of his or her own mind, for all minds worked alike. In this model of invention, the individual authorial mind was privileged over community wisdom, and the written text was regarded as a record of the mind's operations. Clarity and logic were the goals. Pedagogy based on this model emphasized the formal features of texts—correctness and logical organization, for example—that presumably reflected the well-ordered mind at work. The metaphysical principles, supposedly universal, on which this pedagogy is based make it inherently conservative and insensitive to cultural difference. A preferable rhetoric and pedagogy is one that values difference and the diversity of communal treasures as archives for invention.

382 Emig, Janet. "Writing as a Mode of Learning." CCC 28.2 (May 1977): 122–28. Print. Rpt. in Emig [199] and in Young and Liu [387].

Writing is a uniquely valuable mode of learning. It simultaneously engages the hand, the eye, and both hemispheres of the brain. Writing requires an emotional commitment and is self-paced. The written product provides immediate feedback on learning and a record that can be reconsidered and revised at leisure. The stages of the writing process, embodied in notes, outlines, and drafts, also provide a record of the growth of learning.

383 Gage, John T. "Teaching the Enthymeme: Invention and Arrangement." *Rhetoric Review* 2.1 (Sept. 1983): 38–50. Print.

Structural formulae for constructing essays do not acknowledge the extent to which audience affects invention and arrangement. The enthymeme, however, properly understood as a large-scale heuristic and not a sentence-level device, can help the writer consider the questions that concern a particular audience, the probable answers to those questions, potential strategies for presenting those answers, and the shared premises that make reasons persuasive. It can thus provide the basic structure of a whole argument. Teaching the enthymeme helps writers see their rhetorical situation and understand logic as a function of audience assumptions.

384 LeFevre, Karen Burke. *Invention as a Social Act*. Carbondale: Southern Illinois UP, 1987. Print.

American composition pedagogy has long been based on the Platonic view that invention is the act of the individual writer who searches for truth by self-examination. This view is supported by ubiquitous myths of individualism in America. Although there is real value in this perspective, a more complete account must recognize that invention is social and collaborative: the individual author has been influenced by society; all human acts are dialectical responses to context; writing refers to an audience, internal or external; and the classical context of rhetoric is explicitly social. Thus, there are four perspectives on invention. In the Platonic view, invention is private. The internal-dialogic view projects a Freudian self made up of contesting inner voices, strongly influenced by internalized social values. The collaborative view follows George Herbert Mead in locating meaning in the symbolic interactions of a group of people. And the collective view follows Emile Durkheim's theory that social institutions and cultural traditions affect individual choices. The social view of invention suggests ways that composition research and pedagogies can go beyond personal assumptions about authorship.

385 Murray, Donald M. "Write before Writing." CCC 29.4 (Dec. 1978): 375–81. Print.

Professionals go through an elaborate prewriting process, for which teachers would do well to allow time. The first stage is delay, when the writer collects information, develops a concern for the subject and a sense of the audience, and feels the deadline approaching. Next comes rehearsal, talking about what will be written and making notes, outlines, and finally a tentative draft. Eight signals—such as genre, the sense that one's writing is fitting into a known form, or point of view, the development of a strong position on the subject—help the writer to the final draft.

386 Young, Richard E., Alton L. Becker, and Kenneth L. Pike. *Rhetoric: Discovery and Change*. New York: Harcourt, 1970. Print.

Rhetoric is the study of methods for discovering ideas and changing the attitudes of one's audience about those ideas. Humans render the chaos of external reality intelligible through three cognitive activities: sorting perceptions by simple comparison and contrast with other perceptions, looking at the range of variation among the set of similar perceptions, and looking at the distribution of these perceptions across a range of experience. The subject can be considered in three ways in each activity: as an isolated "particle," in itself; as a dynamic "wave"; and as a "field," in relation to other subjects. Out of this nine-part heuristic comes an understanding of the subject as a problem to be solved in writing. To persuade the audience, it is better to avoid an adversarial posture and to adopt a three-step method devised by psychotherapist Carl Rogers: (1) convince your reader that you truly understand his or her position; (2) compare the worldviews that support your position and your reader's, to exploit the similarities between those views; and (3) move your reader toward your position. This textbook, seldom used in undergraduate courses, was a very influential work on invention and persuasion methods derived from psychology and linguistics.

387 Young, Richard, and Yameng Liu, eds. *Landmark Essays on Rhetorical Invention in Writing*. Davis: Hermagoras, 1994. Print.

This text includes nineteen essays arranged chronologically, beginning with Kenneth Burke, "The Five Master Terms" (1943). Essays include Wayne Booth, "The Rhetorical Stance"; Kenneth Pike, "Beyond the Sentence"; D. Gordon Rohman, "Pre-Writing: The Stage of Discovery in the Writing Process"; Chaïm Perelman, "Rhetoric and Philosophy"; S. Michael Halloran, "On the End of Rhetoric, Classical and Modern"; Janet Emig, "Writing as a Mode of Learning" [382]; Walter Ong, "Literacy and Orality in Our Times" [361]; James Britton, "Shaping at the Point of Utterance"; Douglas Park, "The Meanings of 'Audience'" [393]; and James Kinneavy, "Kairos: A Neglected Concept in Classical Rhetoric."

Audience

388 Ede, Lisa, and Andrea Lunsford. "Audience Addressed/Audience Invoked: The Role of Audience in Composition Theory and Pedagogy." CCC 35.2 (May 1984): 155–71. Print. Rpt. in Corbett, Myers, and Tate [150] and in Villanueva [253].

Two divergent views of audience face the writing teacher, one claiming that it is crucial to writing instruction to identify a real audience (the audience addressed), the other claiming that the audience is fictional and a function of signals given in texts (the audience invoked). Both views miss the dynamic quality of rhetorical situations and the interdependence of reading and writing. To emphasize the audience as addressed tends to undervalue both invention and ethics of language use in the effort to adapt to the "real" audience. On the other side, Ong's view of the audience as a fiction (see [392]), which contrasts the speaker's real, present audience with the writer's distant one, tends to overstate the reality of the speaker's audience as compared with the writer's. Rather, both senses of audience must be understood within the larger rhetorical situation and the many possible roles that may be taken by real readers and imagined by the writer. Braddock Award winner.

389 Elbow, Peter. "Closing My Eyes as I Speak: An Argument for Ignoring Audience." *CE* 49.1 (Jan. 1987): 50–69. Print. Rpt. in Graves [571] and in Corbett, Myers, and Tate [150].

Writers should think about their audience, but not always. Some audiences help writers think better, others inhibit or intimidate. Faced with the latter, it is better to ignore the audience or pretend the audience is friendly during the early stages of writing. Not only can this overcome a block, it may lead to new thinking and knowledge. Indeed, this writer-based prose can be better than reader-based prose, in the same way that journal writing can be stronger than formal, audience-directed writing. Writing to an audience has been characterized as the higher level cognitively, yet the ability to turn off the audience, to experiment with a more poetic form of language, should be seen as a higher level still.

390 Kirsch, Gesa, and Duane H. Roen. *A Sense of Audience in Written Communication.* Newbury Park: Sage, 1990. Print.

Ten essays on the history and theory of audience as a rhetorical concern and six essays reporting on empirical studies of writers' conceptions and use of audience include R. J. Willey, "Pre-Classical Roots of the Addressed/Invoked Dichotomy of Audience"; Stuart Brown and Thomas Willard, "George Campbell's Audience"; Barbara Tomlinson, "Ong May Be Wrong: Negotiating with Nonfictional Readers"; Bennett Rafoth, "The Concept of Discourse Community: Descriptive and Explanatory Adequacy"; Louise Wetherbee Phelps, "Audience and Authorship: The Disappearing Boundary"; and Gesa Kirsch, "Experienced Writers' Sense of Audience and Authority: Three Case Studies."

391 Kroll, Barry M. "Writing for Readers: Three Perspectives on Audience." CCC 35.2 (May 1984): 172–85. Print.

Three conceptions of audience are influential in composition teaching: rhetorical, informational, and social. The rhetorical perspective draws from classical theory and recommends adapting speech or writing to the characteristics of the audience. This advice is generally good, but the perspective is flawed: it casts audiences as adversarial, it ignores the impossibility of characterizing most audiences, and it takes an unsophisticated view of reader psychology. The second approach is that writing must convey information to the reader effectively, by attending to the difficulties readers have extracting meaning from texts. But this model, criticized thoroughly by Dillon [194], tends to give a mechanistic and reductive account of text-processing. The third approach is that writing is a social activity like all communication, requiring a decentering from the self that allows the speaker or writer to take another's perspective. Collaborative writing and reader feedback support this approach pedagogically. The "sense of audience" promoted here, though, is vague, and it can be objected that writing is not social but rhetorical, more connected to genre and convention than to social knowledge.

392 Ong, Walter J., S.J. "The Writer's Audience Is Always a Fiction." *PMLA* 90.1 (Jan. 1975): 9–21. Print.

Writers project audiences for their work by imagining the presumptive audiences of other pieces of writing. Readers seem willing to be fictionalized in this way—to be the audience projected by the writer—as long as the reader's role is familiar or the writer creates a new role persuasively. Thus, the writer's style or voice is a way of addressing an imagined audience that will respond in the desired way.

393 Park, Douglas. "The Meanings of 'Audience.'" *CE* 44.3 (Mar. 1982): 247–57. Print. Rpt. in Corbett, Myers, and Tate [150] and in Young and Liu [387].

Audience, a crucial part of teaching writing, is difficult to define and to apply. The meanings tend to diverge, on the one hand, toward real people with a set of beliefs and expectations to which the discourse must be adjusted and, on the other, toward a fictional audience implied by the text itself. In both cases, audience refers to aspects of knowledge and motivation that form the contexts for discourse. Even when identified, its characteristics remain complex; the general audience is that much more elusive. Instead of asking about audience, we might more usefully ask about the conventions that make a piece of writing meaningful to a range of readers, beginning with generally accepted conventions of form and moving toward more particular conventions associated with the subject or genre. Using the class as audience does not solve the problem of defining the appropriate rhetorical contexts. We ask our students to act in sophisticated ways when we call for sensitivity to audience, but we lack a clear understanding of the kinds of writing we ought to teach and fall instead into teaching vaguely defined general writing skills.

394 Petraglia, Joseph. "Spinning Like a Kite: A Closer Look at the Pseudotransactional Function of Writing." *JAC: A Journal of Composition Theory* 15.1 (Winter 1995): 19–33. Print.

Transactional writing aims to get things done in the world, such as informing, persuading, or instructing. Most writing in composition classes, however, is pseudotransactional: while students are asked to consider audience, purpose, and appropriate persona, which seem to be rhetorical concerns, assignments often pose hypothetical cases while serving primarily as occasions for grading. Thus, students do not develop a truly rhetorical, self-reflective grasp of discursive practices. Composition teachers have failed to deal with the problem of pseudotransactionality. They either deny it through expressivist pedagogies claiming that students will provide "their own" purposes for writing or escape it through assigning collaborative work, writing that tests knowledge of reading, or writing across the curriculum. Composition scholars must not let their postmodern skepticism about the possibility of determining assignments' "authenticity" or "reality" prevent them from addressing this problem.

395 Porter, James E. *Audience and Rhetoric: An Archeological Composition of the Discourse Community*. Englewood Cliffs: Prentice, 1992. Print.

From the Western rhetorical tradition, we have inherited a conception of "audience" as a group of real people passively listening to an oral discourse, mere receivers of the communicator's message. Contemporary theory has disrupted this conception, however, with claims that "audience" is actually imagined by the author or called up by the text itself, or even that the notion of discrete individuals who could send or receive messages is problematic. With a survey of conceptions of audience from Aristotle to George Campbell to the New Rhetoric, reader-response criticism, and social constructionism, Porter shows that other disciplinary concerns, as well as cultural and political trends, tend to influence what concept of audience prevails. Porter advocates adherence to a social constructionist view in which the audience collaborates with the writer or speaker in various ways from the beginning of the composing process.

Revision

396 Beach, Richard. "Self-Evaluation Strategies of Extensive Revisers and Non-Revisers." CCC 27.2 (May 1976): 160–64. Print.

In a limited study of revising, the students who typically revised drafts very little tended to evaluate their drafts in terms of form: "choppy," "awkward," "wordy," and the like. They did not consider content important when revising. The more extensive revisers tended to locate the "centers of gravity" in early drafts and to evaluate drafts in terms of the development of ideas. The extensive revisers found that their evaluations of each draft were helpful guides to further revision and occasions for predicting solutions to problems in a draft.

397 Faigley, Lester, and Stephen P. Witte. "Analyzing Revision." CCC 32.4 (Dec. 1981): 400–414. Print.

Revisions can be classified as either surface changes or text-based changes. Surface changes do not affect the information content of the text. They can be subdivided into formal changes, such as spelling, and meaning-preserving changes, such as substitutions. Text-based changes do affect the content. They can be subdivided into microstructure changes, which affect local content only, and macrostructure changes, which affect the gist of the whole text. This taxonomy complements studies of revision such as Sommers' [400] by providing a way of indicating the significance of revision changes. "The major implication of this study . . . is that revision cannot be separated from other aspects of composing." Revision studies have not determined what causes writers to revise.

398 Flower, Linda, John R. Hayes, Linda Carey, Karen Schriver, and James Stratman. "Detection, Diagnosis, and the Strategies of Revision." CCC 37.1 (Feb. 1986): 16–55. Print.

Successful writers revise in order to adapt the text to their goals. Revision requires knowledge about texts, knowledge about strategies for revising, and a clear intention to use this knowledge to achieve a goal. Beginning writers must clear three hurdles in learning revision: detecting problems in the text, diagnosing the problems, and selecting a strategy. Detecting problems calls for a review of the text, testing it against an imagined ideal text that fulfills the writer's intentions. Many beginning writers see not the actual text but the intended text when they read their own drafts, and many do not form a clear sense of the gist of their own writing. These problems are often compounded by too narrow an intention or the lack of a clear sense of intention. Intention reflects knowledge, so beginning writers may focus on proofreading, which they know to be a feature of finished writing. A stronger sense of purpose and audience brings other features into focus. Diagnosis places problems, once detected, into conceptual categories related, for example, to style or audience. Writers may detect problems and simply do local rewriting. But diagnosis suggests more elaborate revising strategies in response to well-defined problems of knowledge and intention. Braddock Award winner.

See: Julie Jung, *Revisionary Rhetoric, Feminist Pedagogy, and Multigenre Texts* [218].

399 Mlynarczyk, Rebecca Williams. "Finding Grandma's Words: A Case Study in the Art of Revising." *Journal of Basic Writing* 15 (Summer 1996): 3–22. Print.

A detailed case study of one basic writer reveals that her tendency to revise for surface features only, typical of many student writers, was encouraged by her teacher's being very focused and directive in written and oral comments on a draft. When the teacher abandoned this evaluative role and stopped trying to "fix" the paper according to her own conception of what it should be, but rather discussed the essay content empathetically with the student, the student revised substantively. Mlynarczyk concludes that more open-ended comments addressed to essay content will best encourage substantive revision.

400 Sommers, Nancy. "Revision Strategies of Student Writers and Experienced Adult Writers." CCC 31.4 (Dec. 1980): 378–88. Print. Rpt. in Enos [641] and in Perl [274].

Revision is a recursive process essential to developing ideas, not merely the last stop in a train of writing tasks. Students usually describe revision as choosing better words and eliminating repetition. They revise to develop ideas only when redrafting the opening paragraph. Adults, on the other hand, usually describe revision as the process of finding the form of an argument and accommodating the audience. Adult writers are more likely to add or delete material and to rearrange sentences and paragraphs as they revise.

401 Yagelski, Robert P. "The Role of Classroom Context in the Revision Strategies of Student Writers." *Research in the Teaching of English* 29.2 (May 1995): 216–38. Print.

Students in a twelfth-grade advanced composition class focused 81.7 percent of revisions on surface and stylistic changes and only 18.3 percent on more substantive structural and content changes. This occurred even though the class emphasized the writing process, requiring two drafts of each of ten papers, reviewed by peers and by the teacher, and providing class time for rewriting. Evidently, the students' revision choices were strongly influenced by the teacher's retaining all authority for determining what constitutes "good" writing and by her emphasizing correctness as its most important criterion.

Grammar and Style

402 Baron, Dennis. *Grammar and Good Taste: Reforming the American Language*. New Haven: Yale UP, 1982. Print.

After the Revolution, English supplanted Latin and Greek as the dominant language of instruction in American schools. Patriots sought to differentiate American from British English by establishing native standards of spelling, grammar, and pronunciation. Some advocated the formation of an American Academy, like the French Academy, to set these standards. The authors of popular grammar textbooks also attempted to set standards. Although no uniform "Federal grammar" emerged, the link between correct grammar and patriotism led to the association of correctness with good morals in general, and hence with social prestige. The link between grammar and morality also fostered intense anxiety about correctness that continues to this day.

403 Baron, Dennis. *Guide to Home Language Repair*. Urbana: NCTE, 1994. Print.

Based on Baron's radio call-in show on grammar and the vagaries of English. Baron answers questions (as "Dr. Grammar") and offers advice on dealing with the Language Police (William Safire and his ilk), the demands of politically correct language, the peculiarities of English spelling, jargon, plagiarism, and sundry other topics.

404 Braddock, Richard. "The Frequency and Placement of Topic Sentences in Expository Prose." *Research in the Teaching of English* 8.3 (Winter 1974): 287–302. Print.

Do good expository paragraphs begin with explicit topic sentences? In twenty-five essays by professional writers, fewer than half of the paragraphs have topic sentences at all, and fewer than half of those topic sentences are simple and direct. Other kinds of topic sentences are delayed-completion, assembled (in which the topic-sentence ideas are scattered through the paragraph), and inferred. First Braddock Award winner.

405 Butler, Paul, ed. *Style in Rhetoric and Composition: A Critical Sourcebook*. Boston: Bedford/St. Martin's, 2010. Print.

Remarking on the importance of style as a teaching strategy as well as a component in individual student writing, this collection of twenty-six essays situates a new view of style within the confines of rhetoric and composition as a discipline: style as a flexible and practical writing tool. Collectively, the anthology's five parts trace the history of the study of the canon of style and investigate the style movement, particularly style's influence on pedagogy, culture, and the future of composition. Contributors include Robert J. Connors, Louis T. Milic, Virginia Tufte, Richard Ohmann, Edward P. J. Corbett, Winston Weathers, Elizabeth D. Rankin, Laura R. Micciche, Peter Elbow, T. R. Johnson, Kathryn Flannery, Paul Butler, and Frank Farmer.

406 Christensen, Francis. "A Generative Rhetoric of the Paragraph." CCC 16.3 (Oct. 1965): 144–56. Print. Rpt. in *The Sentence and the Paragraph* (Urbana: NCTE, 1963); in Francis Christensen, *Notes Toward a New Rhetoric: Six Essays for Teachers* (New York: Harper, 1967); and in Francis Christensen and Bonniejean Christensen, *Notes Toward a New Rhetoric: Nine Essays for Teachers*, 3rd ed., ed. Don Stewart (New York: HarperCollins, 2007).

Paragraph structure resembles sentence structure (cf. [407]). The topic sentence, usually the first sentence, is analogous to the main clause, and supporting sentences, working at lower levels of generality, are analogous to modifying phrases. Relations between sentences in a paragraph are coordinate or subordinate. Most paragraphs exhibit both kinds of relation, even when there is no topic sentence or when the paragraph includes unrelated sentences. Students should practice diagramming paragraphs by level of generality to see where coordinate and subordinate additions are needed. Cf. Braddock [404].

407 Christensen, Francis. "A Generative Rhetoric of the Sentence." CCC 14.3 (Oct. 1963): 155–61. Print. Rpt. in *The Sentence and the Paragraph* (Urbana: NCTE, 1963); in Francis Christensen, *Notes Toward a New Rhetoric: Six Essays for Teachers* (New York: Harper, 1967); and in Francis Christensen and Bonniejean Christensen, *Notes Toward a New Rhetoric: Nine Essays for Teachers*, 3rd ed., ed. Don Stewart (New York: HarperCollins, 2007).

Professional writers write "cumulative" sentences, in which modifying words and phrases are added before, within, or after the base clause. The modifiers work at different levels of abstraction and add to the sentence's texture. Students should practice writing cumulative descriptions of objects and events in single sentences, which will make style and content more complex simultaneously. See also Christensen [406].

See: Robert J. Connors, "The Erasure of the Sentence" [148].

408 Corbett, Edward P. J. "Approaches to the Study of Style." *Teaching Composition: Twelve Bibliographic Essays*. Ed. Gary Tate [44]. Fort Worth: Texas Christian UP, 1987. 83–130. Print.

This bibliographic essay discusses works on literary style and stylistics, the history of English prose style, theories of style, teaching the analysis of prose style, and teaching students how to improve their writing style.

409 Crew, Louie. "Rhetorical Beginnings: Professional and Amateur." CCC 38.3 (Oct. 1987): 346–50. Print.

Most amateurs begin an essay by stating their purpose, giving background, or telling results. Professionals hold those moves in reserve. Sixty percent of professionals, compared with 10 percent of student amateurs (in the given sample), begin with narratives. Such openings dramatize the subject and are brief. Professionals use indirection, drop hints or cite experts in order to contradict them, and use oblique quotations, whereas amateurs attempt to be direct. Amateurs use rhetorical questions and truisms, while professionals rarely do. But when these professional strategies are pointed out, student amateurs learn them quickly.

410 D'Eloia, Sarah. "The Uses—and Limits—of Grammar." *Journal of Basic Writing* 1 (Spring–Summer 1977): 1–20. Print. Rpt. in Corbett, Myers, and Tate [150] and in Enos [641].

Students should learn grammar as part of the writing process. Mina Shaughnessy's work [660] helps us distinguish between true grammar errors and merely accidental errors in student writing. Teachers can address the grammar-based errors through such techniques as dictation, narrowly focused editing, paraphrasing, and imitation. D'Eloia gives much useful advice for teaching grammar.

See: Erasmus, *Copia: Foundations of an Abundant Style* [60].

411 Faigley, Lester. "Names in Search of a Concept: Maturity, Fluency, Complexity, and Growth in Written Syntax." CCC 31.3 (Oct. 1980): 291–300. Print.

Recent research on syntactic maturity in student writing has relied too uncritically on the measures of complexity devised by Kellogg Hunt. Such research, aimed at testing the efficacy of sentence combining, finds increased T-unit and clause lengths in student writing, but no connection has been established between such complexity and the overall quality of the writing. Moreover, designating writing as more or less mature on the basis of such measures is problematic because T-unit and clause length in adult writing vary with discourse aims. Similarly, fluency depends on intersentence, not intrasentence, relations. We have no adequate description of syntactic complexity because we have no reliable generative grammar. Nonetheless, writing pedagogy emphasizes syntax to the detriment of coherence in the essay as a whole.

412 Flannery, Kathryn T. *The Emperor's New Clothes: Literature, Literacy, and the Ideology of Style*. Pittsburgh: U of Pittsburgh P, 1995. Print.

There is no inherently good style. Rather, the style preferred by socially powerful groups becomes established as good. This style is part of the group's cultural capital, helping them maintain their power. Since the late Renaissance, the clear, simple, objective style praised by the Royal Society has been promoted by Western educational institutions. Behind "style talk" that treats style as politically neutral is a conservative agenda of maintaining the cultural status quo, as can be seen in T. S. Eliot's elevation of Francis Bacon's work as model prose. E. D. Hirsch follows the same agenda with his doctrine of "communicative efficiency" in *The Philosophy of Composition*. Literacy education has the institutional role of teaching the plain style to the masses, while literature, with its premium on artifice, remains privileged discourse. Resisting this agenda requires a rhetorical conception of style that valorizes artifice and a range of styles for everyone.

413 Hairston, Maxine. "Working with Advanced Writers." CCC 35.2 (May 1984): 196–208. Print.

Advanced writers—honors freshmen and other students taking an elective advanced expository writing course—are reluctant to change writing habits that are earning them good grades, despite felt dissatisfaction with their own writing. Their writing is correct, wordy (repetitive and inflated), heavily nominalized, impersonal, unrealistically ambitious, overly generalized, and without much sense of audience. Their personalities are hidden behind the mask of a bureaucrat or pedantic scholar. They see this style as officially sanctioned; it has earned them rewards, and it is also safe. To persuade them to try anything new, a safe classroom is necessary, where grades are downplayed, risk is rewarded, and a writing community is formed.

414 Harris, Muriel, and Katherine E. Rowan. "Explaining Grammatical Concepts." *Journal of Basic Writing* 6 (Fall 1989): 21–41. Print.

Editing is a process of detection, diagnosis, and rewriting, not a single final step in the composing process. But prescriptive grammar often does not help unpracticed writers. As Patrick Hartwell [415] argues, most grammar rules are COIK—clear only if known. Learning grammatical terminology, however, is not the same as learning the grammatical concepts necessary for editing. To help students learn the concepts, four techniques are useful: provide background information (i.e., prerequisite concepts) when needed; define critical attributes of the concept; use a variety of examples; and, in practice sessions, lead students to formulate questions they can ask themselves.

415 Hartwell, Patrick. "Grammar, Grammars, and the Teaching of Grammar." *CE* 47.2 (Feb. 1985): 105–27. Print. Rpt. in Enos [641] and in Villanueva [253].

The debate about whether grammar instruction improves writing will not be resolved by empirical studies. These studies suggest that grammar instruction has no effect on writing, and they have been attacked by proponents of such instruction. Grammar may be defined in five ways: (1) The internalized rules shared by speakers of a language. These rules are difficult to articulate and are learned by exposure to the language. (2) The scientific study of the internalized rules. Different theories of language generate different systems of rules. These rules do not dictate the actual use of grammar in the first sense. Researchers find no correlation between learning rules and using them, or between using rules and articulating them. (3) The rules promulgated in schools. These are simplifications of scientific grammars and are therefore even further from grammar as used by speakers of the language. They reflect the questionable belief that poor grammar is a cognitive deficiency. Metalinguistic awareness, including some knowledge of grammar, seems to be central to print literacy, but the awareness appears to follow, not generate, print literacy. (4) Grammar as usage: a set of exceptions to grammar rules. (5) Grammar as style: the use of grammatical terms in manipulating style. Much research suggests that active use of language improves writing more than instruction in any grammar.

See: Richard H. Haswell, "Minimal Marking" [475].

416 Haussamen, Brock. *Revising the Rules: Traditional Grammar and Modern Linguistics*. Dubuque: Kendall, 1993. Print.

The prescriptive rules of grammar were divorced from descriptive linguistics in the nineteenth century, and trying to remarry them is difficult. The tradition of grammar handbooks is long and deeply ingrained, while linguistics has focused on oral language and theory. Descriptive grammar does, however, have much to offer about grammar conventions that can enliven and improve the grammar we teach to students. Haussamen, a community college teacher, offers new descriptions of old conventions including verb tense, agreement, passive voice, pronoun agreement, and punctuation, all in aid of a more rhetorical approach to grammar.

417 Horner, Bruce. "Rethinking the 'Sociality' of Error: Teaching Editing as Negotiation." *Rhetoric Review* 11.1 (Fall 1992): 172–99. Print. Rpt. in Horner and Lu [646].

Writing teachers now generally agree that what counts as "error" in writing is socially determined, yet we continue to treat discrete errors in student papers as failures in the writer's knowledge of correct forms. Rather, we should see errors as instances of the writer's and reader's failure to negotiate an agreement on how their relationship is to be actualized in the text, that is, agreement on the features the text that permits a satisfying relationship will need to have. Such negotiation could help determine, for example, whether a sentence fragment is to be regarded as an error or as a stylistic device. "Basic writers," then, are those who are inept at such negotiation. They need to be taught what it is and how to do it, including how to make decisions about when or whether to use variant dialects of English. Horner concludes with some pedagogical suggestions for how to help basic writers learn to enter into such negotiations while revising their work.

418 Hunter, Susan, and Ray Wallace, eds. *The Place of Grammar in Writing Instruction: Past, Present, Future*. Portsmouth: Heinemann-Boynton/Cook, 1995. Print.

Grammar was long regarded as an essential element in the teaching of writing, an attitude criticized and discarded in more recent times. However, the usefulness and methods of grammar instruction are still debated, with some good arguments appearing for at least limited grammar instruction keyed to students' writing. Sixteen essays explore grammar instruction past, present, and future, including Cheryl Glenn, "When Grammar Was a Language Art"; Gina Claywell, "Reasserting Grammar's Position in the Trivium in American Composition"; John Edlund, "The Rainbow and the Stream: Grammar as System versus Language in Use"; R. Baird Shuman, "Grammar for Writers: How Much Is Enough?"; Stuart Brown, Robert

Boswell, and Kevin McIlvoy, "Grammar and Voice in the Teaching of Creative Writing"; and David Blakesly, "Reconceptualizing Grammar as an Aspect of Rhetorical Invention."

419 Johnson, T. R., and Tom Pace, eds. *Refiguring Prose Style: Possibilities for Writing Pedagogy*. Logan: Utah State UP, 2005. Print.

Over the last two decades, rather than discussing style's definition, context, application, and malleable qualities, instructors have reduced style to clarity. This nineteen-chapter collection, though, works to undo the rigid binaries of composition in order to welcome style in the classroom as a tool for self-expression as well as creative and critical thinking and writing. Framed by an introduction by both editors, each of the four parts also includes a short introduction by either Tom Pace or T. R. Johnson. Part I, What Happened: The Rise and Fall of Stylistics in Composition, includes Tom Pace, "Style and the Renaissance of Composition Studies"; Elizabeth Weiser, "Where Is Style Going? Where Has It Been?"; and Rebecca Moore Howard, "Contextual Stylistics: Breaking Down the Binaries in Sentence-Level Pedagogy." Part II, Belles Lettres and Composition, includes Allison Alsup, "Persuasion, More Than Argument: Moving Toward a Literary Sensitivity in the Classroom"; Melissa A. Goldthwaite, "Playing with Echo: Strategies for Teaching Repetition in the Writing Classroom"; and J. Scott Farrin, "When Their Voice Is Their Problem: Using Imitation to Teach the Classroom Dialect." Part III, Teaching Prose Style, includes Nicole Amare, "Style: The New Grammar in Composition Studies?"; Lisa Baird, "Balancing Thought and Expression: A Short Course in Style"; and William J. Carpenter, "Rethinking Stylistic Analysis in the Writing Class." Part IV, New Definitions of Style, includes Dion C. Cautrell, "Rhetor-Fitting: Defining Ethics through Style"; and Drew Loewe, "Style as a System: Toward a Cybernetic Model of Composition Style."

420 Kline, Charles R., Jr., and W. Dean Memering. "Formal Fragments: The English Minor Sentence." *Research in the Teaching of English* 11.2 (Fall 1977): 97–110. Print.

Grammar handbooks, if they do not simply forbid using sentence fragments, give few guidelines for using them effectively. A survey of samples of formal prose shows that accomplished writers use fragments often and in predictable ways. Kline and Memering list and explain the conditions in which fragments are effectively used and argue that such effective fragments should be called "minor sentences" (following Richard Weaver's suggestion) and taught as a stylistic option.

421 Lanham, Richard A. *Analyzing Prose*. New York: Scribner's, 1983. Print.

The dominant theory of prose style prizes clarity, brevity, and sincerity. This theory tries to make prose transparent; it reduces rhetoric to mere ornament; it runs counter to common sense, to what we value in literature, and to the fact that context defines its three main terms. Classical rhetorical terms provide an alternative way to describe prose style. Noun style relies on "be" verbs, prepositional phrases, and nominalized verbs. Verb style uses active verbs. Parataxis is the absence of connecting words between phrases and clauses, and paratactic style uses simple sentences and prepositional phrase strings. Hypotaxis is the use of connecting words, hence a highly subordinated style. Either style may use asyndeton (few connectors) or polysyndeton (many connectors). The "running" style uses parataxis: it is characterized by a serial record of ideas with many parenthetical additions. "Periodic" style is hypotactic: highly organized, reasoned, and ranked. Other stylistic devices (isocolon, chiasmus) affect these styles differently. Descriptive analysis should also account for visual and vocal form, the use of several common and effective tropes and schemes, and high and low diction. The reader's self-consciousness about style tends to direct judgments of style as clear or opaque, but determining the appropriateness of style to a range of purposes through descriptive analysis is a better way to judge prose.

422 O'Hare, Frank. *Sentence-Combining: Improving Student Writing without Formal Grammar Instruction*. Urbana: NCTE, 1973. Print.

Although teaching transformational grammar is no more helpful in improving student writing than instructing in traditional grammar, practice in sentence-combining (originally used as a way of teaching grammar) leads to increased syntactic maturity, even in the absence of formal grammar training of any kind. See Donald Daiker, Andrew Kerek, and Max Morenberg. "Sentence-Combining and Syntactic Maturity in Freshman English." CCC 29.1 (Feb. 1978): 36–41. Print. Cf. Faigley [411].

423 Ohmann, Richard. "Use Definite, Specific, Concrete Language." *CE* 41.4 (Dec. 1979): 390–97. Print. Rpt. in Corbett, Myers, and Tate [150].

One of the most common revision maxims given in rhetoric textbooks is to substitute concrete for abstract language. This advice springs from an ideology of style that values ahistoricism (focus on the present moment), empiricism (focus on sensory data), fragmentation (objects seen outside the context of social relations), solipsism (focus on individual's perceptions), and denial of conflict (reported facts have the same meaning for everyone). Following this advice may trap students in personal experience and inhibit their ability to think critically about the world. Students need to practice the relational thinking made possible by abstractions and generalizations.

424 Weathers, Winston. "Teaching Style: A Possible Anatomy." CCC 21.2 (May 1970): 144–49. Print. Rpt. in Corbett, Myers, and Tate [150].

To teach style, we should convince students that they must master style to express themselves with individuality and to communicate vividly. We must give students a way to recognize and imitate different styles, to incorporate them into extended discourse, and to suit style to the rhetorical situation. Finally, we must demonstrate our own ability to vary style in writing done in front of the class.

425 Williams, Joseph M. "The Phenomenology of Error." CCC 32.2 (May 1981): 152–68. Print.

When we read student papers, we define "errors" as discrete entities found on the page. But "error" has a more important, social dimension. Our perception of error on the page signals a flawed social transaction between us and the writer, similar to a breach of etiquette. When we read the work of professional writers, we do not expect to find errors, because our social relation to these writers is different from our relation to students. Many highly respected essays on writing breach their own rules, but we tend not to see these errors, although we always find errors when we look for them—in student papers. In guiding students away from error, then, we should redefine it not as structurally deviant but as socially inappropriate in writing situations.

426 Winterowd, W. Ross. "The Grammar of Coherence." *CE* 31.8 (May 1970): 828–35. Print. Rpt. in Corbett, Myers, and Tate [150].

Transformational grammar shows how case and syntax hold sentences together, but these features do not fully explain the coherence either of sentences or of larger units of discourse. Seven transitional relations account for coherence: coordinate (expressed, for example, by *and*); obversative (*but*); causative (*for*); conclusive (*so*); alternative (*or*); inclusive (the colon); and sequential (*first . . . second*).

427 Witte, Stephen P., and Lester Faigley. "Coherence, Cohesion, and Writing Quality." CCC 32.2 (May 1981): 189–204. Print. Rpt. in Villanueva [253].

According to M. A. K. Halliday and Ruqaiya Hasan, cohesive ties—the semantic relations that hold a text together—fall into five classes: substitution and ellipsis, more common in speech than in writing; reference (the use of pronouns and definite articles); conjunction; lexical reiteration (repeating words or synonyms); and collocation (common word groups). Better writers use more ties. Coherence, however, depends on more than cohesive ties. It also requires setting discourse in the appropriate context for the audience. Collocation may be the best indicator of coherence.

See: Kathleen Blake Yancey, *Voices on Voice* [619].

Writing Programs

Writing Program Administration

428 Adler-Kassner, Linda. *The Activist WPA: Changing Stories about Writing and Writers*. Logan: Utah State UP, 2008. Print.

To put different stories about writers and writing into circulation, WPAs can work from points of principle to "shift frames in ways that balance *strategies* and *ideals*." The progressive pragmatic jeremiad, frequently invoked in reports or narratives of American education, can support multiple framings, as illustrated, for example, by a successful reframing of the press coverage of the new SAT writing exam in 2005 by NCTE. Community organizers and media activists follow three models—interest-based, values-based, and issue-based—for taking action to change stories in order to build alliances, identify values, and use short-term goals to achieve long-term objectives. At the heart of change-making processes is a movement from the personal to the social, and activist intellectuals can work productively at the local level to reconceive the role of the WPA.

429 Beaufort, Anne. *College Writing and Beyond: A New Framework for University Writing Instruction*. Logan: Utah State UP, 2007. Print.

A six-year case study relies on seven data sources to track undergraduate Tim through freshman writing, a major in history, another in engineering, and finally workplace writing as an engineer. One of the dilemmas of freshman writing for Tim was that although he encountered multiple discourse communities, the boundaries and differences between these communities were not a topic for study. Tim felt liberated by his freshman composition teacher when he was asked to write in different genres, yet that practice did not necessarily prepare him for writing for historians. Accumulated data, therefore, raise questions about the transfer of learning and suggest that expert writers draw on five knowledge domains: subject matter knowledge, genre knowledge, rhetorical knowledge, writing process knowledge, and discourse community knowledge. For Tim, for example, growth in genre knowledge came from his workplace writing after graduation. A closing chapter indicates new directions for university writing instruction, while an epilogue and appendices share supporting data, including two of Tim's essays.

430 Bishop, Wendy. *Something Old, Something New: College Writing Teachers and Classroom Change*. Carbondale: Southern Illinois UP, 1990. Print.

Ethnographic study of five writing teachers' responses to a graduate seminar in basic writing pedagogy shows that each assimilated the recommended collaborative method in a different way, as a function of his or her developing identity. Writing program administrators and teacher trainers seeking to implement curricula with a diverse staff need to be aware of the factors that may lead to change and resistance.

431 Brown, Stuart C., and Theresa Enos, eds. *The Writing Program Administrator's Resource: A Guide to Reflective Institutional Practice*. Mahwah: Erlbaum, 2002. Print.

WPA work is increasingly specialized and professionalized. Thirty chapters address instituting change and instituting practice, including Douglas D. Hesse, "Politics and the WPA: Traveling Through and Past Realms of Expertise"; Gail Stygall, "Certifying the Knowledge of WPAs"; Edward M. White, "Teaching a Graduate Course in Writing Program Administration"; David E. Schwalm, "Writing Program Administration as Preparation for an Administrative Career"; Stuart C. Brown, "Applying Ethics: A Decision-Making Heuristic for Writing Program Administrators"; Eileen E. Schell, "Part-Time/Adjunct Issues: Working Toward Change"; Sharon Crowley, "How the Professional Lives of WPAs Would Change If FYC Were Elective" [432]; Chris M. Anson, "Figuring It Out: Writing Programs in the Context of University Budgets"; Jeanne Gunner, "Collaborative Administration"; Daniel J. Royer and Roger Gilles, "Placement Issues"; Gregory R. Glau, "Hard Work and Hard Data: Using Statistics to Help Your Program"; Ann-Marie Hall, "Expanding the Community: A Comprehensive Look at Outreach and Articulation"; Ken S. McAllister and Cynthia L. Selfe, "Writing Program Administration and Instructional Computing"; Victoria Holmsten, "This Site Under Construction: Negotiating Space for WPA Work in the Community College"; Martha A. Townsend, "Writing Across the Curriculum"; and Rebecca Jackson and Patricia Wojahn, "Issues in Writing Program Administration: A Select Annotated Bibliography."

432 Council of Writing Program Administrators. "Evaluating the Intellectual Work of Writing Administration." *WPA: Writing Program Administration* 22.1-2 (Fall/Winter 1998): 85–104. Print.

This statement from the council, developed from a draft by Charles Schuster, aims to present a framework by which writing administration can be seen as scholarly work and therefore subject to the same kinds of evaluation as scholarship and teaching. This intellectual work falls into five categories. *Program creation* or reform is work based on disciplinary knowledge, theoretical as well as practical. *Curricular design* draws on the same knowledge base and includes the choice of emphases, selection of textbooks, criteria for evaluation, and so on. *Faculty development* calls on the administrator to develop and implement training programs that reflect disciplinary developments and programmatic goals, to communicate current research to staff, and to provide intellectual leadership in thinking about teaching writing. *Program assessment* requires the development of appropriate measures to evaluate goals, pedagogy, and overall effectiveness and therefore draws on knowledge of scoring, portfolio or other forms of assessment, and descriptive analysis. *Program-related textual production* includes traditional forms of scholarly production, but also such things as innovative model syllabi, funding proposals, statements of program or teaching philosophy, original workshop materials, evaluations of teaching, and resource materials. Evaluation in these categories must consider, of course, whether activities and materials reflect expertise and knowledge and whether they are innovative and effectively disseminated. Finally, peer evaluation—typically by an outside expert—is critical for fair evaluation.

See: Tom Fox, *Defending Access: A Critique of Standards in Higher Education* [343].

433 Crowley, Sharon. "How the Professional Lives of WPAs Would Change If FYC Were Elective." *The Writing Program Administrator's Resource: A Guide to Reflective Institutional Practice*. Ed. Stuart C. Brown and Theresa Enos. Mahwah: Erlbaum, 2002. 219–30. Print.

As the title suggests, Crowley, in response to the conditions of employment for marginal teachers at universities and colleges, outlines the benefits of abandoning the universal requirement of FYC, while addressing the (unwarranted) fear that electivity could result in a loss of teaching positions. If FYC were elective, then "WPAs could begin to work toward installing writing instruction throughout the curriculum, toward strengthening and expanding writing centers, toward establishing departments of writing in institutions where that is appropriate, and toward offering writing courses outside of the academy where that is appropriate." Thereby, WPAs should take back their authority over the universal FYC requirement and, by extension, enrollment, staffing, student placement, curriculum, and the future of their writing programs through the implementation of elective FYC. Crowley also offers a list of supplemental readings that provide a historical context of the issue of labor in FYC as well as commentary on the proposal for elective FYC.

434 George, Diana, ed. *Kitchen Cooks, Plate Twirlers, and Troubadors: Writing Program Administrators Tell Their Stories*. Portsmouth: Heinemann-Boynton/Cook, 1999. Print.

A collection of meaningful stories that offer a portrait of a profession. Sixteen essays include the following: Richard Miller, "Critique's the Easy Part: Choice and the Scale of Relative Oppression"; Doug Hesse, "The WPA as Father, Husband, Ex"; Mary Pinard, "Surviving the Honeymoon: Bliss and Anxiety in a WPA's First Year, or Appreciating the Plate Twirler's Art"; Alice M. Gillam, "Taking It Personally: Redefining the Role and Work of the WPA"; Ralph Walstrom, "Catching Our Tail: A Writing Center in Transition"; Johanna Atwood Brown, "The Peer Who Isn't a Peer: Authority and the Graduate Student Administrator"; Kathleen Yancey, "The Teaching Circle, the WPA, and the Work of Writing in the University"; Beth Daniell, "Establishing E-Mail in a First-Year Program"; and Jeanette Harris (coda), "On Being an Accidental Administrator." Foreword by Patricia Bizzell.

435 Gunner, Jeanne. "Decentering the WPA." *WPA: Writing Program Administration* 18.1-2 (Fall/Winter 1994): 8–15. Print.

Professionalizing the WPA position, as many resolutions have advised, often neglects the larger network that includes writing instructors and often assumes that "tenure" will secure professional status. The belief that a centralized WPA enhances professionalism, or that a program without a tenured director is in a weakened institutional position, is a delusion that excludes nontenure-track faculty from the processes of curricular renewal or program development. Decentering the WPA allows for a collaborative structure that reconsiders a faculty's role in a writing program's direction. Faced with a series of acting directors and a crisis of faculty rights, the program at UCLA designed an administrative structure that de-emphasizes the director's position and allows the faculty to share program authority. A structure made up of committees and individually held positions—positions that rotate and result from elections—and reviews of both individuals and the program contributes to a democratic model that gives all instructors a voice in program governance.

See: Joseph Harris, "Meet the New Boss, Same as the Old Boss: Class Consciousness in Composition" [498].

436 Hartzog, Carol P. *Composition and the Academy: A Study of Writing Program Administration*. New York: MLA, 1986. Print.

A report on the results of a survey of forty-four writing programs at a variety of colleges and universities, as well as extensive descriptions of the programs at Chapel Hill, University of Pennsylvania, and Harvard. The survey data cover administrative structures, program design, staffing, and campus attitudes toward writing. No single model for success is apparent, but good programs seem to be aided to some degree by writing program alliances within the university, the pedagogical skill and scholarly visibility of the director and staff, and a campus commitment to liberal education. Includes an extensive bibliography.

437 Hult, Christine, ed. *Evaluating Teachers of Writing*. Urbana: NCTE, 1994. Print.

Evaluating teachers, whether for development or judgment, is a complex and sensitive task for program administrators. Too often, formative evaluation (for improving teaching) and summative evaluation (for judging overall performance) are insufficiently distinguished by the instruments for gathering information and by our use of the information. The thirteen essays here address three main concerns. The first, theoretical and ideological issues, includes Hult's introduction; David Bleich, "Evaluating the Teaching of Writing: Questions of Ideology"; and Jesse Jones's overview of purposes, objects of evaluation, sources of information, and the process of evaluation. The second, evaluation methods, includes essays on peer review by Ellen Strenski; class observation by Anne Marie Flanagan; Peter Elbow, "Making Better Use of Student Evaluations of Teachers"; and Mark A. Baker and Joyce A. Kinkead, "Using Microteaching to Evaluate Teaching Assistants in a

Writing Program." The third, evaluating specific faculty groups, includes David E. Schwalm, "Evaluating Adjunct Faculty"; Irwin Weiser, "Teaching Assistants as Collaborators in Their Preparation and Evaluation"; John Bean, "Evaluating Teachers in Writing-across-the-Curriculum Programs"; and Deborah Holdstein, "Evaluating Teachers in Computerized Classrooms."

438 Janangelo, Joseph, and Kristine Hansen. *Resituating Writing: Constructing and Administering Writing Programs*. Portsmouth: Heinemann-Boynton/Cook, 1995. Print.

Writing program administration is a significant expression of academic scholarship, as the Portland Resolution strongly states [432]. The eleven essays here extend and substantiate that claim through analysis of the history and current state of the main concerns facing the WPA. Essays include Hansen on part-time teachers; Lester Faigley and Susan Romano on technology; Elizabeth Nist and Helon Raines on two-year college programs; Ellen Strenski on recruitment and retraining; Molly Wingate on writing centers; Susan McLeod on WAC; Christine Hult on the scholarship of administration; and Edward White on program evaluation.

See: Laura R. Micciche, *Doing Emotion: Rhetoric, Writing, Teaching* [224].

439 Miller, Richard E. *As If Learning Mattered: Reforming Higher Education*. Ithaca: Cornell UP, 1998. Print.

Theories that aim to reform education often have very little impact on what actually happens in classrooms, because academics tend to despise the bureaucratic labor that would make change possible. The few successful reforms have adapted to local conditions, not attempting to radically restructure the school day or the curriculum or to retrain teachers, but negotiating minor adjustments while taking these circumstances into account. The reformer who effects such changes must have the administrative ability of the bureaucrat as well as the creative insight of the intellectual. Miller illustrates how the bureaucrat-intellectual could function through case studies: Matthew Arnold in his role as inspector of schools; the Great Books approach; British cultural studies for open-admissions students; and ethnography as a means for student self-study.

440 Myers-Breslin, Linda, ed. *Administrative Problem-Solving for Writing Programs and Writing Centers: Scenarios in Effective Program Management*. Urbana: NCTE, 1999. Print.

Each of the nineteen chapters in three sections (Selection and Training, Program Development, and Professional Issues) presents real-world situations about different aspects of administration; the cases place readers into administrative situations. Chapters include Richard Bullock, "In Pursuit of Competence: Preparing New Graduate Teaching Assistants for the Classroom"; Allene Cooper et al., "What Happens When Discourse Communities Collide? Portfolio Assessment and

Non-Tenure-Track Faculty"; Howard Tinberg, "Examining Our Assumptions as Gatekeepers: A Two-Year College Perspective"; Louise Wetherbee Phelps, "Mobilizing Human Resources to (Re)Form a Writing Program"; Joan A. Mullin, "Writing Across the Curriculum"; Linda S. Houston, "Budgeting and Politics: Keeping the Writing Center Alive"; Deborah H. Holdstein, "From Virtual to Reality: Thinking about Technology and the Composition Program"; Linda Myers-Breslin, "Running a Large Writing Program"; Barry M. Maid, "How WPAs Can Learn to Use Power to Their Own Advantage"; Dave Healy, "Managing the Writing Center/Classroom Relationship"; and Lisa Gerrard, "The WPA, the Composition Instructor, and Scholarship."

441 O'Neill, Peggy, Angela Crow, and Larry W. Burton, eds. *A Field of Dreams: Independent Writing Programs and the Future of Composition Studies*. Logan: Utah State UP, 2002. Print.

Developing a freestanding or independent writing program no longer means standing alone. This seventeen-chapter collection documents lived experiences of the formation of independent writing programs in four-year universities. Includes an introduction by O'Neill and Crow and an afterword by Burton. Section I, Local Scenes: Stories of Independent Writing Programs, includes Daniel J. Royer and Roger Gilles, "The Origins of a Department of Academic, Creative, and Professional Writing"; Anne Aronson and Craig Hansen, "Writing Identity: The Independent Writing Department as a Disciplinary Center"; and Elizabeth J. Deis, Lowell T. Frye, and Katherine J. Weese, "Independence Fostering Community: The Benefits of an Independent Writing Program at a Small Liberal Arts College." Section II, Beyond the Local: Connections among Communities, includes Barry M. Maid, "Creating Two Departments of Writing: One Past and One Future"; Chris M. Anson, "Who Wants Composition? Reflections on the Rise and Fall of an Independent Program"; Peggy O'Neill and Ellen Schendel, "Locating Writing Programs in Research Universities"; and Angela Crow, "Wagering Tenure by Signing on with Independent Writing Programs." Section III, The Big Picture, includes Wendy Bishop, "A Rose by Every Other Name: The Excellent Problem of Independent Writing Programs"; Cynthia L. Selfe, Gail E. Hawisher, and Patricia Ericsson, "Stasis and Change: The Role of Independent Composition Programs and the Dynamic Nature of Literacy"; and Kurt Spellmeyer, "Bigger Than a Discipline."

See: Michael A. Pemberton, "Rethinking the WAC/Writing Center Connection" [531].

442 Rose, Shirley K., and Irwin Weiser, eds. *Going Public: What Writing Programs Learn from Engagement*. Logan: Utah State UP, 2010. Print.

Thirteen essays put the engagement movement, service learning, public writing, and civic rhetoric in conversation with Writing Program Administration in order to sustain a community identity linked to the citizenship missions of such programs. Includes an introduction by the editors. Essays include Jeff Grabill, "Infrastructure Outreach and the Engaged Writing Program"; Michael H. Norton and Eli Goldblatt, "Centering Community Literacy: The Art of Location within Institutions and Neighborhoods"; David A. Jolliffe, "The Arkansas Delta Oral History Project: A Hands-On, Experiential Course on School-College Articulation"; Jonikka Charlton and Colin Charlton, "The Illusion of Transparency at an HSI: Rethinking Service and Public Identity in a South Texas Writing Program"; Timothy Henningsen et al., "A Hybrid Genre Supports Hybrid Roles in Community-University Collaboration"; Susan Wolff Murphy, "Apprenticing Civic and Political Engagement in the First Year Writing Program"; Jessie L. Moore and Michael Strickland, "Wearing Multiple Hats: How Campus WPA Roles Can Inform Program-Specific Writing Designs"; Thia Wolf, Jill Swiencicki, and Chris Fosen, "Students, Faculty and 'Sustainable' WPA Work"; Linda S. Bergmann, "The Writing Center as Site for Engagement"; Linda K. Shamoon and Eileen Medeiros, "Not Politics as Usual: Public Writing as Writing for Engagement"; Dominic DelliCarpini, "Coming Down from the Ivory Tower: Writing Programs' Role in Advocating Public Scholarship"; Linda Adler-Kassner, "The WPA as Activist: Systematic Strategies for Framing, Action, and Representation"; and Jaclyn M. Wells, "Writing Program Administration and Community Engagement: A Bibliographic Essay."

443 Rose, Shirley K., and Irwin Weiser, eds. *The Writing Program Administrator as Researcher: Inquiry in Action and Reflection*. Portsmouth: Heinemann-Boynton/Cook, 1999. Print.

WPAs' work as researchers deserves a greater understanding, and both new and experienced WPAs need to learn to identify opportunities for doing significant intellectual work in the context of their programs. Fourteen chapters follow an introduction by the editors; they include Muriel Harris, "Diverse Research Methodologies at Work for Diverse Audiences: Shaping the Writing Center to the Institution"; Betty Bamberg, "Conflicts Between Teaching and Assessing Writing: Using Program-Based Research to Resolve Pedagogical and Ethical Dilemmas"; Mark Schaub, "The Contributions of Sociolinguistic Profiling and Constituents' Expectations to Writing Program Evaluation"; Sarah Liggett, "After the Practicum: Assessing Teacher Preparation Programs"; Irwin Weiser, "Local Research and Curriculum Development: Using Surveys to Learn about Writing Assignments in the Disciplines"; Ruth M. Mirtz, "WPAs as Historians: Discovering a First-Year Writing Program by Researching Its Past"; Tim Peeples, "'Seeing' the WPA With/Through Postmodern Mapping"; Louise Wetherbee Phelps, "Telling a Writing Program Its Own Story: A Tenth-Anniversary Speech."

444 Rose, Shirley K., and Irwin Weiser, eds. *The Writing Program Administrator as Theorist: Making Knowledge Work*. Portsmouth: Heinemann-Boynton/Cook, 2002. Print.

Successor to *The Writing Program Administrator as Researcher* [443], this volume investigates the role of theory as well as its application and practice in writing program administration. The fifteen-chapter compilation seeks to locate an operational balance "between 'knowing that' and 'knowing how' in the high-stakes world of budgetary planning, program development, and curricular innovation." Begins with an introduction by the editors. Part I, Theorizing Our Writing Programs, includes Jeanne Gunner, "Ideology, Theory, and the Genre of Writing Programs"; Susan Popham, Michael Neal, Ellen Schendel, and Brian Huot, "Breaking Hierarchies: Using Reflective Practice to Re-Construct the Role of the Writing Program Administrator"; William Lalicker, "The Writing Program Administrator and the Challenge of Textbooks and Theory"; and Linda K. Shamoon, Robert A. Schwegler, Rebecca Moore Howard, and Sandra Jamieson, "Reexamining the Theory-Practice Binary in the Work of Writing Program Administration." Part II, Theorizing Writing Program Administration, includes Rita Malenczyk, "Administration as Emergence: Toward a Rhetorical Theory of Writing Program Administration"; Carrie Shively Leverenz, "Theorizing Ethical Issues in Writing Program Administration"; Jeffrey Jablonski, "Developing Practice Theories Through Collaborative Research: Implications for WPA Scholarship"; and Irwin Weiser and Shirley K. Rose, "Theorizing Writing Program Theorizing."

445 Roy, Alice. "ESL Concerns for Writing Program Administrators: Problems and Policies." *WPA: Writing Program Administration* 11.3 (Spring 1988): 17–26. Print.

ESL students may be foreign students planning to return home after college, recent immigrants, or bilingual native students. Current theories of second-language acquisition are similar to current theories of composition for native English speakers, namely, that ESL students need practice in writing to make meaning and to develop strategies for construing meaning rather than grammar drill or audiolingual work. Linguists tend not to be the best writing teachers for ESL students because they are likely to use a grammar-based approach. Specialists in ESL are better because they bring knowledge of cultural diversity and contrastive rhetoric, but often their training has concentrated on oral communication. ESL students may be best served by composition specialists familiar with college-level reading and writing. Mainstreaming ESL students instead of offering a separate ESL course may offer students more sophisticated instruction and oral practice while benefiting native English speakers by providing cultural diversity. Schools should provide support programs for mainstreamed ESL students rather than track them into courses where English competency may not be needed.

446 Tinberg, Howard B. *Border Talk: Writing and Knowing in the Two-Year College*. Urbana: NCTE, 1997. Print.

Tinberg chronicles a summer workshop comprising a writing lab assistant and nine community college professors who had also worked in the lab. Their disciplines included business, dental hygiene, English, ESL, history, mathematics, nursing, and psychology. Their task was to revise a college policy statement on criteria for good writing so that it reflected disciplinary perspectives. In the process, they addressed issues of professional expertise, the nature of knowledge, student and faculty historical consciousness, and cross-disciplinary methods of assessing and responding to writing. They became "border crossers" who had to abandon narrow disciplinary perspectives, to become comfortable with professional discourse that blurred genres, and to recognize and use their own experiences of education and social-class identity in their community college teaching.

See: Eileen E. Schell and Patricia Lambert Stock, eds. *Moving a Mountain: Transforming the Role of Contingent Faculty in Composition Studies and Higher Education* [501].

See: John Trimbur, "The Problem of Freshman English (Only): Toward Programs of Study in Writing" [456].

447 Ward, Irene, and William J. Carpenter, eds. *The Allyn & Bacon Sourcebook for Writing Program Administrators*. New York: Longman, 2002. Print.

Twenty-three essays in five parts, covering teacher training, curriculum design, program assessment, administrative techniques, and professional issues. Includes nine historical documents related to program administration. The eleven essays written specifically for this book are Jeanne Gunner, "Professional Advancement of the WPA: Rhetoric and Politics in Tenure and Promotion"; Doug Hesse, "Understanding Larger Discourses in Higher Education: Practical Advice for WPAs"; Brian A. Huot and Ellen E. Schendel, "A Working Methodology of Assessment for Writing Program Administrators"; Barry M. Maid, "Working Outside of English"; David Schwalm, "The Writing Program (Administrator) in Context: Where Am I, and Can I Still Behave Like a Faculty Member?"; David Smit, "Curriculum Design for First-Year Programs"; Todd Taylor, "Ten Commandments for Computers and Composition"; Martha Townsend, "Writing Across the Curriculum"; Irene Ward and Merry Perry, "A Selection of Strategies for Training Teaching Assistants"; and William J. Carpenter, "Professional Development for Writing Program Staff."

448 White, Edward M. *Developing Successful College Writing Programs*. San Francisco: Jossey-Bass, 1989. Print.

Writing program directors seeking to design or redesign a program can plan for organic development by taking a comprehensive view of the many separate activities that constitute a good program. Ten concise chapters examine the campus climate for writing programs (the roles of the English department, the writing program administrator, and the administration), research on existing programs, prevalent teaching methods, course designs, assessment issues and practices, instructor evaluation, administration (setting policies on placement and credit for remedial courses, setting up ESL and writing-across-the-curriculum programs), training and support of faculty, and evaluation of the program.

449 Witte, Stephen P., and Lester Faigley. *Evaluating College Writing Programs*. Carbondale: Southern Illinois UP, 1983. Print.

Two models dominate writing program evaluation. The qualitative "expert-opinion approach," used by teams from the Council of Writing Program Administrators, confuses description with evaluation. Moreover, team members sometimes differ greatly in the quality of their "expert" credentials and use disparate evaluation methods. The quantitative approach, used in many pre- and posttest studies (four of which are analyzed here), rests on faulty assumptions about the writing process, does not assess either a program's goals or its administrative structure, and tends to produce data with only local applicability. An adequate theory of program evaluation would allow for both qualitative and quantitative measures in assessing a program's cultural and social context, institutional context, administrative structure, curriculum, and pedagogy. See also Faigley et al. [469].

450 WPA Board of Consultant Evaluators. "Writing Program Evaluation: An Outline for Self-Study." *WPA: Writing Program Administration* 4.2 (Winter 1980): 23–28. Print.

A list of seventy-six questions based on the guidelines for WPA Consultant Evaluators covers curriculum (subdivided into courses and goals, syllabus, methods, testing, grading), program administration (institutional and program structure, the writing program administrator's job description), faculty development (current conditions, support), and support services (organization, personnel, administration).

See: Kathleen Blake Yancey, ed., *Delivering College Composition: The Fifth Canon* [257].

First-Year Composition

See: Sharon Crowley, "How the Professional Lives of WPAs Would Change If FYC Were Elective" [433].

451 Downs, Douglas, and Elizabeth Wardle. "Teaching about Writing, Righting Misconceptions: (Re)Envisioning 'First-Year Composition' as 'Introduction to Writing Studies.'" CCC 58.4 (June 2007): 552–84. Print.

By operating as if students can be prepared for academic writing through one or two FYC courses, writing programs ignore research and theory (e.g., on transfer) and reproduce misconceptions about writing and writing studies (e.g., that anyone can teach it). An alternative pedagogy, teaching *about* writing, "recognizes the impossibility of teaching a universal academic discourse and rejects that as a goal for FYC." Introduction to Writing Studies draws on research from the field "to help students understand the nature of writing"; students explore reading and writing in school and in society with readings largely data-driven and research-based. Two case studies and end-of-semester reflections illustrate students' experiences with the material; students begin to see research, for example, as entering an ongoing conversation. Despite acknowledged challenges, this approach professionalizes writing instruction.

See: T. R. Johnson and Tom Pace, eds. *Refiguring Prose Style: Possibilities for Writing Pedagogy* [419].

See: Margaret Price, "Accessing Disability: A Nondisabled Student Works the Hyphen" [732].

452 Robillard, Amy E. "We Won't Get Fooled Again: On the Absence of Angry Responses to Plagiarism in Composition Studies." CE 70.1 (Sept. 2007): 10–31. Print.

Emotional responses to plagiarism—anger and anxiety—are valid and perhaps even necessary if we are to deepen our understanding of it. Prevention and detection methods (i.e., Turnitin.com) may actually encourage plagiarism anxiety, ignore the affective element of this issue, and do little to address the intertextuality of plagiarized work. While largely silent in public discussions about plagiarism, writing teachers have expressed anger in the blogosphere; analyzing these blogs illustrates teachers' conflicting values and the threat of plagiarism to their identity. Most important, theorizing plagiarism requires attention to *readers* as part of the transaction.

453 Slevin, James F. "Inventing and Reinventing the Discipline of Composition." *Introducing English: Essays in the Intellectual Work of Composition.* Pittsburgh: U of Pittsburgh P, 2001. Print.

When it first emerged, composition was an intellectual and social movement, not a disciplinary field. Its intellectual work included "pedagogical self-consciousness, curricular change, and institutional reform." The meaning of "discipline" has shifted to a research-centered guild model and has lost the focus on practices and activities (working *with* rather than working *in*). Composition's work should emphasize a commitment to inclusiveness, where the representation of students in academic disciplines is key, and where students are equal partners in doing the interpretive work of composition. Rather than students being unprepared for college work, maybe institutions are not ready for *them*. Students, in fact, created our discipline.

454 Sommers, Nancy, and Laura Saltz. "The Novice as Expert: Writing the Freshman Year." CCC 56.1 (Sept. 2004): 124–49. Print.

Findings from the Harvard Study of Undergraduate Writing indicate the importance of the freshman year in the arc of writing development. Writing gives students a sense that they *belong* in the academic community and therefore helps in the transition to college. Students report far more understanding or interest in courses that required writing despite the prevalence of the novice-as-expert paradox, which, while it "invites imitative rather than independent behavior," nevertheless enables students to practice with various writing tools and discover their passions. Students who accept their status as novices make the greatest gains in writing development, while those who are able to explore their interests and make assignments matter remain interested in academic writing.

455 Sullivan, Patrick, and Howard Tinberg, eds. *What Is "College-Level" Writing?* Urbana: NCTE, 2006. Print.

A collection of twenty-four chapters arranged in four sections provide diversified accounts and interpretations of the most central question to teaching college composition: What is college-level writing? Includes an appendix titled "Continuing the Conversation: A Dialogue with Our Contributors," which seeks to contextualize the impact of the book on teachers, the authors, and the editors. Section I, High School Perspectives, begins with Patrick Sullivan, "An Essential Question: What Is 'College-Level' Writing?" and continues with entries by Jeanette Jordan et al., "Am I a Liar? The Angst of a High School English Teacher"; and Milka Mustenikova Mosley, "The Truth about High School English." Section II, College Perspectives, includes Lynn Z. Bloom, "Good Enough Writing: What Is Good Enough Writing, Anyway?"; Jeanne Gunner, "The Boxing Effect (An Anti-Essay)"; Ellen Andrews Knodt, "What Is College Writing For?"; and Ronald F. Lunsford, "From Attitude to Aptitude: Assuming the Stance of a College Writer." Section III, Student Perspectives, includes Kimberly L. Nelson, "The Great Conversation (of the Dining Hall): One Student's Experience of College-Level Writing"; and Mike Quilligan, "Putting on the Sunglasses: The Argumentative Thesis as the Keystone to 'Good' College Writing." Section IV, Administrative Perspectives, includes James M. Gentile, "College-Level Writing: A Departmental Perspective"; Chris Kearns, "The Recursive Character of College Writing"; and Sheridan Blau, "College Writing, Academic Literacy, and the Intellectual Community: California Dreams and Cultural Oppositions."

456 Trimbur, John. "The Problem of Freshman English (Only): Toward Programs of Study in Writing." *WPA: Writing Program Administration* 22.3 (Spring 1999): 9–30. Print.

Despite the powerful sense of mission that accompanies the first-year course in writing, our attachment to a single course leads to an oversaturation of the curriculum, while the single-minded focus on the first-year course also makes it difficult to compare models and theorize program design. Programs of study in writing would position the first-year course as introductory to the intellectual study of writing, a move that would help to expand the forum for negotiating differences in the theories and agendas that currently divide the field. The assumption that writing instruction must take place in English-Only environments can be traced to its origins, where the formation of the first-year course severed writing in English from its association with classical languages. English achieved its dominance both as a department and as a modern language in part because of the required first-year course, and mastery of English Only has made Freshman English First Worldist at the level of both language and culture. Program design must intersect with multiple constituencies and serve multiple purposes without departmentalizing knowledge. One of the central challenges facing program design is to imagine writing instruction and curriculum from an internationalist perspective.

Response and Assessment

457 Anson, Chris M. "Response and the Social Construction of Error." *Assessing Writing* 7.1 (Feb. 2000): 5–21. Print.

Writing instructors remain unsettled about the role of error in response and evaluation, perhaps because there has been very little research in teacher *response to error*. Existing scholarship—numerous attempts to qualify errors—might be extended to explore the social dimensions of error in response to student writing; that is, to tell us what teachers are thinking when they encounter errors in student writing. What sources of knowledge *do* teachers act on in responding to students' errors? Many of the socially constructed decisions about hyphen usage, for example, that take place among editors and publishers, are slow to reach writing teachers, who do not always approach "correctness" as a shifting, constantly modified code of language conventions. The relationship between error and response may be explored through reflective practice and the use of instructional "filters," consciously applied to determine when instruction about error will benefit students. Reflection in action brings into the classroom various histories of conventions and more attention to the relationship between rule-breaking and style, persona, or context. Knowing more about the effects of error on our reading processes unites response practices with realistic, context-based instruction.

458 Anson, Chris M. *Writing and Response: Theory, Practice, and Research.* Urbana: NCTE, 1989. Print.

Seventeen essays include Anson, "Response to Writing and the Paradox of Uncertainty"; David Bleich, "Reconceiving Literacy: Language Use and Social Relations"; Louise Phelps, "Images of Student Writing: The Deep Structure of Teacher Response"; Martin Nystrand and Deborah Brandt, "Response to Writing as a Context for Learning to Write"; Susan Wall and Glynda Hull, "The Semantics of Error: What Do Teachers Know?"; Thomas Newkirk, "The First Five Minutes: Setting the Agenda in a Writing Conference"; and Richard Beach, "Demonstrating Techniques for Assessing Writing in the Writing Conference" [459].

459 Beach, Richard. "Demonstrating Techniques for Assessing Writing in the Writing Conference." CCC 37.1 (Feb. 1986): 56–65. Print.

Some students need instruction in assessing writing beyond either reader-based feedback or the teacher's identification of problems in the text. Such instruction can be offered in a conference in which the teacher first demonstrates describing, judging, and selecting appropriate revisions, then describes the rhetorical context of purpose and audience used as criteria for assessment, and finally asks the student to practice this technique. When writers describe their goals in rhetorical terms, they articulate the bases for making judgments, which leads to revision strategies. Students can be given an assessment form before the conference, asking them to describe goals and audience, identify problems, and suggest changes. In conference, the teacher can then focus on the students' difficulties with these categories, helping them see the nature of rhetorical goals, sensing dissonance between goals and the text, and so on.

See: John D. Beard, Jone Rymer, and David L. Williams, "An Assessment System for Collaborative Writing Groups: Theory and Empirical Evaluation" [835].

460 Belanoff, Pat. "The Myth of Assessment." *Journal of Basic Writing* 10 (Spring 1991): 54–66. Print.

There are four myths of assessment. The first is that we know what we're testing for. Tests assume, falsely, that we can judge when writing is good enough for some purpose, to satisfy a requirement or to graduate, and they assume that we know what constitutes improvement. The second myth is that we know what we are testing. We cannot test ability, though: we simply judge the quality of a hastily written product, the result of a meaningless task, without reference to the writer at all. The third is that we agree both on criteria and on whether individual papers meet the criteria. But because texts do not contain meaning, readers inevitably differ about whether abstract criteria have been met. The final myth is that there is a standard of good writing that can be applied uniformly, an obvious misapprehension. Even communal portfolio assessment does not eliminate differences in judgment, but, by promoting discussion of teaching and criteria, it improves teaching, and, moreover, appears to be the best way to approach consensus.

461 Belanoff, Pat, and Marcia Dickson. *Portfolios: Process and Product.* Portsmouth: Heinemann-Boynton/Cook, 1991. Print.

Twenty-three essays on both practical and theoretical dimensions of portfolio assessment. Units cover proficiency testing, program assessment, using portfolios in courses, and political issues. Essays include Peter Elbow and Pat Belanoff, "State University of New York at Stony Brook Portfolio-Based Evaluation Program"; David Smit, Patricia Kolonosky, and Kathryn Seltzer, "Implementing a Portfolio System"; Roberta Rosenberg, "Using the Portfolio to Meet State-Mandated Assessment"; Anne Sheehan and Francine Dempsey, "Bridges to Academic Goals: A Look at Returning Adult Portfolios"; Richard Larson, "Using Portfolios in the Assessment of Writing in the Academic Disciplines"; Jeffery Sommers, "Bringing Practice in Line with Theory: Using Portfolio Grading in the Composition Classroom"; Pamela Gay, "A Portfolio Approach to Teaching a Biology-Linked Basic Writing Course"; and Marcia Dickson, "The WPA, the Portfolio System, and Academic Freedom." Includes a cumulative bibliography of works cited.

462 Belanoff, Pat, and Peter Elbow. "Using Portfolios to Increase Collaboration and Community in a Writing Program." *WPA: Writing Program Administration* 9.3 (Spring 1986): 27–40. Print.

Students prepare portfolios of three composition-course papers—one narrative or expressive, one formal essay conceptually organized, and one text analysis—plus cover sheets describing their writing processes and an unrevised piece of in-class writing. Students submit one or two pieces mid-semester to be evaluated without prejudice. Grades are pass-fail only, assigned by a group of teachers. The student's own teacher can ask for a second reading. This testing process, unlike the proficiency exam, rewards the student for collaboration and revision. It also builds community among the teachers, who have two chances each semester to discuss writing and grading standards and slowly work toward consensus on some issues. The portfolio system encourages collaboration between teachers and students and gives the teacher's coaching role more credibility. Finally, the system increases collaboration between teachers and program directors by bringing the course content into the open.

463 Black, Laurel, Donald A. Daiker, Jeffrey Sommers, and Gail Stygall, eds. *New Directions in Portfolio Assessment: Reflective Practice, Critical Theory, and Large-Scale Scoring*. Portsmouth: Heinemann-Boynton/Cook, 1994. Print.

Twenty-six essays representing a variety of research approaches to the questions of the validity and perceived benefits of portfolio assessment. Essays include Pat Belanoff, "Portfolios and Literacy: Why?"; Edward White, "Portfolios as an Assessment Concept"; Peter Elbow, "Will the Virtues of Portfolios Blind Us to Their Potential Dangers?"; James Berlin, "The Subversions of the Portfolio"; Glenda Conway, "Portfolio Cover Letters, Students' Self-Presentation, and Teachers' Ethics"; John Beall, "Portfolios, Research, and Writing about Science"; James Reither and Russell Hunt, "Beyond Portfolios: Scenes for Dialogic Reading and Writing"; Nedra Reynolds, "Graduate Writers and Portfolios: Issues of Professionalism, Authority, and Resistance"; Irwin Weiser, "Portfolios and the New Teacher of Writing"; Gail Stygall et al., "Gendered Textuality: Assigning Gender to Portfolios"; Robert Broad, "'Portfolio Scoring': A Contradiction in Terms"; David Smit, "A WPA's Nightmare: Reflections on Using Portfolios as a Course Exit Exam"; and Carl Lovitt and Art Young, "Portfolios in the Disciplines: Sharing Knowledge in the Contact Zone."

464 Broad, Bob. *What We Really Value: Beyond Rubrics in Teaching and Assessing Writing.* Logan: Utah State UP, 2003. Print.

How do composition instructors judge their students' work? Dynamic Criteria Mapping (DCM) offers a rigorous method for finding answers to this question, answers that traditional rubrics and scoring guides cannot provide. "City University" (a pseudonym) is the site for this qualitative study of one writing program's portfolio assessment program, particularly the dynamics of its rhetorical values. Interviews, field notes, and documents provided criteria that, once "mapped," presented evidence of how pass/fail judgments were made about students' portfolios. Both textual and contextual criteria impacted judgments; the "hidden" contextual criteria played a much larger role than most evaluators realized. DCM made clear, for example, how much "Teachers' Special Knowledge" influenced the pass/fail rating even though evaluation was supposed to be restricted to the text alone. The final chapter reviews a streamlined version of DCM for programs invested in communal writing assessment.

465 Charney, Davida. "The Validity of Using Holistic Scoring to Evaluate Writing: A Critical Overview." *Research in the Teaching of English* 18.1 (Feb. 1984): 65–81. Print.

A good test of writing ability must be both reliable (it must provide reproducible results) and valid (it must actually test what it claims to test). Many writing teachers have rejected quantitative tests as invalid, feeling that they do not actually measure writing ability. But qualitative tests are often unreliable, as raters disagree over what constitutes good writing. The use of holistically scored writing samples is now widely regarded as a reliable and valid testing method. But holistic scorers are often influenced by legibility, length, and unusual diction, casting doubt on the validity of this method.

466 Cooper, Charles R., and Lee Odell, eds. *Evaluating Writing: Describing, Measuring, Judging.* Urbana: NCTE, 1977. Print.

Six essays explain current techniques for assessing students' writing, including measures of syntactic complexity, intellectual maturity, and self-evaluating ability. Two important testing methods are described in Cooper and Odell, "Holistic Evaluation of Writing," and Richard Lloyd-Jones, "Primary Trait Scoring."

467 Cooper, Charles R., and Lee Odell, eds. *Evaluating Writing: The Role of Teachers' Knowledge about Text, Learning, and Culture.* Urbana: NCTE, 1999. Print.

A collection of seventeen essays covers a number of issues related to response, evaluation, and assessment, including describing students' writing, connecting teaching and evaluation, and examining assumptions and practices. Sections include assessment in four disciplines and the writing of dual-language students. Essays include Charles R. Cooper, "What We Know about Genres, and How It Can Help Us Assign and

Evaluate Writing"; Richard W. Beach, "Evaluating Students' Response Strategies in Writing about Literature"; Arnetha F. Ball, "Evaluating the Writing of Culturally and Linguistically Diverse Students: The Case of the African American Vernacular English Speaker"; Chris M. Anson, "Reflective Reading: Developing Thoughtful Ways to Respond to Students' Writing"; Sandra Murphy and Mary Ann Smith, "Creating a Climate for Portfolios"; and Roxanne Mountford, "Let Them Experiment: Accommodating Diverse Discourse Practices in Large-Scale Writing Assessment."

468 Diederich, Paul. *Measuring Growth in English.* Urbana: NCTE, 1974. Print.

Diederich discusses factor analysis of readers' responses to essay tests; avoidance of reader bias; reliability of statistical results; standard deviation; comparative reliability of objective and essay tests; and design of tests. Appendices describe criteria for evaluating essay tests, sample essay topics, and sample objective questions. See Cooper and Odell [466] for newer testing methods, but Diederich's work is essential for explaining statistical problems.

469 Faigley, Lester, Roger D. Cherry, David A. Jolliffe, and Anna M. Skinner. *Assessing Writers' Knowledge and Processes of Composing.* Norwood: Ablex, 1985. Print.

Current methods of evaluating writing do not adequately reflect the research on composing that has prompted many writing programs to teach the composing process. Better evaluation would consider the literary, cognitive, and social dimensions of composing, and measure what writers know as well as what they do. Two methods developed for this study attempt to assess knowledge and process. In the first method, writers describe the knowledge they will apply to a given writing task (about situation, form, content, and so on). The second method is a "process log" of the actual writing experience. This book presents an extensive overview of research; the results of a study of writers' planning, writing, and revising and their task-related knowledge; and a thorough discussion of the relationship between theories of composing and theories of assessment.

470 Garrison, Roger. "One-to-One: Tutorial Instruction in Freshman Composition." *New Directions for Community Colleges* 2 (Spring 1974): 55–84. Print.

Professional writers learn their craft by writing with the help of an editor. Freshman writers can learn the same way if the classroom is set up as a workshop in which students work independently, at their own pace, and consult the instructor for editorial guidance in brief conferences. The instructor should suggest writing projects tailored to each student's personal or career interests. Garrison provides detailed advice on commenting effectively in a short conference.

471 Greenberg, Karen. "Validity and Reliability Issues in the Direct Assessment of Writing." *WPA: Writing Program Administration* 16.1-2 (Fall/Winter 1992): 7–23. Print.

Writing teachers prefer direct assessment—that is, holistically scored essay tests—to indirect, multiple-choice tests. Yet direct assessment is still criticized by the College Board on grounds of inter-rater unreliability, based on studies through the years that show greater reliability for indirect measures. But multiple-choice tests, scored mechanically, will always produce high reliability. Such tests, moreover, focus on the less important components of writing and reflect cultural bias. Differences in judgment on essays reflect the complexity of reading and writing, and good scoring procedures increase reliability. The validity of indirect assessment has long been challenged, yet the College Board—despite the evidence of its own study showing that a writing sample calling for two or more rhetorical tasks has greatest construct validity—champions a cost-effective test that includes multiple choice. Portfolio assessment is clearly more relevant to theory and classroom practice, but it does not yet include a model of good writing that will boost construct validity. Though research is needed in this area, there is sufficient reason to be comfortable with a commitment to direct assessment.

472 Greenberg, Karen, Harvey S. Wiener, and Richard A. Donovan, eds. *Writing Assessment: Issues and Strategies*. New York: Longman, 1986. Print.

Twelve essays and an annotated bibliography (fifty-three entries) collected by the National Testing Network in Writing, which is based at the City University of New York. Included are Stephen P. Witte, Mary Trachsel, and Keith Walters, "Literacy and the Direct Assessment of Writing: A Diachronic Perspective"; Edward M. White, "Pitfalls in the Testing of Writing"; Gertrude Conlon, "'Objective' Measures of Writing Ability"; Roscoe C. Brown Jr., "Testing Black Student Writers"; and Gordon Brossell, "Current Research and Unanswered Questions in Writing Assessment."

473 Harris, Muriel. *Teaching One-to-One: The Writing Conference*. Urbana: NCTE, 1986. Print.

Conferences should be an integral part of teaching writing. Many teachers find conferences their most helpful pedagogical strategy, useful at every stage of the writing process, and capable of improving the writer's sense of audience and purpose. To have successful conferences, teachers should consider their goals, their role in the conference, meeting formats, and scheduling. Conversation should be purposefully directive or nondirective in keeping with the immediate goals. To diagnose student difficulties and provide help in solving problems, teachers should begin by diagnosing their own criteria, their teaching methods, and the composing styles of the students. Diagnosis leads to strategies for overcoming writer's block, for recognizing cultural differences, and for dealing with learning disabilities. Finally, the conference is a good setting for teaching grammar.

474 Haswell, Richard H., ed. *Beyond Outcomes: Assessment and Instruction within a University Writing Program*. Westport: Ablex, 2001. Print.

An in-depth look at Washington State University's integrated writing instruction and writing assessment programs. Five parts plus appendices include the following chapters: Richard H. Haswell and Susan Wyche, "Authoring an Exam: Adventuring into Large-Scale Writing Assessment"; Galen Leonhardy and William Condon, "Exploring the Difficult Cases: In the Cracks of Writing Assessment"; Lisa Johnson-Shull and Diane Kelly-Riley, "Writes of Passage: Conceptualizing the Relationship of Writing Center and Writing Assessment Practices"; and Fiona Glade et al., "Faculty Opinion and Experience: The Writing Portfolio."

475 Haswell, Richard H. "Minimal Marking." *CE* 45.6 (Oct. 1983): 600–604. Print.

Marking compositions is unpleasant and largely unproductive as well: correcting surface errors has virtually no effect on students' writing. A way to address this level of writing, though, is not to correct errors but to indicate their presence in a line of writing by a check in the margin. This method challenges the student to find and correct the errors, most of which turn out to be careless. Conceptual errors are now easier to address; the teacher's commenting time can be spent on substance; and students move more effectively to mastery.

476 Horvath, Brooke K. "The Components of Written Response: A Practical Synthesis of Current Views." *Rhetoric Review* 2.2 (Jan. 1984): 136–56. Print. Rpt. in Corbett, Myers, and Tate [150].

The consensus of advice on formative evaluation (feedback on drafts as opposed to summative evaluation of final products) suggests that teachers should avoid correcting and rewriting students' papers and should instead ask questions, suggest changes, and assign new tasks. The goal of formative evaluation is to promote learning and help students approximate skilled writers' behavior. Teachers should remember to put responses in appropriate order (large-scale concerns before mechanics), leave the authorship with the student, and avoid unhelpful comments. Bibliography contains eighty-one annotated items.

477 Huot, Brian, and Peggy O'Neill, eds. *Assessing Writing: A Critical Sourcebook*. Boston: Bedford/St. Martin's, 2009. Print.

Organized into three parts, this twenty-four chapter anthology explores assessment theory and practice as it relates to rhetoric and composition instruction and administration. Contains an introduction by the editors and a bibliography of additional readings regarding the history of large-scale assessment, departmentalizing assessment, and evaluating assessment systems. Part I, Foundations, includes L. Ramon Veal and Sally Ann Hudson, "Direct and Indirect Measures for Large-Scale Evaluation of Writing"; Peter Elbow and Pat Belanoff, "Portfolios as a Substitute for Proficiency Examinations"; Kathleen Blake Yancey, "Looking Back as We Look Forward: Historicizing Writing Assessment"; and Brian Huot,

"Toward a New Theory of Writing Assessment." Part II, Models, includes William L. Smith, "The Importance of Teacher Knowledge in College Composition Placement Testing"; Daniel J. Royer and Roger Gilles, "Directed Self-Placement: An Attitude of Orientation"; Richard Haswell and Susan McLeod, "WAC Assessment and Internal Audiences: A Dialogue"; and Michael Carter, "A Process for Establishing Outcome-Based Assessment Plans for Writing and Speaking in the Diciplines." Part III, Issues, includes Brian Huot and Michael M. Williamson, "Rethinking Portfolios for Evaluating Writing: Isues of Assessment and Power"; Liz Hamp-Lyons, "The Challenges of Second-Language Writing Assessment"; Arnetha F. Ball, "Expanding the Dialogue on Culture as a Critical Component When Assessing Writing"; and Michael M. Williamson, "Validity of Automated Scoring: Prologue for a Continuing Discussion of Machine Scoring Student Writing."

478 Huot, Brian. *(Re)Articulating Writing Assessment for Teaching and Learning*. Logan: Utah State UP, 2002. Print.

Reframed for its pedagogical value, writing assessment can be connected fully to teaching rather than researched in isolation by the separate communities of college writing assessment and educational measurement. With validity as a rallying point, writing assessment can become a joint field of study, one that includes students learning to work as writers. *Instructive assessment* is an authentic and practical way of embedding assessment into the writing process, for students need to be *taught* how to assess. In addition, seeing assessment as research shifts the focus away from rubrics, anchor papers, scoring sessions, or grades and recognizes the programmatic, pedagogical, and theoretical reasons for asking questions about students and programs. Principles for a new theory and practice of assessment include the following: site-based, locally controlled, context-sensitive, rhetorically based, and accessible. Two models illustrate situations where those who teach in and administer the programs control the assessment.

479 Huot, Brian. "Toward a New Theory of Writing Assessment." CCC 47.4 (Dec. 1996): 549–66. Print.

Traditional writing assessment practices, rooted in positivism, are beginning to be redefined through revised views of validity that account for context, site specificity, and institutional needs. Placement or exit procedures at three universities illustrate "emergent assessment methods" focused on context while bypassing inter-rater reliability. Concerns about reliability are heightened in "contextually stripped environments" but can be just one way to judge a worthwhile assessment. Specific communicative tasks, created within a meaningful rhetorical situation, can eliminate testing technologies and will require different procedures through which to validate these procedures. An assessment scheme rich in context will emphasize local control and will make inter-rater reliability irrelevant.

480 Lunsford, Andrea A., and Karen J. Lunsford. "'Mistakes Are a Fact of Life': A National Comparative Study." CCC 59.4 (June 2008): 781–806. Print.

Motivated by frequent media reports about language use and by curiosity about the impact of digital technologies, this national study was designed to replicate the 1988 Connors and Lunsford study on the frequency of error in college student writing. A frustrating IRB approval process limited the number of papers collected; a random stratified sample of 877 papers was coded. Significant findings indicated that papers were longer than those evaluated in the 1988 study and represented a range of types or genres, with an emphasis on argument and research. Teachers marked 38 percent of the errors that coders found; generally, teachers are not using computer technologies to mark or comment on student papers. Similarly, students are producing traditional print-based texts without using a variety of tools available. The most common formal errors found in this study were "wrong word," spelling, and incomplete or missing documentation. Student errors are not more prevalent, simply different.

481 McLeod, Susan H., Heather Horn, and Richard H. Haswell. "Accelerated Classes and the Writers at the Bottom: A Local Assessment Story." CCC 56.4 (June 2005): 556–80. Print.

Do accelerated courses do students a disservice by giving them less time to develop? Comparing a six-week section of FYC to a ten-week section taught during one summer by the same teacher (and then compared to a ten-week fall course) suggests that students take courses strategically; for example, taking one class during the summer enables students to focus. Blind readings of student papers with a primary-trait scoring guide showed "no evidence for the received teacher knowledge that time pressure in short courses curtails improvement in writing." The use of multiple measures and multiple methods (including a pre-course questionnaire, focus-group interviews, student test scores on the SAT II Writing Test, and several others) speaks to the importance of designing local assessments, collecting data from many sources, and including students as research participants.

See: Priscilla S. Rogers, "Analytic Measures for Evaluating Managerial Writing" [853].

482 Rubin, Donnalee. *Gender Influences: Reading Student Texts*. Carbondale: Southern Illinois UP, 1993. Print.

Reader-response theories argue that men and women respond differently to literary texts. Nevertheless, research in which a group of male and female teachers were asked to evaluate unidentified essays reveals little gender bias. Longitudinal study of two teachers, one male and one female, also reveals little bias. The better a teacher knows his or her students—through, for example, a pedagogy that uses frequent conferencing—the less gender bias the teacher exhibits. Blind evaluation increases the chance of distortion by essay topics or styles uncongenial to the evaluator's gender identity. A maternal model of teaching, which gives a responsive reading to all students, attends to the contexts of writing, and encourages independence, most tends to obviate gender bias.

483 Smith, Jane Bowman, and Kathleen Blake Yancey, eds. *Self-Assessment and Development in Writing: A Collaborative Inquiry*. Cresskill: Hampton, 2000. Print.

Self-assessment is a phenomenon that can be approached in several ways: historical, theoretical, practical, ethical, and conceptual. Eleven chapters include Thomas L. Hilgers, Edna L. Hussey, and Monica Stitt-Bergh, "The Case for Prompted Self-Assessment in the Writing Classroom"; Susan Latta and Janice Lauer, "Student Self-Assessment: Some Issues and Concerns from Postmodern and Feminist Perspectives"; Rebecca Moore Howard, "Applications and Assumptions of Student Self-Assessment"; Chris M. Anson, "Talking about Writing: A Classroom-Based Study of Students' Reflections on Their Drafts"; Vicki Tolar Collins, "Freewriting in the Middle: Self-Help for College Writers Across the Curriculum"; and Irwin Weiser, "Self-Assessment, Reflection, and the New Teacher of Writing."

484 Smith, Summer. "The Genre of the End Comment: Conventions in Teacher Responses to Student Writing." CCC 48.2 (May 1997): 249–68. Print.

End comments on student papers can be understood as secondary speech genres, with "relatively stable content, style, and structure." Not interested in finding contradictions or measuring specificity in teachers' end comments, this study of 313 representative end comments seeks to determine the features of end comments and the range of options available to commenters. Sixteen primary genres were identified, grouped into three categories: judging, reader response, and coaching. The most frequently identified genres included "evaluation of development" and "suggestion for revision of current paper"; 88 percent of end comments begin with a positive evaluation. When patterns of selecting from the repertoire of commenting conventions do not vary, students may dismiss the commentary as generic and formulaic.

485 Sommers, Nancy. "Responding to Student Writing." CCC 33.2 (May 1982): 148–56. Print. Rpt. in *Teaching Writing: Theories and Practices*. Ed. J. Travers. Glenview: Scott Foresman, 1988.

"Teachers' comments can take students' attention away from their own purposes in writing a particular text and focus that attention on the teachers' purpose in commenting." In this study, comments by teachers directed students to edit sentences and to rethink and expand the topic at the same time. This is contradictory advice, urging students to treat the text as finished while treating the subject as unfinished. Instead of using comments to justify grades, teachers should respond to the meaning and purpose of early drafts and leave editing corrections for later, thus encouraging students to revise more extensively rather than to patch up the text. Winner of the 1983 Braddock Award.

486 Straub, Richard. "The Concept of Control in Teacher Response: Defining the Varieties of 'Directive' and 'Facilitative' Commentary." CCC 47.2 (May 1996): 223–51. Print.

With remarkable consistency in the literature, teachers are urged to be facilitative and not directive in their responses to student writing. However, between these two extremes, teacher commentary can take a number of forms that resist a neat binary. Analyzing teacher commentary by *focuses* and *modes* illustrates the varying degrees of control that teachers exercise. Five teachers who wrote comments on the same student draft used different strategies for giving the student help and direction without usurping the student's choices. This study suggests that we "should not reject all directive styles of response any more than we should all adopt some standard facilitative style."

487 Walvoord, Barbara E. Fassler. *Helping Students Write Well: A Guide for Teachers in All Disciplines*. 2nd ed. New York: MLA, 1990. Print.

To help students write well, teachers should communicate expectations clearly, respond to writing without rewriting students' papers for them, and use grades to coach as well as evaluate writing. Walvoord provides a wealth of practical advice, primarily for the novice writing teacher, with sample assignments, student papers, and comments.

488 White, Edward M. *Teaching and Assessing Writing*. 2nd ed. San Francisco: Jossey-Bass, 1994. Print.

Assessment can have a damaging influence on writing instruction, but, used properly, may improve teaching and demonstrate the value of what we do. Formative assessment should be used to help students progress and to understand that product assessment is the inevitable end of writing in college. Writing teachers should, for example, help students learn how to take essay tests, which students will encounter frequently. External or summative assessment is similarly inevitable, and writing program administrators are well advised to understand the language of testing from a variety of perspectives, in an effort to produce fair and satisfactory tests. White offers much commonsense advice on testing, organizing holistic tests, program evaluation, and using testing and evaluation in teaching.

489 Wiener, Harvey S. "Collaborative Learning in the Classroom: A Guide to Evaluation." *CE* 48.1 (Jan. 1986): 52–61. Print. Rpt. in Corbett, Myers, and Tate [150].

In a collaborative classroom, students work in small groups on a task designed by the teacher. Each group reports its results to the whole class while the teacher mediates differences and highlights important features of the task. The teacher can be evaluated in several roles: as a task-setter who must design problems that involve students in complex negotiations and provide guidelines for reaching consensus; as a classroom manager who must organize groups efficiently; as a facilitator who must help all students to participate while intervening minimally; and as a synthesizer who must help the class compare the groups' results and lead them to appreciate the intellectual purposes of the task rather than simply to seek the right answers.

490 Yancey, Kathleen Blake. "Looking Back as We Look Forward: Historicizing Writing Assessment." CCC 50.3 (Feb. 1999): 483–503. Print.

The history of writing assessment can be traced in various ways. The one located in method sees three waves: the first in the form of objective tests, the second as holistically scored essays, and the third or most current as portfolio and programmatic assessment. In the first wave, reliability and testing specialists dominated the field; in the second wave, validity became a major concern, and the disciplinary machinery was developed to support and disseminate expertise in both writing and assessment. The third wave features a model of assessment that emphasizes validity and re-contextualizes reliability through multiple texts, different genres, and/or portfolios; more important, the third wave is creating knowledge about both assessment and our own practices. Only recently has assessment been seen as a knowledge-making endeavor. Understanding writing assessment as a rhetorical act that is both humane and ethical marks the most significant change of the last fifty years.

491 Yancey, Kathleen Blake, and Irwin Weiser, eds. *Situating Portfolios: Four Perspectives*. Logan: Utah State UP, 1997. Print.

Twenty-four essays in four sections—Theory and Power, Pedagogy, Teaching and Professional Development, and Technology—address themes of collaboration, models, and reflection in classroom portfolios, teacher portfolios, and large-scale portfolio assessment. Essays include Peter Elbow and Pat Belanoff, "Reflections on an Explosion: Portfolios in the '90s and Beyond"; Brian Huot and Michael M. Williamson, "Rethinking Portfolios for Evaluating Writing: Issues of Assessment and Power"; Sandra Murphy, "Teachers and Students: Reclaiming Assessment via Portfolios"; Mary Ann Smith, "Behind the Scenes: Portfolios in a Classroom Learning Community"; William Condon, "Building Bridges, Closing Gaps: Using Portfolios to Reconstruct the Academic Community"; Robert P. Yagelski, "Portfolios as a Way to Encourage Reflective Practice among Preservice English Teachers"; Irwin Weiser, "Revising Our Practices: How Portfolios Help Teachers Learn"; Gail E. Hawisher and Cynthia L. Selfe, "Wedding the Technologies of Writing Portfolios and Computers: The Challenges of Electronic Classrooms"; and Kristine L. Blair and Pamela Takayoshi, "Reflections on Reading and Evaluating Electronic Portfolios."

492 Zak, Frances, and Christopher C. Weaver, eds. *The Theory and Practice of Grading Writing*. Albany: State U of New York P, 1998. Print.

Fifteen essays address "our myopia on the subject of grading" and put grading into dialogue with current theory. Essays include Bruce W. Speck and Tammy R. Jones, "Direction in the Grading of Writing? What the Literature on the Grading of Writing Does and Doesn't Tell Us"; Kathleen Blake Yancey and Brian Huot, "Construction, Deconstruction, and (Over)Determination: A Foucaultian Analysis of Grades"; Michael Bernard-Donals, "Peter Elbow and the Cynical Subject"; Nick Carbone and Margaret Daisley, "Grading as a Rhetorical Construct"; Maureen Neal, "The Politics and Perils of Portfolio Grading"; Cherryl Smith and Angus Dunstan, "Grade the Learning, Not the Writing"; and Peter Elbow, "Changing Grading While Working with Grades."

Contingent Labor and Working Conditions

493 Bousquet, Marc. *How the University Works: Higher Education and the Low-Wage Nation.* New York: New York UP, 2008. Print.

Higher education operates according to the values and practices of corporate management—with revenue enhancement and cost containment the primary goals—where an administrative culture is pitted against faculty culture and where job market theory has changed the relationship of faculty to graduate students as a managerial one. Third-wave academic labor knowledge aims to create a contingent-faculty culture, to develop a consciousness of work, and to expose, for example, how undergraduates become flex workers exploited by big companies (e.g., UPS in Louisville). Composition as a discipline proves to be enormously useful to academic capitalism—in part because its discourse is one of management science—but a class consciousness in composition can emerge if universities eliminate WPAs. Furthermore, an analysis of the rhetoric of "job market" concludes that "it simply does not follow that reducing the graduate student population will alter the labor system." Instead, it should be more expensive for universities to use flex labor than to use faculty labor.

494 Bousquet, Marc, Tony Scott, and Leo Parascondola, eds. *Tenured Bosses and Disposable Teachers: Writing Instruction in the Managed University.* Carbondale: Southern Illinois UP, 2004. Print.

This collection exposes the "managed-labor problem in composition" from a variety of perspectives and collectively offers a range of solutions. Twenty-two chapters, with a foreword by Randy Martin, an introduction by Marc Bousquet, and an afterword by Gary Rhoades, are divided into four parts: Disciplinarity and Capitalist Ideology, Putting Labor First, Critiques of Managerialism, and Pedagogy and Possibility. Contributions include Marc Bousquet, "Composition as Management Science"; Donna Strickland, "The Managerial Unconscious of Composition Studies"; Bill Hendricks, "Making a Place for Labor: Composition and Unions"; Eileen E. Schell, "Toward a New Labor Movement in Higher Education:

Contingent Labor and Organizing for Change"; Eric Marshall, "Teaching Writing in a Managed Environment"; Ruth Kiefson, "The Politics and Economics of the Super-Exploitation of Adjuncts"; Tony Scott, "Managing Labor and Literacy in the Future of Composition Studies"; Amanda Godley and Jennifer Seibel Trainor, "Embracing the Logic of the Marketplace: New Rhetorics for the Old Problem of Labor in Composition"; Walter Jacobsohn, "Composition and the Future of Contingency: Labor and Identity in Composition"; Leo Parascondola, "'Write-to-Earn': College Writing and Management Discourse"; and Christopher Ferry, "Knowledge Work, Teaching Work, and Doing Composition."

495 CCCC Committee on Professional Standards. "A Progress Report from the CCCC Committee on Professional Standards." CCC 42.3 (Oct. 1991): 330–44. Print.

As the Statement of Professional Standards circulates around the country, its controversial points, as well as its supporters and detractors, have emerged. Clarifying the statement will encourage discussion and local implementation; thus, in the quest for "long-term systemic and curricular changes," committee members respond directly to criticism of the Statement of Professional Standards, e.g., the position that part-time positions should be maintained because some instructors *choose* to teach (only) part-time. The ambivalence of English departments toward "Freshman English" constitutes a great deal of the problem, but departments who claim to be content with the status quo should make sure that all those who teach writing are heard and are entitled to institutional support. Request for advisement, mediation, or censure must originate at the local level. Making the Wyoming Resolution a reality requires the help of all CCCC members as well as provosts, deans, chairs, WPAs, and faculty. The report ends with three recommendations for implementing and enforcing the provisions of the Wyoming Resolution.

496 CCCC Executive Committee. "Statement of Principles and Standards for the Postsecondary Teaching of Writing." CCC 40.3 (Oct. 1989): 329–36. Print.

The quality of writing instruction is "seriously compromised" by conditions for college teachers of writing. In response to this crisis at post-secondary institutions, the CCCC provides guidelines for effective writing programs to ensure that future generations of American students can read and write critically. The first set of recommendations, "Professional Standards That Promote Quality Education," refers to reports from the MLA and AAUP and addresses issues related to tenure-line faculty, graduate students, part-time faculty, and full-time temporary faculty. For example, "When more than ten percent of a department's course sections are taught by part-time faculty, the department should reconsider its hiring practices." The second set of recommendations pertains to "Teaching Conditions Necessary for Quality Education," for example, "No more than twenty students should be permitted in any writing class. Ideally, classes should be limited to fifteen." (This document was developed by the Wyoming Task Force and as a direct result of the Wyoming Resolution.)

497 Fontaine, Sheryl I., and Susan Hunter, eds. *Writing Ourselves into the Story: Unheard Voices from Composition Studies*. Carbondale: Southern Illinois UP, 1993. Print.

Every academic professional does not follow composition's proclaimed teaching norms. Pedagogical labels cannot classify every academic professional nor can every academic professional locate a specific point of entrance in the central narrative of composition studies, past or future. This collection serves as a response to trends in composition that make it "increasingly difficult for individuals to be heard in the rush of strengthening academic hierarchies." More important, though, it celebrates composition's eclectic, multivocal community of teachers and researchers by publishing the unheard perspectives of those who counter mainstream descriptions of the field through their teaching methods and written scholarship. Begins with an introduction by the editors, while each of the four parts of this collection ends with an "At the Risk of Being Personal . . ." narrative essay where the author shares a personal history with the discipline. Part I, Lives Under Cover, undermines the invisible pedagogy and includes Sarah Sloane, "Invisible Diversity: Gay and Lesbian Students Writing Our Way into the Academy"; Frances Ruhlen McConnel, "Freeway Flyers: The Migrant Workers of the Academy"; and Susan Hunter, "The Dangers of Teaching Differently." Part II, Seduction and Suspicion, rebels against the power structures within the discipline and includes Jeanne Gunner, "The Fate of the Wyoming Resolution: A History of Professional Seduction"; Marcia Dickson, "Directing Without Power: Adventures in Constructing a Model of Feminist Writing Programs Administration"; and Michael A. Pemberton, "Tales Too Terrible to Tell: Unstated Truths and Underpreparation in Graduate Composition Programs." Part III, But You Never Asked!, welcomes student voices and includes Wendy Bishop, "Students' Stories and the Variable Gaze of Composition Research"; Carol Lea Clark and Students of English 1803, "Student Voices: How Students Define Themselves as Writers"; and Patricia Prandini Buckler, Kay Franklin, and Thomas E. Young, "Privacy, Peers, and Process: Conflicts in the Composition Classroom." Part IV, Staking a Claim, raises the excluded professional voices of those within the discipline and includes Elizabeth A. Nist and Helon Howell Raines, "Writing in the Margins: A Search for Community College Voices"; and Nancy Mellin McCracken, Lois I. Green, and Claudia M. Greenwood, "Gender in Composition Research: A Strange Silence."

498 Harris, Joseph. "Meet the New Boss, Same as the Old Boss: Class Consciousness in Composition." CCC 52.1 (Sept. 2000): 42–68. Print.

Tenured professors in English studies have participated in "the ongoing exploitation of composition teachers." In the professional middle class, knowledge workers are neither capital nor labor, making discussions of class in America difficult and "fears of falling" endemic in academe. Despite attention to the issue of the exploitation of part-time teachers of writing, compositionists have turned this concern into an argument for disciplinary status, one that ignores working conditions for all. The key to improving the teaching of writing does *not* lie in establishing composition as a research field. A new form of class-consciousness might present opportunities for change if bosses and workers can work together to promote good teaching for fair pay. Harris presents three proposals for change.

499 Robertson, Linda R., Sharon Crowley, and Frank Lentricchia. "The Wyoming Conference Resolution Opposing Unfair Salaries and Working Conditions for Post-Secondary Teachers of Writing." *CE* 49.3 (Mar. 1987): 274–80. Print.

CCCC Committee on Professional Standards for Quality Education. "CCCC Initiatives on the Wyoming Conference Resolution: A Draft Report." *CCC* 40.1 (Feb. 1989): 61–72. Print.

MLA Commission on Writing and Literature. "Report of the Commission on Writing and Literature." *Profession* 88 (1988): 70–76. Print.

At the 1986 University of Wyoming summer conference on composition and literature, a protest was raised against the generally low professional status of composition scholars and the economic exploitation of many writing teachers. The resolution resulting from this protest calls on the CCCC to formulate standards for the working conditions of postsecondary writing teachers and to prescribe grievance and sanction procedures where these standards are not met. The resolution was unanimously endorsed at the Business Meeting of the 1987 CCCC Convention, and, in response, the CCCC Executive Committee created the Committee on Professional Standards for Quality Education, charged with delineating such standards and developing ways for the CCCC to support efforts at reform. The committee's draft report concludes with appendices on professional organizations and accrediting bodies to which teachers might appeal. At the 1989 CCCC Convention, the Executive Committee promulgated an official statement on professional standards. This statement offers guidelines on optimal teaching conditions as well as on the placement and evaluation of writing teachers who are tenure-line faculty, graduate students, part-time faculty, and full-time temporary faculty members. This statement also refers positively to the report of the MLA Commission on Writing and Literature, which provides guidelines for evaluating scholarship and professional activities in composition studies.

500 Schell, Eileen E. *Gypsy Academics and Mother Teachers: Gender, Contingent Labor, and Writing Instruction.* Portsmouth: Heinemann-Boynton/Cook, 1998. Print.

Research methodologies informed by socialist feminism—interviews, published narratives, and survey responses—document the perspectives of women who are disproportionally employed as contingent labor in writing instruction and allow intervention into the debates surrounding the erosion of faculty working conditions. Women seek or end up in nontenure-track positions for complex reasons, some of which date back to nineteenth-century gender ideologies and the disciplinary formation of English studies, but none of which can be neatly explained as women's desire for a "psychic income." Critiquing the maternal ethic of care in feminist pedagogy, building coalitions to reform working conditions, and developing professional development programs are all strategies to address women's roles in the academy. Schell ends with an analysis of four proposed solutions to reform working conditions for all contingent faculty; without endorsing any of the four, Schell argues for "academic citizenship" as essential to preserving academic freedom.

501 Schell, Eileen E., and Patricia Lambert Stock, eds. *Moving a Mountain: Transforming the Role of Contingent Faculty in Composition Studies and Higher Education*. Urbana: NCTE, 2001. Print.

A fiscal and historical context surrounds this fourteen-chapter collection, which proactively seeks a future with ethical employment practices for part-time and nontenure-track writing faculty. Aware of increasing enrollment rates, downward economic trends, and an ever-present pressure to teach despite these conditions, contributors write to persuade the academy that a working environment appropriate for both teaching and learning is needed. Includes an introduction by the editors and a select bibliography of Contingent Labor Issues in Composition Studies and Higher Education. Part I, Transforming the Cultural and Material Conditions of Contingent Writing Faculty: The Personal and the Institutional, consists of chapters written by Chris M. Anson and Richard Jewell, Barry M. Maid, Eva Brumberger, Carol Lipson and Molly Voorheis, and Helen O'Grady. Part II, Collectivity and Change in Non-Tenure-Track Employment: Collective Bargaining, Coalition Building, and Community Organizing, explores the importance of dialogue between the academy and faculty in order to change the current working environment, and includes contributions from Walter Jacobsohn, Karen Thompson, John C. Lovas, Nicholas Tingle and Judy Kirscht, Elana Peled et al., and Debra A. Benko. Part III, Rethinking Non-Tenure-Track Faculty Roles and Rewards, includes chapters by Danielle DeVoss, Dawn Hayden, Cynthia L. Selfe, and Richard J. Selfe Jr.; Patricia Lambert Stock, Amanda Brown, David Franke, and John Starkweather; and Eileen E. Schell.

Writing Centers and Supplemental Instruction

502 Blythe, Stuart. "Networked Computers + Writing Centers = ? Thinking about Networked Computers in Writing Center Practice." *Writing Center Journal* 17.2 (Spring 1997): 89–110. Print.

Writing centers have been rushing to add networked computer technologies to their services, but logistical questions have dominated ("How can this be done?") rather than theoretical questions. The latter are necessary for examining conceptions of technology that underlie discussions of networked writing-center services. Instrumental theories, the idea that technology is neutral, lead to a focus on purely logistical concerns and the belief that a center's basic mission will not change; substantive theories focus on the power of technology and the inevitable changes (for good or bad) that it will bring. Both theories are inadequate for researching theoretical questions; what's needed is a critical theory of technology (Feenberg) that can help to shape the designs of writing-center technologies.

503 Boquet, Elizabeth. *Noise from the Writing Center*. Logan: Utah State UP, 2002. Print.

Paying attention to the noise in (and about) the writing center allows for a new representation of writing centers. By embracing, even amplifying, the noise of the writing center—the feedback, distortion, dissonance, harmony, and repetition—we can come to recognize the writing center as a powerful place—a place where people go in search of information that might be excluded in more "efficient" systems, and as a place where teaching and learning are transformed into more performative processes.

504 Boquet, Elizabeth H. "'Our Little Secret': A History of Writing Centers, Pre- to Post-Open Admissions." CCC 50.3 (Feb. 1999): 463–82. Print.

Some forms of "secrecy" are endemic to the institutional position of writing centers because of the tension enacted there between institutional goals and individual pedagogies. A history of writing centers reveals a tension between time and space: "between the writing center whose identity rests on method and the writing center whose identity rests on site." Early writing centers evolved from a method of instruction but by the 1940s became a site—a place where, for example, students were sent by the institution for remediation. Open admissions writing centers, forced to take a defensive stance within their institutions, began to train peer tutors, furthering the implications of the site-method dichotomy. Boquet is most interested in the "excessive institutional possibilities" of writing centers—the ways in which they exceed their spaces and methods.

505 Boquet, Elizabeth H., and Neal Lerner. "Reconsiderations: After 'The Idea of a Writing Center.'" CE 71.2 (Nov. 2008): 170–89. Print.

Despite the number of writing-center publications in the past twenty-five years that cite it, Stephen North's 1984 article, "The Idea of a Writing Center," has functioned mostly as lore or as a shared ethos and has not led to a marked increase in writing-center research and scholarship or to a more central role for writing centers. The intellectual work of writing centers remains largely invisible in the major journals of English Studies. Ironically, North's article "became an ossifying force for the assumptions inherent in writing center work." Still, using reception studies can illuminate the processes by which a field becomes defined.

506 Brooks, Jeff. "Minimalist Tutoring: Making the Student Do All the Work." *Writing Lab Newsletter* 15.6 (Feb. 1991): 1–4. Print.

The tutor's job is not to improve papers (tempting though that is) but to improve writers. To avoid the temptation to edit, the tutor should follow simple rules: sit beside the student, keep the paper close to the student, don't hold a pen or pencil, and have the student read the paper aloud at the start of the conference to reinforce the student's authority and engagement. In addition, be sure to praise something in the paper, ask questions rather than give suggestions, and, if possible, have students do some writing. Don't allow students to force you to edit: they will ultimately appreciate your refusal to do so.

507 Bruffee, Kenneth A. "The Brooklyn Plan: Attaining Intellectual Growth through Peer-Group Tutoring." *Liberal Education* 64.4 (Dec. 1978): 447–68. Print.

Student tutors are sometimes more effective than teachers in helping other students gain confidence and ability in writing because the students are engaged socially and intellectually at once. In the Brooklyn Plan, tutors who have been trained in an advanced composition course help other students in expository composition. The tutors gain, too, by becoming more committed to quality in their own writing. Bruffee describes the tutor-training program.

508 Carino, Peter. "Open Admissions and the Construction of Writing Center History: A Tale of Three Models." *Writing Center Journal* 17.1 (Fall 1996): 30–48. Print.

A cultural model of writing-center history—drawing upon poststructuralist assumptions, thick descriptions, and untidy versions of progress—challenges both evolutionary and dialectic models, neither of which is adequate to representing center history from 1968 to 1983. Open admissions initiatives did not give birth to writing centers and were not central to debates on remediation. The evolutionary model—the idea that labs "have come a long way"—serves a political and rhetorical purpose but is too seamless as a narrative. The dialectic model offers a "heroic tale of resistance" to the lab as a remedial operation and reinforces the idea of centers as radically innovative. Using the Purdue lab in 1975 as one example, Carino demonstrates the more detailed history of the cultural model.

509 Geller, Anne Ellen, Michele Eodice, Frankie Condon, Meg Carroll, and Elizabeth H. Boquet. *The Everyday Writing Center: A Community of Practice*. Logan: Utah State UP, 2007. Print.

The idea of communities of practice (drawn from Etienne Wenger) invites writing-center directors to slow down, notice everyday exchanges, and cultivate habits of mind that resist the usual managerial modes.

"Trickster" moments, for example, provide opportunities to attend more closely to coincidences or unplanned occurrences; the Trickster rubs against tutor training textbooks and suggests the importance of more spontaneous, creative forms of staff development. Being a slave to time and efficiency structures writing centers in ways that squelch reflection or limit functional leadership. Supporting a learning culture for tutors is not simply about giving tips or advice; it means facilitating writerly identities. Embracing communities of practice also means breaking the silence about race in writing-center work.

510 Grimm, Nancy Maloney. *Good Intentions: Writing Center Work for Postmodern Times*. Portsmouth: Heinemann-Boynton/Cook, 1999. Print.

Postmodern theory, particularly because of its emphasis on diversity, subjectivity, and agency, engages writing-center practices in a reconsideration of literacy, fairness, and social justice. The good intentions of those who do and do not fully understand writing-center work must be disrupted. Given the regulatory nature of literacy, and given the fact that writing centers facilitate both literacy and assimilation into academic discourses, writing-center work is neither innocent nor ideologically neutral. Writing centers can, however, rise above their normalizing and gatekeeping functions. Writing centers can be not only places where students gain access to literacy, but also places where public and political action occurs. Recipient of the IWCA Outstanding Scholarship Award.

511 Grimm, Nancy Maloney. "The Regulatory Role of the Writing Center: Coming to Terms with a Loss of Innocence." *Writing Center Journal* 17.1 (Fall 1996): 5–29. Print.

Writing centers are often implicated in regulatory uses of literacy despite the innocence with which writing-center work is currently theorized. The institutional role of the writing center and its implication in disciplinary forms of power (Foucault) assumes that the problem of literacy has been located in the individual rather than in institutional practices and in academic discourse. The stories of two "successful" students who encountered normalizing practices illustrate how writing-center instruction is tied to an autonomous view of literacy, where individuals must master the code, rather than to an ideological view of literacy, where "proofreading," for example, becomes a complex "normalized cultural belief" that requires critical engagement.

512 Harris, Jeanette, and Joyce Kinkead, eds. *Writing Centers in Context: Twelve Case Studies*. Urbana: NCTE, 1993. Print.

Twelve circumstantial descriptions of working writing centers provide concrete details about how centers work. Each description follows the same outline: history, physical description (including a floor plan), chronology of a typical day, clientele, selection and training of tutors, types of services (including tutoring, testing, computers, WAC, etc.), administration (management, staff, budget), evaluation, research, and plans for the future. Centers described are at Purdue, Medgar Evers College, University of Toledo, Lehigh University, University of Southern California, Harvard, University of Puget Sound, Johnson County Community College, University of Washington, Utah State, and Colorado State. A concluding essay by Kinkead examines themes raised in the text. Includes bibliography and index.

513 Harris, Muriel. "Talking in the Middle: Why Writers Need Writing Tutors." *CE* 57.1 (Jan. 1995): 27–42. Print.

Tutoring should not be seen as an extension of other forms of instruction. In the one-to-one experience of working with a tutor, student writers gain knowledge that does not arise in other settings. The tutor is a middleperson mediating between the teacher and the student, a role teachers cannot truly take. The tutorial relationship is, moreover, flexible and conversational and therefore more personal than classroom interaction. Students feel helped rather than instructed by the tutor. Writing-center evaluations show that students prefer to do their own work, to reach their own conclusions—again, a situation not usually available in a class setting. Talking to a teacher, students feel pressured to perform rather than to think freely, as they can with a tutor. In the tutoring experience, students actually write, reread, and revise, gaining practical knowledge in collaboration with the tutor. Students can also express anxiety with a tutor, rarely if at all with a teacher. In their intermediate position, tutors are able to interpret academic language and ease the transition to a new discourse community. In short, writing instruction without a writing center would lack activities essential for students to mature as writers.

See: Muriel Harris, *Teaching One-to-One: The Writing Conference* [473].

514 Healy, Dave. "Countering the Myth on (In)dependence: Developing Life-Long Clients." *Writing Lab Newsletter* 18.9 (May 1994): 1–3. Print.

Metaphors of writing centers as clinics and clients as diseased cast the center as a place that should cure and discharge the client. One who returns is not fully cured. Although these metaphors have been thoroughly criticized, we still assume that the goal of the center is to make the client independent, to leave the center and not return. Those who do return signal the center's failure. But this view misrepresents the center's mission. Centers are not storehouses dispensing knowledge, but Burkean parlors where writers can discuss writing and get feedback. Writing, we know, is ongoing collaboration. The image of the solitary writer is a throwback. Why stigmatize those who seek the presence of others? A place where talk about writing occurs should hardly be seen as a place where there is an impoverished understanding of writing.

515 Hobson, Eric H., ed. *Wiring the Writing Center*. Logan: Utah State UP, 1998. Print.

An introduction by the editor and fourteen chapters discuss the possibilities and limitations of online applications for writing centers. Essays include David Coogan, "Email 'Tutoring' as Collaborative Writing"; Sara Kimball, "WAC on the Web: Writing Center Outreach to Teachers of Writing Intensive Courses"; Stuart Blythe, "Wiring a Usable Center: Usability Research and Writing Center Practice"; Neal Lerner, "Drill Pads, Teaching Machines, and Programmed Texts: Origins of Instructional Technology in Writing Centers"; and Ellen Mohr, "The Community College Mission and the Electronic Writing Center."

516 Hult, Christine, and Joyce Kinkead, eds. *Writing Centers Online*, a special issue of *Computers and Composition* 12.2 (1995). Print.

Twelve essays comprise this special issue, including Jane Nelson and Cynthia Wambeam, "Moving Computers into the Writing Center: The Path to Least Resistance"; Muriel Harris and Michael Pemberton, "Online Writing Labs (OWLS): A Taxonomy of Options and Issues"; David Coogan, "E-Mail Tutoring, a New Way to Do New Work"; Irene Clark, "Information Literacy and the Writing Center"; Gail Wood, "Making the Transition from ASL [American Sign Language] to English: Deaf Students, Computers, and the Writing Center"; and Cindy Johanek and Rebecca Rickly, "Online Tutor Training: Synchronous Conferencing in a Professional Community."

517 Kail, Harvey, and John Trimbur. "The Politics of Peer Tutoring." *WPA: Writing Program Administration* 11.1-2 (Fall/Winter 1987): 5–12. Print.

Peer tutoring may be based in the writing center or in the curriculum. The writing-center model makes tutoring voluntary and open with regard to the stage of writing or questions addressed. Its success depends on publicity and image. In the curriculum-based model, tutoring is required of writing students. More students see tutors this way, and the program is easier to administer. But in the curriculum-based model, tutors are part of the institution and share its authority, and this situation inhibits collaboration. The writing-center model is superior in this regard. Writing-center collaboration also challenges institutional authority and may demystify the institution's ideology of knowledge delivery.

518 Konstant, Shoshana Beth. "Multi-Sensory Tutoring for Multi-Sensory Learners." *Writing Lab Newsletter* 16.9-10 (May–June 1992): 6–8. Print.

Learning-disabled students—who are of average intelligence but have perceptual or processing problems—require a bit more creativity from tutors. First, find the student's strongest perceptual channel—visual, auditory, or kinesthetic. Many LD students know their best learning style or channel, so ask first. For visual learners, use charts, diagrams, colors, and gestures; for auditory learners, read aloud, use the tape recorder, and encourage the student to record classes and assignments; for kinesthetic learners, use physical objects and act out ideas. But don't be formulaic. Try a variety of approaches, use whatever works, and be patient.

519 Lerner, Neal. "Confessions of a First-Time Writing Center Director." *Writing Center Journal* 21.1 (Fall/Winter 2000): 29-48. Print.

Despite progress made since the 1981 CCCC resolution and the 1985 NWCA position statement on professional status for writing-center directors, the quest for professionalism remains a dilemma. A review of three surveys of writing-center directors reveals that the field continues to be split between the haves and the have-nots: those who have full-time or tenure-track positions, and those who have part-time, contingent, or staff positions. While tenure-track status may not be the goal of all involved in writing-center work, and while some argue that the pursuit of professional status may have more risks than benefits, a two-tiered system of writing-center directors harms the field as a whole. Ultimately, writing-center directors who "make it" to positions of institutional stability and leverage should work not only to transform their own institutions, but also to prevent this "haves and have-nots" structure of writing-center directors for the good of writing centers themselves. Winner of the IWCA Outstanding Scholarship Award.

520 Lerner, Neal. "Rejecting the Remedial Brand: The Rise and Fall of the Dartmouth Writing Clinic." CCC 59.1 (Sept. 2007): 13–35. Print.

The story of Dartmouth's Writing Clinic (1939–1960) offers a cautionary tale for writing programs when the perception of student abilities and achievements is at odds with the increasing popularity of universities' "branding" initiatives. Maintaining the institution's identity conflicted with the day-to-day workload for faculty: despite repeated efforts to persuade faculty to refer students to the clinic who were deficient rather than careless and to "get tough on student writing," faculty retreated to assigning less and less writing. When Dartmouth received a grant from the Carnegie Foundation to study student writing, Albert Kitzhaber argued for closing the Writing Clinic because it was, in fact, a barrier to developing a comprehensive writing program. Archival research and correspondence with alumni contribute to the conclusion that institutions are eliminating remedial services in order to build an identity—when underprepared students are unlikely to go away.

521 Lunsford, Andrea. "Collaboration, Control, and the Idea of a Writing Center." *Writing Center Journal* 12.1 (Fall 1991): 3–10. Print.

The idea of collaboration is based on a view of knowledge as socially constructed. Collaboration threatens the idea of the writing center as a storehouse of knowledge that prescribes skills and strategies to individual learners, given that the storehouse approach incorporates the assumption that knowledge is external and accessible. Collaboration also threatens the idea of the center as a writer's garret because that approach incorporates the assumption that knowledge is interior, within the student. Both kinds of centers do good work, but we must acknowledge the superiority of collaboration as a model of real-world writing, as an aid in problem-solving and to critical thinking, and as a route to excellence.

Collaborative centers are difficult to create because they require appropriate tasks and group cooperation. But the need to help students learn to work with others is paramount. Collaborative centers engage students not only in solving problems set by teachers but in identifying problems for themselves, negotiating issues of control, and valuing diversity.

522 Maxwell, Martha, ed. *When Tutor Meets Student*. 2nd ed. Ann Arbor: U of Michigan P, 1994. Print.

Fifty-four stories of tutoring encounters by student writing tutors at UC Berkeley. The tutors describe tutoring sessions and the process of defining their roles, dealing with cultural diversity and gender difference, and learning from their experiences. The stories, addressed to new tutors, reveal successes and failures, insights, techniques, personal dilemmas, and awkward situations (plagiarism, unwanted advances, problems with a teacher, tutor dependency). Includes, in appendices, descriptions of and paperwork for the UC Berkeley peer-tutoring center.

523 Meyer, Emily, and Louise Z. Smith. *The Practical Tutor*. New York: Oxford UP, 1987. Print.

Experienced writers who serve as tutors may take for granted the very skills most difficult for inexperienced writers to attain. The fourteen chapters of this textbook lead tutors through sets of problems and strategies for dealing with them: establishing a tutorial dialogue that maintains trust; dealing with anger and frustration; avoiding evaluation; using open-ended questions; promoting fluency through heuristics; deepening critical analysis and concept formation; using teachers' comments productively during revision; reclaiming the writer's authority over the text; addressing sentence-level errors, punctuation, spelling, vocabulary, and dialect-based errors; helping writers to develop reading strategies; and tutoring with computers. Writing assignments, suggestions for class activities, and a bibliography end each chapter.

524 Mullin, Joan, and Ray Wallace, eds. *Intersections: Theory-Practice in the Writing Center*. Urbana: NCTE, 1994. Print.

Fifteen essays explore and critique composition theories, particularly those concerning collaboration, as they have been and might be applied to writing-center practices. Included are Eric Hobson, "Writing Center Practice Often Counters Its Theory. So What?"; Sallyanne Fitzgerald, "Collaborative Learning and Whole Language Theory"; Christina Murphy, "The Writing Center and Social Constructionist Theory"; Alice Gillan, "Collaborative Learning Theory and Peer Tutoring Practice"; Julie Neff, "Learning Disabilities and the Writing Center"; Muriel Harris, "Individualized Instruction in Writing Centers: Attending to Cross-Cultural Differences"; Jay Jacoby, "'The Use of Force': Medical Ethics and Center Practice"; and Mary Abascal-Hildegrand, "Tutor and Student Relations: Applying Gadamer's Notions of Translation."

525 Murphy, Christina, and Joe Law, eds. *Landmark Essays on Writing Centers*. Davis: Hermagoras, 1995. Print.

Writing centers have had a place in American universities since the 1930s, and their methods have generally followed the theoretical directions of the profession as a whole. Twenty-one previously published essays examine the history, theory, and praxis of writing centers, including Lou Kelly, "One-on-One, Iowa City Style: Fifty Years of Individualized Writing Instruction"; Muriel Harris, "What's Up and What's In: Trends and Traditions in Writing Centers"; Gary Olson and Evelyn Ashton-Jones, "Writing Center Directors: The Search for Professional Status"; Judith Summerfield, "Writing Centers: A Long View"; Stephen North, "The Idea of a Writing Center"; Kenneth Bruffee, "Collaborative Learning and the 'Conversation of Mankind'" (see [186]); Lisa Ede, "Writing as a Social Process: A Theoretical Foundation for Writing Centers?"; Andrea Lunsford, "Collaboration, Control, and the Idea of a Writing Center"; Marilyn Cooper, "Really Useful Knowledge: A Cultural Studies Agenda for Writing Centers"; Harvey Kail and John Trimbur, "The Politics of Peer Tutoring"; and Meg Woolbright, "The Politics of Tutoring: Feminism within the Patriarchy."

526 Murphy, Christina, Joe Law, and Steve Sherwood. *Writing Centers: An Annotated Bibliography*. Westport: Greenwood, 1996. Print.

Part of a series of bibliographies and indexes in Education. Brief annotations accompany more than fourteen hundred entries in such categories as History, Program Descriptions, Professional Concerns, Writing Center Theory, Writing across the Curriculum, and Tutoring.

527 Murphy, Christina, and Byron L. Stay, eds. *The Writing Center Director's Resource Book*. Mahwah: Erlbaum, 2006. Print.

Thirty-nine chapters work conjointly to answer the central question in writing-center communities: "What knowledge do writing-center professionals need to have in order to do their best work?" Essays in Part I include Carl Glover, "Kairos and the Writing Center: Modern Perspectives on an Ancient Idea"; Stephen Ferruci and Susan DeRosa, "Writing a Sustainable History: Mapping Writing Center Ethos"; Pamela B. Childers, "Designing a Strategic Plan for a Writing Center"; Brad Peters, "Documentation Strategies and the Institutional Socialization of Writing Centers"; Kevin Dvorak and Ben Rafoth, "Examining Writing Center Director–Assistant Director Relationships"; Albert C. DeCiccio, "There's Something Happening Here: The Writing Center and Core Writing"; and Joan Mullin, Peter Carino, Jane Nelson, and Kathy Evertz, "Administrative (Chaos) Theory: The Politics and Practices of Writing Center Location." Part II includes Rebecca Moore Howard and Tracy Hamler Carrick, "Activist Strategies for Textual Multiplicity: Writing Center Leadership on Plagiarism and Authorship"; Christina Murphy, "On Not 'Bowling Alone' in the Writing Center, or Why Peer Tutoring Is an Essential Community for Writers and for Higher Education"; Muriel Harris, "Using Tutorial Principles to Train Tutors: Practicing Our Praxis"; Carol Peterson Haviland and Marcy Trianosky, "Tutors Speak: What Do We Want from Our Writing Center Directors?"; David

M. Sheridan, "Words, Images, Sounds: Writing Centers as Multiliteracy Centers"; Lisa Eastmond Bell, "Preserving the Rhetorical Nature of Tutoring When Going Online"; and Michael A. Pemberton, "Working with Faculty Consultants in the Writing Center: Three Guidelines and a Case History."

528 Nelson, Jane, and Kathy Evertz. *The Politics of Writing Centers*. Portsmouth: Heinemann-Boynton/Cook, 2001. Print.

Divided into two parts, "The Politics of Conversation," and "The Politics of Location," this collection of twelve essays examines conflict in writing center politics, and points out opportunities and recommendations for change. Included are Peter Carino, "Writing Centers and Writing Programs: Local and Communal Politics"; Pat McQueeney, "What's in a Name?"; Carrie Shirley Leverenz, "Graduate Students in the Writing Center: Confronting the Cult of (Non)Expertise"; Carol Peterson Haviland, Carmen M. Fye, and Richard Colby, "The Politics of Administrative and Physical Location"; Pamela B. Childers and James K. Upton, "Political Issues in Secondary School Writing Centers"; Eric Hobson and Kelly Lowe, "An Audit of the National Writing Centers Association's Growth"; and Christina Murphy and Joe Law, "The Disappearing Writing Center Within the Disappearing Academy: The Challenges and Consequences of Outsourcing in the Twenty-First Century." Winner of the IWCA Outstanding Scholarship Award.

See: Marie Nelson, *At the Point of Need: Teaching Basic and ESL Writers* [781].

529 North, Stephen M. "The Idea of a Writing Center." *CE* 46.5 (Sept. 1984): 433–46. Print. Rpt. in Graves [571].

English-department faculty have a false sense of what goes on in the writing center. This makes it difficult to dispel their notion of the center as a fix-it shop that deals with "special problems" in composition, corrects mechanical errors, and serves only poor writers. Such ideas created the skill-and-drill model that most writing centers have battled to escape. Writing centers attempt to produce better writers, not better writing, through a student-centered, process-oriented approach, which chiefly means talking to writers about writing. Teachers should not send students to the center—students must come when they are ready to talk about writing. Writing centers are gaining recognition, but institutional and faculty support leave much room for improvement.

530 Olson, Gary A., ed. *Writing Centers: Theory and Administration*. Urbana: NCTE, 1984. Print.

Nineteen essays on theory, administration, and special concerns include Kenneth A. Bruffee, "Collaborative Learning and the 'Conversation of Mankind'" (see [186]); Stephen M. North, "Writing Center Research: Testing Our Assumptions"; Patrick Hartwell, "The Writing Center and the Paradoxes of Written-Down Speech"; Linda Bannister-Wills,

"Developing a Peer Tutor Program"; and Alexander Friedlander, "Meeting the Needs of Foreign Students in the Writing Center."

531 Pemberton, Michael A. "Rethinking the WAC/Writing Center Connection." *Writing Center Journal* 15.2 (Spring 1995): 116–33. Print.

The relationship between writing-across-the-curriculum programs and writing centers needs to be reconsidered because, despite the pedagogical focus they share, their epistemologies and assumptions about rhetorical and textual features differ significantly. The "pedagogy of the generic" common to writing centers — where tutors apply common principles to all academic texts and genres — may do a disservice to students in WAC programs, where writers are expected to follow discipline-specific practices. "Conscious myopia" and the "myth of disciplinarity" characterize the typical ways that WAC and writing centers work together, both of which allow tutors to sidestep the challenges of disciplinary discourse. Pemberton recommends two roles that writing centers can play to support WAC programs.

532 Pemberton, Michael A., and Joyce Kinkead, eds. *The Center Will Hold: Critical Perspectives on Writing Center Scholarship*. Logan: Utah State UP, 2003. Print.

In honor of the contributions of Muriel Harris, who published the first issue of *Writing Lab Newsletter* in 1977, this volume offers a critical perspective on writing-center scholarship. Ten chapters follow an introduction by the editors: Michael A. Pemberton, "The Writing Lab Newsletter as History: Tracing the Growth of a Scholarly Community"; Nancy M. Grimm, "In the Spirit of Service: Making Writing Center Research a 'Featured Character'"; Neal Lerner, "Writing Center Assessment: Searching for the 'Proof' of Our Effectiveness"; Harvey Kail, "Separation, Initiation, and Return: Tutor Training Manuals and Writing Center Lore"; Peter Carino, "Power and Authority in Peer Tutoring"; Michele Eodice, "Breathing Lessons, or Collaboration Is"; Rebecca Jackson, Carrie Leverenz, and Joe Law, "(RE)Shaping the Profession: Graduate Courses in Writing Center Theory, Practice, and Administration"; Josephine A. Koster, "Administration across the Curriculum: Or Practicing What We Preach"; Leslie Hadfield, et al., "An Ideal Writing Center: Re-Imagining Space and Design"; and James A. Inman and Donna N. Sewell, "Mentoring in Electronic Spaces: Using Resources to Sustain Relationships." Winner of the IWCA Outstanding Scholarship Award.

533 Rafoth, Ben, ed. *A Tutor's Guide: Helping Writers One to One*. Portsmouth: Heinemann-Boynton/Cook, 2000. Print.

Fifteen essays offer experienced perspectives on dealing with problems in tutorial sessions. Each essay describes a particular problem, contextualizes it in writing-center theory and practice, offers concrete suggestions for handling the problem, and then discusses counterarguments and complications. Each essay also includes an annotated list of further reading. Selections include William J. Macauley Jr., "Setting the Agenda for the Next 30 Minutes"; Molly Wingate, "What Line? I Don't See Any Line"; Muriel Harris, "Talk to Me: Engaging Reluctant Writers"; Lea Masiello, "Style in the Writing Center: It's a Matter of Choice and Voice"; Ben Rafoth, "Helping Writers to Write Analytically"; Jennifer J. Ritter, "Recent Developments in Assisting ESL Writers"; Beth Rapp Young, "Can You Proofread This?"; and Mary Mortimore Dossin, "Using Others' Words: Quoting, Summarizing and Documenting Sources." The collection ends with six topics for staff discussion and reflection.

534 Silk, Bobbie Bayliss, ed. *The Writing Center Resource Manual.* Emmitsburg: National Writing Centers, 1998. Print.

This collection of practical essays is designed for those starting or managing a writing center. Essays include Jeanne Simpson, "Assessing Needs, Identifying an Institutional Home, and Developing a Proposal"; Clinton Gardner, "Centering the Community College Writing Center"; Stuart Blythe, "Technology in the Writing Center: Strategies for Implementation and Maintenance"; Paula Gillespie and Jon Olson, "Tutor Training"; Anne E. Mullin, "Serving Clients with Learning Disabilities"; Joe Law, "Serving Faculty and Writing across the Curriculum"; and Neal Lerner, "Research in the Writing Center."

535 Simpson, Jeanne. "The Challenge of Innovation: Putting New Approaches into Practice." *Writing Lab Newsletter* 18.1 (Sept. 1993): 1–3. Print.

Writing centers face, like the rest of the academy, threats of budget cuts and calls for accountability. It would be a mistake to be defensive in this situation. Rather, we should see opportunities here. It is important to participate in the processes of institutional change. The growth of writing centers so far has come from steady work and innovation, not from revolution, a process to be continued in the new era. We must tell our stories better to all academic constituencies, connecting with institutional governance in ways that are presently not typical. Institutional service has not been seen as part of the career path for center directors, but it is the path of change.

536 Vandenberg, Peter. "Lessons of Inscription: Tutor Training and the 'Professional Conversation.'" *Writing Center Journal* 19.2 (Spring/Summer 1999): 59–83. Print.

The role of student tutors warrants careful consideration in writing-center work. Because of the nature of writing-center work, the "student" status of student tutors, and the view of the interaction between tutors and directors as "education," student tutors run the risk of perpetuating institutional and professional values in which authority and hierarchy are already inscribed. While student tutors may come to writing centers already understanding writing practices, they may not necessarily understand the academic institutional practices that use literacy to measure competence and establish hierarchy. Those who work in tutor training should be cautious not to engage student tutors in the replication of problematic models of professionalism.

Writing across the Curriculum and Writing in the Disciplines

537 Anderson, Worth, Cynthia Best, Alycia Black, John Hurst, Brandt Miller, and Susan Miller. "Cross-Curricular Underlife: A Collaborative Report on Ways with Academic Words." CCC 41.1 (Feb. 1990): 11–36. Print.

Five students and their teacher observed language use in several courses, discovering how it differed from the freshman-composition image of academic discourse. Teachers and students did not seem to form discourse communities but maintained separate views of their roles and of appropriate language use. The writing course did prepare students to analyze and imitate writing in other courses, but its model of collaborative knowledge-making did not match the practice in other courses. Recording their motives for taking courses, enrollment and attendance, and types of writing assigned for each of sixteen courses, the students describe teachers', students', and their own uses of language for learning—or, rather, for succeeding in each class. There were few formal assignments; the audience approach taught in the writing course did help students decide what was called for in each class in all language interactions. Note taking was the writing skill most needed in all courses.

538 Anson, Chris M., John E. Schwiebert, and Michael M. Williamson. *Writing across the Curriculum: An Annotated Bibliography*. Westport: Greenwood, 1993. Print.

A bibliography of 1,067 items, with annotations of about fifty words each, in eleven categories. Part I, on scholarship, is subdivided into bibliographies, collections, history and implementation, research studies, and theory. Part II, on pedagogy, is subdivided into general, arts and humanities, math and science, social science, business and economics, and textbooks.

539 Bazerman, Charles, and David R. Russell, eds. *Landmark Essays on Writing across the Curriculum*. Davis: Hermagoras, 1994. Print.

Thirteen essays on history, programs, pedagogy, and writing in disciplines include Bazerman and Russell, "The Rhetorical Tradition and Specialized Discourses"; David Russell, "American Origins of the Writing-across-the-Curriculum Movement"; Toby Fulwiler, "How Well Does Writing across the Curriculum Work?" [542]; James L. Kinneavy, "Writing across the Curriculum" [547]; Susan McLeod, "Writing across the Curriculum: The Second Stage, and Beyond"; Janet Emig, "Writing as a Mode of Learning" [382]; Charles Bazerman, "What Written Knowledge Does: Three Examples of Academic Discourse" [172]; and Greg Myers, "The Social Construction of Two Biologists' Proposals."

540 Blair, Catherine Pastore. "Only One of the Voices: Dialogic Writing across the Curriculum." *CE* 50.4 (Apr. 1988): 383–89. Print.

The social theory of knowledge that informs the writing-across-the-curriculum movement suggests that each academic discipline has its own way of using language, which makes sense only in the disciplinary context. The discipline of English studies knows only its own discourse, not all the others, and not some generic academic discourse. There is, therefore, no reason to entrust all writing instruction to the English department. A better writing-across-the-curriculum program would be taught by professors from all disciplines, whose dialogues over the common writing curriculum would reveal the discursive properties of each discipline in contrast to the others. Composition specialists could serve as consultants to such programs. See Smith [558].

541 Fulwiler, Toby. "The Argument for Writing across the Curriculum." *Writing across the Disciplines: Research into Practice*. Ed. Art Young and Toby Fulwiler. Upper Montclair: Boynton/Cook, 1986. 21–32. Print.

Three principles that underlie writing across the curriculum should be elaborated in faculty workshops: that composing is a complex intellectual process of making choices and making meaning; that writing is a mode of learning that calls for expressive as well as transactional composing; and that writing problems arise from a variety of sources, including attitude, skills, and knowledge. Two pedagogical challenges are also at issue in workshops: making good assignments and evaluating or responding to student writing. Good assignment design includes setting up a context, allowing time for the composing process, varying the audience, and giving clear directions. Evaluation should, among other things, be positive and specific and focus on content.

542 Fulwiler, Toby. "How Well Does Writing across the Curriculum Work?" *CE* 46.2 (Feb. 1984): 113–25. Print. Rpt. in Fulwiler [541].

The interdisciplinary writing workshops at Michigan Technological University introduced the idea that writing can promote learning in all areas. After six years, the program seems to have enjoyed uneven success. Problems have included misunderstanding of special terminology (chiefly "expressive writing"); resistance by suspicious faculty members; conflicts with some members of the English and philosophy departments about language theory; inability to apply the ideas generated in the workshops to some classes, especially large ones; distrust of the peer-review technique and lack of commitment to methods that require it; and lack of reinforcement by the administration. But benefits have included the growth of a community of scholars, a general sense that the program has helped improve students' ability to communicate, more writing by faculty members in the program, greater sensitivity to pedagogy, development of collaborative projects among participants in the program, and more cohesion in the writing department itself.

543 Fulwiler, Toby, and Art Young, eds. *Language Connections: Writing and Reading across the Curriculum*. Urbana: NCTE, 1982. Print.

Twelve essays describe the writing-across-the-curriculum program at Michigan Technological University. Essays include Toby Fulwiler, "The Personal Connection: Journal Writing across the Curriculum"; Toby Fulwiler and Robert Jones, "Assigning and Evaluating Transactional Writing"; Peter Schiff, "Responding to Writing: Peer Critiques, Teacher-Student Conferences, and Essay Evaluation"; Diana Freisinger and Jill Burkland, "Talking about Writing: The Role of the Writing Lab"; and Bruce Petersen, "A Select Bibliography" (annotated).

544 Goldblatt, Eli. *Because We Live Here: Sponsoring Literacy Beyond the College Curriculum*. Cresskill: Hampton, 2007. Print.

Relationship building in local communities can lead to a comprehensive writing program that goes beyond the curriculum, one that continually asks the question, "Who is serving whom?" John Dewey's work inspires a set of principles for writing-program design that emphasize the relationships between student, school, and the larger society. In addition, Saul Alinsky's work on community organizing offers a model for putting neighborhood needs first—before traditional curricular requirements—and to see community-based learning from the point of view of the community. Metropolitan universities like Temple can benefit from various forms of knowledge activism. Data—statistical and observational—collected through a project of visiting schools helps build an understanding of where Temple's students come from and establishes the need for joint literacy sponsorship and deep alignment between community and institutional programs. A framework for literacy sponsorship that includes multiple partnerships within a region will serve most postsecondary students better than a traditional view of writing contained by campus boundaries. The chapters profile such partnerships and suggest ways to reconsider writing programs.

545 Griffin, C. Williams, ed. *Teaching Writing in All Disciplines*. San Francisco: Jossey-Bass, 1982. Print.

Ten essays on writing-across-the-curriculum programs, teaching writing in disciplines other than English, and teaching techniques for using writing as learning include Toby Fulwiler, "Writing: An Act of Cognition"; Barbara King, "Using Writing in the Mathematics Class: Theory and Practice"; Dean Drenk, "Teaching Finance Through Writing"; and Elaine P. Maimon, "Writing across the Curriculum: Past, Present, and Future" [550].

546 Herrington, Anne, and Charles Moran, eds. *Writing, Teaching, and Learning in the Disciplines*. New York: MLA, 1992. Print.

Fourteen essays examine the history, theoretical coherence, and pedagogical practices of writing across the curriculum, including Nancy

Martin, "Language across the Curriculum: Where It Began and What It Promises"; David Russell, "American Origins of the Writing-across-the-Curriculum Movement"; James Britton, "Theories of the Disciplines and a Learning Theory"; Charles Bazerman, "From Cultural Criticism to Disciplinary Participation: Living with Powerful Words"; Jacqueline Jones Royster, "From Practice to Theory: Writing across the Disciplines at Spelman College"; Toby Fulwiler, "Writing and Learning American Literature"; Joy Marsella, Thomas Hilgers, and Clemence McLaren, "How Students Handle Writing Assignments: A Study of Eighteen Responses in Six Disciplines"; Louise Dunlap, "Advocacy and Neutrality: A Contradiction in the Discourse of Urban Planners"; and Anne Herrington and Charles Moran, "Writing in the Disciplines: A Prospect."

547 Kinneavy, James L. "Writing across the Curriculum." *ADE Bulletin* 76 (Winter 1983): 14–21. Print.

Writing across the curriculum responds to concerns about declining literacy and reasserts the importance of rhetoric in the liberal arts curriculum. Writing across the curriculum takes two forms: writing-intensive courses in all departments and courses in writing for other disciplines offered by the English or writing department. In the first kind of program, the teacher is an expert in the discipline and knows its vocabulary and genres. Students can thus use highly technical language and discipline-specific forms of writing. But such programs reinforce disciplinary isolation and create a heavy burden of writing instruction for teachers untrained in composition. In the second kind of program, esoteric material, technical vocabulary, subtle methodology, and distinctiveness may be sacrificed, but with gains in writing expertise and an opportunity to open a large academic conversation and perhaps, ultimately, an educated public discourse. A well-designed program benefits from both approaches by offering different kinds of writing courses "vertically" throughout the college experience.

548 Kirscht, Judy, Rhonda Levine, and John Reiff. "Evolving Paradigms: WAC and the Rhetoric of Inquiry." CCC 45.3 (Oct. 1994): 369–80. Print.

The WAC movement continues to be divided between the writing-to-learn model—in which writing is seen as an integral part of the learning process in all disciplines—and the writing-in-the-disciplines model—which studies the discourse communities of the disciplines and brings that knowledge to the writing class. WAC proponents are deeply divided along these lines. The social-constructionist view of disciplines as rhetorically negotiated territory resolves the conflict by treating writing-to-learn as an inquiry into the ways that knowledge is produced in the disciplines. Disciplinary forms and conventions are not separated from the writing process but are presented as communally accepted ways of looking at a particular subject matter, forms that can then be analyzed to determine how they shape the knowledge they produce.

549 Maimon, Elaine P. "Maps and Genres: Exploring Connections in the Arts and Sciences." *Composition and Literature: Bridging the Gap*. Ed. Winifred Bryan Horner [626]. Chicago: U of Chicago P, 1983. 110–25. Print.

We need to know the forms and traditions of writing in all disciplines in order to fill in the largely uncharted territory we label "nonfiction prose" on our maps of the genres of writing. Trained in literary criticism, we are well suited to exploring the relation of discipline-specific genres to modes of thought in the discipline. Just as the lyric poet writes within and against the structure of his genre, so too the scientist works through the conventions, rituals, and assumptions of lab reports and other genres. Writing students should understand the concept of genre and practice several academic genres. The "modes of discourse" and "composing process" approaches may obscure questions of audience, purpose, and disciplinary method—questions that concern writing as it is used in the academic community—but these approaches can lead to writing that does enter the academic conversation.

550 Maimon, Elaine P. "Writing across the Curriculum: Past, Present, and Future." *Teaching Writing in All Disciplines*. Ed. C. Williams Griffin [545]. San Francisco: Jossey-Bass, 1982. 67–73. Print.

The development of writing-across-the-curriculum programs has been an effort to make writing an integral part of the learning process in all courses. This effort reinforced the shift in composition pedagogy from a product to a process orientation because the learning process and the writing process work together. Writing across the curriculum has also promoted collaborative-learning techniques. Process pedagogy requires many drafts and much feedback, and small groups of students can provide each other with audience feedback that may be even more valuable than the teacher's responses. Writing-across-the-curriculum programs are helping students find "an authentic voice in the community of educated people."

551 Martin, Nancy, ed. *Writing across the Curriculum Pamphlets: A Selection from the Schools Council and London University Institute of Education Joint Project: Writing across the Curriculum*. 1973, 1974, 1975. Rpt. Upper Montclair: Boynton/Cook, 1983. Print.

James Britton's colleagues, who worked with British schoolchildren of elementary and high school age, offer assignment suggestions and samples of student writing. Included are Nancy Martin, Peter Medway, and Harold Smith, "From Information to Understanding: What Children Do with New Ideas"; Nancy Martin, Peter Medway, Harold Smith, and Pat D'Arcy, "Why Write?"; Peter Medway, "From Talking to Writing"; Pat D'Arcy, "Keeping Options Open: Writing in the Humanities"; and selections from *Writing in Science* (essays by Sue Watts and Jeff Shapland) and *Language and Learning in the Humanities* (essays by Bryan Newton, and Peter Medway and Ivor Goodson).

552 McLeod, Susan H., and Margot Iris Soven, eds. *Composing a Community: A History of Writing Across the Curriculum*. West Lafayette: Parlor, 2006. Print.

This eleven-chapter collection serves as a history of early WAC programs as told by the scholars who played a significant part in the launch of the movement. Includes an introduction by David R. Russell, "WAC's Beginnings: Developing a Community of Change Agents." Contributions are as follows: Elaine P. Maimon, "It Takes a Campus to Teach a Writer: WAC and the Reform of Undergraduate Education"; Christopher Thaiss, "A University-Schools Partnership: WAC and the National Writing Project at George Mason University"; Charles Bazerman and Anne Herrington, "Circles of Interest: The Growth of Research Communities in WAC and WID/WIP"; Carol R. Holder and Susan H. McLeod, "The Start of Writing in the Disciplines/Writing Across the Curriculum in the California State University System"; Margot Soven, "WAC Becomes Respectable: The University of Chicago Institutes on Writing and Higher Order Reasoning"; Peshe Kuriloff and Linda Peterson, "Writing Across the Curriculum in the Ivy Consortium"; John C. Bean, "Montana, Mina Shaughnessy, and Microthemes: Reflections on WAC as a Community"; Christopher Thaiss, "Still a Good Place to Be: More than 20 Years of the National Network of WAC Programs"; Barbara E. Walvoord, "Gender and Discipline in Two Early WAC Communities: Lessons for Today"; Toby Fulwiler, with additions by Art Young, "Writing Across the Michigan Tech Curriculum"; and Sam Watson, "My Story of Wildacres, 1983–1998."

553 McLeod, Susan H., Eric Miraglia, Margot Iris Soven, and Christopher Thaiss, eds. *WAC for the New Millennium: Strategies for Continuing Writing-Across-the-Curriculum Programs*. Urbana: NCTE, 2001. Print.

Twelve chapters actively address how WAC programs have maintained stability within the ever-changing academic environment and suggest strategies and possible new research directions to ensure that WAC programs continue to help shape the future of higher education. Includes a foreword by Elaine P. Maimon and the following chapters: Susan H. McLeod and Eric Miraglia, "Writing Across the Curriculum in a Time of Change"; William Condon, "Accommodating Complexity: WAC Program Evaluation in the Age of Accountability"; Donna Reiss and Art Young, "WAC Wired: Electronic Communication Across the Curriculum"; David A. Jolliffe, "Writing Across the Curriculum and Service Learning: Kairos, Genre, and Collaboration"; Terry Meyers Zawacki and Ashley Taliaferro Williams, "Is It Still WAC? Writing within Interdisciplinary Learning Communities"; Ann M. Johns, "ESL Students and WAC Programs: Varied Populations and Diverse Needs"; Victor Villanueva, "The Politics of Literacy Across the Curriculum"; Joan A. Mullin, "Writing Centers and WAC"; Margot Soven, "Curriculum-Based Peer Tutors and WAC"; Martha A. Townsend, "Writing Intensive Courses and WAC"; David R. Russell, "Where Do the Naturalistic Studies of

WAC/WID Point? A Research Review"; and Christopher Thaiss, "Theory in WAC: Where Have We Been, Where Are We Going?"

554 McLeod, Susan, and Margot Soven, eds. *Writing across the Curriculum: A Guide to Developing Programs.* Newbury Park: Sage, 1992. Print.

Twelve essays on the practical elements of setting up and developing WAC programs include Barbara Walvoord, "Getting Started"; Joyce Neff Magnetto and Barbara Stout, "Faculty Workshops"; Linda Peterson, "Writing across the Curriculum and/in the Freshman English Program"; Christine Farris and Raymond Smith, "Writing-Intensive Courses: Tools for Curricular Change"; Christopher Thaiss, "WAC and General Education Courses"; Muriel Harris, "The Writing Center and Tutoring in WAC Programs"; and Tori Haring-Smith, "Changing Students' Attitudes: Writing Fellows Programs."

555 Parks, Steve, and Eli Goldblatt. "Writing beyond the Curriculum: Fostering New Collaborations in Literacy." *CE* 62.5 (May 2000): 584–606. Print.

The standard structure of college writing programs makes it difficult to respond to increasing external demands, such as building stronger relationships with surrounding communities. As several voices in the field call for an expanded WAC, one that can combine discipline-based instruction with increased literacy experiences for undergraduates, the Institute for the Study of Literature, Literacy, and Culture at Temple University is one response to that call. The Institute reconceptualizes WAC with its alliance of university, public school, and community educators. An advisory board, fellows, and a director contribute to achieving the overall goal of integrating educational communities. One result is New City Press, designed to publish community-based histories and narratives or such publications as a coach's handbook for local baseball leagues. Maintaining focus, gathering support, and building alliances will continue to be significant challenges for sustaining university writing programs that stretch beyond the curriculum and campus.

556 Reiss, Donna, Dickie Selfe, and Art Young, eds. *Electronic Communication across the Curriculum.* Urbana: NCTE, 1998. Print.

Three sections of essays—programs, partnerships, and classrooms—explore the intersections of WAC theory and practice and electronic communication and present a number of strategies for approaching ECAC. Essays include Gail E. Hawisher and Michael A. Pemberton, "Writing across the Curriculum Encounters Asynchronous Learning Networks"; Mary E. Hocks and Daniele Bascelli, "Building a Writing-Intensive Multimedia Curriculum"; Stuart A. Selber and Bill Karis, "Composing Human-Computer Interfaces across the Curriculum in Engineering Schools"; Todd Taylor, "Teacher Training: A Blueprint for Action Using the World Wide Web"; Teresa M. Redd, "Accommodation and Resistance on (the Color) Line: Black Writers Meet White Artists on the Internet"; Margaret Portillo and Gail Summerskill

Cummins, "Creativity, Collaboration, and Computers"; Paula Gillespie, "E-Journals: Writing to Learn in the Literature Classroom"; and Maryanne Felter and Daniel F. Schultz, "Network Discussions for Teaching Western Civilization."

See: David R. Russell, *Writing in the Academic Disciplines: A Curricular History* [166].

557 Smagorinsky, Peter. "Constructing Meaning in the Disciplines: Reconceptualizing Writing across the Curriculum as Composing across the Curriculum." *American Journal of Education* 103.2 (Feb. 1995): 160–84. Print.

Writing is only one way to promote thinking across the curriculum; its appropriateness as a medium depends on several factors. Theories based on semiotics and multiple intelligences challenge the privileged status of writing for the development of thought. Instead of embracing writing as a unique mode of learning, "each discipline should endorse the notion that meaning construction is the goal of learning," with the medium dependent on the discipline's values as well as the participants' consensus in the transaction. The author's exploratory research on the production of nonwritten texts suggests that an exclusive focus on writing as a mode of learning limits students' abilities to develop conceptual knowledge. Nonwritten texts are also valuable in English classes, where students should be invited to compose and develop interpretations of literature from a variety of media.

558 Smith, Louise Z. "Why English Departments Should 'House' Writing across the Curriculum." *CE* 50.4 (Apr. 1988): 390–95. Print.

Catherine Blair's account [540] of writing-across-the-curriculum theory is correct. She errs, however, in asserting that English departments can know only their own discipline-specific discourse. Postmodern literary theory blurs disciplinary boundaries by analyzing the influence of canonical cultural artifacts on the supposedly value-neutral discourse of other academic disciplines and by denying the distinction between literary and nonliterary language. Thus, English departments contain many scholars, including composition specialists, who have expertise in examining the relationship between language and knowledge and how these relationships might be taught. The authoritative influence of compositionists may be necessary to prevent mere editing across the curriculum even as we learn about disciplinary discourses from novice writing teachers from other departments.

See: Christopher Thaiss and Terry Myers Zawacki, *Engaged Writers, Dynamic Disciplines: Research on the Academic Writing Life* [589].

559 Walvoord, Barbara E. "The Future of WAC." *CE* 58.1 (Jan. 1996): 58–79. Print.

The twenty-fifth anniversary of Writing across the Curriculum provides an opportunity for long-range planning and for interpreting WAC's past—both of which can be done through examining WAC as a social movement organization. For example, the literature on "movements" highlights early choices made by WAC to focus on micro, rather than on macro, concerns; to choose strategies that depended on changing behavior by persuasion; and to make workshops the backbone of the movement. Now, WAC must refocus its attention on macro issues, most significantly the need to work with other organizations and to become active in national debates about educational reform. WAC must also define its relationship to administrations, explore the implications of new technologies, and contribute to debates on assessment. As a mature reform organization, WAC must draw upon the power of community so evident in early workshops.

See: Vivian Zamel, "Strangers in Academia: The Experiences of Faculty and ESL Students across the Curriculum" [793].

Curriculum Development

Course Development

560 Adams, Katherine H. "Bringing Rhetorical Theory into the Advanced Writing Class." *Rhetoric Review* 3.2 (1985): 184–89. Print.

Rhetorical theory and research in writing can enhance advanced writing courses. Advanced students are capable of appreciating empirical research. They identify, for example, with the problems attested to by writers in protocol analyses and learn from the research on the effects of revision. Testimony by professional writers can encourage students to see the connection between writing and their own disciplines and careers. Grounding in the history of rhetoric reinforces students' sense of the importance and value of speaking to real audiences. The theories of Plato and others can be effectively applied to current examples of attempted persuasion. Research on heuristics can be an antidote to the current-traditional model that most students learned in freshman composition. This material does not need to become the course, but can be incorporated in workshops and discussions.

561 Adams, Katherine H., and John L. Adams, eds. *Teaching Advanced Composition: Why and How?* Portsmouth: Heinemann-Boynton/Cook, 1991. Print.

Nineteen essays, seven on theory and the problem of distinguishing advanced from freshman courses, and twelve on approaches to teaching. Essays include Elizabeth Penfield, "Freshman English/Advanced Writing: How Do We Distinguish the Two?"; William Covino, "The Grammar of Advanced Writing"; Michael Carter, "What Is Advanced about Advanced Composition? A Theory of Expertise in Writing"; Michael Keene and Ray Wallace, "Advanced Writing Courses and Programs"; Mary Fuller, "Teaching Style in Advanced Writing Courses"; Sam Watson, "Letters on Writing—A Medium of Exchange with Students of Writing"; Jeanne Fahnestock, "Teaching Argumentation in the Junior-Level Course"; Timothy Donovan and Janet Carr, "'Real World' Research: Writing Beyond the Curriculum"; and Lynn Bloom, "Creative Nonfiction, Is There Any Other Kind?" Includes "Afterword: Needed Scholarship in Advanced Composition" by Gary Olson, and an annotated bibliography of twenty-eight articles on advanced composition.

562 Bartholomae, David, and Anthony R. Petrosky. *Facts, Artifacts, and Counterfacts*. Upper Montclair: Boynton/Cook, 1986. Print.

Basic writers can learn to use academic discourse in a course that asks them to read difficult nonfiction books and write about their reading processes. The students find that all reading requires interpretation and that interpretive methods are inevitably culture-bound. They thus come to see that their "problem" as basic writers exists in their use of nonacademic or imperfectly assimilated academic interpretive methods. As they become more familiar with the language and methods of the university, they can create authoritative, academically successful personae in their writing. This book explains the theory behind the authors' University of Pittsburgh course and reproduces course materials, including twenty-four sequenced writing assignments. It also includes chapters by their colleagues on revising, correcting errors, and using personal writing to develop a dialogue between student and text.

563 Brooke, Robert. *Writing and Sense of Self: Identity Negotiation in Writing Workshops*. Urbana: NCTE, 1991. Print.

Learning to write requires seeing oneself as a person who uses writing to solve problems and accomplish purposes in many areas of one's life, not only in school. To foster this vision, the writing class should encourage students to try on various social roles in their writing and to negotiate a writer's identity for themselves. The teacher should coach apprentices and offer instruction about writing (writing processes, formal rules, etc.) only as needed to help students write what they want. This approach also encourages students to use writing to address public problems beyond the classroom.

564 Brooke, Robert, Ruth Mirtz, and Rick Evans. *Small Groups in Writing Workshops*. Urbana: NCTE, 1994. Print.

Writing groups facilitate four elements that are essential to a writer's life: time for writing, ownership of the uses of writing, a community of responders, and exposure to other people's writing. Groups are complex communities, with social and emotional challenges for students. Such challenges are opportunities for learning to deal with differences of many kinds. Teachers are challenged, too, to see themselves as writers in communities and to formulate successful pedagogies. Teachers must, for example, facilitate student role experimentation in groups, design writing activities, provide rules for response, adjust rules as needed, monitor group dynamics, and evaluate group work. The authors give specific, detailed advice about teaching courses with small group workshops.

565 Carroll, Lee Ann. *Rehearsing New Roles: How College Students Develop as Writers*. Carbondale: Southern Illinois UP, 2002. Print.

Longitudinal studies illustrate that student writing develops over time. Tracking twenty students over four years in a Digital Portfolio Assessment Project suggests that repeated practice is needed for proficiency. First-year writing courses mark only a beginning stage in the development of academic discourse. Rather than expecting that skills developed in first-year writing courses will transfer, faculty should focus on developing rich literacy environments and "hands on" learning projects that become increasingly challenging. As they face greater intellectual challenges, students' writing may feature lapses in style or coherence that illustrate their struggle with sophisticated ideas or their unfamiliarity with certain conventions. Faculty, in addition, may underestimate the complex literacy skills required to succeed with their assignments. Scaffolding (i.e., models and guidelines), including peer response, can provide substantial support for students as they try on new roles as writers.

566 Cooper, Marilyn M., and Michael Holzman. *Writing as Social Action*. Portsmouth: Heinemann-Boynton/Cook, 1989. Print.

Fifteen essays, eight previously published by the authors separately and collaboratively, focusing on literacy education, include "The Ecology of Writing" [260], "Women's Ways of Writing," and "Why Are We Talking about Discourse Communities? or, Foundationalism Rears Its Ugly Head Once More" (all by Cooper); "A Post-Freirean Model for Adult Literacy Education" [353] and "The Social Context of Literacy Education" (both by Holzman); and "Talking about Protocols" (by Cooper and Holzman).

567 Dickson, Marcia. *It's Not Like That Here: Teaching Academic Writing and Reading to Novice Writers*. Portsmouth: Heinemann-Boynton/Cook, 1995. Print.

A major problem for novices entering the academic discourse community is that they do not understand how they can use their nonacademic literacies and personal knowledge there. The Distanced/Personal writing course project attacks this problem by having students research and write about a topic like high school education, about which they have some personal experience, a topic that can be explored both in the library and by ethnographic research in their home communities. Final papers synthesize these disparate sources. Several chapters give advice on how to help students read difficult academic material and interview others effectively.

568 Dixon, John. *Growth through English*. 3rd ed. London: Oxford UP for the National Association for the Teaching of English, NCTE, and MLA, 1975. Print.

"Language is learnt in operation, not by dummy runs." Children need to do more writing in school for their own purposes of self-exploration or communicating personal experience. The development of writing ability thus becomes a social and cognitive process. English education should be based on a "growth model" rather than a "skills" or "cultural heritage" model. Reporting on his conclusions following the 1966 Dartmouth Conference, Dixon gives examples of student writing and suggestions for classroom practice at the elementary and middle-school levels, but his curriculum theory has also influenced college teachers. In this edition, Dixon recommends paying more attention to the students' social world and encouraging students to write in a wider variety of modes.

See: Douglas Downs and Elizabeth Wardle, "Teaching about Writing, Righting Misconceptions: (Re)Envisioning 'First-Year Composition' as 'Introduction to Writing Studies'" [451].

569 Elbow, Peter. *Writing with Power*. New York: Oxford UP, 1981. Print.

Learning to master our writing makes us feel that we can express our ideas powerfully and move our audience. Writing well thus becomes an important way of relating to the world. This book works from the same premises as *Writing without Teachers* [152] with many more teaching suggestions, particularly on making writing responsive to audience.

570 Foster, David. *A Primer for Writing Teachers: Theories, Theorists, Issues, Problems*. 2nd ed. Portsmouth: Heinemann-Boynton/Cook, 1993. Print.

The teaching of writing has been influenced by a number of theories and traditions, including the handbook tradition of error-correcting and the rhetorical tradition. The work of Piaget, Vygotsky, and Bruner in cognitive psychology has led to the development of a variety of cognitive-process models of writing that have been vastly influential in teaching and research; however, constructivist views, drawing on the work of Rorty, Bakhtin, and Freire [344, 345], oppose the cognitivist view of language as expression of thought. Several discourse systems offer additional theoretical bases for teachers of writing. Relational systems (Burke [188, 189], Moffett [576], Britton [259]) emphasize the interaction between writer and audience; categorical systems (Kinneavy [221]) classify topics, strategies, forms, and styles; "micro-rhetorics" (Christensen [406], Alton Becker) focus on the shaping of sentences and paragraphs. Writing teachers must also be aware of the relationship between literacy and dialect, the problems of measuring writing skills, and research in basic writing. Foster concludes with a chapter each on course planning and teaching methods.

See: Paulo Freire and Donaldo Macedo, *Literacy: Reading the Word and the World* [345].

571 Graves, Richard L., ed. *Rhetoric and Composition: A Sourcebook for Teachers and Writers*. 3rd ed. Portsmouth: Heinemann-Boynton/Cook, 1990. Print.

Thirty-one previously published essays collected as a resource for practicing writing teachers. Few of the essays from the previous edition appear in this one. There are sections on theory, motivating student writing, and style, as well as stories from the writing classroom. Essays include Maxine Hairston, "The Winds of Change"; Lester Faigley, "Competing Theories of Process: A Critique and a Proposal" [262]; Robert Brooke, "Underlife and Writing Instruction"; Gabriele Lusser Rico, "Tapping Creative Potential for Writing"; Donald Murray, "Writing and Teaching for Surprise"; Valerie Krishna, "The Syntax of Error"; Francis Christensen, "A Generative Rhetoric of the Sentence" [407]; Winston Weathers, "Grammars of Style: New Options in Composition"; Stephen M. North, "The Idea of a Writing Center" [529]; Peter Elbow, "Closing My Eyes as I Speak: An Argument for Ignoring Audience" [389]; Linda Brodkey, "On the Subjects of Class and Gender in 'The Literacy Letters'" [637]; and Ann Berthoff, "Paulo Freire's Liberation Pedagogy."

See: Bruce Herzberg, "Community Service and Critical Teaching" [691].

572 Jarratt, Susan C., Katherine Mack, Alexandra Sartor, and Shevaun E. Watson. "Pedagogical Memory: Writing, Mapping, Translating." *WPA:*

The Journal of Writing Program Administration 33.1-2 (Fall/Winter 2009): 46–73. Print.

Rather than being concerned with transfer, which is so difficult to track, writing researchers and instructors might turn to contemporary memory theory and the concept of cultural memory to discern what students remember about writing instruction. Interviews with ninety-two junior- and senior-level college students from a wide range of majors give insight into how students find their way from first-year writing instruction to disciplinary-specific writing in their majors. What accommodations have students made to "the complex demands of university writing, expressed through acts of remembering or forgetting"? Students who were thriving as writers "had a stronger ability to narrate their writing experiences, to see themselves in relationship to writing teachers and other audiences, and to confront the emotional challenges writing poses." Pedagogical memory work helps students to map their own pasts and to imagine their futures as writers.

573 Kail, Harvey. "Narratives of Knowledge: Story and Pedagogy in Four Composition Texts." *Rhetoric Review* 6.2 (Spring 1988): 179–89. Print.

A course or a textbook is like a story about acquiring knowledge, a heroic quest; in the texts considered here, it is a myth of separation, initiation, and return. In Young, Becker, and Pike's *Rhetoric: Discovery and Change* [386], the hero's quest is to reunite the post-Babel world of epistemic alienation by overcoming barriers to communication through the exercise of tortuous heuristics and the disarming of opponents by Rogerian rhetoric, at once winning the trust of the audience and a glimpse of unclouded reality. In Berthoff's *Forming/Thinking/Writing: The Composing Imagination* [377], the hero assails the Castle of Positivism to reclaim the imagination, sailing off on assisted invitations to examine magical objects that lead first to chaos and then to self-recognition. In Coles' *Teaching Composing*, the hero awakens from enchantment by the school, abandons its familiar language, enters the gap of silence between languages, and, with the help of classmate-comrades, gains the freedom of true individual identity. These and other such narratives are founded on social traditions—the Christian search for salvation or the romantic quest for a natural form of individual identity.

574 Lindemann, Erika. *A Rhetoric for Writing Teachers*. 3rd ed. New York: Oxford UP, 1995. Print.

Writing is a means of communication (sending a message to a reader in a particular context) as well as a process involving prewriting, writing, and rewriting. Psychology and linguistics inform modern methods of teaching students to find ideas; choose words; shape effective sentences, paragraphs, and forms of discourse; and revise what they have written. Lindemann provides chapters on each step in the writing process, on premodern rhetoric, on modern grammar, on the evaluation of writing, and on the design of courses. The third edition provides an expanded bibliography and an outline of the history of composition and rhetoric.

575 McComiskey, Bruce, and Cynthia Ryan, eds. *City Comp: Identities, Spaces, Practices*. Albany: State U of New York P, 2003. Print.

Michel de Certeau's "walking/composing" metaphor gives this collection navigational freedom as the authors detail the unique "paths/texts" created at urban universities in cities such as Pittsburgh, Chicago, Atlanta, and Birmingham. The fourteen essays illustrate how students and teachers can both reevaluate and transform their metropolitan classrooms into learning spaces appropriate to their geography and writerly identities. Foreword by Linda Flower and an introduction by the editors. Essays from Part I, Negotiating Identities, include Tracey Baker, Peggy Jolly, Bruce McComiskey, and Cynthia Ryan, "Myth, Identity, and Composition: Teaching Writing in Birmingham, Alabama"; Krista Hiser, "A Paragraph Ain't Nothin' but a Sandwich: The Effects of the GED on Four Urban Writers and Their Writing"; Paula Mathieu, "'Not Your Mama's Bus Tour': A Case for 'Radically Insufficient' Writing"; and Susan Swan, "From Urban Classroom to Urban Community." Essays from Part II, Composing Spaces, include Van E. Hillard, "A Place in the City: Hull-House and the Architecture of Civility" and Jeffrey T. Grabill, "The Written City: Urban Planning, Computer Networks, and Civic Literacies." Essays from Part III, Redefining Practices, include David A. Jolliffe, "Composition by Immersion: Writing Your Way into a Mission-Driven University"; Lynee Lewis Gaillet, "Writing Program Administration in a 'Metropolitan University'"; and Patrick Bruch, "Moving to the City: Redefining Literacy in the Post–Civil Rights Era."

576 Moffett, James. *Teaching the Universe of Discourse*. Boston: Houghton, 1968. Print.

English classes in grades K through 12 should focus on language as a symbol system that enables increasingly abstract thought. This view of language is realized in a curriculum that moves students through a "spectrum" of kinds of discourse — interior dialogue, conversation, correspondence, public narrative, and public generalization and inference — that are classified according to the distance between speaker/writer, hearer/reader, and subject. Moving through the spectrum requires increasing efforts to imagine one's audience and what they need to be told about the subject. Lessons can begin with drama performed in class, followed by narrative, moving from diaries and letters to memoirs and biographies. As narration becomes more anonymous, older students move to abstract reasoning. This curriculum is student-centered because it reflects children's cognitive development and because student writing is the principal content. An influential curriculum model, based on the principles developed at the 1966 Dartmouth Conference.

577 Muller, Herbert J. *The Uses of English*. New York: Holt, 1967. Print.

Summarizing the conclusions agreed upon at the 1966 Dartmouth Conference, Muller makes several recommendations. Children in a democratic school system should not be grouped according to ability; the classroom should also be ethnically and socially diverse. The English curriculum should center on the child's cognitive development, and "good English" should not be taught prescriptively. Literature, not literary criticism, should be taught, with respect for personal responses. English teachers should connect writing with speaking to break down students' tendency to use academic jargon; bring drama into the classroom to foster social maturity and creativity; and use audiovisual media in the classroom and make the study of film, television, and other mass media part of English study. Alternatives to formal examinations should also be sought.

578 Murray, Donald M. *A Writer Teaches Writing*. 2nd ed. Boston: Houghton, 1985. Print.

Murray advocates teaching writing through a workshop approach, in which students and teachers seek the surprise of hearing the written voices that engage readers. Drawing on his experience as a Pulitzer Prize–winning journalist, Murray gives detailed advice on teaching the whole writing process, from syllabus design ("inviting writing") to evaluation (helping students learn to evaluate their own drafts).

579 Olson, Gary A., and Julie Drew, eds. *Landmark Essays on Advanced Composition*. Mahwah: Erlbaum, 1996. Print.

Twenty-four previously published essays and an extensive bibliography on the history, curriculum, and theory of advanced composition. Included are several surveys of the field from 1980 and 1990; the 1967 CCCC guidelines for advanced composition; William A. Covino, "Defining Advanced Composition: Contributions from the History of Rhetoric" [91]; Carol Snyder, "Analyzing Classifications: Foucault for Advanced Writers"; Susan Hilligoss, "Preoccupations: Private Writing and Advanced Composition"; Katherine H. Adams, "Bringing Rhetorical Theory into the Advanced Writing Class" [560]; and Kate Ronald, "The Politics of Teaching Professional Writing."

See: Wayne Campbell Peck, Linda Flower, and Lorraine Higgins, "Community Literacy" [696].

580 Petrosky, Anthony R., and David Bartholomae, eds. *The Teaching of Writing: Eighty-Fifth Yearbook of the National Society for the Study of Education, Part II*. Chicago: U of Chicago P, 1986. Print.

Eleven comprehensive essays directed to an audience of educators who are not composition specialists. Included are David Bartholomae, "Words from Afar"; John Gage, "Why Write?"; Patricia Bizzell, "Composing Processes: An Overview"; Arthur N. Applebee, "Problems in Process Approaches: Toward a Reconceptualization of Process Instruction"; Rexford Brown, "Evaluation and Learning"; and Paul Kameen, "Coming of Age in College Composition."

581 Ramage, John. "From Profession to Discipline: The Politics of Establishing a Writing Concentration." Rpt. in *Coming of Age: The Advanced Writing Curriculum* [583]. Ed. Linda K. Shamoon, Rebecca Moore Howard,

Sandra Jamieson, and Robert A. Schwegler. Portsmouth: Heinemann-Boynton/Cook, 2000. 137. Print.

The development of an advanced undergraduate writing program usually entails the following: resistance from literature colleagues worried about encroachment; the necessity of collectively defining and enacting a disciplinary identity; and the likelihood of having to debate "secession" (from the English department) and "abolition" (of first-year composition). The toughest issues often have less to do with resources and institutional support than with internal department politics. Local circumstances will guide answers, but critical factors can be identified that need to be accounted for by any program undergoing the change of identity.

582 Reynolds, Mark, ed. *Two-Year College English: Essays for a New Century*. Urbana: NCTE, 1994. Print.

Nineteen essays on a variety of issues facing teachers of English in two-year colleges, including Janice Albert, "I Am Not the Look in Your Eyes"; Mary L. Needham, "This New Breed of College Students"; Mary Kay Morrison, "'The Old Lady in the Student Lounge': Integrating the Adult Female Student into the College Classroom"; Smokey Wilson, "What Happened to Darlene? Reconstructing the Life and Schooling of an Underprepared Learner"; Kate Mangelsdorf, "Latina/o College Writing Students: Linguistic, Cultural, and Gender Issues"; Raelyn Agustin Joyce, "Aliteracy among Community College Students"; Claudia Barrett and Judith Wootten, "Today for Tomorrow: Program and Pedagogy for 21st-Century College Students"; Myrna Goldenberg and Barbara Stout, "Writing Everybody In"; Judith Rae Davis and Sandra Silverberg, "The Integration Project: A Model for Curriculum Transformation"; Ellen Andrews Knodt, "If at First You Don't Succeed: Effective Strategies for Teaching Composition in the Two-Year College"; Nell Ann Pickett, "A Quarter Century and Beyond: My Story of Teaching Technical Writing"; Jean Bolen Bridges, "Honors English in the Two-Year Colleges"; Mark Harris and Jeff Hooks, "Writing in Cyberspace: Communication, Community, and the Electronic Network"; Al Starr, "Community College Teaching: Endless Possibilities"; Bertie E. Fearing, "Renewed Vitality in the 21st Century: The Partnership between Two-Year College and University English Departments"; and Keith Kroll, "(Re)Viewing Faculty Preservice Training and Development."

583 Shamoon, Linda K., Rebecca Moore Howard, Sandra Jamieson, and Robert A. Schwegler. *Coming of Age: The Advanced Writing Curriculum*. Portsmouth: Heinemann-Boynton/Cook, 2000. Print.

Advanced composition has come to take a wide range of shapes and forms, reflecting new developments in the teaching of writing. The thirty-four entries here reflect the emerging variety of advanced composition from traditional business and technical writing courses to visual communication, civic discourse, and cultural studies courses. Each short essay provides both theoretical discussion and practical information on assignments and syllabi. Included are Lynn Bloom, "Advancing Composition"; Deepika Bahri, "Postcolonial Writing"; Rebecca Howard, "Style, Race, Culture, Context"; Richard Leo Enos, "The History of Rhetoric"; Sandra Jamieson, "Theories of Composing"; Dennis Baron, "Literacy and Technology"; John C. Bean, "Seeking the Good: A Course in Advanced Argument"; Patricia Bizzell, "Writing as a Means of Social Change"; Diana George, "Cultural Studies"; Bruce Herzberg, "Civic Literacy and Service Learning"; Johndan Johnson-Eilola, "Computers and Communication"; Mary Lay, "Technical Communication"; Kitty O. Locker, "Writing for and about Business and Nonprofit Organizations"; and John Ramage, "From Profession to Discipline: The Politics of Establishing a Writing Concentration" [581].

584 Shor, Ira. *Critical Teaching and Everyday Life*. Boston: South End Press, 1980. Print.

Open-admissions policies have brought increasing numbers of working-class students into American colleges. They need to learn how to distance themselves from their everyday experience in order to analyze it critically, a first step toward understanding and acting on their political situation. Shor shows how to design a writing course that encourages such analysis while reducing the teacher's authority. The most complete application of the ideas of Paulo Freire [344] to American education. Cf. Berthoff [175].

585 Shor, Ira, and Caroline Pari. *Critical Literacy in Action*. Portsmouth: Heinemann-Boynton/Cook, 1999. Print.

Seventeen previously published essays elaborating Freirean critical pedagogy, with a new introductory essay by Shor, "What Is Critical Literacy?" Other essays include Elsa Auerbach's essay on adult ESL teaching, "Teacher, Tell Me What to Do"; Beverly Tatum, "Teaching White Students about Racism: The Search for White Allies and the Restoration of Hope," which proposes alternatives to the oppressor/victim roles of whites and blacks; Tom Fox's critique of extant models of racial and linguistic differences, "Basic Writing as Cultural Conflict"; Terry Dean, "Multicultural Classrooms, Monocultural Teachers" [744]; Houston Baker's 1992 Presidential Address to the MLA, "Local Pedagogy; or, How I Redeemed My Spring Semester"; Jane Nagle, "Social Class and School Literacy," which challenges middle-class assumptions about the goals of working-class students; Dale Bauer, "The Other 'F' Word: The Feminist in the Classroom" [704]; Bruce Herzberg, "Community Service and Critical Teaching" [691]; and James Berlin, "Students (Re)Writing Culture," from *Rhetorics, Poetics, and Cultures: Refiguring English Studies* [741].

586 Spear, Karen. *Sharing Writing: Peer Response Groups in English Classes*. Portsmouth: Heinemann-Boynton/Cook, 1988. Print.

Peer-response groups must first learn how groups work. Peer interaction needs to be seen as part of the composing process, and students need instruction in how to read each other's drafts to overcome confusion about sharing writing. Students' tendency to stand in for the teacher should be replaced by real collaborative behavior. The teacher's role is to recognize successful group work and foster it. Spear offers detailed advice on running a class with groups, focusing on interpersonal relationships.

587 Summerfield, Judith, and Geoffrey Summerfield. *Texts and Contexts: A Contribution to the Theory and Practice of Teaching Composition*. New York: Random, 1986. Print.

Human discourse is produced in reaction to social contexts. People adopt a variety of roles constructed in discourse, roles that can be understood as occupying a position on a spectrum from participant in the social context to spectator of it. Participant texts tend to offer many sensory impressions of the context but little explanation of it. They also tend to be structured paratactically. Spectator texts tend to evaluate the social context from a critical distance, to seek connections among contexts, and to be structured hypotactically. Students can be stimulated to write in a variety of participant and spectator roles as they react to texts by others. They can thus test the purposes and effects of taking different roles, develop commitment in writing, and become more critical as readers.

588 Tate, Gary, Amy Rupiper, and Kurt Schick, eds. *A Guide to Composition Pedagogies*. New York: Oxford UP, 2001. Print.

This collection of twelve original essays serves as an introduction to composition studies and its wide range of current pedagogies and also offers an overview of the pedagogical approaches important in the discipline. Process, expressive, rhetorical, collaborative, cultural studies, critical, feminist, community service, writing center, and basic writing pedagogies, as well as writing across the curriculum and technology and the teaching of writing, are each explained in a separate essay which includes bibliographic guides. Contributors include Lad Tobin, Christopher Burnham, William A. Covino, Rebecca Moore Howard, Diana George, John Trimbur, Ann George, Susan C. Jarratt, Laura Julier, Susan McLeod, Eric H. Robinson, Deborah Mutnick, and Charles Moran.

589 Thaiss, Christopher, and Terry Myers Zawacki. *Engaged Writers, Dynamic Disciplines: Research on the Academic Writing Life*. Portsmouth: Heinemann-Boynton/Cook, 2006. Print.

A five-year empirical study seeks a more precise understanding of the relationship between academic writing standards and alternative discourses and how those distinctions have developed for writers in different fields. Responses from fourteen faculty informants combined with departmental assessment rubrics indicate a remarkable similarity of terms by which faculty describe "good writing"—with faculty knowledge of standards accruing over time. In most cases, what faculty said they valued about writing were enacted in their assignments. A survey administered to 183 students, student focus groups, and proficiency exam essays contributed to findings that suggest, for example, students' development progresses largely in three stages; moreover, their confidence and abilities depend upon writing frequently for a variety of teachers and courses as well as ample opportunities to reflect on their writing and learning. Alternative discourses might be better understood as "*variations within* academic expectations." The final chapter offers implications for teaching and program building.

See: Barbara E. Fassler Walvoord, *Helping Students Write Well: A Guide for Teachers in All Disciplines* [487].

590 Williams, James D. *Preparing to Teach Writing: Research, Theory, and Practice*. 2nd ed. Mahwah: Erlbaum, 1998. Print.

Teachers of writing in college face an extensive field of theory and practice related to writing, rhetoric, classroom management, assignments, and assessment. In ten chapters, Williams presents exceptionally clear summaries of these concerns, offering theoretical background as well as practical options. Chapters include an overview of the history of rhetoric and its relation to writing instruction; explanations of the main current theories of composition; the workshop classroom; how to teach reading, grammar, and style; ESL, Ebonics, and nonstandard English; and commenting on and assessing writing.

Essay and Personal Writing

591 Adler-Kassner, Linda. "Ownership Revisited: An Exploration in Progressive Era and Expressivist Composition Scholarship." CCC 49.2 (May 1998): 208–33. Print.

Writing teachers want students to feel ownership of their own words, yet ideas of ownership are the product of culture, constructions that promote and reflect value systems, in the past and today. Progressive-era writing scholars valued democratic individualism, and expressivist composition scholars valued writing "for me" rather than writing "for teacher," both facilitating student ownership of writing. New "hybrid discourse" models for composition, from service learning to portfolios, also seek to promote student ownership of writing. But these "hybrid discourse" models seek to place student experience in the mix with other voices and to allow writing to express student perspectives as well as social and institutional values. The key difference is that student ownership is reflected in genre and language, not just in the content of the writing. Students' personal and academic literacies have always been complex. Despite the best intentions, many students have been silenced, and efforts to promote student ownership do not always work. Yet, by recognizing the ways that ownership is itself a changing cultural value, and by recognizing the transactional nature of language and culture, we can move toward new notions of ownership.

592 Anderson, Chris, ed. *Literary Nonfiction: Theory, Criticisms, Pedagogy*. Carbondale: Southern Illinois UP, 1989. Print.

New Journalism and personal essays by contemporary men and women of letters are often studied in composition classes. This intersection of literature and rhetoric is explored in the seventeen essays in this volume, presenting readings of individual authors, theoretical commentary on the essay form, and pedagogical strategies. Essays include Charles Schuster, "The Nonfictional Prose of Richard Selzer"; Suzanne Clark, "Annie Dillard"; Carl H. Klaus, "Essayists on the Essay"; George L. Dillon, "Fiction in Persuasion: Personal Experience as Evidence and Art"; Peter Elbow, "Gretel Ehrlich and Richard Selzer"; John Clifford, "Responding to Loren Eiseley's 'The Running Man'"; and Pat Hoy II, "Students and Teachers under the Influence: Image and Idea in the Essay."

See: Akua Duku Anokye, "Oral Connections to Literacy: The Narrative" [633].

593 Atkins, G. Douglas. *Tracing the Essay: Through Experience to Truth.* Athens: U of Georgia P, 2005. Print.

The essay has traditionally been seen as a second-class citizen to other literary forms and to critical writing, yet it has survived and sometimes thrived. What the essay offers is a certain form of truth, what Atkins calls embodied truth—the form and pattern of the essay unfold in order to flesh out the writer. The essay inhabits the space in between philosophy (reflection) and fiction (experience). The essay is modest, yet has a moral focus, and often tells the reader what to do.

594 Bloom, Lynn Z. "The Essay Canon." *College English* 61.4 (Mar. 1999): 401–30. Print.

The essay is now read primarily in composition anthologies, whose contents thus reveal the essay canon of the time. In anthologies, an "essay" may be virtually any nonfiction prose piece, such as the Gettysburg Address. Short or abridged pieces are favored. They must also be teachable (not too difficult for first-year students, for example), provocative (according to writing teachers' proclivities), and suitable as models of form and style for undergraduate writing. Permissions costs must also be affordable. Bloom surveyed fifty-eight best-selling anthologies in multiple editions from World War II to the present, to compile the list printed here of most-anthologized authors and essays (in first place is George Orwell's "Politics and the English Language"). Bloom deplores the dull study questions that usually accompany essays in anthologies and the neglect of the genre by MLA and CCCC. More serious pedagogical and scholarly attention to the genre might result in a less conservative canon.

595 Bloom, Lynn Z. "The Ineluctable Elitism of Essays and Why They Prevail in First-Year Composition Courses." *Open Words* 1.2 (Spring 2007): 62–78. Print.

Essays, as taught in first-year composition, "are an elusive, elitist genre difficult to write and nearly impossible to imitate." Further, essays reflect elitist class values while they model normative, middle-class language, thus creating a "split-level" that promotes upward aspirations and degrades "working-class locutions." Alternatively, service-learning and community involvement in composition classes might allow teachers and students to resist dominant establishment values, but these programs seem nearly impossible to promote and maintain in the modern corporate university.

596 Bryant, Lizbeth A. *Voice as Process*. Portsmouth: Heinemann-Boynton/Cook, 2005. Print.

In student writing, there is conflict between "home voices" and "school voices." The case studies in this book trace this conflict and recognize the ways that students find resolution, developing their own personalized academic voices with varying degrees of success. This process is shown to be fraught with uneven power relations, is recursive and nonlinear, and can be difficult for students. Teachers need to allow students to experiment with voice, in order to find their own words and to better understand academic conventions in their own ways.

597 Chandler, Sally. "Fear, Teaching Composition, and Students' Discursive Choices: Re-Thinking Connections between Emotions and College Student Writing." *Composition Studies* 35.2 (Fall 2007): 53–70. Print.

Effective pedagogy takes into account students' cognitive *and* emotional worlds. Writing is a matter of emotional positioning as much as it is a mastery of discursive patterns. We can't simply teach essays or forms of academic discourse. Instead, we need to create full emotional contexts for discourse and facilitate interactive reflection about both words and feelings. Chandler illustrates and analyzes such contexts and reflective practices, and suggests that compositionists must do much more to recognize the affective patterns and strategies of student writers.

598 Coles, William E., Jr. *The Plural I: The Teaching of Writing*. Upper Montclair: Boynton/Cook, 1988. Print.

Students produce "themewriting"—correct but meaningless prose—when teachers correct only for mechanics and style and never comment on content. Coles sets forth a thirty-lesson writing course that focuses on content by identifying an intellectual problem that the class will work on together throughout the semester. Assignments pose increasingly difficult questions about the common problem. Class discussion of students' essays creates a productive self-consciousness about using language.

599 Connors, Robert J. "Personal Writing Assignments." CCC 38.2 (May 1987): 166–83. Print.

Through most of its history, instruction in rhetoric aimed to equip students to write or speak on any objective topic. The rhetor was to be knowledgeable and impersonal in treating subjects. In the seventeenth and, especially, the eighteenth centuries, personal tastes and feelings became more acceptable, particularly in essays and narratives.

Nineteenth-century romanticism brought a dramatic shift in the direction of personal writing, and rhetoric instruction, following suit, came to emphasize everyday language (as opposed to Ciceronian high style), assignments that called upon personal experience (rather than abstract ideas), and invention methods for probing personal experience (rather than for searching academic knowledge). By the early twentieth century, novelty—one's own new experience—became a criterion for good writing. Several objective modes remained—impersonal or public topics were still assigned for exposition and argument exercises—but personal assignments remained an important, if contested, element of the composition curriculum.

600 Elbow, Peter. *Everyone Can Write: Essays toward a Hopeful Theory of Writing and Teaching Writing*. New York: Oxford UP, 2000. Print.

As the title says, *Everyone Can Write*. This essential (and hopeful) belief in our inherent ability for expression fuels all of Elbow's work. This "greatest hits" selection brings together most of Elbow's very influential arguments and ideas. Key themes from Elbow's more than thirty years of active publishing in the field include the promotion of (and defense of) expressivism and process pedagogy, the importance of the individual voice, the embrace of contraries and binary thinking, and the virtues of withholding judgment and assessment. Many of Elbow's more controversial ideas have been revisited, sometimes revised, and often defended. For instance, he includes sections that allow for the "brambles" one walks into when championing individual voices, and he concedes that texts are made up of voices—plural—thus acknowledging social-constructivist critiques of his work. Teachers can also find explanations of and justifications for specific practices: free-writing, private writing, the "believing game," "liking," "closing one's eyes," collage, and portfolios, for example.

601 Elbow, Peter, ed. *Landmark Essays on Voice and Writing*. Davis: Hermagoras, 1994. Print.

Seventeen essays, beginning with an analytical introduction by Elbow and including Mikhail Bakhtin, "Discourse in Life and Discourse in Art"; Walker Gibson, "The 'Speaking Voice' and the Teaching of Composition"; Barbara Johnson, "Translator's Introduction to Dissemination"; bell hooks, "When I Was a Young Soldier for the Revolution: Coming to Voice"; June Jordan, "Nobody Mean to Me Than You: And the Future Life of Willie Jordan"; I. Hashimoto, "Voice as Juice: Some Reservations about Evangelic Composition"; Lester Faigley, "Judging Writing, Judging Selves"; Toby Fulwiler, "Looking and Listening for My Voice"; and Randall Freisinger, "Voicing the Self: Toward a Pedagogy of Resistance in a Postmodern Age."

See: Peter Elbow, *Writing without Teachers* [152].

602 Fishman, Stephen, and Lucille McCarthy. "Is Expressivism Dead?" *CE* 54.6 (Oct. 1992): 647–61. Print.

Expressivism has been attacked with, but can be defended from, the charges that it is tied to the ideal of the isolated writer and that it does not allow students to learn academic discourses. Expressivism has romantic roots, and romanticists are seen to possess a "naive view of the writer as independent, as possessing innate abilities to discover truth." Yet the expressivism of scholars such as Peter Elbow is connected most closely to a more social, and social-constructive, romantic tradition. Elbow's theory and practice of "believing" allows students to identify with one another and seek social communion. Further, the goal of helping students make sense of their own lives and experiences—a key goal of expressivism—is not at odds with the pedagogical goal of helping students master disciplinary discourses. If expression is seen as open-ended exploration, this exploration need not just focus on self-understanding, but can also lead to trying on other, sometimes unfamiliar, voices and ideas.

603 Harris, Jeanette. *Expressive Discourse*. Dallas: Southern Methodist UP, 1990. Print.

All discourse can be described as expressive of the writer's ideas and feelings, and virtually no discourse is entirely expressive—that is, devoid of a desire to communicate. Thus, although the category "expressive discourse" is in a sense false, the concept has aided the development of composition pedagogy. Four types of expressive discourse have been promoted. (1) The interior text is the unwritten text in a writer's mind. It serves as the model of the text to be created and may drive the desire to see the text realized. (2) Generative texts include reading journals, summaries, position papers, personal reaction papers, and so on, which help prepare students for more formal writing. (3) Aesthetic discourse forms—poems, stories, and plays—are often taught on the questionable assumption that practicing these forms improves writing generally. (4) Experience-based discourse, or the essay on personal experience, is the type most often assigned in composition classes. There is no evidence that it helps students improve their writing. Moreover, such assignments tend to dichotomize personal writing and information-based writing when a preferable approach is to help students integrate the two.

604 Heilker, Paul. *The Essay: Theory and Pedagogy for an Active Form*. Urbana: NCTE, 1996. Print.

The essay is in need of rehabilitation. This rehabilitated and revised form of the personal essay should be taught in the composition classroom, just as often as the more "serious" thesis/support form is. The thesis/support form favors masculine discourse, linearity, and positivism. The thesis is seen as the key to all academic writing, as having "talismanic" properties. But a return to the essay as a skeptical, reflective, exploratory form might allow for a focus on what the essay *does*, rather than what the form should look like or what idea or argument the essay contains. We should see the essay as an action or activity, a process by which, ideally, we move toward wisdom and understanding but do so often indirectly, via uncertainty, a wild ride, a journey.

605 Hesford, Wendy. *Framing Identities: Autobiography and the Politics of Pedagogy*. Minneapolis: U of Minnesota P, 1999. Print.

More than an expressionistic inquiry into one's hidden, essential, or true self, autobiographical acts—be they written texts, speech acts, visual forms, or symbolic gestures—are social, contradictory, and ideologically encoded acts of self-representation. Historically marginalized groups can use autobiography to refuse the identities imposed upon them by dominant groups. However, autobiography is not automatically an empowering tool. An understanding of the ways in which power is claimed, negotiated, and resisted through autobiography is necessary. In order to justify the attention to the personal in the classroom, and to move beyond naïve politics of identity, self-reflections must be integrated with cultural, material, and rhetorical analysis.

606 Hollis, Karyn. "Liberating Voices: Autobiographical Writing at the Bryn Mawr Summer School for Women Workers, 1921–1938." CCC 45.1 (Feb. 1994): 31–60. Print.

The Bryn Mawr Summer School boasted a distinguished faculty, an innovative interdisciplinary curriculum, and an equally innovative pedagogy that included peer collaboration, guided revision, student publication, and links between personal experience and academic disciplines. Writing an autobiography was a key assignment. Today, some critics charge that the autobiographical sensibility is compromised by the masculine belief in a unified self. The Summer School assignments, however, show awareness of the need to be critical of the status quo and not present the themes of bourgeois life as norms. The most popular topic in the autobiographies is work. Most of the autobiographies show a shift from a narrative "I," typical of the unitary bourgeois consciousness, to "we," along with a shift from past to present tense, the "I" being critical and the "we" offering responses to exploitation. This identification with other workers, or with women, or with the family, is the voice of public resistance and empowerment, counteracting the powerless social atom represented by the "I" narrator. Follow-up studies show that many of the students went back to their communities to become civic, religious, and union leaders. The "we" of collective subjectivity is rarely seen in student autobiography, but the sense of collective endeavor that supports it might well be encouraged as a way to change consciousness.

607 Joeres, Ruth-Ellen Boetcher, and Elizabeth Mittman, eds. *The Politics of the Essay: Feminist Perspectives*. Bloomington: Indiana UP, 1993. Print.

The essay as a form is both dynamic and "utterly traditional." Women were historically excluded from the form, as it valued the agency and experience that women weren't seen to have—women were observed, not observers. Thus, it has been somewhat radical for women to appropriate the essay form. The result is that the essay has changed. Feminist perspectives on the essay highlight the politicization of subjectivity and authority; the involvement of the audience; the classed, raced, gendered history of the genre; and the possibility for new forms of feminist discourse. Contents include Amy Kaminsky, "Essay, Gender, and *Mestizaje*: Victoria Ocampo and Gabriela Mistral"; Tuzyline Jita Allan, "A Voice of One's Own: Implications of Impersonality in the Essays of Virginia Woolf and Alice Walker"; Ruth-Ellen Boetcher Joeres, "The Passionate Essay: Radical Feminist Essayists"; Lourdes Rojas and Nancy Saporta Sternbach, "Latin American Women Essayists: 'Intruders and Usurpers'"; Pamela Klass Mittlefehldt, "'A Weaponry of Choice': Black American Women Writers and the Essay"; and Arlene A. Teraoka, "Terrorism and the Essay: The Case of Ulrike Meinhof."

608 Lopate, Phillip. "Introduction." *The Art of the Personal Essay: An Anthology from the Classical Era to the Present*. New York: Anchor, 1994. xxiii–liv. Print.

The essay is seen, in our culture, as either a test or an indulgent art. The essay must be perfectly organized and executed, ready to be scanned and judged by a computer (or a roboticized teacher). Or the essay contains the hint of a "vulnerable humanity" and is "pure pleasure" to read. (It depends, of course, on whether you are a high school senior sitting at an ETS center or not.) Lopate argues that the essay should be the former, an experience that "awakens our capacity for mental adventure." He also suggests that the essay need not contain an argument; it might instead digress and meander. The essayist can be as much a poet as a lawyer, so long as her reader is not a computer.

609 Macrorie, Ken. *Telling Writing*. Rochelle Park: Hayden, 1970. Print.

College students are urged to write dull, impersonal prose: "Engfish." They will write better and learn more if they see writing as a way of telling the truth about their experiences. This textbook contains lessons on telling facts, working through facts to large meanings, using a journal, sharpening word choice, and writing critically. See also *Uptaught* (Rochelle Park: Hayden, 1970), in which Macrorie describes how his dissatisfaction with his own teaching and school standards led him to develop the "telling writing" pedagogy.

See: Richard E. Miller, "Fault Lines in the Contact Zone" [225].

See: James Moffett, *Teaching the Universe of Discourse* [576].

610 Morgan, Dan. "Ethical Issues Raised by Students' Personal Writing." *CE* 60.3 (Mar. 1998): 318–25. Print. Rpt. in Corbett, Myers, and Tate [150].

Teachers who assign personal writing are often distressed by students' apparent disclosure of criminal behavior or severe emotional problems. Administrators should provide clear guidelines for when and how such self-disclosure should be reported; but teachers should realize that counseling services at many schools are inadequate. Sometimes, teachers just need to listen sympathetically while maintaining appropriate professional distance. Morgan also suggests that teachers emphasize audience and purpose in writing assignments, using sample papers from earlier classes to show what kinds of problems arise when explosively self-disclosing pieces are offered for class discussion. Teachers may also rule some topics out of bounds—illegal activities, for example—and may deal with self-disclosing drafts in conference. Teachers should seek readings (not commonly found in composition anthologies) that deal with the kinds of personal topics students usually choose, such as divorce or alcoholism, in appropriate ways. Morgan sensibly acknowledges the limitations of all these suggestions, but deplores the solution that abandons all personal writing assignments.

611 Paley, Karen Surman. *I-Writing: The Politics and Practice of Teaching First-Person Writing*. Carbondale: Southern Illinois UP, 2001. Print.

Expressivist pedagogy is much more sophisticated and complicated than it has been given credit for. In particular, expressivist pedagogy can engage with issues of identity and critical consciousness in ways that bring the personal and political together, openly addressing bias, student self-doubt, agency, authority, even racism and homophobia. First-person writing always has social and cultural significance, despite the fact that many compositionists have dismissed expressivism as romantic or even sentimental. Paley presents an ethnographic study of two "expressivist" writing teachers, and she interacts with these teachers and engages with student writing to better understand the risks, difficult moments, and conflicts that arise when we teach personal writing. Finally, she advocates for similar interactions between all teachers; the creation of engaged communities of practice instead of hierarchies of form or entrenched schools of thought.

612 Petrosky, Anthony R. "From Story to Essay: Reading and Writing." CCC 33.1 (Feb. 1982): 19–36. Print.

Reading comprehension is not a simple matter of seeing the information in the text but of formulating it through schemata, or culturally determined cognitive frameworks of understanding. Bartholomae's work on basic writers [634] suggests that writing, like reading, is a process of forming through schemata. The literary pedagogy of Louise Rosenblatt, Norman Holland, and David Bleich provides a way to unite reading and writing instruction productively.

613 Sanders, Scott Russell. "The Singular First Person." *Essays on the Essay: Redefining the Genre*. Ed. Alexander J. Butrym. Athens: U of Georgia P, 1989. 31–42. Print.

The essayist, like an orator on a soapbox, has nowhere to hide, has only a singular voice and an individual mind. Yet the essay form is thriving, perhaps because its boundaries invite blurring, because it encourages verbal play, because it also allows for deep thinking, because it has an intention and an argument—a singularity—because it can aim for a "truth" that isn't literal, and because the true subject of any essay is the author herself.

614 Schilb, John. "Reprocessing the Essay." *Post-Process Theory: Beyond the Writing-Process Paradigm*. Ed. Thomas Kent. Carbondale: Southern Illinois UP, 1999. 198–216. Print.

Frequently, defenders of the essay have argued that the form mirrors the workings of the human mind. The flux and uncertainty of the essay mirrors the messy and loopy process of thinking. Yet this mess and recursion has solidified into convention, and authors of the personal essay tap into this convention by openly mapping their own thought processes across their writing, perhaps in disingenuous ways. This can often obscure the social processes of writing and thinking. At best, an essay can represent, but not recreate, the process of thought. Understanding this, teachers can encourage students to *also* see their writing within its social contexts.

615 Schroeder, Christopher, Helen Fox, and Patricia Bizzell, eds. *ALT DIS: Alternative Discourses and the Academy*. Portsmouth: Heinemann-Boynton/Cook, 2002. Print.

Debate continues over the fundamental assumption that all students need to learn traditional academic discourse while many academics and students develop "hybrid," "mixed," "alternative," or "constructed" forms of academic discourse. Fifteen essays include the following: Patricia Bizzell, "The Intellectual Work of 'Mixed' Forms of Academic Discourses"; Malea Powell, "Listening to Ghosts: An Alternative (non)Argument"; Jacqueline Jones Royster, "Academic Discourses or Small Boats on a Big Sea"; Sidney I. Dobrin, "A Problem with Writing (about) 'Alternative' Discourse"; Haixia Lan, "Contrastive Rhetoric: A Must in Cross-Cultural Inquiries"; Christopher Thaiss and Terry Myers Zawacki, "Questioning Alternative Discourses: Reports from across the Disciplines"; LuMing Mao, "Re-Clustering Traditional Academic Discourse: Alternating with Confucian Discourse"; Laura Lai Long, "Full (dis)Course Meal: Some Words on Hybrid/Alternative Discourses"; and Michael Spooner, "An Essay We're Learning to Read: Responding to Alt.Style."

616 Spellmeyer, Kurt. "A Common Ground: The Essay in the Academy." *CE* 51.3 (Mar. 1989): 262–76. Print.

Proponents of teaching academic discourse depict learning to write as constructing one's knowledge and one's very self through a discourse given by tradition. This approach ignores something universal in all uses of discourse, namely the individual writer's attempts to work out interpretations of experience that make sense to him or her, that allow him or her to retain or reconstruct a feeling of personal coherence. Unity within the writer and within the discourse is best achieved through a form that owes as little as possible to tradition, that contravenes convention for the sake of reproducing the personal viewpoint, yet recognizes stylistic constraints imposed by the attempt to make the personal viewpoint public. The essay best meets this need. Students should be encouraged to write essays in order to learn to put their own stamps on any discourse they employ.

617 Tobin, Lad. "Car Wrecks, Baseball Caps, and Man-to-Man Defense: The Personal Narratives of Adolescent Males." *CE* 58.2 (Feb. 1996): 158–75. Print.

Many male students write personal essays that celebrate acts of machismo in clichéd language. Both male and female teachers tend to overreact negatively to such essays. To better understand both these students' writing and their personal development, teachers should study how masculine identities are constructed in American culture—considering, for example, the significance of the automobile. They should be especially careful not to impose their own cultural agendas when coaching revision. They should force themselves to respond empathetically even to the most openly defiant or disengaged students. Tobin illustrates the success of these approaches through a semester's experience with one male student's writing.

618 Trimmer, Joseph F., ed. *Narration as Knowledge: Tales of the Teaching Life.* Portsmouth: Heinemann-Boynton/Cook, 1997. Print.

Deliberately avoiding academic methods of empirical or ethnographic reporting, the nineteen teachers included here tell stories about their teaching experiences in ways that attempt to make full use of the literary resources of the essay genre. Among the essays, which both exemplify and discuss personal writing, are Victor Villanueva Jr., "Shoot-Out at the I'm OK, You're OK Corral"; Lad Tobin, "Reading and Writing about Death, Disease, and Dysfunction; or, How I've Spent My Summer Vacations"; Lynn Z. Bloom, "Subverting the Academic Master Plot"; Cecelia Tichi, "The Teflon Lesson and Why It Didn't Stick"; Sondra Perl, "Facing the Other: The Emergence of Ethics and Selfhood in a Cross-Cultural Writing Classroom"; and Wendy Bishop, "What We Don't Like, Don't Admit, Don't Understand Can't Hurt Us, Or Can It? On Writing, Teaching, Living."

619 Yancey, Kathleen Blake, ed. *Voices on Voice.* Urbana: NCTE, 1994. Print.

Voice as a metaphor for style signals a focus on the writer as an individual, on the drive to express oneself, and on the search for personal authenticity, for a distinctive or a natural sound, and for control of various personae that may inhabit a text or speak to a particular discourse community or speak within a particular culture. Eighteen essays explore the range of meanings and pedagogical uses of the idea of voice, including Peter Elbow, "What Do We Mean When We Talk about Voice in Texts?"; Nancy Allen and Deborah Bosley, "Technical Texts/Personal Voice: Intersections and Crossed Purposes"; John Albertini, Bonnie Meath-Lang, and David Harris, "Voice as Muse, Message, and Medium: The Views of Deaf College Students"; Tom Carr, "Varieties of the 'Other': Voice and Native American Culture"; John Powers and Gwendolyn Gong, "East Asian Voice and the Expression of Cultural Ethos"; Susan Brown Carlton, "Voice and the Naming of Woman"; and Peter Elbow and Kathleen Blake Yancey, "An Annotated and Collective Bibliography of Voice."

Literature and Composition

620 Anderson, Judith H., and Christine R. Farris, eds. *Integrating Literature and Writing Instruction: First-Year English, Humanities Core Courses, Seminars*. New York: MLA, 2007. Print.

This collection provides accounts of some "promising models" for integrating literature and composition in undergraduate classes and focuses on describing and assessing courses currently being implemented. Fourteen essays provide descriptions and discussions of curriculum and include John Cyril Barton, Douglas Higbee, and Andre Hulet, "Reading Detectives: Teaching Analysis and Argument in First-Year Writing"; Lori Robison and Eric A. Wolfe, "Writing on Boundaries: A Cultural Studies Approach to Literature and Writing Instruction"; Clyde Moneyhun, "Literary Texts as Primers in Meaning Making"; Rona Kaufman and Lee Torda, "On Not Being Only One Thing: Book Clubs in the Writing Classroom"; and Judith H. Anderson and Christine R. Farris, "Language and Metaphor: The Ways We Think in Words."

621 Bergmann, Linda S., and Edith M. Baker. *Composition and/or Literature: The End(s) of Education*. Urbana: NCTE, 2006. Print.

The status quo relationship between literature and composition should be challenged and reshaped. But can composition and literature coexist? Several essays openly argue for the separation of composition from departments of English. Yet, other contributors also examine the many ways that composition faculty currently interact with literature faculty, across diverse institutional contexts. These unique arrangements, as well as possibly radical rearrangements, hold the potential to change writing instruction, but also to alter the "shape and purpose of the university." The collected essays are divided into three sections: Institutional Contexts, Departmental Cultures, and Applications in the Classroom, and include Dominic DelliCarpini, "Composition, Literary Studies, and the End(s) of Civic Education"; Timothy J. Doherty, "Restructuring in Higher Education and the Relationship between Literature and Composition"; Edward A. Kearns, "Causes and Cures for Our Professional Schizophrenia"; Eve Wiederhold, "Rhetoric, Literature, and the Ruined University"; Barry M. Maid, "In this Corner . . ."; John Heyda, "Along the DMZ between Composition and Literature"; Dennis Ciesielski, "Whole English, Whole Teachers: Maintaining the Balance between Rhetorical and Literary Expertise"; Katherine Fischer, Donna Reiss, and Art Young, "Computer-Mediated Communication and the Confluence of Composition and Literature"; Edith M. Baker, "Composing English 102: Reframing Students' Lives through Literature"; and Mary T. Segall, "The Missing Voice in the Debate: What Students Say about Literature in Composition."

622 Crowley, Sharon. "Literature and Composition: Not Separate but Certainly Unequal." *Composition in the University: Historical and Polemical Essays* [193]. Pittsburgh: U of Pittsburgh P, 1998. 79–117. Print.

English as a university discipline at first studied not literature but philology and composition. Literature came to be the focus only in the late nineteenth century with the professionalization of academic work in English, providing both material to study and a justification for studying it, namely that literature was supposedly an ideal repository of human experience that cultivated moral sensibility. Good taste in literature, then, because it was based on moral qualities, seemed to justify the social privilege of those who possessed it. Concomitantly, composition was despised because to need such instruction was to show that one did not possess good taste. Yet composition was able to displace rhetoric in English departments because at least it focused on self-expression, as literature does, and not on public persuasive discourse, as rhetoric does. What has been taught in composition since 1900? Process has been suppressed because literary scholars did not want to sully the glamour of their artists' inspiration by imagining them revising. One prevailing approach has taught literature as an aid to elevating students' taste—and therefore their morals. The other most prevalent approach has aimed to teach universally applicable writing skills as a service to the university. A third approach, which taught literature as a source of stylistic models and community values, dwindled along with rhetoric generally. Crowley discusses the use of the first approach at Harvard, Yale, and Princeton. The second approach, usually found at less elite schools, encouraged a lot of writing on personal topics, which the teacher corrected—this developed into what is now known as "current-traditional rhetoric," with its focus on form and correctness. Crowley discusses a few challenges to approaches one and two but says that the skills approach, leavened with more or less literature, prevailed in most programs until around 1970.

623 Eberly, Rosa A. *Citizen Critics: Literary Public Spheres*. Urbana and Chicago: U of Illinois P, 2000. Print.

Four case studies of nonexpert citizen critics writing in literary public spheres offer an account of discursive processes and forms of public criticism. Texts considered "literary" can be studied empirically: the interpretive practices of actual readers writing publicly about problematic literary texts (James Joyce's *Ulysses*, Henry Miller's *Tropic of Cancer*, Bret Easton Ellis's *American Psycho*, and Andrea Dworkin's *Mercy*) illustrate rhetorical approaches to the study and practice of interpretation. Interpretations are shaped not only by broad cultural assumptions but also by inventional strategies, topoi in particular, with cultural texts playing an important role in reinvigorating participatory democratic practice. Public criticism rather than literary criticism may offer a way to study how literature has affected society. Rhetorical theory offers possibilities for studying how fictional texts and the public debate around them influence social practices around such topics as obscenity, community standards, public interest, or social value vs. literary merit. This book ends with a discussion of classrooms as protopublic spaces.

624 Elbow, Peter. "The Cultures of Literature and Composition: What Could Each Learn from the Other?" *CE* 64.5 (May 2002): 533–46. Print.

Writing teachers most often focus on "the most obvious problems: political and material issues" in the relationship between literature and composition. However, we might instead interrogate the "*cultures* or *traditions* or *identities* of literature and composition." Composition has always been comfortable with a multiplicity of approaches and a dynamic pedagogical model, yet also offers practicality. Literature, on the other hand, offers "sophistication" and the power of a coherent disciplinary identity. Currently, though, both fields are trending away from these identities – composition is gaining a disciplinary and scholarly foothold as literature is "relinquishing pretensions." Elbow uses the metaphor of the two disciplines passing one another on opposite escalators at Macy's. Yet, because of this movement, each field has important things to learn from the other.

625 Foley, Colleen, and Kate Huber, eds. *Lore: Special Issue on the Intersection of Literature and Composition* (Spring 2009). Web. 1 Dec. 2009.

A divide exists between composition and literature that can be difficult to navigate. This divide is often created by "lore," the conversations, sharing, even venting we do with other teachers. Yet, the healing of this divide can also be facilitated through the exchange of "lore." This collection values lore as a body of experiences, practices, and ideas that must be shared if we hope to become better writing teachers. Essays include Colleen Foley and Kate Huber, "Introduction: Exchanging Lore at the Intersection of Composition and Literature"; Nicole Warwick and Jennifer Johnson, "Considering the Comp/Lit Divide: Contention, Context, and Cooperation"; Emily Sorensen, "Literature, Composition, and the Student: A New Writing Triangle"; Jaime Harker, "Composition, Literature, and the 'Practice of Writing'"; Jeff Sommers and Moira Casey, "Exploring the Social Nature of Reading: The Literary Interview Assignment"; Brad Lucas, "A Novel Underlife: Faculty Aims, Student Perceptions, and the Marketplace of Literature in Composition"; Vera A. Klekovkina, "Proust to the Rescue or Writing with Style"; Melissa Ianetta, Melissa Sullivan, Corey Taylor, Kathleen R. Slaugh-Sanford, and Michelle Filling, "A Great Divide?: Literature Graduate Students as WPAs"; Katherine Gillen and Jim Webber, "Discussing the Rhetoric We 'Do' as Graduate Students in Literature and Composition: A (Very) Small Peer-Study"; and Betsy A. Bowen, "Literature Faculty at the CCCC Convention: Exploring Professional Identities."

626 Horner, Winifred Bryan, ed. *Composition and Literature: Bridging the Gap*. Chicago: U of Chicago P, 1983. Print.

This important collection of twelve essays on the theoretical and pedagogical relationships between composition and literature includes J. Hillis Miller, "Composition and Decomposition: Deconstruction and the

Teaching of Writing"; Wayne C. Booth, "LITCOMP: Some Rhetoric Addressed to Cryptorhetoricians about a Rhetorical Solution to a Rhetorical Problem"; Nancy R. Comley and Robert Scholes, "Literature, Composition, and the Structure of English"; Elaine P. Maimon, "Maps and Genres: Exploring Connections in the Arts and Sciences" [549]; Walter J. Ong, S.J., "Literacy and Orality in Our Times" [361]; and E. D. Hirsch Jr., "Reading, Writing, and Cultural Literacy."

627 Isaacs, Emily. "Teaching General Education Writing: Is There a Place for Literature?" *Pedagogy* 9.1 (Winter 2009): 97–120. Print.

Arguments in support of "writing about lietrature" composition courses tend to focus on the "special, superior quality of literature and literary language." In response, compositionists have formulated many persuasive critiques of such courses, focusing on the top-down flow of knowledge and the lack of applicability and transfer of learning. Successful composition and literature courses can, however, refute the usual critiques. While one's perspective on a "composition and literature" course would be necessarily influenced by one's unique institutional placement, such courses also encourage literature faculty to invest in composition and create opportunities for composition teachers to collaborate with literature faculty in productive ways.

628 Lindemann, Erika, and Gary Tate. "Two Views on the Use of Literature in Composition." *CE* 55.3 (Mar. 1993): 311–21. Print. Rpt. in Corbett, Myers, and Tate [150].

Lindemann and Tate recap here a debate staged at the 1992 CCCC. In "Freshman Composition: No Place for Literature," Lindemann argues against including imaginative literature—poetry, fiction, and drama—in the first-year composition course. This course should focus on academic discourse, and students should read and write texts from a variety of disciplines. Including literature risks shifting the focus from students' active composing processes to their passive consuming of texts and the teacher's ideas about the texts or about current critical theory. In "A Place for Literature in Freshman Composition," Tate implies that literature has already been eliminated from first-year classes merely to satisfy a fad for rhetoric. But writing teachers usually are not competent to teach the discourses of disciplines other than their own, and deciding which ones to treat becomes problematic in a class of diverse majors. Moreover, teaching literature allows teachers and students to discuss and enjoy the most stylistically accomplished products of the human imagination that our culture has produced, a powerful inspiration to student writers. For further discussion of the issues raised here, see a symposium in the March 1995 *College English* with essays by Lindemann, Tate, Erwin R. Steinberg, Michael Gamer, and Jane Peterson.

See: Steven Mailloux, *Reception Histories: Rhetoric, Pragmatism, and American Cultural Politics* [223].

629 McQuade, Donald. "Composition and Literary Studies." *Redrawing the Boundaries: The Transformation of English and American Literary Studies.* Ed. Stephen Greenblatt and Giles Gunn. New York: MLA, 1992. 482–520. Print.

Composition studies continues to be an academic borderland, a contested territory, seen by outsiders as the site of political struggle over institutional resources and by insiders as a burgeoning area of scholarship and pedagogy dealing with critical issues of power, race, class, gender, and ethnicity at the beginning of every instructional hour. Despite efforts to cast it in a healing role, composition remains a fracture separating literary criticism and rhetoric. In the nineteenth century, as belletristic rhetoric spawned literary studies, composition was placed in a subservient role, a development that was exacerbated by New Criticism and by the general degradation of teaching. The class division persists today. Composition has, in the past two decades, developed and professionalized through vigorous scholarship, while scholars like Wayne Booth, Richard Lanham, and Robert Scholes have shown ways to draw the two fields together by extending our understanding of textuality—all without healing the rift. The work should not be abandoned; however, our students should be taught that there is a continuum from literature to composition on which they can locate their own work.

630 Schilb, John. "Preparing Graduate Students to Teach Literature: Composition Studies as a Possible Foundation." *Pedagogy* 1.3 (Fall 2001): 507–27. Print.

For most literature graduate students, teaching composition is their first and their primary teaching experience. Literature graduate students rarely get any explicit pedagogical training, except for composition theory. So, what would happen if literature students were more deeply engaged in discussions about pedagogy in their own fields? The creation of a graduate course focusing on literature pedagogy would afford students an important opportunity to develop new knowledge about literary studies and to recognize composition pedagogy in new ways as well. All graduate programs must acknowledge the value of learning *both* literature and composition pedagogy, and should actively "encourage their symbiosis."

631 Steinberg, Erwin R., Michael Gamer, Erika Lindemann, Gary Tate, and Jane Peterson. "Symposium: Literature in the Composition Classroom." *CE* 57.3 (Mar. 1995): 265–318. Print.

Five scholars respond to an earlier debate between Lindemann and Tate [628] on whether imaginative literature—poetry, fiction, and drama—should be taught in the first-year composition course.

Basic Writing

632 Adler-Kassner, Linda, and Susanmarie Harrington. *Basic Writing as a Political Act: Public Conversations about Writing and Literacies*. Cresskill: Hampton, 2002. Print.

Making basic writing a political act requires acknowledging the ideological contexts in which literacy skills are used, not simply the strategies that students need to be successful in college. The autonomous model of literacy, as defined by Brian V. Street, dominates literacy education, where literacy skills exist divorced from social context. In this model, students are responsible for their own problems with writing, with little attention to their prior literacy experiences or to institutional mechanisms. Interviews with thirty-eight students about literacy inside and outside of school, analysis of mainstream media accounts of basic writing and basic writers, and a review of syllabi collected from a variety of institutions provide material for complicating basic writing and raising serious questions about how literacy is represented in classes as well as what the consequences are for students and teachers. In order to make basic writing a political act, teachers and administrators must defy the institutional impulse toward perpetuating an autonomous notion of literacy.

633 Anokye, Akua Duku. "Oral Connections to Literacy: The Narrative." *Journal of Basic Writing* 13.2 (Fall 1994): 46–60. Print.

Oral narratives can help students appreciate their classmates' cultural and racial diversity and generate a variety of themes for writing. Class discussion of the secrets of storytelling and the ways that tales are told in different cultures is a preliminary to an assignment to tell a familiar folktale that represents some strongly held value. Folktales reveal both common themes and cultural differences, oral presentation makes students aware of the need to adapt to the audience, and the stories lead to self-awareness as well as cross-cultural understanding. A second assignment is to tell a family story that goes as far back in history as possible, and a third is to tell a personal life narrative. These assignments generate exciting class discussion about cultures and about composition—anticipating questions and confusion, choosing language both for comprehension and effect, clarifying central ideas, and choosing rhetorical forms. Moving to journal and essay writing, students write the stories themselves or reflect on cultural difference, stereotypes, customs, or history. Discussions also generate criteria for peer-group response. Such assignments help us fulfill our obligation to open windows on the world for our students.

634 Bartholomae, David. "The Study of Error." CCC 31.3 (Oct. 1980): 253–69. Print. Rpt. in Corbett, Myers, and Tate [150].

"Basic writing" is not a simplified course for the cognitively or linguistically deficient, but a kind of writing produced by an adult who is, in effect, learning a second language called formal written discourse. While learning the new language, the writer produces a personal version of it, an "interlanguage." More research is needed to discover how students produce their interlanguages. One research technique is to ask students to read their work aloud: students will often orally correct written errors without noticing the difference between written and spoken versions. The researcher can point this out and discuss the reasons for the error. Bartholomae uses error analysis and miscue analysis procedures developed by English as a Second Language (ESL) and reading instructors. Winner of the 1981 Braddock Award.

635 Bartholomae, David. "The Tidy House: Basic Writing in the American Curriculum." *Journal of Basic Writing* 12.1 (Spring 1993): 4–21. Print.

Basic writing cannot be a course in which students are taught skills preparatory to reading and writing: it must be a course that engages them in the difficult materials the academy regards as its best possessions and should treat their writing seriously as texts in the course. Even a basic writing course that strives for these laudable goals risks patronizing basic writers as recipients of liberal outreach—and worse, ensuring that the category "basic writer" will remain marked and filled—if the course asks students to shape their writing under a single controlling idea, to produce linear arguments, and to exclude the tangential. Such writing makes it impossible to acknowledge the very specifics of race, gender, and class that have contributed to their status as basic writers. Basic writing should adopt the arts of the contact zone (see Pratt [239]), in which unequal cultures struggle and, in so doing, produce texts of uncertain genre. At the same time, we must remember that students need to become more accomplished at controlling their writing to bring in their history and culture; we should not see all nonstandard features as deliberately unconventional. Basic writing, which once served the strategic purpose of making us change the way we talked about students and curriculum, has tended to become fixed. That status must be questioned.

636 Bizzell, Patricia. "What Happens When Basic Writers Come to College?" CCC 37.3 (Oct. 1986): 294–301. Print. Rpt. in Bizzell [179].

When basic writers begin to learn academic discourse, they are acquiring not only a new dialect (Standard English) and new genres but also a new worldview. Their difficulties may often stem more from conflicts between this new worldview and their home worldviews than from purely linguistic differences. Therefore, to understand and help them, writing teachers should learn more about both the worldviews basic writers bring to college and the academic worldview. The final position in William Perry's scheme of college-level intellectual development can be taken as a model of the academic worldview. We should be cautious about applying models from orality-literacy theory or European class-based analyses of educational differences to American basic writers; still, we might explore whether the relativism described by Perry is especially off-putting to basic writers from communities that cohere around traditional authorities. Even so, there are some grounds for hope that basic writers can become bicultural in their own and the academic worldviews.

637 Brodkey, Linda. "On the Subjects of Class and Gender in 'The Literacy Letters.'" *CE* 51.2 (Feb. 1989): 125–41. Print. Rpt. in Graves [571].

In the postmodern view, the self is constructed in discourse along ideological lines that determine who can create a privileged position and who will be denied such "authority." Basic writers' resistance to academic discourse may be construed as their rejection of the vulnerable subject position this discourse offers them. Academic discourse, therefore, was eschewed for the sake of encouraging fluency in the "Literacy Letters"—personal letters exchanged between six teachers taking a graduate course in teaching composition and six adult students in a basic writing class. The teachers did not correct the letters they received, and the students did not ask for corrections. Still, the teachers asserted their authority to control the discourse by refusing to respond to passages that suggested social-class or gender differences between teacher and student. The teachers maintained the image of classless and sexless academic writing. To authorize basic writers, class, race, and gender issues that affect them must be acknowledged as classroom realities, even if such acknowledgment threatens the teacher's privileged position.

638 Brooks, Charlotte K., ed. *Tapping Potential: English and Language Arts for the Black Learner*. Urbana: NCTE, 1985. Print.

Produced by the NCTE Black Caucus, this collection of forty-three essays on teaching reading, writing, and literature at levels K through 16 includes Clara Alexander, "Black English Dialect and the Classroom Teacher"; Darwin Turner, "Black Students, Language, and Classroom Teachers" and "Black Experience, Black Literature, Black Students, and the English Classroom"; Geneva Smitherman, "'What Go Round Come Round': *King* in Perspective" (see [368]); Miriam Chaplin, "Implications in Personal Construct Theory for Teaching Reading to Black Students"; Robert Fowler, "The Composing Processes of Black Student Writers"; Vivian Davis, "Teachers as Editors: The Student Conference"; William Cook, "The Afro-American Griot"; and Mildred Hill-Lubin, "Putting Africa into the Curriculum through African Literature."

See: Shannon Carter, *The Way Literacy Lives: Rhetorical Dexterity and Basic Writing Instruction* [332].

639 Del Principe, Ann. "Paradigm Clashes among Basic Writing Teachers: Sources of Conflict and a Call for Change." *Journal of Basic Writing* 23.1 (Spring 2004): 64–81. Print.

Significant differences in philosophy among basic writing teachers stand in the way of strong BW programs. The "linear narrative of writing ability," transmitted through lore, views writers as incapable of writing researched arguments, for example, unless they have mastered paragraphing and summarizing. This narrative combines with one of "cognitive deficiency," and basic writing teachers who adhere to these beliefs often do not think their students are capable of text-based research or analysis, despite evidence from recent research. A contrasting paradigm situates basic writers as "literate performers" who simply lack knowledge of conventions or experience with academic reading and writing. Writers who are challenged to do college-level work, and are supported by instructors who have been trained in basic writing research and practice, can respond.

640 DiPardo, Anne. *A Kind of Passport: A Basic Writing Adjunct Program and the Challenge of Student Diversity*. Urbana: NCTE, 1993. Print.

Case studies focus on four basic writers—a Mexican American woman, a Native American woman, an African American man, and a recently arrived Salvadoran man—and on the adjuncts assigned to them for tutorial support—two more accomplished undergraduate writers, an African American woman and a European American woman. Their struggles and successes suggest that the tensions aroused by campus diversity and educational-opportunity programs should be discussed openly by faculty and students, that basic writers need help finding personal meaning in the academic work in a cultural environment that is often unfamiliar or hostile, and that peer tutors need to establish their role as facilitators without being undermined by student resistance or riding roughshod over it.

641 Enos, Theresa, ed. *A Sourcebook for Basic Writing Teachers*. New York: Random, 1987. Print.

Forty-two essays and parts of books and three bibliographies, some previously published. Included are Walter J. Ong, S.J., "Literacy and Orality in Our Times" [361]; Mike Rose, "Remedial Writing Courses: A Critique and a Proposal" [657]; E. D. Hirsch Jr., "Cultural Literacy"; Paulo Freire, "The Adult Literacy Process as Cultural Action for Freedom"; David Bartholomae and Anthony R. Petrosky, "Facts, Artifacts, and Counterfacts: A Basic Reading and Writing Course for the College Curriculum" [562]; Patrick Hartwell, "Grammar, Grammars, and the Teaching of Grammar" [415]; Sarah D'Eloia, "The Uses—and Limits—of Grammar" [410]; Ira Shor, "Reinventing Daily Life: Self-Study and the Theme of 'Work'"; Mina P. Shaughnessy, "Vocabulary" and "Beyond the Sentence" [660]; Nancy Sommers, "Revision Strategies of Student Writers and Experienced Adult Writers" [400]; Ann E. Berthoff, "Recognition, Representation, and Revision"; and Kenneth A. Bruffee, "Writing and Reading as Collaborative or Social Acts." This collection is an excellent introduction to the field of composition studies as a whole.

642 Greene, Nicole Pepinster, and Patricia J. McAlexander, eds. *Basic Writing in America: The History of Nine College Programs*. Cresskill: Hampton, 2008. Print.

This collection shares basic writing histories of nine different campuses in an effort to save such programs from funding cuts or elimination. Includes an introduction by the editors. Contributions are as follows: Gorge Otte, "Sunrise, Sunset: Basic Writing at CUNY's City College"; Michelle Gibson and Deborah T. Meem, "The Life and Death and Life of a College, a Department, and a Basic Writing Program"; Nicole Pepinster Greene, "Basic Writing, Desegregation, and Open Admissions in Southwest Louisiana"; Mark Wiley, "Basic Writing at 'The Beach';

Mary Kay Crouch, "Basic Writing at Cal State Fullerton: The Ongoing Battle to Abolish 'Remediation'"; Karen S. Uehling, "From Community College to Urban University: Beginning Writing Instruction for Diverse Students at Boise State University"; Patricia J. McAlexander, "The Evolution of a Division: Basic Writing at the University of Georgia"; Mindy Wright, "The Writing Workshop: The Ohio State University's Basic Writing Program"; and Linda J. Stine, "Just What Is 'Basic'?: Computer-Enhanced Basic Writing for a Non-traditional Graduate Program."

643 Gunner, Jeanne. "Iconic Discourse: The Troubling Legacy of Mina Shaughnessy." *Journal of Basic Writing* 17.2 (Fall 1998): 25–42. Print.

Examining the constraining discursive rules that are the legacy of Mina Shaughnessy (in the iconic sense) helps to understand the nature of the conflicts in the field of basic writing. Two primary discourses—iconic and critical—have shaped discussions in basic writing over the last twenty years and operate as systems of linguistic constraint. Iconic discourse reproduces the field according to certain laws, while critical discourse is transgressive. Iconic discourse makes it impossible within the discourse to reconceptualize without seeming at once to betray and dehistoricize; it also constructs an idealized identity for the basic writing teacher, a heroic teacher-figure that remains as the central value in the academic enterprise. Iconic discourse contextualizes and thus constrains its subject(s), evident by the degree of resistance met by authors who engage in critical discourse, which constructs no heroes and is highly theoretical and political. Speaking outside of established discursive parameters, critical discourse is perceived as betrayal.

644 Harris, Joseph. "Negotiating the Contact Zone." *Journal of Basic Writing* 41.1 (Spring 1995): 27–42. Print.

Metaphors of growth and initiation dominated discussions of teaching writing until the late 1980s, when the idea of struggle or conflict became popular, largely through Mary Louise Pratt's "contact zones." Pratt imports difference into her classroom (through her choices of texts) but does not engage with differences among *students* or offer strategies for students to communicate about and across differences. Pratt's conceptualization of the contact zone is problematic because of the superficiality of the engagement with otherness. When students retreat to "safe houses," for example, difference is valorized but the conflict remains. Working on *how* differences get negotiated promises a more expansive view of intellectual life.

See: Muriel Harris and Katherine E. Rowan, "Explaining Grammatical Concepts" [414].

645 Haswell, Richard. *Gaining Ground in College Writing: Tales of Development and Interpretation*. Dallas: Southern Methodist UP, 1991. Print.

How does students' writing change during college? An assortment of interpretive frames causes clashes between developmental and nondevelopmental tales of interpretation, many of which compromise the engagement between teacher and student. Writing teachers should conceive of pedagogical tasks—evaluation, models, diagnosis, curriculum—as *narrative*, and see writing development as three-dimensional. Evaluation and course content should be based not on the growth but on the *maturing* of students when maturing is defined as generative change toward cultural standards. The transformative approach offers idiographic frames of action for individuals to try rather than nomothetic categories—general interpretations rather than explanatory laws. The paradoxical bind between writing instruction and writing style cannot be entirely overcome, but the transformative approach offers a guide for such issues as solecisms, rate of production, sentence sense, organization, and remediality. An instrumental perspective generates a distinct understanding of pedagogical sequencing; however, a lifework tale of sequence has teachers joining students in some work, not imitating educational disciplines. Similarly, lifework developmental perspectives should inform curriculum and (true) diagnosis. Parts of this book are informed by empirical data from a study analyzing first-week diagnostic essays, end-of-course essays, and similar essays written by college graduates employed in business, government, and industry.

646 Horner, Bruce, and Min-Zhan Lu. *Representing the "Other": Basic Writers and the Teaching of Basic Writing.* Urbana: NCTE, 1999. Print.

An analysis of the dominant discourse on basic writing begins by situating basic writing socially and historically and by examining representations of basic writers. Key terms and assumptions work to privilege some practices and marginalize others; these cultural materialist readings address a range of research and teaching practices. Essays include four by Horner—"The 'Birth' of Basic Writing"; "Mapping Errors and Expectations for Basic Writing: From the 'Frontier Field' to 'Border Country'"; "Rethinking the 'Sociality' of Error: Teaching Editing as Negotiation"; and "Some Afterwords: Intersections and Divergences"—and four by Lu—"Conflict and Struggle: The Enemies or Preconditions of Basic Writing?" [649]; "Importing 'Science': Neutralizing Basic Writing"; "Redefining the Legacy of Mina Shaughnessy: A Critique of the Politics of Linguistic Innocence"; and "Professing Multiculturalism: The Politics of Style in the Contact Zone."

See: Bruce Horner, "Rethinking the 'Sociality' of Error: Teaching Editing as Negotiation" [417].

647 Kiniry, Malcolm, and Ellen Strenski. "Sequencing Expository Writing: A Recursive Approach." CCC 36.2 (May 1985): 191–202. Print.

The basic-writing program at the University of California, Los Angeles uses a sequence of expository assignments, in order of increasing cognitive complexity, to introduce students to academic writing: listing, definition, seriation (e.g., chronology), classification, summary, comparison/contrast, analysis, and academic argument. These schema, abstracted from a survey of writing assignments in all departments, allow for development, recursivity (repetition of earlier tasks in later assignments), the use of model academic writing, and an introduction to the methods of reasoning in different academic disciplines.

648 Labov, William. *The Study of Nonstandard English.* Urbana: NCTE, 1970. Print.

Nonstandard dialects of English, such as Black English, should not be seen as error-ridden deviations from the standard form—but neither should they be seen as separate languages. Comparative studies reveal that nonstandard forms express many of the same logical relations among elements in a sentence that the standard form does, in different yet regular ways. Almost all native speakers of English can use more than one dialect of the language, and almost all have at least some acquaintance with the standard form. Social class tends to determine which dialect a person feels most comfortable using. Nonstandard dialects tend to be socially stigmatized, even by those who feel most comfortable using them. Teachers must be aware of the grammatical structures and conventions governing social use of dialects to mediate between the dialects and Standard English. Some in-class speaking, reading, and writing in the students' dialects may help them to learn the standard form more quickly with less damage to their self-esteem.

649 Lu, Min-Zhan. "Conflict and Struggle: The Enemies or Preconditions of Basic Writing?" *CE* 54.8 (Dec. 1992): 887–913. Print. Rpt. in Horner and Lu [646].

When students from marginalized cultures enter the academy, they experience the pain of learning to live with multiple, conflicting points of view, but also the exhilarating creativity and insight that their borderland consciousness makes possible. Early work in basic-writing pedagogy sought to alleviate this pain, ignoring the accompanying benefits. Thomas Farrell and Kenneth Bruffee proposed acculturation as the cure, welcoming students into the intellectually superior academic community. This approach calmed colleagues who feared that basic writers would bring destructive change to the academy. Mina Shaughnessy, in contrast, offered accommodation, promising that students could accept the academic worldview without abandoning home allegiances. This approach also spared the academy from change. But the real task of the basic writer is neither to conform to nor abandon a monolithic discourse community, but to find innovative discursive strategies for negotiating the boundaries. Basic writers are complex selves, not to be essentialized as products of a single cultural group. The academy must adjust to these border-crossers' new discursive forms.

650 Lu, Min-Zhan. "From Silence to Words: Writing as Struggle." *CE* 49.4 (Apr. 1987): 437–48. Print. Rpt. in Perl [274].

Lu describes her experiences in negotiating among different worlds: her early schooling in Maoist China, her parents' Western education, her graduate work in Pittsburgh. Dealing with the often painful conflicts among these worlds, Lu attests, helped her grow as a thinker and writer. She concludes that writing teachers should avoid making only one kind of discourse acceptable in their classrooms. Students, however, should not be led to believe that they can move freely among the discourses they know and at the same time keep each discourse pure. Instead, the conflict of discourses—in the classroom and in one's head—should be a topic of reflection.

651 Lunsford, Andrea A. "The Content of Basic Writers' Essays." CCC 31.3 (Oct. 1980): 278–90. Print.

A sample of five hundred entrance exams suggests that basic writers focus on personal experience, using it as conclusive evidence or evaluating abstract questions solely in terms of personal effects; rely on clichéd maxims in place of generalizations; see themselves as passive victims of authority; and use stylistic features (such as personal pronouns) that reflect these content characteristics. All of this suggests that basic writers are arrested in what Piaget and Vygotsky call the "egocentric stage" of cognitive development. A similar study by Susan Miller suggests that they are also stuck in what Kohlberg calls the "conventional" stage of moral development. Basic writers might be helped, therefore, by a curriculum that asks them to solve increasingly abstract cognitive problems.

652 McNenny, Gerri, and Sallyanne H. Fitzgerald, eds. *Mainstreaming Basic Writers: Politics and Pedagogies of Access*. Mahwah: Erlbaum, 2001. Print.

Recent challenges posed to basic writing instruction demand alternative configurations that attempt to do justice to both students' needs and administrative constraints. Twelve chapters, including the following, address a wide representation on the issue of mainstreaming basic writers at the college level: Gerri McNenny, "Writing Instruction and the Post-Remedial University: Setting the Scene for the Mainstreaming Debate in Basic Writing"; Ira Shor, "Errors and Economics: Inequality Breeds Remediation"; Mary Soliday, "Ideologies of Access and the Politics of Agency"; Eleanor Agnew and Margaret McLaughlin, "Those Crazy Gates and How They Swing: Tracking the System That Tracks African-American Students"; Barbara Gleason, "Returning Adults to the Mainstream: Toward a Curriculum for Diverse Student Writers"; Mark Wiley, "Mainstreaming and Other Experiments in a Learning Community"; and Trudy Smoke, "Mainstreaming Writing: What Does This Mean for ESL Students?"

653 Moran, Michael G., and Martin J. Jacobi, eds. *Research in Basic Writing: A Bibliographic Sourcebook*. Westport: Greenwood, 1990. Print.

Ten extensive bibliographic essays, including Andrea Lunsford and Patricia Sullivan, "Who Are Basic Writers?"; Donn Haisty Winchell, "Developmental Psychology and Basic Writers"; Mariolina Salvatori and Glynda Hull, "Literacy Theory and Basic Writing"; Ronald Lunsford, "Modern Grammar and Basic Writers"; Michael Montgomery, "Dialects and Basic Writers"; Sue Render, "TESL Research and

Basic Writing"; Michael Hood, "Basic Writing Courses and Programs"; Stephen Bernhardt and Patricia Wojahn, "Computers and Writing Instruction"; Donna Beth Nelson, "Writing Laboratories and Basic Writing"; and Richard Filloy, "Preparing Teachers of Basic Writing."

See: Marie Nelson, *At the Point of Need: Teaching Basic and ESL Writers* [781].

654 Ritter, Kelly. *Before Shaughnessy: Basic Writing at Yale and Harvard, 1920–1960.* Carbondale: Southern Illinois UP, 2009. Print.

Basic writing is exclusively an institutional construct with locally specific course designations, but it has never been confined to one type of educational location. Examining basic writing at Harvard and Yale challenges associations of basic writers as enrolled only in non-elite institutions or as members of only lower socioeconomic classes. Prior to Shaughnessy's study at CUNY, elite institutions classified and separated students and debated how to assist underprepared writers while also protecting the institution's image. At Yale, "the Awkward Squad" served as an early version of a lab attached to a first-semester course and enrolled a quarter of the freshman class by midcentury, although that fact was not publicized. Harvard was far less secretive, but even historians don't always acknowledge that Harvard's English A had several outgrowths: English C, D, and F, postadmission remedial instruction serving its privileged students. Eliminating the term "basic" altogether (in lieu of "introductory") would be a responsible, humane, and practical act.

655 Rose, Mike. *Lives on the Boundary: The Struggles and Achievements of America's Underprepared.* New York: Free Press, 1989. Print.

"Deprived" and "deficient" elementary school children, "vocational-track" high school students, and "remedial" college students have all been judged negatively by teachers, by parents, and often by themselves on the basis of their inability to perform a very small set of intellectual activities. But these students possess knowledge and mental capacities fully representative of the richness of human creativity. Their difficulties should be understood in terms of the intellectual and, especially, the affective dissonances evoked by their experiences of crossing boundaries into school from relatively marginalized social positions. Rose offers poignantly detailed anecdotes from his own life as an "underprepared" student and as a teacher of such students, illustrating how teachers, parents, students, and others can sensitively acknowledge the boundary-crossing experience and avoid treating the boundaries as unbreachable walls. Winner of the 1989 Mina P. Shaughnessy Prize and the 1991 CCCC Outstanding Book Award.

656 Rose, Mike. "Narrowing the Mind and the Page: Remedial Writers and Cognitive Reductionism." CCC 39.3 (Oct. 1988): 267–302. Print.

The misguided effort to find a single cognitive explanation for complex and varied student problems—cognitive reductionism—has many avatars: studies of cognitive style characterize people as field-dependent or field-independent, brain research uses hemisphericity to account for logical and verbal abilities, the work of Piaget offers stages of cognitive development and logical thinking, and orality-literacy theorists connect literacy to logic and thinking ability. Applying these theories to student writers is problematic because they tend to level differences between individuals, they describe mental processes that can be linked only inferentially to writing, they deflect attention from student writers' immediate social contexts, and they often reproduce cultural stereotypes that should themselves be questioned—as the overrepresentation of socially marginal students at the low end of every scale suggests. Cognition is too complex to be captured in such schemes.

657 Rose, Mike. "Remedial Writing Courses: A Critique and a Proposal." *CE* 45.2 (Feb. 1983): 109–28. Print. Rpt. in Enos [641] and in Corbett, Myers, and Tate [150].

The remedial writing course should not assign simple, personal topics so that errors can be more easily isolated. Rather, it should emphasize connections with other college work by challenging students with academic reading and writing and by focusing on strategies for coping with these tasks as part of the composing process.

658 Schwalm, David E. "Degree of Difficulty in Basic Writing Courses: Insights from the Oral Proficiency Interview Testing Program." *CE* 47.6 (Oct. 1985): 629–40. Print.

The Foreign Service Institute's Oral Proficiency Interview (OPI) rates adults' conversational competence in a second language according to "function," or ability to interact at an appropriate level of formality; "context/content," or mastery of vocabulary suited to the topic; and "accuracy," or ability to speak correctly and intelligibly. On the six-level OPI scale, movement from level 2 to level 3 is most significant because here the speaker becomes able to explain and argue rather than simply narrate or describe, to employ more abstract and formal vocabulary and demonstrate broad cultural awareness, and to use more complex grammatical structures. The linguistic resources on which basic writers draw in written communication correspond to the characteristics of OPI level 2. Basic writing curricula should be designed specifically to move students into writing tasks requiring the equivalent of OPI level-3 abilities.

659 Shaughnessy, Mina P. "Basic Writing." *Teaching Composition: Twelve Bibliographical Essays*. Ed. Gary Tate. Fort Worth: Texas Christian UP, 1987. 177–206. Print.

Little work on college-level basic writing had been done when this bibliographic essay was written in 1976. It cites work on remedial education in general, Black English, social and cultural factors in educational success, Standard English grammar, philosophy of language, and composition pedagogy. All are selected according to Shaughnessy's sense of what might be useful to the basic-writing teacher. The essay thus provides an interesting picture of the development of her thought.

660 Shaughnessy, Mina P. *Errors and Expectations: A Guide for the Teacher of Basic Writing*. New York: Oxford UP, 1977. Print.

Basic writers' errors in Standard English fall into patterns derived from systematic gaps in students' knowledge of the written form and from students' own idiosyncratic but regular plans for using unfamiliar writing conventions. Chapters 1 to 5 catalog students' problems with handwriting, punctuation, syntax, and spelling. Chapters 6 to 8 show that basic writers are unfamiliar with the concepts and argument forms that are customary in academic writing. To help these students learn Standard English and academic discourse, teachers should not rely on atomized drills. They should instead discuss the grammatical and argumentative principles that inform academic writing. Teachers should remember that basic writers are intelligent adults. This book has had enormous influence on the study of basic writing, not primarily for its ideas on classroom practice, but for its way of understanding the writing that basic writers produce.

661 Soliday, Mary. "From the Margins to the Mainstream: Reconceiving Remediation." CCC 47.1 (Feb. 1996): 85–100. Print.

Within a volatile atmosphere for remedial writing programs, the Fund for the Improvement of Postsecondary Education (FIPSE) funded the Enrichment Approach at City College, featuring a two-course, six-credit sequence that bypassed test scores and mainstreamed students into a well-supported curriculum centered on language variety and cultural differences. A close reading of one student's portfolio illustrates the effectiveness of the mainstreamed curriculum. For example, in learning to approximate academic discourse, "Derek" begins to formulate generalizations more sophisticated than simple agreement or disagreement with a topic and uses both subordination and metalanguage. This student's portfolio illustrates "the promise of responsible mainstreaming" when the curriculum emphasizes linguistic self-consciousness, the study of language and culture, and social interactions with readers; however, what remains is to account for the complex institutional politics of remediation.

662 Soliday, Mary. *The Politics of Remediation: Institutional and Student Needs in Higher Education*. Pittsburgh: U of Pittsburgh P, 2002. Print.

Remediation at the college level exists to serve institutional needs and to resolve social conflicts and cannot be attributed to students' backgrounds or socioeconomic status. A crisis management tool aimed at what are perceived as singular crises in student preparation, remedial English appeared not as a response to student skill levels but only as the dividing lines between institutions—college, university, academy, public high school—were firmly fixed. Historical analyses of remedial English are needed, rather than studies of individual students and classroom pedagogy, to explode the assumption of today's students as anomalous or "always new," to examine the underpinnings of a discourse of student need, and to distinguish the politics of representation from the politics of access. We must challenge the rhetoric of needs that assumes remediation is a "special" need of nontraditional students, and we must disentangle curricular reforms from institutional ones with, for example, translation theory. City University of New York and City College of New York are used throughout to illustrate the broader dynamics of institutional growth in American higher education: how institutions adopt new standards as a management strategy or use remediation to stratify higher education.

663 Soliday, Mary. "Towards a Consciousness of Language: A Language Pedagogy for Multicultural Classrooms." *Journal of Basic Writing* 16.2 (Fall 1997): 62–73. Print.

The Language Research Project was designed as a year-long course to increase students' understanding of the nature of human language and to move them beyond the view that language (merely) conveys information. Beginning with a literacy narrative, students described a language group and kept a field notebook of language samples; they also wrote weekly self-assessments, analytical and interpretive drafts, and a final research paper. The emphasis on the sociolinguistic nature of language asked students to investigate the relationship between their private and public languages and encouraged them to develop a literate attitude toward language.

664 Sternglass, Marilyn S. *Time to Know Them: A Longitudinal Study of Writing and Learning at the College Level.* Mahwah: Erlbaum, 1997. Print.

In this first longitudinal study dedicated to tracing the same students through their entire college experience, extensive data for nine students at City College provide a full picture of writing development in a multicultural urban population. Interviews and student writing demonstrate the effect of complex social histories on academic performance, but students also showed metacognitive awareness of the relationship between writing and learning, suggesting that engagement with writing moves students to reflect more deeply on materials and ideas. Chapter 4 illustrates the crucial but also limited role that composition instruction has in the development of writing abilities, especially if the instructor ignores content or relies on generic commentary. Other chapters examine institutional testing, instructional settings, case studies of how the writing process changes over time, and implications for instruction and research. Informed by research in basic writing, ESL, feminist pedagogy, and sociocognitive theories, this in-depth study presents "the true complexity of writing development." Winner of the 1999 CCCC Outstanding Book Award.

665 Stygall, Gail. "Resisting Privilege: Basic Writing and Foucault's Author Function." CCC 45.3 (Oct. 1994): 320–41. Print.

Just as Foucault's author function organizes the curriculum in English studies and defines its proper object for study, the teaching of basic writing, too, is formulated around the educational discursive practices necessary to keep the author function dominant. Designed to increase consciousness of how teachers and institutional practices participate in constructing basic writers, a "letters" project—exchanges between graduate students enrolled in a seminar designed to study basic writing and basic writing students at two other universities—highlighted claims of neutrality, constructions of educational identities, and attempts to resist privilege. Differences in length between the two sets of letters, for example, placed graduate students firmly in the author category and served to reinscribe the basic writers' positions. Reflection on the "success" of the project is included, as recommended changes in basic writing pedagogy.

666 Stygall, Gail. "Unraveling at Both Ends: Anti-Undergraduate Education, Anti-Affirmative Action, and Basic Writing at Research Schools." *Journal of Basic Writing* 18.2 (Fall 1999): 4–12. Print.

While they remain an important facet of work and thought in issues of basic writing, when pressed financially, Research 1 universities cut courses deemed less central to their mission. At the same time, recent successful anti-affirmative action ballot initiatives make diverse student populations less likely. These two intertwined movements—cutting courses and shutting doors—foreground the need for rhetoric and composition specialists to act as public intellectuals and to participate in the forums available for debate. In particular, we should analyze public documents on education—administrative reports as well as newspaper stories. For example, just as predictions are made that future growth in the college population is likely to be from underrepresented groups, university "master plans" position all lower division writing courses as remedial or superfluous in an "efficient" system. Ideologies of fairness and quantification, pervasive in education, undercut commitments to diversity yet are the most difficult to counter among the public. The use of critical discourse analysis—with its attention to agency, action, stakes, absence, and presence—helps to explain how underrepresented students can be both welcomed and rejected, among other contradictions.

Genre Studies

667 Bawarshi, Anis. "The Genre Function." *CE* 62.3 (Jan. 2000): 335–60. Print.

Genre plays a role not only in the constitution of texts but also in the *contexts*; genres are the rhetorical environments within which situations and practices are recognized, enacted, and reproduced. Because genres constitute all communicative action, genre provides an alternative to Foucault's author function, which cannot account for how *all* discourses function, only privileged ones. Genres function on conceptual, discursive, and ideological levels, and they carry with them social motives. For genre theorists in literary studies, literary genres constitute and regulate literary activities or literary textual relations rather than being seen as constituting social reality. Building from Bakhtin, genre theorists in several fields are beginning to synthesize how the genre function makes possible and meaningful many kinds of relations and identities. Halliday defines genre through register; however, genre has a more constitutive role, an integral part of genre as social semiotic, part of an activity system. Giddens' theory of structuration also has much to offer genre studies, as an extended example of a medical history form makes clear. The genre function accounts for all discursive activities, not just those endowed with a certain literary value.

668 Bawarshi, Anis. *Genre and the Invention of the Writer: Reconsidering the Place of Invention in Composition*. Logan: Utah State UP, 2003. Print.

Analyzing genres as sites of action or as rhetorical ecosystems contributes to our understanding of how and why writers invent. Because genres are not passive backdrops or containers, the writer is, accordingly, *not* the primary locus for invention. Instead, writers are located within discursive ecologies, at an intersection of various relations, practices, and commitments. In this sense, the genre function works to maintain the desires that genres help writers to fulfill. Generic conventions of the course syllabus, for example, both generate and organize rhetorically the teacher's intentions and "mask power as solidarity" in the service of writing programs. In addition to offering several examples of genres as constitutive of communicative action, including greeting cards, social workers' assessment reports, and writing prompts, Bawarshi also reviews the history of invention in composition studies.

669 Bazerman, Charles, Adair Bonini, and Débora Figueiredo, eds. *Genre in a Changing World*. West Lafayette: Parlor, 2009. Print.

A product of SIGET IV (the Fourth International Symposium on Genre Studies) held on the campus of UNISUL in Tubarão, Santa Catarina, Brazil, in August 2007, this compilation offers a snapshot of the current movement toward using genre in educational scenarios across the globe, from Argentina, Chile, Brazil, Finland, and Australia to France, Portugal, England, Canada, and the United States. Twenty-four chapters are broken into sections exploring advances in genre theories, genre and the professions, genre and media, genre in teaching and learning, and genre in writing across the curriculum; also includes an introduction by the editors. Contributors include John M. Swales; Paul Prior; Maria Antónia Coutinho and Florencia Miranda; Cristiane Fuzer and Nina Célia Barros; Anthony Paré, Doreen Starke-Meyerring, and Lynn McAlpine; Adair Bonini; Helen Caple; Charles Bazerman; Amy Devitt; David R. Russell, Mary Lea Jan Parker, Brian V. Street, and Tiane Donahue; Estela Inés Moyano; and Solange Aranha.

670 Bishop, Wendy, and Hans Ostrom, eds. *Genre and Writing: Issues, Arguments, Alternatives*. Portsmouth: Heinemann-Boynton/Cook, 1997. Print.

A collection that draws upon rhetorical criticism, critical pedagogy, feminist and psychoanalytic criticism, linguistic analysis, curricular debate, case studies, cultural criticism, autobiography, and personal reflection to explore a breadth of perspectives on genre. Seven sections and twenty-two chapters include the following: Charles Bazerman, "The Life of Genre, the Life in the Classroom"; Amy J. Devitt, "Genre as Language Standard"; Gregory Clark, "Genre as Relation: On Writing and Reading as Ethical Interaction"; Wendy S. Hesford, "Autobiography and Feminist Writing Pedagogy"; Aviva Freedman, "Situating 'Genre' and Situated Genres: Understanding Student Writing from a Genre Perspective"; and Ruth M. Mirtz, "The Territorial Demands of Form and Process: The Case for Student Writing as a Genre."

671 Coe, Richard, Lorelei Lingard, and Tatiana Teslenko, eds. *The Rhetoric and Ideology of Genre: Strategies for Stability and Change*. Cresskill: Hampton, 2002. Print.

Seventeen chapters investigate the idea of genre as action and conceptualize the "sociality of discourse" through rhetorical assessment. Section I takes a cultural studies approach to genre and includes Charles Bazerman, "Genre and Identity: Citizenship in the Age of the Internet and the Age of Global Capitalism." Section II connects professional discourse and genre theory and includes Anthony Paré, "Genre and Identity: Individuals, Institutions, and Ideology"; Catherine Schryer, "Genre and Power: A Chronotopic Analysis"; and JoAnne Yates and Wanda Orlikowski, "Genre Systems: Chronos and Kairos in Communicative Interaction." Section III situates genre within a school setting and includes Janet Giltrow, "Meta-Genre"; Gillian Fuller and Alison Lee, "Assembling a Generic Subject"; and David R. Russell, "The Kind-ness of Genre: An Activity Theory Analysis of High School Teachers' Perception of Genre in Portfolio Assessment Across the Curriculum." In the final section, the authors use theoretical studies and applications to explore social and political discourse; selections include Peter Knapp's "Disembodied Voices: The Problem of Context and Form in Theories of Genre"; and Sigmund Ongstad, "Genres: From Static, Closed, Extrinsic, Verbal Dyads to Dynamic, Open, Intrinsic, Semiotic Triads."

672 Devitt, Amy J. *Writing Genres*. Carbondale: Southern Illinois UP, 2004. Print.

Traditional views of genre do not capture the complexity of genre as types of rhetorical actions that people perform in everyday situations, a definition established by Carolyn Miller in her 1984 article "Genre as Social Action." The relationship between genre and situation is reciprocal and dynamic, and genres mediate between individual action and cultural context as they also function socially and culturally according to six basic principles, e.g., *genres usually develop through the actions of many people, in groups*. In studies of specific practice, however, these basic principles show variation. In fact, genres change over time or in their daily uses; genres must be "flexible synchronically and changeable diachronically," and new genres emerge from others. In addition, genres both constrain and enable writers' choices; constraint *and* creativity are not mutually exclusive but are equally necessary. The challenge for genre theory is to demonstrate not only how genre enables creativity but also how and why creativity is valued. Chapters include a number of cases to illustrate genre change, for example, the rhetorical and social significance of genres in a professional community of tax accountants. Devitt's final chapter is a proposal for teaching genre awareness.

673 Herrington, Anne, and Charles Moran, eds. *Genre Across the Curriculum*. Logan: Utah State UP, 2005. Print.

Contributors from a variety of disciplines and institutions define genre, identify learning goals, and address teaching and evaluating strategies. The collection is organized into three parts. Part I, Genre Across the Curriculum: General Education and Courses for Majors, includes Elizabeth A. Petroff, "Reading and Writing, Teaching and Learning Spiritual Autobiography"; Anne Beaufort and John A. Williams, "Writing History: Informed or Not by Genre Theory?"; Mary Soliday, "Mapping Classroom Genres in a Science in Society Course"; and Anne Ellen Geller, "'What's Cool Here?' Collaboratively Learning Genre in Biology." Part II, Genres in First-Year Writing Courses, consists of Rochelle Kopp and Bongi Bangeni, "'I Was Just Never Exposed to This Argument Thing': Using a Genre Approach to Teach Academic Writing to ESL Students in the Humanities"; Carmen Kynard, "'Getting on the Right Side of It': Problematizing and Rethinking the Research Paper Genre in the College Composition Course"; and Shane Peagler and Kathleen Blake Yancey, "The Resumé as Genre: A Rhetorical Foundation for First-Year Composition." Part III, Mixing Media, Evolving Genres, includes Chris M. Anson, Deanna P. Dannels, and Karen St. Clair, "Teaching and Learning a Multimodal Genre in a Psychology Course"; Mike Edwards and Heidi McKee, "The Teaching and Learning of Web Genres in First-Year Composition"; and Mike Palmquist, "Writing in Emerging Genres: Student Web Sites in Writing and Writing-Intensive Classes."

674 Johns, Ann M., ed. *Genre in the Classroom: Multiple Perspectives*. 2002. New York: Routledge, 2008. Print.

Seventeen chapters draw from international classrooms—from Australia, Hong Kong, and the Middle East to Canada and the United States—to demonstrate just how effectively genre can fit into classroom pedagogy and lesson plans from both a theoretical and a practical perspective. This collection attests to the fact that there is not one "'true way' to approach genre theory or practice," but rather a multitude of applications and creative methods to bridge text, audience, and context. Organized into seven parts titled for different schools of genre theory, the collection begins with an introduction by the editor and ends with a unique conclusion: a chapter written by William Grabe titled "Narrative and Expository Macro-Genres," which contests many of the arguments presented in the text, followed by three responses from members of The Sydney School, English for Specific Purposes, and The New Rhetoric. Contributions include Mary Macken-Horarik, "'Something to Shoot For': A Systematic Functional Approach to Teaching Genre in Secondary School Science"; Brian Paltridge, "Genre, Text Type, and the English for Academic Purposes (EAP) Classroom"; John Flowerdew, "Genre in the Classroom: A Linguistic Approach"; John M. Swales and Stephanie Lindemann, "Teaching the Literature Review to International Graduate Students"; Sunny Hyon, "Genre and ESL Reading: A Classroom Study"; Terence T. T. Pang, "Textual Analysis and Contextual Awareness Building: A Comparison of Two Approaches to Teaching Genre"; Christine Adam and Natasha Artemeva, "Writing Instruction in English for Academic Purposes (EAP) Classes: Introducing Second Language Learners to the Academic Community"; Virginia Guleff, "Approaching Genre: Prewriting as Apprenticeship to Communities of Practice"; Tony Dudley-Evans, "The Teaching of the Academic Essay: Is a Genre Approach Possible?"; and Ann M. Johns, "Destabilizing and Enriching Novice Students' Genre Theories."

Service Learning, Civic Engagement, and Public Writing

675 Adler-Kassner, Linda, Robert Crooks, and Ann Watters, eds. *Writing the Community: Concepts and Models for Service-Learning in Composition.* Washington: American Assoc. for Higher Education, 1997. Print.

Thirteen essays and an annotated bibliography on service-learning theories and practices. Included are Tom Deans, "Writing across the Curriculum and Service Learning"; Nora Bacon, "Community Service Writing: Problems, Challenges, Questions"; Bruce Herzberg, "Community Service and Critical Teaching" [691]; David Cooper and Laura Julier, "Democratic Conversations: Civic Literacy and Service-Learning in the American Grains" [682]; Linda Flower, "Partners in Inquiry: A Logic for Community Outreach"; and Chris Anson, "On Reflection: The Role of Logs and Journals in Service-Learning Courses" [676].

676 Anson, Chris. "On Reflection: The Role of Logs and Journals in Service-Learning Courses." *Writing the Community: Concepts and Models for Service-Learning in Composition.* Ed. Linda Adler-Kassner, Robert Crooks, and Ann Watters [675]. Washington: American Assoc. for Higher Education, 1997. 167–80. Print.

Service-learning courses require an element of reflection that is typically served by journal writing. The complexity and personal engagement in such courses make journals an ideal medium for recording events and personal reactions. However, with direction and modeling, journals can become quite sophisticated ways for students to engage in more focused reflection and critical examination of ideas. A direct way to do this is simply to assign students to first record reactions and then reflect on them. The reflection assignment can be enriched by specifying theoretical frameworks—drawn from readings or class presentation—for examining experience. In responding to these journals, teachers have the opportunity to deepen reflection within the framework, to shift to other perhaps more fruitful frames, or to encourage deeper reflection on social practices.

677 Bacon, Nora. "Building a Swan's Nest for Instruction in Rhetoric." CCC 51.4 (June 2000): 589–609. Print.

Community-based writing assignments highlight the need for writing instruction that attends to matters of rhetorical variation. Students need to understand the rhetorical function of the texts they are asked to produce; they need to analyze language in a wide range of texts and contexts, academic as well as nonacademic, in order to discover the ways in which form corresponds to rhetorical function. The evolution of one teacher's community-based writing curriculum demonstrates the possibility of rendering the teaching of rhetorical awareness from the classroom a less contradictory and more manageable task.

678 Bacon, Nora. "Setting the Course for Service-Learning Research." *Reflections on Community-Based Writing Instruction* 2.1 (Fall 2001): 1–7. Print.

Pragmatic issues, such as whether service learning actually works, have typically dominated service-learning research. Responding to a call put forth at the First Annual International Conference on Service-Learning Research, future research will prove more rigorous in terms of both questions and design. An increase in empirical work focused on academics, on students' mastery of course content, will be seen, as will an increase in studies that compare service-learning pedagogy to more traditional pedagogy. Further, the impact of service learning on community (in all its multiple meanings) and on faculty, as well as on particular higher education institutions, is also likely to play a significant role in future investigations of service learning. Of most significance for composition studies, however, will be the expanded role of qualitative research. As questions shift from "does service learning work?" to "*how* does service learning work?", methodological approaches will shift and yield new insights into teaching and learning.

679 Ball, Kevin, and Amy Goodburn. "Composition Studies and Service Learning: Appealing to Communities?" *Composition Studies* 28.1 (Spring 2000): 79–94. Print.

Although much of composition's literature on service learning calls for reciprocity and community empowerment, the value of service learning is debated among professionals and peers, rather than the community or public being served. Furthermore, the professional literature on service learning does not address the learning of community participants. Community perspectives as well as all participants' experiences, not just students' and teachers', in service-learning endeavors might be integrated more fully into service-learning curricula by conducting community problem-solving dialogues, as described by Linda Flower, and by assigning students research projects that ask them not only to study the community contexts in which they will be working but also to include community participants' perspectives in their papers and reflections.

680 Coogan, David. "Counterpublics in Public Housing: Reframing the Politics of Service-Learning." *CE* 67.5 (May 2005): 461–82. Print.

Through the application of a Christian love ethic, an investigation of Afrocentric rhetoric, and an analysis of how student community leader "portraits" can capture the connotative and community transformations of the phrase "housing project" to "public homeplace," a pedagogical alteration can be achieved in service learning. Writing public texts for the community *and* writing personal narratives about the community simultaneously can serve as a "source of civic potential" and lead to more interactive public ventures for students. Implementation of such a pedagogy would encourage institutions of higher learning to "generate [public] writing projects that build 'sustainable' partnerships," thus "influenc[ing] public discourse *and* private convictions" regarding race, gender, and class in an effort to maintain personal responsibility and a human capacity for interaction within the community as it develops.

681 Coogan, David. "Service Learning and Social Change: The Case for Materialist Rhetoric." *CCC* 57.4 (June 2006): 667–93. Print.

Effective advocacy begins with an analysis of the historical and material conditions that have made some arguments more viable than others within particular communities or organizations. Service learning needs a materialist rhetoric, which extends the unit of analysis well beyond the text, in order to carve a path from rhetorical discovery to practical outcomes. A materialist rhetoric suggests beginning with everyday texts of the CBOs (community-based organizations) and outlines a pedagogical framework of discovery, analysis, production, and assessment as one concrete way to initiate community-based writing projects. Ideographs—for example, the terms "local control" and "accountability"—illustrate the link between techniques of rhetoric and techniques of power and how these play out through two case studies: one of public school reform in Chicago and one of a two-semester service-learning project. In both cases, there were significant constraints on agencies; however, more important was the necessity for rhetorical analysis to precede rhetorical production. Such analysis might point to alternative pathways into an ongoing public debate about the relationship between institutions and community service-learning projects.

682 Cooper, David D., and Laura Julier. "Democratic Conversations: Civic Literacy and Service-Learning in the American Grains." *Writing the Community: Concepts and Models for Service-Learning in Composition*. Ed. Linda Adler-Kassner, Robert Crooks, and Ann Watters [675]. Washington: American Assoc. for Higher Education, 1997. 79–94. Print.

In a service-learning composition course called Public Life in America, students examine what it means to be a member of a community and a citizen in a democracy and ask how civic, religious, economic, and social traditions shaped moral life in America. Students read works by civic writers such as Jefferson, King, and Dorothy Day, study civic problems such as inequality and prejudice, and analyze the many outlets for political persuasion that flood citizens with information and propaganda. For their service work, students engage in writing projects for nonprofits in the area. Research papers focus on local issues of civic importance such as civil rights cases and include surveys, interviews, and attending public meetings. Quite often, as a result of this work and their growing ability to write for public agencies, students engage in the civic debate on the issues they are studying and thus participate in the search for solutions to problems. In this process, the vocabulary of democracy comes alive, students gain both academic discourse skills and civic literacy, and they begin to participate in the conversation that constitutes democracy.

683 Cushman, Ellen. "The Rhetorician as an Agent of Social Change." CCC 47.1 (Feb. 1996): 7–28. Print.

Academics can be activists for progressive social change if they tear down the barriers, both literal and socioeconomic, between them and the communities surrounding their schools. They can find ways to use their specialized academic knowledge to work with literacy activities already happening in the community. Social change need not be defined in terms of sweeping mass movements; it can happen in people's everyday uses of language as well. Rhetoricians can help bring about such changes by sharing academic resources, such as libraries and computers; by tutoring written and oral language, such as that used in a social-service application or job interview; and by implementing service-learning courses according to Bruce Herzberg's model (see [691]). This activist work is reciprocal, not altruistic, because the academic gains such benefits as interesting research sites. Cushman's appendices make clear that she intends her argument here to stand as a powerful critique of the tendency of some cultural studies scholars and Freirean educators to hold aloof from people whom they regard as unenlightened about the functions of oppressive ideologies. Winner of the 1997 Braddock Award.

684 Cushman, Ellen. "Sustainable Service Learning Programs." CCC 54.1 (Sept. 2002): 40–65. Print.

Obstacles to sustainable service-learning programs arise from an undefined role for the professor. The reciprocity and risk-taking that characterize successful programs emerge when the professor treats the site as a place for collaborative inquiry with both students and community members. When they enter into service-learning initiatives as both teachers *and* researchers, professors can address the limitations of the end-of-semester project model. Service-learning projects that focus on methodology and involve actual research lead to curricular tasks that are connected, appropriate, and meaningful; such projects become sustainable programs when they continue to develop trust, commitment, and consistency between students and community members. Research-based service learning can help to meet those goals if the professor takes an active research role and maintains an on-site presence.

685 Deans, Thomas. *Writing Partnerships: Service-Learning in Composition.* Urbana: NCTE, 2000. Print.

The works of John Dewey and Paulo Freire provide a theoretical framework for setting up community writing initiatives. Such initiatives can be categorized according to where the primary learning takes place, which literacies (workplace, academic, critical, and hybrid) are privileged, and which discourses (academic, workplace, and hybrid) are most highly valued. Whether writing *for*, *with*, or *about* the community (the three classifications in the taxonomy of community writing paradigms), community-based composition courses emphasize experiential learning, community work paired with academic study, community outreach experiences blended with research and writing projects, and a commitment to investigating social justice and community problems through writing and rhetoric.

686 Ervin, Elizabeth. "Learning to Write with a Civic Tongue." *Blundering for a Change: Errors and Expectations in Critical Pedagogy*. Ed. John Paul Tassoni and William H. Thelin. Portsmouth: Heinemann-Boynton/Cook, 2000. 144–57. Print.

Errors can serve useful heuristic functions. When considered as honestly and generously as student errors, teacher/researcher errors can prompt the necessary reflection and action that lead to new understandings. If service learning is to be the microrevolution many enthuse it can be, those who practice it and record their practices must straightforwardly own up to their blunders. Only by revealing the "messy realities" of pedagogy can teachers truly practice teaching that is both radical and democratic.

687 Flower, Linda. *Community Literacy and the Rhetoric of Public Engagement.* Carbondale: Southern Illinois UP, 2008. Print.

Influenced by John Dewey, Paulo Freire, and Ira Shor, community literacy is an expressive action and practice that asks participants to "*speak with* others or to *speak for* our commitments in a nonfoundational way" while creating the rhetorical space, a counterpublic, to do so effectively, "a space not only for examining competing values, histories, assumptions, and goals but for actually negotiating a common life—one that accepts, even highlights, rather than avoids difference." Documentation of "an experiment in local public rhetoric" at the Community Literacy Center (CLC) in Pittsburgh demonstrates how powerful community literacy in action can be in understanding a problem from rivaling perspectives in an attempt to negotiate *with* others, instead of *for* a specific side. Through a multitude of engaging public and personal writing activities, products of which are sampled in the text, participants at the CLC are encouraged to always engage in "multivoiced intercultural inquiry" and develop, as a result, a "hybrid community, built around talk, writing, reflection, persuasion, and performance." Incorporating such pedagogy into the classroom or in service-learning projects will, undoubtedly, lead to the creation of local public dialogues that spark open conversations between urban writers and college mentors, between community centers and universities.

688 Flower, Linda, and Shirley Brice Heath. "Drawing on the Local: Collaboration and Community Expertise." *Language and Learning Across the Disciplines* 4.3 (Oct. 2000): 43–55. Print.

Service-learning initiatives should work toward creating relationships that respect, nurture, and draw on local expertise. In doing so, however, student and faculty participants in service learning face the problem not only of hearing local expertise, but also of constructing an understanding of that expertise that has the power to change the participants themselves and the communities they encounter. The "rival hypotheses" that develop from a community problem-solving dialogue suggest that sustainability in service-learning initiatives requires more than good intentions. Sustainability also requires stepping out of one's own discourse and framework as well as off campus; and reciprocity must come in multiple forms: recognition of a community institution's history and contributions, commitment to a relationship beyond the single-semester parameter, and a respect for community expertise that shows itself via engaged dialogue.

See: Eli Goldblatt, *Because We Live Here: Sponsoring Literacy Beyond the College Curriculum* [544].

689 Grabill, Jeffrey T. *Writing Community Change: Designing Technologies for Citizen Action*. Cresskill: Hampton, 2007. Print.

How do people write with ICTs (information communication technologies) for community change? Most people assume that information is the key to civic action, but "information" is a concept characterized by instability. The work of citizenship involves coordination of tasks, specialist technologies, and expertise, but it requires, most importantly, infrastructure. Information infrastructure—dynamic and contingent—can become both a tool for and a focus of rhetorical activity. A risk communication project in the city of "Harbor" and a community information project that tests existing tools (like Web sites or databases) with usability methods and then tries to provide better ones are methodologically different studies but are both informed by action research and community-based research and demonstrate how people write with advanced information technologies to support their work in communities. The design of infrastructure to support effective knowledge work in communities must support invention; thus, citizens in the twenty-first century must learn to write databases because some, like "Grassroots," have the potential to change dramatically the local information infrastructure. As a public and rhetorical forum, writing programs can become part of the infrastructure of civic life.

690 Green, Ann E. "Difficult Stories: Service-Learning, Race, Class, and Whiteness." CCC 55.2 (Dec. 2003): 276–301. Print.

Telling more explicit stories about race and class will allow for more complex theorizing about the relationship between those who serve and those who are served. Because students often seek service-learning opportunities in order to feel good about helping others, they may find it difficult to explore cultural and systemic racism and classism or to talk about white privilege. The silences performed by whiteness make it difficult for students to connect theories about race and class to their individual experiences. The author shares her own difficult stories about performing community service as a white, working-class college student and reflects on teaching practices that break silences and make power relationships visible.

691 Herzberg, Bruce. "Community Service and Critical Teaching." CCC 45.3 (Oct. 1994): 307–19. Print. Rpt. in Adler-Kassner, Crooks, and Watters [675] and in Shor and Pari [585].

Students in service-learning courses who go into the community as volunteers are performing needed work. Moreover, they report a heightened sense of the reality of homelessness and need. But their perceptions of these problems tend to be personal rather than social and systemic. They see illiteracy, for example, as the consequence of not studying hard enough. Bandage volunteer work thus masks the causes of social problems. Service learning must promote critical analysis and social change: students must therefore do more than write about their experiences. Studying and writing about social forces and how they operate through institutions like schools challenges students' long-held beliefs in meritocracy and individualism, but finally leads to deeper reflection on the nature of the problems they see in their community-service work.

692 Herzberg, Bruce. "Service Learning and Public Discourse." *JAC* 20.2 (Spring 2000): 391–404. Print.

Those who contend that the composition course is truly about rhetoric and civic virtue, and about public discourse as well as academic, need to develop convincing conceptualizations about the connections between society and the academy. One approach in a service-learning course asks students to write research papers that draw on their experiences in service projects. However, while this approach enables a deeper understanding of the issues, it does not lead students into an exploration of the gap between academic research and public policy. Students need both academic discourse and public discourse; they need to practice both and to find a way to bring academic knowledge to bear in public argument. One way students can do this in a service-learning course is to identify a number of ways to go public with their community service-related academic research—phone calls, letters, personal appearances, Web postings, interactive Web pages, fliers, demonstrations, tee shirts, running for office, seeking organizations, and establishing organizations are some—and then to examine the rhetorical characteristics of these forms and choose one through which to go public with their arguments. This exercise teaches students to make use of arguments that they develop in academic research papers; it sharpens their awareness of the purposes of different forms, and it enables them to better recognize rhetorical dimensions of both academic and public discourse.

693 Himley, Margaret. "Facing (Up To) 'The Stranger' in Community Service Learning." CCC 55.3 (Feb. 2004): 416–38. Print.

Discourses of volunteerism or experiential learning often conceal "asymmetries of power," making "the stranger" a figure that haunts community-service projects. Students in community-service learning projects are often situated in a "deceptive" relationship, where they are the ones who can leave or where their service experience may resemble breaking and entering or a hit and run. These debates about representation and interpretation are important to community-service initiatives, and critical feminist ethnographers have examined the role of otherness and acknowledge the dilemmas. Reciprocity, for example, has been suggested as one way to even the playing field, but no methodology can erase the privilege of the researcher or "manage" difference adequately. Facing up to the stranger creates "noisy encounters" but ones worth having. However, ways to disrupt reproducing the stranger might include analytical genres as alternatives to narratives and journal entries.

694 Huckin, Thomas N. "Technical Writing and Community Service." *Journal of Business and Technical Communication* 11.1 (Jan. 1997): 49–59. Print.

Technical-writing courses have long sent students off campus to do projects in businesses, government agencies, and nonprofit organizations. These projects successfully motivate students, help them learn audience awareness and collaboration, and develop project management skills. In addition to these benefits, students in service-learning courses develop civic awareness and help the larger community. Agencies with technical-writing needs abound. Instructors should, however, work with each agency to define the project clearly, establish goals, and assure agency support. Small groups for each project work well. Students will need to learn on-site consulting skills, such as interviewing. Once projects are under way, students should work independently, producing progress reports and meeting with the instructor, though full-class meetings may not be necessary every week. The instructor should monitor the projects for quality control and maintain contact with the agencies. Civic education, a major benefit, requires classroom reflection periodically and at the end of the semester. Such a course prepares technical writers for a life of active citizenship.

695 Mathieu, Paula. *Tactics of Hope: The Public Turn in English Composition.* Portsmouth: Heinemann-Boynton/Cook, 2005. Print.

The public turn in composition has brought students and instructors into the heart of communities as members of university-community partnerships. These partnerships demand the existence and development of community-based literacy as a discourse central to local exchanges that promote sensitivity to and an awareness of real community issues. However, service-learning projects and public writing assignments often have strict time constraints implemented by university calendars. To maintain these community partnerships and work within university agendas, instructors need to begin creating long-term student programs that develop from the bottom up *and* consider community members as sources of expertise. Instructors must also involve students in work that has rhetorical exigencies specific to community needs in order to help them become active citizens. Such pedagogy relies heavily on Michel de Certeau's definition of tactics as an extension of kairos and Ernst Bloch's interpretation of hope as an active, conscious decision to take on risk and responsibility while maintaining a source of motivation to persevere. Only then, while working with hope in conjunction with the notion of public accountability as a product of writing, can instructors take advantage of "tactical projects that create social opportunities" within local communities and strengthen university-community partnerships.

696 Peck, Wayne Campbell, Linda Flower, and Lorraine Higgins. "Community Literacy." CCC 46.2 (May 1995): 199–222. Print.

The Community Literacy Center, a collaboration between a Pittsburgh settlement house and Carnegie Mellon, seeks to foster literacy as action and reflection. It promotes collaborative, intercultural efforts to write public texts as a form of community action. Unlike cultural literacy, which seeks to build community by minimizing difference, and unlike social critique, which seeks community through ideological struggle, community literacy seeks alternative discourses that promote social change, intercultural conversation, inquiry, and strategic rhetoric. Community literacy approaches difference with the goal of negotiating meanings as a way of responding to conflicts. In the CLC collaboration, CMU student mentors do not work to "improve" community residents' writing or help them "find their own voice." Their approach instead is rhetorical: finding ways to use writing as a tool in a literate transaction. This process, to be successful, requires intercultural conversation, problem solving, and negotiation. Several examples illustrate the successes of the community literacy approach.

See: Shirley K. Rose and Irwin Weiser, eds., *Going Public: What Writing Programs Learn from Engagement* [442].

697 Roswell, Barbara. "Service-Learning and Composition: Towards an Engaged Academy." *Reflections on Community-Based Writing Instruction* 1.3 (Winter 2000): 1–7. Print.

Service learning increases students' concepts of the social and personal significance of the skills that composition teaches and can heighten students' awareness of their own sense of themselves as agents of change. Service-learning courses underscore a dual responsibility: to develop effective learning strategies and to promote meaningful, productive change. To live up to both responsibilities, service-learning courses should involve long-term partnerships, rather than placements that change from term to term.

698 Schutz, Aaron, and Anne Ruggles Gere. "Service Learning and English Studies: Rethinking 'Public' Service." *CE* 60.2 (Feb. 1998): 129–49. Print.

If students in service-learning composition courses are not gaining a critical social perspective from their service work, as some have complained, the problem may be that one-on-one work such as tutoring—a frequent type of project—naturally emphasizes a model of "caring" over a model of public policy advocacy. The "caring" approach focuses on the needs of the individual being served and displaces engagement with larger social dimensions. To gain a more public perspective, tutors would need a connection to the tutee's larger community. Students are, however, already connected to a community that they can serve: the campus. In on-campus service and research projects, students explore social and political forces and are participants in the policy issues they investigate. Writing projects can contribute to the local public debate on the issue. Moreover, in such projects, students are not "experts" serving others; they are, rather, relative equals seeking to define a public space and take social action to benefit a community of which they are a part.

699 Welch, Nancy. *Living Room: Teaching Public Writing in a Privatized World.* Portsmouth: Heinemann-Boynton/Cook, 2008. Print.

Overwhelmingly, as history has demonstrated, public voice and organization of ordinary citizens *can* result in a strong momentum for change. Teachers need to adapt a pedagogy that welcomes the voices of students who bring new perspective to a prolonged public issue and who are tired of leaving arguments and decisions for the "experts" to negotiate over in the next election, a pedagogy that views rhetoric, grounded in public writing, as "a mass practical art" that can lead to tangible results. Welch offers a discussion of her community-based literacy politics class and explains the public forums and tools used to structure such a pedagogy, one that encourages students to not only "imagine and build rhetorical space but also to anticipate and think through the discursive and extra-discursive obstacles they'll face in attempting to do so." By rediscovering the canons of delivery and memory, coupled with a historical understanding of the public channels that have, in the past, led to public awareness, demonstration, and change, students will be able to recognize and read "combinations of kairotic appeal" in order to enter the public sphere, gain publicity, resist "privatizing rhetoric," and induce reform.

700 Wells, Susan. "Rogue Cops and Health Care: What Do We Want from Public Writing?" CCC 47.3 (Oct. 1996): 325–41. Print.

The public sphere we want our students to enter is not unitary and must be constructed, as an analysis of Clinton's failed health-care initiative shows. A pre-established national forum where citizens make decisions face to face does not exist. Civic discursive spaces are local, ephemeral, and often crisis-driven. As Jürgen Habermas explains, public discourse comprises a shifting ensemble of practices into which individuals enter and try to make their private experiences intelligible. Access varies with individuals' different social locations. If we want to teach our students to write for this kind of public sphere, assignments that focus on a general topic, such as gun control, or a genre, such as a letter to the (imaginary) editor, are inadequate. Rather, the focus should be on the problem of constructing a public sphere. Students can be given practice negotiating the agreements that allow local public spheres to exist, concentrating on actions to be accomplished, not on the identities of the communicators. Wells suggests four strategies: focus classroom activities on cultural studies and thus make the classroom itself, at least potentially, a public sphere; analyze examples of public discourse, especially those that express resistance to the dominant culture; provide students with internships that require writing that enters a public sphere; and ask students to analyze and produce examples of academic writing that is intended for a public sphere rather than an expert audience.

Gender, Race, Class, and Abilities

701 Alexander, Jonathan. *Literacy, Sexuality, Pedagogy: Theory and Practice for Composition Studies*. Logan: Utah State UP, 2008. Print.

Some of the most critical debates of our time circulate around issues of sex and sexuality. To participate in these debates requires a critical sexual literacy, the ability to speak and write about sexuality (a topic composition has treated as taboo) and to understand it in economic, cultural, and political terms. Connecting work in queer theory with literacy studies helps us to understand sex and sexuality as literacy events and the importance of sexuality in becoming literate. Pedagogical practices that contribute to developing a critical sexual literacy would explore relationships among gender, sexuality, and identity and how these are intertwined with issues of power. Sexual literacy can become a key component of a socially conscious critical pedagogy—one designed to recognize the ways sexuality is constructed in language; to confront how we are socialized to see sexuality as only a personal issue; to acknowledge acts of resistance; and to encourage transgression. Methods include case studies of classroom practices, interviews with students and teachers, reviews of teaching materials, and surveys of forums (e.g., Facebook) that students are already using to write critically about sexuality and literacy.

702 Ball, Arnetha, and Ted Lardner. "Dispositions Toward Language: Teacher Constructs of Knowledge and the Ann Arbor Black English Case." CCC 48.4 (Dec. 1997): 469–85. Print.

The 1979 Ann Arbor case ruled that teachers' language attitudes impeded children's literacy learning; however, the court's ruling left pedagogical issues unresolved. One strategy, to inform teachers about sociolinguistics, does not necessarily translate into classroom practice. The authors outline three constructs of teacher knowledge that help to explain the gaps between knowledge and practice: teacher as technician, teacher knowledge as lore, and teacher efficacy. Teachers' attitudes toward racially inflected language cannot be addressed adequately by knowledge constructs that emphasize either a technical or lore-based approach. Teacher efficacy, however, emphasizes affect and the "emotional tone of classroom interactions." Efficacy begins with a knowledge base of linguistic diversity and cultural discourse patterns but must extend into an understanding of pedagogical theory within a wider sociocultural context. Winner of the 1998 Braddock Award.

703 Barnett, Timothy. "Reading 'Whiteness' in English Studies." *CE* 63.1 (Sept. 2000): 9–37. Print.

As leaders in reading, writing, and literacy training, English studies should better historicize its difficulties with multicultural education and should more vigorously promote the understanding of race as a construct of language and culture rather than as a result of biology. Engaging more fully with the concept of whiteness (in a broader sense, that "whiteness" as an essentialist notion of race) is the first step in this direction. Discourses on whiteness should be read and rewritten in order to foster stronger ties between academic work and social justice. A look at the development of basic and multicultural education at the Universities of Washington and Michigan in the 1960s and 1970s exemplify the type of exploration needed.

704 Bauer, Dale. "The Other 'F' Word: The Feminist in the Classroom." *CE* 52.4 (Apr. 1990): 385–96. Print.

Students frequently attack a teacher's feminist perspective as something personal that does not belong in the classroom. Indeed, students do not wish to acknowledge any value contradictions in their academic work. Feminist teachers should recognize that teaching these students will be a form of persuasion, in which they need to adopt an authoritative but not authoritarian position in setting the course's ethical agenda. They should not reject all forms of authority as patriarchal. Moreover, in seeking to persuade students to feminism, teachers should aim to provoke not only resistance to sexism but also identification (in Kenneth Burke's sense) with feminism's egalitarian vision of the social order. In short, feminist teachers should see themselves as rhetors and aim to develop a feminist rhetoric.

705 Blair, Kristine, and Pamela Takayoshi, eds. *Feminist Cyberspaces: Mapping Gendered Academic Space*. Stamford: Ablex, 1999. Print.

The complex relationship between women and technology is explored through multiple locations in a feminist cyberscape: the body, online identities, discourse communities, coalitions and collaborations, and the future. Thirteen chapters include Joanne Addison and Susan Hilligoss,

"Technological Fronts: Lesbian Lives 'On the Line'"; Barbara Monroe, "Re-Membering Mama: The Female Body in Embodied and Disembodied Communication"; Shannon Wilson, "Pedagogy, Emotion, and the Protocol of Care"; Donna LeCourt, "Writing (Without) the Body: Gender and Power in Networked Discussion Groups"; Dene Grigar, "Over the Line, Online, and Gender Lines: E-mail and Women in the Classroom"; Mary E. Hocks, "Designing Feminist Multimedia for the United Nations Fourth World Conference on Women"; Margaret Daisley and Susan Romano, "Thirteen Ways of Looking at an M-Word"; Lisa Gerrard, "Feminist Research in Computers and Composition." Also featured are interviews with Helen Schwartz, Gail Hawisher, Mary Lay and Elizabeth Tebeaux, and Cynthia Selfe, and an online dialogue with the contributors.

See: Linda Brodkey, "On the Subjects of Class and Gender in 'The Literacy Letters'" [637].

See: Miriam Brody, *Manly Writing: Gender, Rhetoric, and the Rise of Composition* [185].

706 Brueggemann, Brenda Jo, et al., "Becoming Visible: Lessons in Disability." CCC 52.3 (Feb. 2001): 368–98. Print.

Increased awareness of disability reveals, for both teachers and students of composition, the harmful constructions of ability, difference, and normalcy that pervade higher education and society in general. Because differences in ability resemble differences in race, class, gender, and ethnicity insofar as they have the potential to generate learning, compositionists are in a unique position to disrupt accepted notions about disability. By introducing disability texts, by allowing for a multimodal classroom, and by considering disability within a cultural context rather than just a medical one, composition teachers can make disability visible and can challenge such binaries as normal/not normal and us/them.

707 Canagarajah, A. Suresh. "Safe Houses in the Contact Zone: Coping Strategies of African-American Students in the Academy." CCC 48.2 (May 1997): 173–96. Print.

First-year ethnic minority students construct and use "safe houses" to negotiate between their vernacular discourses and academic conventions. In a networked classroom organized around argumentative writing, African American students began the course by practicing traditional topic-centered argumentation but later used person-centered and topic-associated argumentation to reframe classroom matters, to celebrate their ethnic solidarity, and to practice acts of "fronting" characterized by vernacular discourses, parody, and subtle messages to outsiders. These strategies helped to develop meta-pedagogical awareness and prepared students to move into the public sites of the contact zone. If teachers become ethnographers and examine their own locations, the safe house can become a pedagogically significant site, integral to the contact zone.

708 Catano, James V. "The Rhetoric of Masculinity: Origins, Institutions, and the Myth of the Self-Made Man." *CE* 52.4 (Apr. 1990): 421–36. Print.

The myth of self-making is powerful because it provides identities that seem to fit naturally into the requirements of society. The myth errs in equating masculine growth with an escape from origins—sex, race, and class—and from institutions. In the American tradition of individualism, fulfillment comes from applying the virtues of perseverance, loyalty, and so on, virtues that are supposedly not dependent on origins or institutions. The very egalitarianism of this appeal masks social reality, for it is, of course, easier to gain personal fulfillment when supported by the institutions one supposedly spurns. Twentieth-century versions of the myth substitute prowess in corporations for independence from institutions but retain the dichotomy between male identity as self-contained and female identity as interpersonal. In composition pedagogy, the rhetoric of authentic, expressive prose embodies the myth of self-making. Its goal is to free the writer to experience a true self. Ken Macrorie [609], Peter Elbow [152, 198], and William E. Coles Jr. [598], although they reject masculine self-aggression, use traditionally masculine images to define the personae of their self-made teachers and writers, call upon the Emersonian tradition of individualism, and seek freedom from institutions rather than Freirean confrontation with them.

709 DeGenaro, William. "Class Consciousness and the Junior College Movement: Creating a Docile Workforce." *JAC* 21.3 (Fall 2001): 499–520. Print.

The archives of the development and growth of two-year colleges in the early twentieth century reveal a rich narrative of contradiction, diversity, and class consciousness that should provide an historical context for understanding, and possibly undoing, problematic educational practices, such as gatekeeping. The elite scholars who led the junior college movement were motivated in part by the desire to rid prestigious American universities of the masses, in order to more closely approximate the German research model of a university. Discipline and assessment (in the form of intelligence and personality tests), as well as training in taste, civics, and lawfulness, were used to transform junior college students into members of the middle class—though only ideologically, not materially. Movement leaders were also influenced by philosophical trends of the time, such as scientization and social efficiency. Rather than delivering on the promise to prepare students to transfer to four-year colleges and universities (a promise which turned out to be little more than a marketing ploy aimed at students and their parents), junior colleges created poorly respected campuses and a passive working class.

710 DeGenaro, William, ed. *Who Says?: Working-Class Rhetoric, Class Consciousness, and Community*. Pittsburgh: U of Pittsburgh P, 2007. Print.

In an effort to bridge the study of rhetoric and social class and build a "working-class consciousness," this fifteen-chapter collection attempts to uncover "the numerous vernacular discursive traditions of ordinary people" using ethnography, case studies, and historic archives. Includes an introduction by the editor, "What Are Working-Class Rhetorics?" Part I, Toward a Working-Class Rhetorical Tradition, includes James V. Catano, "Articulating the Values of Labor and Laboring: Civic Rhetoric and Heritage Tourism"; Judith D. Hoover, "'Miners Starve, Idle or Working': Working-Class Rhetoric of the Early Twentieth Century"; and Anne F. Mattina, "'Don't Let Them Step On You': Gender, Class, and Ethnicity in the Rhetoric of the Great Strikes, 1909–1913." Part II, Rhetorics of the Workplace, includes contributions from Emily Plec, "The Rhetoric of Migrant Farmworkers"; Melanie Bailey Mills, "Miles of Trials: The Life and Livelihood of the Long-Haul Trucker"; Dale Cyphert, "Rhetoric on the Concrete Pour: The Dance of Decision Making"; Lew Caccia, "Workplace Risk Communication: A Look at Literate Practice within Rhetorical Frameworks"; and Kristen Lucas, "Problematized Providing and Protecting: The Occupational Narrative of the Working Class." Part III, Rhetorical Critiques of Working-Class Pop Culture, includes Catherine Chaput, "The Rhetorics of Reality TV and the Feminization of Working-Class Identity"; Kathleen LeBesco, "Fatness as the Embodiment of Working-Class Rhetoric"; and Julie Lindquist, "Conclusion: Working-Class Rhetoric as Ethnographic Subject."

711 Delpit, Lisa. *Other People's Children: Cultural Conflict in the Classroom.* New York: New Press, 1995. Print.

Progressive educational movements, in the name of liberation from oppression, often silence and exclude minority voices. For example, writing process advocates assume that black students need to develop fluency rather than technical skills, while many black parents and educators want direct instruction in the "culture of power." White middle-class teachers and parents often use indirect communication to deemphasize power; however, not all children have access to the same codes. Children accustomed to more direct instruction and to more authoritative figures will struggle to understand the rules of (white) classroom culture. In this collection of nine articles and essays, Delpit offers ways of appreciating linguistic diversity, shares her research on schooling in multilingual Papua New Guinea, and outlines teacher education for a multicultural society.

712 Enos, Theresa. *Gender Roles and Faculty Lives in Rhetoric and Composition.* Carbondale: Southern Illinois UP, 1996. Print.

Results of a national study of college writing teachers illustrate the variety of experiences writing faculty have had with gender and disciplinary bias in rhetoric and composition and in English departments. Respondents to a survey were invited to share narrative accounts in addition to statistical data; follow-ups to the questionnaires included informal interviews and campus visits as well as other invited stories. Topics include nontraditional careers, glass ceilings, and tenure cases. Enos argues for broadening the definition of intellectual work in rhetoric and composition and suggests ways in which her study can direct change.

713 Fleckenstein, Kristie S. "Bodysigns: A Biorhetoric for Change." *JAC* 21.4 (Winter 2001): 761–90. Print.

Biorhetoric, or a discourse of bodysigns, can arm one to meet the challenges of transformative teaching and thinking. Transformation must encompass three aspects: a way of seeing that enables recognition of the status quo as constructed through rules and the enactment of those rules, a way of speaking that enables the use of language in ways that surpass representation, and a way of living that enables change. A discourse of bodysigns focuses on the inextricable connection between materiality and semiosis, on the point at which the material and the semiotic blur. Biorhetoric makes transformation possible because it provides a double way of seeing, speaking, and living—a perspective that can recognize the material-semiotic nature of both the status quo and change. The work of feminist writing teachers demonstrates the idea of double vision, while a paradigm shift in science illustrates the effect of double speaking. A teaching and writing narrative serves as the site where double being occurs when the boundaries of the who, what, and how of a student-teacher exchange blur.

714 Flynn, Elizabeth A. "Composing as a Woman." CCC 39.4 (Dec. 1988): 423–35. Print. Rpt. in Perl [274] and in Villanueva [253].

The work of Nancy Chodorow on differences between male and female children's relations to their mothers, of Carol Gilligan on female moral development, and of Mary Field Belenky and her colleagues on female intellectual development all suggest that women value collaboration and organize knowledge in networks, whereas men value individual achievement and organize knowledge hierarchically. These differences are reflected in the writing of first-year college students. Material on gender should be included in the composition course so that women students will be encouraged to compose in ways congenial to their gender rather than in the male ways traditionally followed in the academy.

715 Frank, Francine Wattman, and Paula A. Treichler, with H. Lee Gershuny, Sally McConnell-Ginet, and Susan J. Wolfe. *Language, Gender, and Professional Writing: Theoretical Approaches and Guidelines for Nonsexist Usage*. New York: MLA, 1989. Print.

Six essays on language and sexual equality are followed by a set of guidelines with full analysis and explanation of problems and ambiguities. The essays review work on gender and language, give a history of male-chauvinist influences in linguistics, and call for changing sexist language to foster feminist social goals. Essays include Sally McConnell-Ginet, "The Sexual (Re)Production of Meaning: A Discourse-Based Theory"; Paula Treichler, "From Discourse to Dictionary: How Sexist Meanings Are Authorized"; and Susan Wolfe, "The Reconstruction of Word Meanings: A Review of the Scholarship." Extensive bibliography and annotated list of suggestions for further reading.

716 Gannett, Cinthia. *Gender and the Journal*. Albany: State U of New York P, 1992. Print.

For centuries, women have written journals and diaries to explore their sense of self and to maintain their social networks, although these texts, unlike many men's journals, were never intended for publication. More recently, journal writing has become an accepted part of composition pedagogy because it is seen as fostering prewriting processes. Social constructionist theory has also supported journal writing through the idea that discourse is constitutive of identity. Expressive writing in journals thus becomes an important way to learn and grow. Feminist theory supports journal writing as a way for women muted by society to come to voice. Research shows that women students are often more comfortable with journal writing and write more than men. Nevertheless, academics remain uneasy with the expressive, personal aspects of journal writing and tend to emphasize its academic function. Journal writing should be treated more seriously as literature and not marginalized.

717 Gibson, Michelle, Martha Marinara, and Deborah Meem. "Bi, Butch, and Bar-Dyke: Pedagogical Performances of Class, Gender, and Sexuality." CCC 52.1 (Sept. 2000): 69–95. Print.

Compositionists who wish to create classrooms that critique traditional academic power structures must do more than incorporate readings on class, race, gender, and sexuality. The inclusion model does not adequately challenge the centrality of white, middle-class, male heterosexuality. Academic discussions of race, class, and gender downplay the political aspects of identity performance and remain informed by essentialist identity politics. Narratives of the ways in which three writing teachers perform gender, class, and sexual identity illustrate how academic assumptions can be disrupted.

718 Gilyard, Keith, ed. *Race, Rhetoric, and Composition*. Portsmouth: Heinemann-Boynton/Cook, 1999. Print.

A collection of nine essays that critically examine race and discourses of race and identity in rhetoric and composition. Essays include Malea Powell, "Blood and Scholarship: One Mixed Blood's Story"; Meta G. Carstarphen, "News-Surfing the Race Question: Of Bell Curves, Words, and Rhetorical Metaphors"; Anissa Janine Wardi, "Terrorists, Madmen, and Religious Fanatics?: Revisiting Orientalism and Racist Rhetoric"; Keith Gilyard, "Higher Learning: Composition's Racialized Reflection"; David G. Holmes, "Fighting Back by *Writing* Black: Beyond Racially Reductive Composition Theory"; Amy Goodburn, "Racing (Erasing) White Privilege in Teacher/Research Writing about Race"; Robert D. Murray Jr., "Power, Conflict, and Contact: Re-Constructing Authority in the Classroom"; Brad Peters, "Coming to Voice: 'Anger Disguised and Complex, Not Anger Simple and Open'"; and Gail Okawa, "Removing Masks: Confronting Graceful Evasion and Bad Habits in a Graduate English Class."

See: Ann E. Green, "Difficult Stories: Service-Learning, Race, Class, and Whiteness" [690].

See: Karyn Hollis, "Liberating Voices: Autobiographical Writing at the Bryn Mawr Summer School for Women Workers, 1921–1938" [606].

719 hooks, bell. *Talking Back: Thinking Feminist, Thinking Black.* Boston: South End, 1989. Print.

hooks describes her experiences challenging race, gender, and class barriers to higher education. She analyzes the intersections of race, gender, and class oppressions and articulates a pedagogy to deal with them.

See: Jennifer Horsman, *Something in My Mind besides the Everyday: Women and Literacy* [354].

See: Daphne A. Jameson, "Using a Simulation to Teach Intercultural Communication in Business Communication Courses" [849].

720 Jarratt, Susan C., and Lynn Worsham. *Feminism and Composition Studies: In Other Words.* New York: MLA, 1998. Print.

An introduction and afterword, thirteen essays, and six responses contribute to a growing dialogue between feminism and composition across discourses, pedagogies, alliances, and discontinuities. Essays include Laura Brady, "The Reproduction of Othering"; Shirley Wilson Logan, "'When and Where I Enter': Race, Gender, and Composition Studies"; Pamela L. Caughie, "Let It Pass: Changing the Subject, Once Again"; Christy Desmet, "Equivalent Students, Equitable Classrooms"; Min-Zhan Lu, "Reading and Writing Differences: The Problematic of Experience"; Gail Stygall, "Women and Language in the Collaborative Writing Classroom"; and Harriet Malinowitz, "A Feminist Critique of Writing in the Disciplines." Response essays by Suzanne Clark, Ellen M. Gil-Gomez, Lisa Ede and Andrea Lunsford, and others.

721 Jung, Julie. "Textual Mainstreaming and Rhetorics of Accommodation." *Rhetoric Review* 26.2 (May 2007): 160–78. Print.

Disability narratives anthologized in composition readers reproduce a view of accommodation as something individuals must do to fit in rather than something institutions have the responsibility to enact. Articulation theory and feminist disability theory work together to redefine accommodation "as a social process that demands both material *and* ideological change." Disability narratives can construct rhetorics of "sentiment" or "wonder," but both allow nondisabled readers to keep intact their notions of normalcy. A third rhetoric, that of coming-to-terms, is perhaps "more insidious because its narrative arc . . . affirms normative privilege." Redefining accommodation requires the methodology of feminist disability theory, the goal being to "disarticulate" personal narrative from individual subjectivity.

722 Kirsch, Gesa. *Women Writing in the Academy: Audience, Authority, and Transformation.* Carbondale: Southern Illinois UP, 1993. Print.

Interviews with thirty-five women (twenty students and fifteen faculty members) in five academic disciplines suggest that even successful academic writers struggle to maintain confidence in their own authorial authority. Authority issues can become more salient for women in the higher academic ranks because these women often feel both greater freedom and greater need to challenge disciplinary boundaries and conventional discourse forms. Women should continue to push for more collaborative academic work and more acceptance of a personal dimension in scholarly writing.

723 Kirsch, Gesa E., and Joy S. Ritchie. "Beyond the Personal: Theorizing a Politics of Location in Composition Research." CCC 46.1 (Feb. 1995): 7–29. Print.

Feminist scholarship has helped to validate personal experience as a source of knowledge in composition research. It is not enough, though, to locate ourselves in our research. To do so risks creating the kind of master narrative that feminism rejects because it silences other views. Rather, the feminist researcher should trace her personal views to their cultural and ideological sources, recognize her multiple and contradictory locations, and use the positions of others to gain critical insight into her own. Specifically, these ends can be served by research practices in which those being studied collaborate with the researcher in designing and interpreting the research. Even so, the researcher, although she cannot avoid being in a position of power, should be sensitive to abuse of power, such as soliciting overly personal information or editing out testimony that supports values different from her own. Ethical issues are critical in such research.

724 Kraemer, Don J., Jr. "Gender and the Autobiographical Essay: A Critical Extension of the Research." CCC 43.3 (Oct. 1992): 323–40. Print.

Much research suggests that men write personal narratives in which they are heroic agents struggling for independent achievement. Women's narratives, in contrast, depict the protagonist as one agent among several struggling to forge connections or sort out competing loyalties. Although student writers cannot set aside these gendered discourses, neither are their narratives wholly determined by them. Rather, most personal narratives show authors shaping a complex identity and negotiating among a range of discourses, the events of personal history, and classroom demands. We should read, and encourage students to read, personal narratives with an eye to the complexities, not just the stereotypes.

725 Lamb, Catherine E. "Beyond Argument in Feminist Composition." CCC 42.1 (Feb. 1991): 11–24. Print.

Monologic argument, in which an author seeks to establish the correctness of his or her view by knocking down all other views, is the dominant form of scholarly writing, a form uncongenial to women, who value relationships and negotiate responsibilities. But monologic argument cannot simply be replaced by autobiography as a preferred form. Women's very concern for others will motivate them to use persuasive power to rectify injustice, although without violence. More collaborative forms of argument are needed, however, in which the parties negotiate a resolution by exploring each other's needs in detail, brainstorming multiple solutions, and discussing alternatives to find a mutually agreeable resolution. Such forms of dealing with conflict, beneficial to both men and women, can be modeled in the composition class.

726 Lewiecki-Wilson, Cynthia, and Brenda Jo Brueggemann, eds. *Disability and the Teaching of Writing: A Critical Sourcebook.* Boston: Bedford/St. Martin's, 2008. Print.

Learning about disability from the viewpoint of the disabled can lead to a fuller, more informed understanding of the practices needed in the classroom. This thirty-two-chapter collection of new and previously published articles encourages "reflective classroom practice" by including sections titled "Reflecting on Your Teaching" and "Suggestions for Student Activities" and a bibliography to assist in achieving a pedagogy rich in embodied learning. Introduction by the editors. Articles from Part I, Disability Awareness in Teacher Training, include Jay Dolmage, "Mapping Composition: Inviting Disability in the Front Door," and Margaret Price, "Writing from Normal: Critical Thinking and Disability in the Composition Classroom." Articles from Part II, Embodied Writing: Perspectives from Teachers with Disabilities, include Kristin Lindgren, "Body Language: Disability Narratives and the Act of Writing," and Georgina Kleege, "Reflections on Writing and Teaching Disability Autobiography." Included in Part III, Resources for Teaching Disability Concepts in the Writing Classroom, are James C. Wilson and Cynthia Lewiecki-Wilson, From *Constructing a Third Space: Disability Studies, the Teaching of English, and Institutional Transformation*; Mark Mossman, From *Visible Disability in the College Classroom*; G. Thomas Couser, From *Conflicting Paradigms: The Rhetorics of Disability Memoir*; Jacqueline Rinaldi, From *Rhetoric and Healing: Revising Narratives about Disability*; Eli Clare, *Gawking, Gaping, Staring*; Jim Swan, From *Disabilities, Bodies, Voices*; Michael Bérubé, From *Citizenship and Disability*; and Tobin Siebers, From *What Can Disability Studies Learn from the Culture Wars?*

See: Andrea A. Lunsford, ed. *Reclaiming Rhetorica: Women in the Rhetorical Tradition* [118].

727 Lyons, Scott Richard. "Rhetorical Sovereignty: What Do American Indians Want from Writing?" CCC 51.3 (Feb. 2000): 447–68. Print.

For American Indians, the end goal of literacy can be described as rhetorical sovereignty—as peoples' inherent right and ability to determine their own communicative needs and desires. While the field of composition and rhetoric has exhibited increased interest in American Indian and Native knowledge and voice, some of the literature expressing that interest has contained Indian stereotypes and cultural appropriations, and has excluded any discourse on sovereignty, a central concept in Indian discourse. Such literature actually hinders rhetorical sovereignty, which demands a radical rethinking of what gets taught as the written word. In the interest of rhetorical sovereignty, canons and curricula need to expand; specifically, graduate and writing programs might start by examining American Indian rhetoric, taking treaties and federal laws as rhetorical texts.

728 Malinowitz, Harriet. *Textual Orientations: Lesbian and Gay Students and the Making of Discourse Communities*. Portsmouth: Heinemann-Boynton/Cook, 1994. Print.

Gay, lesbian, and bisexual students continue to face a deeply homophobic environment in writing classes, making assignments to reflect on the self, narrate personal events, or otherwise reveal the writer's subjectivity highly problematic. The field of composition needs to recognize the existence of lesbian and gay discourses and discourse communities and allow these students to explore the social construction of their identities. Lesbian and gay students in gay-themed writing courses find that sexual identity is a significant epistemological context and social location. They discover the history and thematics of their community; analyze the ways that "gay" and "straight" have been constructed and valued in dominant discourses; excavate social meanings that underlie mainstream attitudes, complicating the very idea of sexual identity; and escape the disenfranchising individualism that confines them in mainstream views of sexual identity. The theories of social construction and critical pedagogy facilitate this understanding and allow further investigation of complex cross-cultural community definitions with similarly disabling mainstream constructions.

729 Parks, Steven. *Class Politics: The Movement for the Students' Right to Their Own Language*. Urbana: NCTE, 2000. Print.

The CCCC 1974 resolution of the Students' Right to Their Own Language (SROTL) represents much more than a moment in the history of the discipline. When considered in conjunction with the political and social organizations and movements of the time, such as the civil rights movement, Black Power, and anti-Vietnam protests, the SROTL brings to light the importance of collective action by academics. The SROTL exemplifies both the possibilities and difficulties of progressive coalition politics; and its history can be read as a guide for new university-community alliances and community-based pedagogy.

730 Phelps, Louise Wetherbee, and Janet Emig, eds. *Feminine Principles and Women's Experience in American Composition and Rhetoric*. Pittsburgh: U of Pittsburgh P, 1995. Print.

Fourteen essays explore many aspects of women's work as teachers and writers, including Patricia Bizzell, "Praising Folly: Constructing a Postmodern Rhetorical Authority as a Woman"; Lillian Bridwell-Bowles, "Discourse and Diversity: Experimental Writing within the Academy";

Robert Connors, "Women's Reclamation of Rhetoric in Nineteenth-Century America"; Mary Kay Crouch, with Son Kim Vo, "The Role of Vietnamese Women in Literacy Processes: An Interview"; Janice Hays, "Intellectual Parenting and a Developmental Feminist Pedagogy of Writing"; Sara Dalmas Jonsberg, with Maria Salgado and the Women of the Next Step, "Composing the Multiple Self: Teen Mothers Re-write Their Roles"; Louise Wetherbee Phelps, "Becoming a Warrior: Lessons of the Feminist Workplace"; and Nancy Sommers, "Between the Drafts." In addition, six essays comment on the previous fourteen, identifying recurring themes, significant omissions, and directions for further study.

731 Prendergast, Catherine. "Race: The Absent Presence in Composition Studies." CCC 50.1 (Sept. 1998): 36–53. Print.

Heath's *Ways with Words* forms a point of departure for this analysis of the ways in which race has been ignored in its relationship to the composing process and how race takes the form of other tropes. Studying the "deliberately dissonant" rhetorical stances of critical race theorists—namely, Patricia Williams and Derrick Bell—can help to foreground race in the discourses of composition studies and to uncover composition's colonial sensibilities. Through a rhetoric of double-consciousness, including features of irrationality and other departures from argumentation, these authors use voices that "refuse to be socialized" to reflect experiences of discrimination. Williams creates allegories, for example, to confront myths of black women—a textual act of double-consciousness that the author contends should not be manufactured in the composition classroom. More important is to track the ways race appears and disappears in "the collective unconscious" of composition, for example, in the discourses of basic writing. Critical race theory teaches us that our rhetoric inscribes students as foreigners and leaves whiteness uninvestigated. Winner of the 1999 Braddock Award.

732 Price, Margaret. "Accessing Disability: A Nondisabled Student Works the Hyphen." CCC 59.1 (Sept. 2007): 53–76. Print.

Including disability in first-year composition courses is often done uncritically; instead, disability studies needs to be incorporated as a *critical modality*. As illustrated by a case study of Tara, nondisabled students are often silenced by disability and tend to see it as an "us" and "them" issue. Discourse analysis shows that Tara's essay, "Lack of Access," uses pronouns in ways that draw a sharp boundary between disabled (third-person pronouns) and nondisabled (first-person pronouns) subjects. Tara's choices in this (tidy, coherent) essay also illustrate a "view from nowhere," in that she never identifies herself as either disabled or non-disabled. Disability studies, when treated as a *critical modality* rather than as a moral lesson, contribute to complicating binary thinking. While the use of disability studies in composition classrooms does not guarantee critical thinking, it can shift teachers' attention away from the search for measurable, text-based progress and toward a more layered, complex view of critical thought processes.

733 Ratcliffe, Krista. "Eavesdropping as Rhetorical Tactic: History, Whiteness, and Rhetoric." *JAC* 20.1 (Winter 2000): 87–119. Print.

Using a composite definition formed in part by Mary Daly's method of gynocentric writing, eavesdropping can be redefined, or reconsidered, as an ethical rhetorical tactic and as a way to study history, whiteness, and rhetoric. If we deliberately place ourselves at the edges of our own knowledge, we can overhear—without the demeaning, gossip-related connotations—and learn from others and ourselves. Further, if we shift our gaze in historical exploration from origins to usage as the focal point, we can eavesdrop on history in productive ways. Within the usage-directed framework, the past empowers us and leads to accountability. By eavesdropping on historical moments when the trope of whiteness was used in the United States, we can disengage dysfunctional realities of the past and dysfunctional idealizations of the present. Eavesdropping prompts scholars to reflect on the role of whiteness in the field and all its embodiments and enables teachers to better equip students with a rhetorical tactic for examining the role whiteness plays in their lives.

See: Krista Ratcliffe, *Rhetorical Listening: Identification, Gender, Whiteness* [241].

See: Jacqueline Jones Royster, *Traces of a Stream: Literacy and Social Change Among African American Women* [131].

See: Jacqueline Jones Royster and Jean C. Williams, "History in the Spaces Left: African American Presence and Narratives of Composition Studies" [130].

See: Donnalee Rubin, *Gender Influences: Reading Student Texts* [482].

See: Eileen E. Schell, *Gypsy Academics and Mother Teachers: Gender, Contingent Labor, and Writing Instruction* [500].

734 Severino, Carol, Juan C. Guerra, and Johnnella E. Butler, eds. *Writing in Multicultural Settings*. New York: MLA, 1997. Print.

Twenty essays and four cross-talks engage with the challenges of multiculturalism. Four sections address Cultural and Linguistic Diversity, The Roles of Teachers and Texts, ESL Issues, and Sociocultural and Pedagogical Tensions. Essays include Bonnie Lisle and Sandra Mano, "Embracing a Multicultural Rhetoric"; Michelle Grijalva, "Teaching American Indian Students: Interpreting the Rhetorics of Silence"; Kermit E. Campbell, "Real Niggaz's Don't Die: African American Students Speaking Themselves into Their Writing"; Carol Severino, "Two Approaches to 'Cultural Text': Toward Multicultural Literacy"; Esha Niyogi De and Donna Uthus Gregory, "Decolonizing the Classroom: Freshman Composition in a Multicultural Setting"; Wendy S. Hesford, "Writing Identities: The Essence of Difference in Multicultural Classrooms"; Muriel

Harris, "Cultural Conflicts in the Writing Center: Expectations and Assumptions of ESL Students"; Juan C. Guerra, "The Place of Intercultural Literacy in the Writing Classroom"; Mary Soliday, "The Politics of Difference: Toward a Pedagogy of Reciprocity"; and Kate Mangelsdorf, "Students on the Border."

735 Shepard, Alan, John McMillan, and Gary Tate, eds. *Coming to Class: Pedagogy and the Social Class of Teachers*. Portsmouth: Heinemann-Boynton/Cook, 1998. Print.

Reflective, autobiographical essays about the relationship of socioeconomic class to teaching, or how teachers' social class or experiences with class issues influence their teaching practices. Twenty-one essays, including Jim Daniels, "Class and Classroom: Going to Work"; Louise DeSalvo, "Digging Deep"; Donald Lazere, "Class Conflict in the English Profession"; Cecilia Rodrigues Milanes, "Color and Class"; Beverly J. Moss, "Intersections of Race and Class in the Academy"; Hephzibah Roskelly, "Rising and Converging: Race and Class in the South"; Patricia A. Sullivan, "Passing: A Family Dissemblance"; and Gary Tate, "Halfway Back Home."

See: Ira Shor and Caroline Pari, *Critical Literacy in Action* [585].

See: Lad Tobin, "Car Wrecks, Baseball Caps, and Man-to-Man Defense: The Personal Narratives of Adolescent Males" [617].

736 Vidali, Amy. "Texts of Our Institutional Lives: Performing the Rhetorical Freak Show: Disability, Student Writing, and College Admissions." *CE* 69.6 (July 2007): 615–41. Print.

Composition scholarship on embodiment must begin to acknowledge disability. Considering disability draws attention to all forms of diversity and resists the framing of disability as a personal phenomenon. Freak-show theory, particularly its contradictory nature, becomes a useful rhetorical tool to shed light on how disability can become "an object of rhetorical or textual curiosity." Students with disabilities who write college admissions essays are under intense pressure to perform. A small case study adapts theories of the freak show to "emphasize the rhetorical risks and rewards of disclosing disability." One of the three essays in this textual analysis takes on the politics of disability disclosure and upends the rhetorical expectations of the admissions essay, while all three illustrate a tension between standing out and blending in—even at the risk of discrimination.

737 Wallace, David L., and Annissa Bell. "Being Black at a Predominantly White University." *CE* 61.3 (Jan. 1999): 307–27. Print.

Interviews with three African American men—English or education majors at a university with a 7.1 percent minority enrollment rate—challenge the results of quantitative retention studies and offer a richer understanding of minority students' experiences. The three students resisted the label of "success stories," forcing the researchers to rethink how to tell these stories without being reductive or essentialist and without reproducing the dominant culture. Three critical issues from the literature frame the narratives: an educational system that reproduces inequality; the paradoxical position of "being a victim"; and assimilation and resistance. African American men, in particular, face social adjustment problems on predominantly white college campuses that are unknown to white students, but positive contact with faculty—and opportunities to explore the consequences of assimilation or resistance—may determine which students persevere.

738 Wilson, James C., and Cynthia Lewiecki-Wilson, eds. *Embodied Rhetorics: Disability in Language and Culture*. Carbondale: Southern Illinois UP, 2001. Print.

Separated into three parts—Identity and Rhetoricity: The (Dis)Abled Subject; Rhetorics of Literacy: Education and Disability; and Cultural and Spatial Rhetorics of Disability—thirteen chapters challenge current socially prescribed labels surrounding the disabled, the body, and the idea of disability. The collection as a whole explores the rhetorical implications of these labels and the prospects for turning everyday social interactions away from intolerance and toward awareness. Contributions include James C. Wilson and Cynthia Lewiecki-Wilson, "Disability, Rhetoric, and the Body"; Martha Stoddard Holmes, "Working (with) the Rhetoric of Affliction: Autobiographical Narratives of Victorians with Physical Disabilities"; Catherine Prendergast, "On the Rhetorics of Mental Disability"; Miriamne Ara Krummel, "Am I MS?"; G. Thomas Couser, "Conflicting Paradigms: The Rhetorics of Disability Memoir"; Nirmala Erevelles, "In Search of the Disabled Subject"; Brenda Jo Brueggemann, "Deafness, Literacy, Rhetoric: Legacies of Language and Communication"; Deshae E. Lott, "Going to Class with (Going to Clash with?) the Disabled Person: Educators, Students, and Their Spoken and Unspoken Negotiations"; Hannah Joyner, "Signs of Resistence: Deaf Perspectives on Linguistic Conflict in a Nineteenth-Century Southern Family"; Ellen L. Barton, "Textual Practices of Erasure: Representations of Disability and the Founding of the United Way"; Rod Michalko and Tanya Titchkosky, "Putting Disability in Its Place: It's Not a Joking Matter"; Emily F. Nye, "The Rhetoric of AIDS: A New Taxonomy"; and Beth Franks, "Gutting the Golden Goose: Disability in Grimms' Fairy Tales."

Cultural Studies

739 Berlin, James A., and Michael J. Vivion, eds. *Cultural Studies in the English Classroom*. Portsmouth: Heinemann-Boynton/Cook, 1992. Print.

Scholars in English studies and composition contribute nine essays that address issues involved in designing literature and/or writing courses with a cultural studies focus, including Michael Blitz and C. Mark Hurlbert, "Cults of Culture"; Philip E. Smith II, "Composing a Cultural Studies

Curriculum at Pitt"; Delores K. Schriner, "One Person, Many Worlds: A Multi-Cultural Composition Curriculum"; and Richard Penticoff and Linda Brodkey, "'Writing about Difference': Hard Cases for Cultural Studies." These essays are followed by ten essays that describe cultural studies courses on such varied topics as the research paper, visual texts, and Shakespeare.

740 Berlin, James A. "Poststructuralism, Cultural Studies, and the Composition Classroom." *Rhetoric Review* 11.1 (Fall 1992): 16–33. Print.

The postmodern critique of traditional liberal-humanist epistemology has been useful to social-epistemic rhetoricians. In place of the traditional view of the individual as a unified consciousness unencumbered by historical circumstances, postmodernism posits a subject shaped by history and conflicting discourses, making individual consciousness contradictory and mutable. In place of the view of language as a neutral device for conveying truth, postmodernism sees language as constructing reality and deriving its meaning from differences among the signs themselves. Postmodernism critiques master narratives of human experience as part of, not external to, experience, and locates their meanings in what they exclude. These views mesh with the social-epistemic treatment of the writer as a construct, the audience as an unstable repertoire of constructed selves, and language as the constructive medium—hence as the site of the struggle to define reality in one's best interests. All texts are thus ideological. In studying texts, rhetoric cannot accept claims of transcendence. The writing course, then, should study many ways of using language, emphasizing the need to negotiate among textual and contextual meanings. This approach fosters democratic values by enabling students to analyze claims made on them by competing discourses.

741 Berlin, James A. *Rhetorics, Poetics, and Cultures: Refiguring English Studies*. Urbana: NCTE, 1996. Print.

For almost three centuries, English studies in America served to secure the hegemony of the dominant social group by valorizing their cultural capital. Until about 1970, this meant educating a professional elite—lawyers, ministers, politicians, and business leaders. But after 1970, the global economy began to change rapidly and radically. The American economy deindustrialized, and social power now devolved upon a managerial class, those who could best communicate, collaborate, and learn new tasks quickly. Moreover, American society changed rapidly as well, with immigrants coming in record numbers in the 1980s, rich and poor suddenly moving much farther apart culturally and economically, and families developing models other than the nuclear to organize their lives. The traditional English department simply cannot cope with all of these rapid changes. Literary theorists and cultural studies scholars understand that they need to redesign their profession, but they may not realize that they need to enlist the aid of workers in social-epistemic rhetoric. These rhetoricians can help them because they are already accustomed to dealing with a wide range of texts, visual and musical as well as print; because they deal with texts that exert power in the world (political, legal, ceremonial, etc.) and not merely those that exist to be appreciated aesthetically; because they have always focused on the production rather than the reception of texts; and because they are comfortable crossing disciplinary boundaries. They can help create a new English studies discipline that erases the split between rhetoric and poetic and studies all forms of signifying practices, their genres, ideologies, and supporting social institutions. The new English studies will equip students not only for work in a postindustrial age but also for participatory citizenship in a multicultural democracy. Berlin concludes with detailed descriptions of two cultural studies courses that enact the pedagogy for which he calls, and three English departments that have already reorganized themselves along the lines he recommends.

742 Bullock, Richard, and John Trimbur. *The Politics of Writing Instruction, Postsecondary*. Portsmouth: Heinemann-Boynton/Cook, 1991. Print.

Eighteen original essays (and a foreword by Richard Ohmann) that develop a political critique of writing instruction and demonstrate the inseparability of teaching writing from social, cultural, and economic forces. Essays include James S. Slevin, "Depoliticizing and Politicizing Composition Studies"; James A. Berlin, "Rhetoric, Poetic, and Culture: Contested Boundaries in English Studies"; Susan Miller, "The Feminization of Composition"; Robert Connors, "Rhetoric in the Modern University: The Creation of an Underclass"; Bruce Herzberg, "Composition and the Politics of the Curriculum"; Elizabeth Flynn, "Composition Studies from a Feminist Perspective"; Richard Bullock, "Autonomy and Community in the Evaluation of Writing"; Robert Schwegler, "The Politics of Reading Student Papers"; Victor Villanueva Jr., "Considerations of American Freireistas"; and John Trimbur, "Literacy and the Discourse of Crisis." Winner of the 1993 CCCC Outstanding Book Award.

743 Canagarajah, A. Suresh. "The Place of World Englishes in Composition: Pluralization Continued." CCC 57.4 (June 2006): 586–619. Print.

Multilingual users of English will soon outnumber native speakers, and as local Englishes travel, World English speakers use creative strategies to accomplish various purposes. Composition students, therefore, need to become proficient in negotiating a repertoire of World Englishes in order to shuttle between different discourse communities. Code meshing (rather than code switching) embraces the reality of multilingualism demanded by globalization; users have to know when it is rhetorically appropriate to blend dominant varieties of English with their own preferred varieties. The negotiation of different codes can actually facilitate language competence and encourage awareness of conventions. Texts by African American scholar Geneva Smitherman demonstrate her infrequent but careful uses of AAVE in ways that show her control over a number of Englishes while they also demonstrate that change is possible "*even within the system*."

744 Dean, Terry. "Multicultural Classrooms, Monocultural Teachers." CCC 40.1 (Feb. 1989): 23–37. Print. Rpt. in Corbett, Myers, and Tate [150].

The greater the distance between a student's home culture and American academic culture, the greater the likelihood that the student will not succeed in school. This problem can be addressed by including the home culture in the curriculum, involving people from the home culture in the school, allowing students to shape some learning tasks according to their own interests and needs, and encouraging teachers to be advocates who will prevent culture-conflict "problems" from being blamed on the students. If the negotiation between home and school culture is studied sensitively in class, students can become comfortably bicultural. Students can write about cultural similarities and contrasts that they have observed, about their own cultural identities, and about their experiences in language learning. Monocultural teachers should avoid making assumptions about how students view their cultural identities and the transition to school culture.

745 Farmer, Frank. "Dialogue and Critique: Bakhtin and the Cultural Studies Writing Classroom." CCC 49.2 (May 1998): 187–207. Print.

A besetting problem in cultural studies pedagogy is the cultural studies critic's apparent stance of superiority over consumers of mass culture, who do not, as the critic does, notice and resist its ideological messages. Students usually resent this superior role for their teacher and reject it for themselves. Two concepts from the work of literary theorist Mikhail Bakhtin can help address this difficulty. One is his notion of "anacrisis," or critical questioning. The teacher can use questions to bring out the students' "going truths" or ingrained ideologies and also to reveal his or her own positions. The second is the concept of the "superaddressee," a hypothetical listener or reader who is imagined to understand the speaker or writer perfectly. Bakhtin says that one imagines this audience in order to overcome the fear of being misunderstood or ignored and thus to be willing to take the risk of uttering or writing. This concept can be used to analyze popular culture artifacts for the vision of a better life that they project. For example, *The Cosby Show*, attacked by television cultural critic Mark Crispin Miller as racist, can be analyzed as providing with its images of affluence a symbolic corrective to social inequities that make such affluence especially hard for African Americans to obtain. Such an analysis helps to acknowledge the sources of pleasure in popular culture, which students soon become weary of hearing relentlessly denounced.

746 Gilyard, Keith, and Vorris Nunley, eds. *Rhetoric and Ethnicity*. Portsmouth: Heinemann-Boynton/Cook, 2004. Print.

Ethnic identity cannot be reduced to a single, all-encompassing profile. Instead, it is an important ingredient in the personal make-up and expression of individuals inside neighborhoods and through conversation and writing. Sixteen chapters engage with Gilyard's term "critical ethnicity," which serves as a political and social process and discourse that seeks a more civilized society based on tolerance and open-mindedness.

Part I, History, includes Geneva Smitherman, "Meditations on Language, Pedagogy, and a Life of Struggle"; Jessica Enoch, "'Semblances of Civilization': Zitkala Sa's Resistance to White Education"; Malea Powell, "Extending the Hand of Empire: American Indians and the Indian Reform Movement, a Beginning"; and Barry Thatcher, "Contrastive U.S. and South American Rhetorics." Part II, Identity and Pedagogy, includes Marilyn M. Cooper, "Nonessentialist Identity and the National Discourse"; Xin Liu Gale, "Community, Personal Experiences, and Rhetoric of Commitment"; Janice Chernekoff, "Challenging the Constraints of First-Year Composition Through Ethnic Women's Narratives"; and Laurie Grobman, "Challenging Racial Authority, Rewriting Racial Authority: Multicultural Rhetorics in Literary Studies and Composition."

747 Gray-Rosendale, Laura, and Steven Rosendale, eds. *Radical Relevance: Toward a Scholarship of the Whole Left*. Albany: State U of New York P, 2005. Print.

This thirteen-chapter collection is divided into three parts—Legacies of Marxism; Left Coalitions Beyond the Triad; and The Academic Left, Critical Theory, and the Global Context—and examines the role of the academic left in emerging scholarship, activism, and student work in the classroom. Framed by an introduction by Steven Rosendale, essays include Alan Wald, "Black Nationalist Identity and Internationalist Class Unity: The Political and Cultural Legacy of Marxism"; Barbara Foley, "Race, Class, and Communism: The Young Ralph Ellison and the 'Whole Left'"; Victor Villanueva, "Toward a Political Economy of Rhetoric (or a Rhetoric of Political Economy)"; Scott Richard Lyons, "The Left Side of the Circle: American Indians and Progressive Politics"; Michael Bennett, "Reconciling Red and Green"; Brenda Jo Brueggemann, Wendy L. Chrisman, and Marian E. Lupo, "A Monstrous Emerge-agency: Cripping the 'Whole Left'"; Derek Owens, "What the Left Left Out"; Henry A. Giroux, "Globalizing Dissent and Radicalizing Democracy: Politics, Pedagogy, and the Responsibility of Critical Intellectuals"; Noah De Lissovoy and Peter McLaren, "Toward a Contemporary Philosophy of Praxis"; Wendy S. Hesford, "Global/Local Labor Politics and the Promise of Service Learning"; Evan Watkins, "Between Schools and Work: Classroom and Class"; Mark Wood, "Another World Is Possible"; and Laura Gray-Rosendale, "Feminism(s) and the Left: A Discussion with Linda Martín Alcoff."

See: Gail E. Hawisher and Cynthia L. Selfe, with Yi-Huey Guo and Lu Liu, "Globalization and Agency: Designing and Redesigning the Literacies of Cyberspace" [351].

748 Howard, Rebecca Moore. "Sexuality, Textuality: The Cultural Work of Plagiarism." *CE* 62.4 (Mar. 2000): 473–91. Print.

The discourse of plagiarism is laden with gendered, sexualized metaphors of weakness, collaboration, disease, adultery, rape, and property. These metaphors connote a sense of sexual as well as textual violation. The term *plagiarism*, therefore, does as much (or more) cultural work as pedagogical; it regulates sexuality (insisting on compulsory heterosexuality) and student bodies as well as textuality and student papers. However, the metaphors that construct the term *plagiarism* are not the real problem; the term itself is, and should therefore be abandoned. Instead, we should concern ourselves with fraud, insufficient citation, and excessive repetition—pedagogical concerns rather than moral or sexual issues.

749 Lunsford, Andrea A., and Lahoucine Ouzgane, eds. *Crossing Borderlands: Composition and Postcolonial Studies*. Pittsburgh: U of Pittsburgh P, 2004. Print.

By breaking away from the Eurocentric view of postcolonialism and, instead, "considering the position of Mexican Americans, African Americans, and Native Americans," this thirteen-chapter collection explores various borderlands in America and the impact of student voices on the "colonizing modes of English." Contributors investigate the preventative mechanisms that inhibit student access and agency to language and the individuality of their own voices. Such exposure will undoubtedly lead to "the liberatory potential of teaching and practicing writing," a landmark theme central to borderland pedagogy. Framed by an introduction by the editors, essays include Min-Zhan Lu, "Composing Postcolonial Studies"; Deepika Bahri, "Terms of Engagement: Postcolonialism, Transnationalism, and Composition Studies"; Gary A. Olson, "Encountering the Other: Postcolonial Theory and Composition Scholarship"; Susan C. Jarratt, "Beside Ourselves: Rhetoric and Representation in Postcolonial Feminist Writing"; Aneil Rallin, "(Im)migrant Crossings"; David Dzaka, "Resisting Writing: Reflections on the Postcolonial Factor in the Writing Class"; Jaime Armin Mejía, "Arts of the U.S.–Mexico Contact Zone"; Louise Rodríguez Connal, "Hybridity: A Lens for Understanding Mestizo/a Writers"; and C. Jan Swearingen, "The New Literacy/Orality Debates: Ebonics and the Redefinition of Literacy in Multicultural Settings."

750 Lunsford, Andrea A. "Toward a Mestiza Rhetoric: Gloria Anzaldúa on Composition and Postcoloniality." *JAC: A Journal of Composition Theory* 18.1 (Winter 1998): 1–27. Print.

A mestiza lives in geographical and cultural borderlands and must learn to tolerate contradiction and ambiguity, to juggle cultures, and to imagine spaces not limited by dichotomies. For writing, this means using a rich variety of genres, languages, and registers, while also engaging in collaboration. In this interview, Anzaldúa discusses her earliest writings and drawings, her composing rituals, and issues that range from internal censorship to precolonial histories and activism. In addition to her poetry and children's books, one of Anzaldúa's current book projects is about composition and postcolonial issues of identity, based on the theme of *compustura*, or seaming together fragments to make a garment that represents oneself.

See: Paul Kei Matsuda, "The Myth of Linguistic Homogeneity in U.S. College Composition" [776].

751 McComiskey, Bruce. "Social-Process Rhetorical Inquiry: Cultural Studies Methodologies for Critical Writing about Advertisements." *JAC: A Journal of Composition Theory* 17.3 (Fall 1997): 381–400. Print.

Classical Marxism focuses on a cycle that begins with the production of material things, which are then distributed for purchase, and finally consumed in such a way as to produce more things, so that the cycle continues. Cultural studies applies this cycle to ideology, focusing first on the production of desires for things. Next, cultural studies looks at distribution not in terms of transportation systems and the like but in terms of cultural institutions, such as workplaces, schools, or organs of the mass media, that provide contexts for the values that produce desires. Consumption, for cultural studies, focuses not on the use of material things but on the use of values to construct identities, a process that, in turn, creates new desires. An adequate cultural studies pedagogy must address all three moments in this cycle. It must ask: How do cultural artifacts (advertisements, in this case) construct their ideal consumers through the values they project? How do media that circulate artifacts and their values create larger contexts for them (e.g., how does a fashion magazine create a context for the perfume ad placed in it)? How do the values thus circulated impact consumers, that is, how do people accept, reject, or modify the subject positions these artifacts offer them? Cultural studies critics are often negative about consumers who accept the subject positions offered to them by mass culture as if these were natural or universal. But this view errs by neglecting the extent to which people negotiate with what's offered and shape it to their own ends. McComiskey concludes with specific examples from his own cultural studies pedagogy to teach all three moments in the cycle.

752 Reynolds, Nedra. "Interrupting Our Way to Agency: Feminist Cultural Studies and Composition." *Feminism and Composition Studies: In Other Words*. Ed. Susan C. Jarratt and Lynn Worsham. New York: MLA, 1998. 58–73. Print.

Women need an idea of agency that reflects postmodernism's insights into the multiple and competing subjectivities within the self but that still conceptualizes the possibility of individual action amid and on one's circumstances. A rhetorical dimension of this notion of agency might draw upon interruption as a deliberate strategy for those who are all too often interrupted or silenced when they try to speak. A cultural-studies analysis of the impact of feminist work on British cultural studies shows just such a strategy of interruption in action. Similarly, American feminists need to interrupt cultural-studies work in composition. Cultural-studies scholars John Trimbur and James Berlin replicate British male chauvinism when they allow their Marxist-inspired focus on labor and class issues to cause them to neglect gender issues and feminist scholarship. Lester Faigley can also be faulted for relying too heavily on the work of French cultural critic Jean-François Lyotard, leading him to deny metanarratives, such as the critique of patriarchy, that are vital to feminism, and to portray academic discourse as unrelentingly agonistic. Feminist writing teachers can encourage students to interrupt the academy's expectations for traditional academic discourse, with its emphasis on clarity, coherence, and linear organization to prove a thesis, and help students to devise forms more congenial to women.

753 Rosteck, Thomas, ed. *At the Intersection: Cultural Studies and Rhetorical Studies*. New York: Guilford, 1999. Print.

Scholars from American Studies, Speech Communication, and English contribute thirteen essays that focus on connections between the theoretical discourses of cultural studies and rhetoric or that trace such links through analysis of cultural artifacts. Contributors include Carole Blair and Neil Michel, "Commemorating in the Theme Park Zone: Reading the Astronauts Memorial"; Steven Mailloux, "Reading the Culture Wars: Traveling Rhetoric and the Reception of Curricular Reform"; Barry Brummett and Detine L. Bowers, "Subject Positions as a Site of Rhetorical Struggle: Representing African Americans"; Elizabeth Walker Mechling and Jay Mechling, "American Cultural Criticism in the Pragmatic Attitude"; Cary Nelson, "The Linguisticality of Cultural Studies: Rhetoric, Close Reading, and Contextualization"; and Thomas S. Frentz and Janice Hocker Rushing, "Courting Community in Contemporary Culture."

See: Carol Severino, Juan C. Guerra, and Johnella E. Butler, eds., *Writing in Multicultural Settings* [734].

754 Sirc, Geoffrey. "Never Mind the Tagmemics, Where's the Sex Pistols?" CCC 48.1 (Feb. 1997): 9–29. Print.

Composition teachers were drawn to teaching popular music and encouraging self-exploration and self-expression in the 1960s. But the field returned to more academic materials and goals in the 1970s. Therefore, composition studies ignored the phenomenon of Punk music when it emerged in the mid-1970s. Punk's ethos was both nihilistic and playful, unconcerned in either case with success or problem-solving. In the 1980s the neglect of Punk continued—its demise as a popular music form around 1980 was ignored—because composition studies wanted irony-free reproduction of academic discourse while Punk art abounded in irreverent transformations of familiar images of respect and power. Composition studies favored mastery and control over one's medium, whereas Punk artists attempted above all to generate energy and emotion, with musicianship taking a back seat. Composition studies could have benefited from admitting the Punk perspective—it would have made writing more fun, put more emphasis on process as opposed to product, and given students permission, too, to hate writing and to fail. Punk's negative perspective is still present, fortunately, and beginning to influence composition studies after all, such as in the work of

Richard Miller and Joseph Harris. Sirc's essay exemplifies cultural-studies criticism.

755 Trimbur, John. "Articulation Theory and the Problem of Determination: A Reading of Lives on the Boundary." *JAC: A Journal of Advanced Composition* 13.1 (Winter 1993): 33–50. Print.

Cultural studies can help explain Mike Rose's *Lives on the Boundary* [655]. In this book, Rose tells the story of his own life according to a familiar American pattern: the poor boy who makes good through his own efforts, especially through acquiring advanced literacy. His moments of resistance to the dominant order—when he just wants to be "average" rather than to excel in school—are mediated by adult mentors, and Rose himself eventually enters adult life successfully and takes a secure place in a profession, teaching. This story could be faulted for undercutting the book's larger purpose by suggesting that the educational reforms Rose advocates would not be necessary if everyone worked as hard as he did. Trimbur argues, however, that the presence of this familiar American narrative in Rose's book should be understood as a "conjuncture," in cultural-studies terms, that is, an historical moment when ideas converge and take their meaning from one another. The meaning of the narrative is changed here by its use in a larger project of education reform. It does not simply celebrate individual effort but rather provides a vehicle for demonstrating the many social constraints on educational success. As in Stuart Hall's "articulation" theory, Rose puts together seemingly contradictory discursive elements in order to make meaning out of his life and to make a persuasive case for reform. We know that he is not simply advocating conformity to traditional literacy as the sole path to success because he also dramatizes the unfairness of traditional standards of evaluation and the richness of nontraditional students' literacy experiences outside of school. Rose's use of a familiar autobiographical trope, therefore, should be understood as a strategy to gain broader popular acceptance for his valuable educational views.

756 Trimbur, John. *Popular Literacy: Studies in Cultural Practices and Poetics.* Pittsburgh: U of Pittsburgh P, 2001. Print.

This book poses the question of how people make literacy popular, using reading and writing for their own ends rather than for official purposes, and offers fourteen essays that explore that question, including these: Mariolina Salvatori, "Porque no puedo decir mi cuento: Mexican Ex-votos' Iconographic Literacy"; Cheryl Glenn, "Popular Literacy in the Middle Ages: *The Book of Margery Kempe*"; Todd S. Gernes, "Recasting the Culture of Ephemera"; Patricia Bizzell, "'Stolen Literacies in *Iola Leroy*"; Stephanie Almagno, Nedra Reynolds, and John Trimbur, "Italian-American Cookbooks: Authenticity and the Market"; Nicholas Coles, "Joe Shakespeare: The Contemporary British Worker Movement"; Diana George, "Changing the Face of Poverty: Nonprofits and the Problem of Representation"; Lundy Braun and John Trimbur,

"Popularizing Science: At the Boundary of Expert and Lay Biomedical Knowledge"; and Lester Faigley, "Understanding Popular Digital Literacies: Metaphors for the Internet."

Teaching English as a Second Language and Language Policy

757 Belcher, Diane, and George Braine, eds. *Academic Writing in a Second Language: Essays on Research and Pedagogy*. Norwood: Ablex, 1994. Print.

Sixteen essays exploring the social perspective on ESL writing issues. Included are Ilona Leki, "Good Writing: I Know It When I See It"; George Braine, "Writing in the Natural Sciences"; Diane Belcher, "Writing Critically across the Curriculum"; Ulla Connor and Melinda Kramer, "Writing from Sources: Case Studies of Graduate Students in Business Management"; Diane Tedick and Maureen Mathison, "Holistic Scoring on ESL Writing Assessment: What Does an Analysis of Rhetorical Features Reveal?"; Ann Johns, "Teaching Classroom and Authentic Genres: Initiating Students into Academic Cultures and Discourses"; and Sally Jacoby, David Leech, and Christine Holten, "A Genre-Based Developmental Writing Course for Undergraduate ESL Science Majors."

758 Belcher, Diane, and Alan Hirvela, eds. *Linking Literacies: Perspectives on L2 Reading-Writing Connections*. Ann Arbor: U of Michigan P, 2001. Print.

Examining a wide range of issues within the general rubrics of L2 reading-writing connections and L2 academic literacy illustrates the many ways in which L2 reading-writing relations can be manifested. Following an introduction by the editors, thirteen chapters in four sections consider the theories, history, and research that influence L2 literacy pedagogy, including William Grabe, "Reading-Writing Relations: Theoretical Perspectives and Instructional Practices"; Paul Kei Matsuda, "Reexamining Audiolingualism: On the Genesis of Reading and Writing in L2 Studies"; Alan Hirvela, "Connecting Reading and Writing through Literature"; George Newell, Maria C. Garriga, and Susan S. Peterson, "Learning to Assume the Role of Author: A Study of Reading-to-Write One's Own Ideas in an Undergraduate ESL Composition Course"; Barbara Dobson and Christine Feak, "A Cognitive Modeling Approach to Teaching Critique Writing to Nonnative Speakers"; Joel Bloch, "Plagiarism and the ESL Student: From Printed to Electronic Texts"; Debbie Barks and Patricia Watts, "Textual Borrowing Strategies for Graduate-Level ESL Writers"; and Georgette Jabbour, "Lexis and Grammar in Second Language Reading and Writing."

See: A. Suresh Canagarajah, "The Place of World Englishes in Composition: Pluralization Continued" [743].

759 Carson, Joan G., and Ilona Leki, eds. *Reading in the Composition Classroom: Second Language Perspectives*. Boston: Heinle, 1993. Print.

After many years of being taught separately as technical skills, reading and writing are increasingly being taught together in ESL courses that recognize the inextricable links between them. Eighteen essays examine how individual readers process text, how cultural contexts affect understanding, and how reading can be taught in writing classes. Essays include Ilona Leki, "Reciprocal Themes in ESL Reading and Writing"; Joy Reid, "Historical Perspectives on Writing and Reading in the ESL Classroom"; Barbara Kroll, "Teaching Writing Is Teaching Reading: Training the New Teacher of ESL Composition"; Joan Carson, "Reading for Writing: Cognitive Perspectives"; Douglas Flahive and Nathalie Bailey, "Exploring Reading/Writing Relationships in Adult Second Language Learners"; Ruth Spack, "Student Meets Text, Text Meets Student: Finding a Way into Academic Discourse"; Sarah Benesch, "ESL Authors: Reading and Writing Critical Autobiographies"; and Ann Johns, "Reading and Writing Tasks in English for Academic Purposes Classes: Products, Processes, and Resources."

760 Casanave, Christine Pearson. *Controversies in Second Language Writing: Dilemmas and Decisions in Research and Instruction*. Ann Arbor: U of Michigan P, 2003. Print.

Teachers can make informed decisions about L2 writing pedagogy by "understanding some of the key issues and conflicting opinions" in the field. One might begin by recognizing a series of false dichotomies, from process/product to the debate over the explicit teaching of genres. These dichotomies can be neither dismissed nor necessarily resolved. Understanding the ongoing and evolving nature of controversies in second-language writing allows for critical and progressive pedagogy. Each chapter in this book begins with a provocative question, then surveys opinions, looks at classroom perspectives and practices, reinvokes "ongoing questions," and ends with further references and relevant readings.

761 Connor, Ulla. *Contrastive Rhetoric: Cross-Cultural Aspects of Second-Language Writing*. New York: Cambridge UP, 1996. Print.

Contrastive rhetoric studies the ways that a first language interferes with learning a second language. Contrastive rhetoric has become increasingly complex, moving beyond the analysis of merely negative effects to include, today, insights from rhetoric, composition studies, discourse theory, genre theory, theoretical and applied linguistics, and literacy theory. Moreover, studies of ESL learners from different cultures have produced detailed analyses of cultural and educational differences that influence second-language learning. Connor summarizes the relevant aspects of each set of theories and of the major empirical studies and draws implications for further study of ESL, EFL, and ESP research.

762 Cummins, Jim. "The Sanitized Curriculum: Educational Disempowerment in a Nation at Risk." *Richness in Writing: Empowering ESL Students*.

Ed. Donna M. Johnson and Duane H. Roen. White Plains: Longman, 1989. 19–38. Print.

The 1983 report "A Nation at Risk" shifted policy emphasis from equity to "excellence." Subsequent reports focus on raising standards and getting tough. This reform movement threatens to disempower students, particularly minority students, by fostering a "transmission" approach to teaching that ignores students' need to develop a sense of efficacy in their relations with educators. Transmission especially harms ESL students by excluding student experience and suppressing the meaningful communication needed to learn language. Moreover, the reforms reflect an autocratic image of society that is counterdemocratic. In addition, the focus on excellence promotes passivity rather than critical thinking. An alternative conception of reform can be based on a more productive interaction between students and teachers, active use of written and oral language for critical thinking, and use of students' cultural resources that will enrich all students. Our children's generation will need critical skills and intercultural understanding in the future and cannot reach the goals set out in "A Nation at Risk" by following the path of "excellence" laid out there.

763 Ferdman, Bernardo M., Rose-Marie Weber, and Arnulfo G. Ramirez, eds. *Literacy across Languages and Cultures*. Albany: State U of New York P, 1994. Print.

Meeting the English literacy needs of members of linguistic and cultural minorities in the United States requires rethinking many assumptions about literacy itself, especially because most research concentrates on first-language literacy. The eleven essays in this volume probe the meaning of literacy in a multiethnic context, the processes of second-language and second-culture acquisition, and the application of current research to these concerns. Essays include Stephen Reder, "Practice-Engagement Theory: A Sociocultural Approach to Literacy across Languages and Cultures"; Nancy Hornberger, "Continua of Biliteracy"; Concha Delgado-Gaitan, "Sociocultural Change through Literacy: Toward the Empowerment of Families"; Barbara McCaskill, "Literacy in the Loophole of Retreat: Harriet Jacobs's Nineteenth-Century Narrative"; and Alison d'Anglejan, "Language and Literacy in Quebec."

764 Ferris, Dana, and John S. Hedgcock. *Teaching ESL Composition: Purpose, Process, and Practice*. 2nd ed. Mahwah: Erlbaum, 2005. Print.

In this second edition, Ferris and Hedgcock update pedagogical approaches to teaching ESL composition. These approaches are grounded in current research and offer very practical advice and materials for teachers. The initial chapters lay out theoretical and practical issues, but the bulk of the book focuses on the development of teaching materials and strategies, from course and lesson planning, to text selection and task construction, to teacher and peer response, to error treatment, to assessment, to technology. Within each of these themes, the authors offer a wide range of materials, from syllabi examples, to student worksheets, to rubrics and grade conversion charts. Each chapter concludes with "Application Activities" for readers, not to teach from but to help process the issues raised in the chapter. Thus, the book is useful not just for teachers of ESL students or those interested in ESL issues, but also for those who are learning about ESL issues in teacher-preparation programs.

765 Harklau, Linda. "From the 'Good Kids' to the 'Worst': Representations of English Language Learners Across Educational Settings." *TESOL Quarterly* 34.1 (Spring 2000): 35–67. Print.

Learners' identities affect their experiences in school; the institutional label *ESOL student*, largely accepted as unchanging and self-evident, played a crucial role in three students' transitions from high school to college. Three year-long ethnographic case studies of language minority students, each a U.S. high school graduate, illustrate how educators' representations of ESOL student identity are reproduced in broader institutional discourses and how representations have direct effects on classroom behavior and achievement in both settings—keeping students engaged in high school but turning them away in community college. The representation of what it meant to be an ESOL student in high school (immigrants as model students) facilitated favorable conditions for learning, while the dominant representation of ESOL students in their community college (new to the United States) led to student resistance. In the context of the high school, images of immigrants informed a representation of ESOL students as hardworking and highly motivated; in the ESOL program of the urban community college, however, the curriculum reflected an image of ESOL students as cultural novices—with goals diametrically opposed to these students' self-perceptions and expectations as seasoned school-goers and residents of the United States. Labels given to students have consequences for students' classroom behavior and investment in learning; at the same time, institutional representations, in determining how entering students are placed and evaluated, have significant educational implications.

766 Harklau, Linda, Kay M. Losey, and Meryl Siegal, eds. *Generation 1.5 Meets College Composition: Issues in the Teaching of Writing to U.S.-Educated Learners of ESL*. Mahwah: Erlbaum, 1999. Print.

The "1.5 generation" represents the student population of U.S. high school graduates who enter higher education while in the process of learning English; their traits and experiences lie somewhere in between those of first- or second-generation immigrants. Twelve chapters address instructional issues presented by this group and include Ilona Leki, "'Pretty Much I Screwed Up': Ill-Served Needs of a Permanent Resident"; Judith Rodby, "Contingent Literacy: The Social Construction of Writing for Nonnative English-Speaking College Freshmen"; Yuet-Sim D. Chiang and Mary Schmida, "Language Identity and Language Ownership: Linguistic Conflicts of First-Year University Writing Students"; Beth Hartman and Elaine Tarone, "Preparation for College Writing: Teachers Talk About Writing Instruction for Southeast Asian

American Students in Secondary School"; Dana R. Ferris, "One Size Does Not Fit All: Response and Revision Issues for Immigrant Student Writers"; and Kate Wolfe-Quintero and Gabriela Segade, "University Support for Second-Language Writers Across the Curriculum."

767 Horner, Bruce, and John Trimbur. "English Only and U.S. College Composition." CCC 53.4 (June 2002): 594–630. Print.

U.S. writing programs and writing instruction have been strongly influenced by a tacit language policy of unidirectional English monolingualism. In the modern university, "the triumph of the vernacular" had consequences beyond a curriculum with less Greek and Latin. In a view of modern languages where texts were privileged, English became the (only) language for writing instruction—a consequence of several overlapping beliefs, for example, that the study of modern languages is but a means to mastering English. These assumptions about language along with persistent fears of the foreign show up in English Only legislation as well as in debates over basic writers. Debates *for* as well as *against* English Only develop from the same troubling assumptions—that, for example, language or language learning are fixed and uniform with the goal of mastery. Overcoming the tacit compliance with English Only means seeing language competence as arbitrary and fluctuating. Winner of the 2003 Braddock Award.

768 Huckin, Thomas, Margot Haynes, and James Coady. *Second Language Reading and Vocabulary Learning*. Norwood: Ablex, 1993. Print.

Fourteen essays report on research into the ways that ESL students learn vocabulary, including analyses of L1 vocabulary learning and the efficacy of contextual guessing, investigation of the assumption that reading improves vocabulary acquisition, and evaluation of pedagogical practices for improving vocabulary. Essays include Frederika Stoller and William Grabe, "Implication for L2 Vocabulary Acquisition from L1 Research"; Margot Haynes, "Patterns and Perils of Guessing in Second Language Reading"; Chion-Lan Chern, "Chinese Students' Word-Solving Strategies in Reading in English"; Kate Parry, "Too Many Words: Learning the Vocabulary of an Academic Subject"; Mark Stein, "The Healthy Inadequacy of Contextual Definition"; and Cheryl Brown, "Factors Affecting the Acquisition of Vocabulary: Frequency and Saliency of Words."

769 Kells, Michelle Hall, and Valerie Balester, eds. *Attending to the Margins: Writing, Researching, and Teaching on the Front Lines*. Portsmouth: Heinemann-Boynton/Cook, 1999. Print.

So-called nontraditional students, including those whose native language is not English, whose home culture is not derived from northern Europe, and/or whose social class is disadvantaged, now make up the majority of students in many classrooms. The so-called marginalized have come to the center of the educational enterprise in the schools where the ten contributors to this volume teach. These students need to learn traditional academic discourse, but in order to learn, they need to draw on the cultural resources they bring to the classroom. Specific suggestions on pedagogies to help these students do so can be found in Donna Dunbar-Odom, "Speaking Back with Authority: Students as Ethnographers in the Research Writing Class"; Caroline Pari, "Developing Critical Pedagogy for Basic Writing at a CUNY Community College"; Mike Palmquist, Donna LeCourt, and Kate Kiefer, "Talking Across Differences: Building Student/Teacher Dialogue Through Instruction in Computer-Supported Writing Classrooms"; Randall Popken, "Adult Writers, Interdiscursive Linking, and Academic Survival"; Maureen Neal, "Abdominal Conditions and Other Cretins of Habit: Hyperfluency and the Acquisition of Academic Discourse"; Barbara Gleason, "Something of Great Constancy: Storytelling, Story Writing, and Academic Literacy"; Margaret A. McLaughlin and Eleanor Agnew, "Teacher Attitudes Toward African American Language Patterns: A Close Look at Attrition Rates"; Michelle Hall Kells, "Leveling the Linguistic Playing Field in First-Year Composition"; Alan Hirvela, "Teaching Immigrant Students in the College Writing Classroom"; and Sharon Dean and Barbara Wenner, with Rosalyn Haugabrook, "Skin Deep: Toward an Equality of Disclosure." Sections of the book are introduced by Kells and Balester, Ira Shor, Victor Villanueva, and Akua Duku Anokye.

770 Kubota, Ryoko. "Japanese Culture Constructed by Discourses: Implications for Applied Linguistics Research and ELT." *TESOL Quarterly* 33.1 (Spring 1999): 9–35. Print.

Conceptions of culture tend to dichotomize Western culture and Eastern culture, drawing boundaries between them in areas of inquiry such as contrastive rhetoric. In the applied linguistic literature, Japanese culture is essentialized, the result of discourse that defines the subordinate group as exotic Other. Another way of understanding cultural differences comes from a critique of cultural representations from the concepts of discourse and power/knowledge, not to dismiss the existence of diversity within a culture but to escape the binary logic of same versus different. In this view, characteristics of the Japanese people and culture are seen as ideological constructs that promote homogeneity and thus serve the interest of the government and corporations, as illustrated through *nihonjinron*. The pedagogical tension between acculturation and pluralist approaches in teaching ESL students suggests an alternative model, that of critical multiculturalism that supports both cultural pluralism and critical acquisition of the dominant language.

771 Kutz, Eleanor, Suzy Q. Groden, and Vivian Zamel. *The Discovery of Competence: Teaching and Learning with Diverse Student Writers*. Portsmouth: Heinemann-Boynton/Cook, 1993. Print.

Teachers of writing, especially to ESL students, should begin with students' competencies and not focus on correcting their deficiencies. Understanding the complexities of language acquisition allows teachers to help students acquire new competencies in academic discourse. The academy is a culture with a discourse and mindsets that are alien to many students, particularly to ESL students. Teachers can, however, make the transition to the new culture less frustrating and alienating by designing courses that allow students to discover and build on existing abilities and knowledge as they investigate new conditions and expectations. Language learning comes from the desire to make meaning, not from building up incremental linguistic units; so, too, with a second language or dialect. Moreover, intellectual development and cognitive orientations to learning that characterize extant competencies need to be respected and not forced into academic molds. Teachers can use the classroom as a research site for discovering students' abilities and examining their own teaching methods, taking a critical view of their curricular frameworks. The authors include many excerpts from student papers reflecting on their language-learning experiences, describe classroom research practices, suggest ways to assess student competencies, and offer advice about creating multicultural frameworks for curriculum development.

772 Leki, Ilona. "Coping Strategies of ESL Students in Writing Tasks across the Curriculum." *TESOL Quarterly* 29.2 (Summer 1995): 235–60. Print.

A naturalistic study examines five ESL visa students' experiences in disciplinary courses and identifies strategies that students both bring with them and develop in response to writing demands. Through interviews, observations, student journals, and various documents, ten categories of strategies are cataloged, including relying on past writing experiences, looking for models, and accommodating (and resisting) teachers' demands. Each student is profiled, and then each of the ten categories is illustrated.

773 Leki, Ilona. *Undergraduates in a Second Language: Challenges and Complexities of Academic Literacy Development.* Mahwah: Erlbaum, 2007. Print.

Leki presents a large qualitative study of the literacy experiences of a group of L2 students across their undergraduate careers. The focus is on students' writing, but also on the full range of their academic lives, and the study examines the "social nature" of literacy and the degree to which literacy learning transfers from the writing classroom to other classes and contexts. Leki offers detailed pictures of each of her student subjects and includes sections of interview transcript to allow students to speak in their own words. The students in the study have diverse backgrounds and goals, and through their stories a cross-curricular perspective on writing is uncovered—one student is an engineer, another is in nursing, another in social work, for instance. Based on this extensive research, Leki makes unique conclusions about university literacy, socio-academic factors in literacy learning, and finally recognizes that L2 writing courses actually serve a much more minor role in literacy development than we might imagine. This recognition should allow educators to understand the complex and varied ways in which literacy learning happens at the university and to facilitate learning beyond the classroom.

774 Leki, Ilona. *Understanding ESL Writers: A Guide for Teachers.* Portsmouth: Heinemann-Boynton/Cook, 1992. Print.

Although teaching writing to ESL students is not radically different from teaching writing to native speakers, it helps to understand the difficulties of learning to write in an L2. Native speakers must orchestrate many skills and strategies to write. ESL writers face, in addition, limited vocabulary, cultural and idiomatic complexities, unfamiliar style and audience expectations, and the frustration of not being able to express their real thoughts or knowledge. Only slowly has ESL teaching shifted from structure-based language instruction to process-based instruction. Research confirms that the desire to communicate aids language acquisition, whereas knowledge of rules and error correction does not. Immersion in language, especially reading, is vital for writing. At the same time, social comfort increases the desire to communicate. Leki sensitively discusses the characteristics of ESL students and ways to distinguish ESL students from basic writers in classes where they are mixed, recommends classroom practices for teachers in ESL and mixed classes, analyzes ESL-student writing behavior (concerning personal writing, plagiarism, sophistication, and so on), describes L2 writing processes, surveys findings of contrastive rhetoric for several cultures, discusses sentence-level correction, and offers advice about responding. Includes an extensive, unannotated bibliography.

775 Matsuda, Paul Kei. "Composition Studies and ESL Writing: A Disciplinary Division of Labor." CCC 50.4 (June 1999): 699–721. Print.

There is a clear lack of scholarship on ESL issues in composition studies, in spite of the fact that there are an increasing number of ESL students in writing classes. Though these students are often much like "regular" students, they do have some specific needs and learning styles. These needs differ from student to student and school to school, so it isn't possible to create a single solution—just as there is no one way to teach any group of students. But what is certain is that useful pedagogical strategies and disciplinary knowledge will not be discovered or created when first-language scholarship and second-language scholarship are seen as divided. This "disciplinary division of labor," as mentioned in the article's title, was created to develop the identity of each field and has become institutionalized. Yet for any field, isolation from other disciplinary perspectives can be severely limiting. In particular, ESL scholarship has benefited from the use of insights from the field of composition, so composition should benefit from a greater familiarity with ESL scholarship.

776 Matsuda, Paul Kei. "The Myth of Linguistic Homogeneity in U.S. College Composition." *CE* 68.6 (July 2006): 637–51. Print.

The myth of linguistic homogeneity has persisted despite evidence that many college students are functional bilinguals or native speakers of traditionally underprivileged varieties of English rather than, as the dominant image portrays them, native speakers of privileged varieties of

English. College composition courses contribute to linguistic containment by creating conditions that make it acceptable to dismiss language variety or differences. The history of international ESL students in U.S. higher education illustrates how effectively composition has participated in a policy of containment rather than pursuing genuine pedagogical reform. The college composition classroom should be reimagined as a multilingual space, not a monolingual one.

777 Matsuda, Paul Kei, Christina Ortmeier-Hooper, and Xiaoye You, eds. *The Politics of Second Language Writing: In Search of the Promised Land.* West Lafayette: Parlor, 2006. Print.

This edited collection grew out of a 2004 Symposium on Second Language Writing examining the "intersection of institutional policies and politics and classroom practices." This book thus offers a unique perspective, placing classroom practice always within larger institutional contexts, with a focus on the politics of ESL writing. Authors discuss these politics in a variety of contexts, from K-12 classrooms to writing centers to online directed self-placement, as well as the university writing classroom. Contents include Danling Fu and Marylou Matoush, "Writing Development and Biliteracy"; Angela M. Dadak, "No ESL Allowed: A Case Exploring University and College Writing Program Practices"; Xiaoye You, "Globalization and the Politics of Teaching EFL Writing"; Jessie Moore Kapper, "Mapping Postsecondary Classifications and Second Language Writing Research in the United States"; and Barbara Kroll, "Toward a Promised Land of Writing: At the Intersection of Hope and Reality."

778 Matsuda, Paul Kei, Michelle Cox, Jay Jordan, and Christina Ortmeier-Hooper. *Second-Language Writing in the Composition Classroom: A Critical Sourcebook.* Boston: Bedford/St. Martin's, 2011. Print.

A broad collection of the key essays in this field. Contents range from classics to contemporary debates, spanning nearly forty years of scholarship. Essays are divided into five major sections, focused on situating ESL within composition, understanding second-language writers, theoretical frameworks, curriculum, and response/assessment. Contents include "CCCC Statement on Second-Language Writing and Writers"; Paul Kei Matsuda, "Second-Language Writing in the Twentieth Century: A Situated Historical Perspective"; Awad El Karim M. Ibrahim, "Becoming Black: Rap and Hip-Hop, Race, Gender, Identity, and the Politics of ESL Learning"; Tony Silva, "On the Ethical Treatment of ESL Writers"; A. Suresh Canagarajah, "Understanding Critical Writing"; Janet Bean, Maryann Cucchiara, Robert Eddy, Peter Elbow, Rhonda Grego, Rich Haswell, Patricia Irvine, Eileen Kennedy, Ellie Kutz, Al Lehner, and Paul Kei Matsuda, "Should We Invite Students to Write in Home Languages? Complicating the Yes/No Debate"; Paul Kei Matsuda and Tony Silva, "Cross-Cultural Composition: Mediated Integration of U.S. and International Students"; and Martha C. Pennington, "The Impact of the Computer in Second-Language Writing."

779 Matsuda, Paul Kei, and Tony Silva. "Cross-Cultural Composition: Mediated Integration of U.S. and International Students." *Composition Studies* 27.1 (Spring 1999): 15–30. Print.

A cross-cultural composition course, designed to integrate U.S. and international students, provides an alternative placement option for ESL writers and promotes intercultural understanding for both groups of students. Integrating ESL writers into existing writing courses has an economic advantage; however, traditional mainstreaming has several problems when ESL writers are a distinct minority. ESL-friendly courses provide a mediated integration of NES and ESL writers; not conflict-free, such a course foregrounds difference. The cross-cultural aspect of this placement option may be especially valuable at institutions where linguistic and cultural diversity is not prevalent.

780 Matsuda, Paul Kei, and Tony Silva, eds. *Second Language Writing Research: Perspectives on the Process of Knowledge Construction.* Mahwah: Erlbaum, 2005. Print.

Traditional composition research methods are not easily transportable into second-language writing research. Knowledge construction in the field of second-language writing research cannot be simply understood through the delineated categories of composition research. Researchers need to combine various methodological tools and to develop situated research practices unique to the contexts of second-language writing. This volume seeks to recognize the variety of research methods germane to the study of second-language writing and thus to better understand second-language writing and writers. The editors bring together sixteen scholars who explain and reflect on their own methods and methodologies through the lens of a specific research project. Philosophical, narrative, historical, qualitative, quantitative, and mixed approaches to research are examined. The contributions shed light on the messy and complex process of constructing knowledge in the field of second-language writing research.

See: Min-Zhan Lu, "From Silence to Words: Writing as Struggle" [650].

781 Nelson, Marie W. *At the Point of Need: Teaching Basic and ESL Writers.* Portsmouth: Heinemann-Boynton/Cook, 1991. Print.

Beginning with the premise that attending closely to students' own descriptions of the writing help they need would improve their pedagogy, teams of writing-center tutors over five years carefully recorded their interactions with basic-writing and ESL students—and with one another—as they sought to discover how best to teach writing. The teams discovered significant similarities between ESL and basic writers in writing behaviors, assumptions, and development. Students also had unrecognized skills of invention and language production that could be tapped once they were given permission to use them. Allowing students to be independent of the teacher produced the best results in the long term, a condition accomplished by establishing a safe atmosphere, modeling successful writing behaviors, unteaching misperceptions about how to write, pointing out strengths in student writing, rewarding critical attitudes and risk taking, and so on. The tutors refined the process of working with students and the steps that might be taken to help writers become independent and fluent. Many case studies illustrate the development of students—basic writers and ESL students from many cultures—and of the tutors. Chapters examine longitudinal studies of writers, types of writing assignments, the organization of the writing center, the training of tutors, and research design.

782 Ortmeier-Hooper, Christina. "English May Be My Second Language, but I'm Not 'ESL.'" CCC 59.3 (Feb. 2008): 389–419. Print.

Terms such as "ESL" and "Generation 1.5," while often used by teachers and scholars in composition, are generally not favored by students, as Ortmeier-Hooper shows through a series of case studies. These terms, which can obscure differences between students, have taken on emotional and political meanings that make them problematic. We know that writing is inextricably linked to identity formation, and, thus, the labels used to recognize students must also be recognized as impacting them as writers and individuals. The "ESL" label is based upon a deficit model. "Generation 1.5" has become a highly amorphous term, and not in a useful way. Labeled students are seen as outsiders, impoverished, undeveloped. We need to move away from the sense of singular identity that these labels encourage us to embrace. Students who write in English as their second language are whole individuals with multiple experiences. They, like all of our students, deserve the right to compose their own identities.

783 Pennycook, Alastair. "Borrowing Others' Words: Text, Ownership, Memory, and Plagiarism." *TESOL Quarterly* 30.2 (Summer 1996): 201–30. Print.

Memorizing the words of others and other acts of language learning differ significantly across cultures, and understanding the complex issues related to textual borrowing makes Western notions of plagiarism confusing and hypocritical. A brief history of authorship and the individual shows that the author is a modern invention and that famous authors have often borrowed from the texts of others. Changing textual practices (through writing technologies) mark yet another shift in notions of originality and authorship and illustrate how different cultural practices (here, Chinese educational practices) represent fundamentally different beliefs about the relationship between language and reality. Informal interviews with ESL students challenge our traditional views of plagiarism and reveal "the extent to which these students feel the English language remains a language of colonialism."

See: Mary Louise Pratt, "Arts of the Contact Zone" [239].

784 Raimes, Ann. "Out of the Woods: Emerging Traditions in the Teaching of Writing." *TESOL Quarterly* 25.3 (Fall 1991): 407–30. Print.

Four approaches characterize ESL teaching since the mid-1960s. At the beginning of this period, the audiolingual method made writing subservient to oral learning. Students wrote only to practice grammatical or rhetorical forms. In the late 1970s, influenced by L1 scholars' research on composing processes, L2 teachers began to think about writers, meaning-making, multiple drafts, and journals, downplaying linguistic accuracy—at least in early drafts. In the late 1980s, some reacted against process, arguing that academic writing was what students would need to do, resulting in the adjunct course model to provide academic content. At the same time, a focus on academic readers' expectations generated English for academic purposes and a concern for socializing students into the academic discourse community. These methods all continue to stir controversy. Should students do personal writing or practice "real" academic writing? When we teach to the academic discourse community, mustn't we beware of simply enforcing submission to a set of rules (as L1 researchers warn)? In this same period, contrastive rhetoric has developed. Although it offers no pedagogical suggestions, contrastive rhetoric raises consciousness about composing conventions in different cultures. This consciousness makes us aware not only of English forms, but of alternate rhetorics from many cultures. The field of ESL teaching must continue to recognize the complexity of composing, the diversity of students and their composing processes, the politics of pedagogy, and the need for classroom-based research.

See: Mike Rose, "The Language of Exclusion: Writing Instruction at the University" [244].

See: Alice Roy, "ESL Concerns for Writing Program Administrators: Problems and Policies" [445].

785 Roberge, Mark, Meryl Siegal, and Linda Harklau, eds. *Generation 1.5 in College Composition: Teaching Academic Writing to U.S.-Educated Learners of ESL*. New York: Routledge, 2009. Print.

"Generation 1.5" is both a population and a heuristic that allows educators to move beyond simplified definitions and understandings of ESL. This collection is a sequel to Harklau, Losey, and Siegal [766] and covers Frameworks (Part I), Student Characteristics and Schooling Paths (Part II), and Curricular and Pedagogical Approaches (Part III). The new edition extends the first edition without duplication and updates some of the debates and discussions introduced in the first edition, with a focus on promoting educational access, success, and equity.

786 Silva, Tony. "An Examination of Writing Program Administrators' Options for the Placement of ESL Students in First Year Writing Classes." *WPA: Writing Program Administration* 18.1-2 (Fall/Winter 1994): 37–43. Print.

Writing programs can recognize the diversity of the student population, and respect the equal rights of all students to an education, by offering a range of approaches to ESL pedagogy. Research shows that L1 and L2 writing are broadly similar, but with important distinctions. In some important ways, ESL students are different from native English-speaking students. Yet, there is great diversity within any group of ESL or L2 students as well. These students should be offered as many options for their education as resources permit. Options should include more than just segregated ESL classes, but not just mainstreaming, basic writing, or cross-cultural classes. Each approach has benefits and drawbacks, depending on the individual students and their needs and goals. A useful approach for one student might be wholly inappropriate for another. To better understand what will work, and to better develop a range of approaches, writing programs should seek collaboration with ESL programs.

787 Silva, Tony, and Paul Kei Matsuda, eds. *Landmark Essays on ESL Writing.* Mahwah: Erlbaum, 2001. Print.

Sixteen essays, arranged chronologically (beginning with Anita Pincas, "Structural Linguistics and Systematic Composition Teaching to Students of English as a Foreign Language"), make available previously published ESL writing scholarship over the last four decades. Includes Robert B. Kaplan, "Cultural Thought Patterns in Inter-Cultural Education"; Vivian Zamel, "Teaching Composition in the ESL Classroom: What We Can Learn from Research in the Teaching of English"; Ann Raimes, "What Unskilled ESL Students Do as They Write: A Classroom Study of Composing"; Ulla Connor, "Research Frontiers in Writing Analysis"; Ruth Spack, "Initiating ESL Students into the Academic Discourse Community: How Far Should We Go?"; Ann M. Johns, "Interpreting an English Competency Examination: The Frustrations of an ESL Science Student"; Ilona Leki, "Reciprocal Themes in ESL Reading and Writing"; Tony Silva, "Toward an Understanding of the Distinct Nature of L2 Writing: The ESL Research and Its Implications"; and Liz Hamp-Lyons and Barbara Kroll, "Issues in ESL Writing Assessment: An Overview."

788 Silva, Tony, and Paul Kei Matsuda, eds. *On Second Language Writing.* Mahwah: Erlbaum, 2001. Print.

Second-language writing specialists systematically address basic concerns in the field, including theory, research, instruction assessment, politics, and articulation with other disciplines and standards. Fifteen chapters include the following: Ilona Leki, "Hearing Voices: L2 Students' Experiences in L2 Writing Courses"; Diane Belcher, "Does Second Language Writing Theory Have Gender?"; Lynn Goldstein, "For Kyla: What Does the Research Say About Responding to ESL Writers"; Liz Hamp-Lyons, "Fourth Generation Writing Assessment"; Trudy Smoke, "Instructional Strategies for Making ESL Students Integral to the University"; Sarah Benesch, "Critical Pragmatism: A Politics of L2 Composition"; Carol Severino, "Dangerous Liaisons: Problems of Representation and Articulation"; and Alister Cumming, "The Difficulty of Standards, For Example in L2 Writing."

789 Spack, Ruth. "The Acquisition of Academic Literacy in a Second Language: A Longitudinal Case Study." *Written Communication* 14.1 (Jan. 1997): 3–62. Print.

A three-year study of an undergraduate L2 student, "Yuko," combines qualitative methods to understand how this student drew upon multiple resources or developed strategies for reading and writing successfully in a university setting. Beginning with an account of Yuko's acquisition of academic literacy in early childhood, this study follows Yuko through nine courses in English and social science classes. The longitudinal narrative, informed by interviews, observations, writing samples, and other data, attributes Yuko's lack of confidence, despite her strong TOEFL score, to her educational background in Japan. Deliberate avoidance of reading courses and a struggle to analyze rather than summarize were replaced by the third year with her recognition that "acquisition involves being engaged in a process of constructing knowledge."

790 Trimbur, John. "Linguistic Memory and the Politics of U.S. English." *CE* 68.6 (July 2006): 575–88. Print.

Language policy in the colonial and national period operated covertly but systematically to suppress languages or restrict communication, and American ambivalence toward multilingualism was produced by, in part, a laissez-faire language policy and a "systematic forgetting" of the multiple languages spoken and written in North America. For example, versions of American English (like Webster's) ignore plantation Creole as well as linguistic hybrids of the borderlands. The linguistic memory that emerges from decolonization and nation building has influenced the language policy of college composition. Rather than asking how academic literacy in English operates, writing studies should ask how available linguistic resources could be utilized to promote biliteracy and multilingualism. Such a national language policy would work beyond the discourse of linguistic rights in order to abolish English monolingualism altogether.

791 Tucker, Amy. *Decoding ESL: International Students in the American College Classroom.* Portsmouth: Heinemann-Boynton/Cook, 1995. Print.

Teaching writing to international students is not training in an isolated skill but in a way of experiencing the world. Contrastive rhetoric shows that the errors of ESL writers can be read not as random mistakes but as patterns that are inevitable in cultural transformation. In our readings of other cultures, we must be students of cultural difference, conscious of the rhetorical limitations placed on both writer and reader (the teacher) by limitations of language, the clash of conventions, deep ideological differences, and current political situations. These are not incapacitating differences but challenges that ultimately deepen cross-cultural understanding. Tucker illustrates with case studies of students from Afghanistan, Russia, Greece, China, and Japan, examining their experience in writing and literature courses.

792 Valdes, Guadalupe. "Bilingual Minorities and Language Issues in Writing." *Written Communication* 9.1 (Jan. 1992): 85–136. Print.

The teaching of English is divided into segments, with mainstream and basic writers in one group and ESL students in the other. This division fails to take into account the complexity of bilingualism in America. A bilingual individual's ability to function in a second language depends on a large number of social factors such as age, previous language learning, and degree of contact with fluent speakers of the second language. These factors also affect the time it takes to pass through the incipient (nonfluent) bilingual stage. The difficulty of identifying these factors causes confusion about some students' instructional needs in our simple bipartite system. The very same nonnative-like features in their writing can be variously interpreted. Some nonidiomatic forms persist, for example, in the writing of fluent bilinguals who don't need ESL instruction. ESL research has focused on some groups of bilinguals, but the profession as a whole must deal with the entire range of bilinguals. To do so, we must do more research on the kinds of writing bilingual minorities are exposed to, the ways that mainstream teachers respond to the writing of these students, and the linguistic and social factors that affect their writing. To address these pressing issues, we must break out of our current compartmentalization.

793 Zamel, Vivian. "Strangers in Academia: The Experiences of Faculty and ESL Students across the Curriculum." CCC 46.4 (Dec. 1995): 506–21. Print. Rpt. in Corbett, Myers, and Tate [150].

Faculty across the disciplines, surveyed about ESL students in their classes, often conflated students' "deficient and inadequate" language use with intellectual ability. When instructors believe in a deficit model of learning, students are not invited to participate in intellectual work. Two faculty responses to working with nonnative speakers of English illustrate very different sets of assumptions about language and knowledge, one rich and complicated, the other static and limited to gate-keeping. At the same time, ESL students enrolled in various courses were asked about how they learn best and what they want faculty to know, and their responses clarify much about ESL students' academic lives. When faculty hold reductive approaches to teaching academic discourse, they need more information about the process of language acquisition and ways to represent the distinct culture of each discipline.

794 Zamel, Vivian. "Writing One's Way into Reading." *TESOL Quarterly* 26.3 (Fall 1992): 463–85. Print.

Both reading and writing are acts of meaning-making, yet reading continues to be taught by a transmission or information-retrieval model. Reading ought not to be passive, but a transaction between the text and the reader's knowledge and experience. Writing can reveal and enhance this transaction by enabling students to engage the text through their responses. Reading journals or logs are effective for this purpose, as research attests. Sequencing assignments around readings is another way of allowing students to approach a text from different perspectives, avoiding the sense that there is a single meaning to extract. Students can become better readers by becoming better writers.

795 Zamel, Vivian, and Ruth Spack, eds. *Negotiating Academic Literacies: Teaching and Learning across Languages and Cultures*. Mahwah: Erlbaum, 1998. Print.

Essays from several different fields—composition studies, education, applied linguistics, anthropology, and others—explore how students acquire literacies but also reconsider how academic discourse is typically conceptualized. Essays include Mina Shaughnessy, "Diving In: An Introduction to Basic Writing"; Eleanor Kutz, "Between Students' Language and Academic Discourse: Interlanguage as Middle Ground"; Ruth Spack, "Initiating ESL Students into the Academic Discourse Community: How Far Should We Go?"; Fan Shen, "The Classroom and the Wider Culture: Identity as a Key to Learning English Composition"; Robert E. Land Jr. and Catherine Whitley, "Evaluating Second Language Essays in Regular Composition Classes: Toward a Pluralistic U.S. Rhetoric"; Linda Lonon Blanton, "Discourse, Artifacts, and the Ozarks: Understanding Academic Literacy"; and Norma Gonzalez, "Blurred Voices: Who Speaks for the Subaltern?"

Technical Communication

796 Alred, Gerald J. *St. Martin's Bibliography of Business and Technical Communication*. New York: St. Martin's, 1997. Print.

An extensively annotated bibliography of 376 items divided into sections on research and history, theory and rhetoric, profession and curriculum, genre studies, technology and visual theory, and interdisciplinary connections, each with several subcategories. Includes complete contact information for journals, professional associations, conferences, and Internet discussion groups, as well as an author index and a subject index.

797 Anderson, Paul V., R. John Brockmann, and Carolyn R. Miller, eds. *New Essays in Technical and Scientific Communication: Research, Theory, Practice*. Farmingdale: Baywood, 1983. Print.

Twelve essays take a serious scholarly approach to empirical research, theory, pedagogy, and historical study in the field of technical communication. Essays include Lee Odell, Dixie Goswami, Anne Herrington, and Doris Quick, "Studying Writing in Non-Academic Settings"; Linda Flower, John Hayes, and Heidi Swarts, "Revising Functional Documents: The Scenario Principle"; Lester Faigley and Stephen Witte, "Topical Focus in Technical Writing"; Jack Selzer, "What Constitutes a 'Readable' Technical Style?"; James Zappen, "A Rhetoric for Research in Sciences and Technologies"; Charles Bazerman, "Scientific Writing as a Social

Act: A Review of the Literature of the Sociology of Science"; and David Dobrin, "What's Technical about Technical Writing?" Winner of a 1984 NCTE Award in Technical and Scientific Communication.

See: Charles Bazerman and James Paradis, eds., *Textual Dynamics of the Professions: Historical and Contemporary Studies of Writing in Professional Communities* [834].

798 Barker, Thomas, and Natalia Matveeva. "Teaching Intercultural Communication in a Technical Writing Service Course: Real Instructors' Practices and Suggestions for Textbook Selection." *Technical Communication Quarterly* 15.2 (Apr. 2006): 191–214. Print.

Intercultural communication needs to be taught in technical communication courses. Therefore, textbooks must better represent the issues and components involved in intercultural communication. Further, and most important, it is not enough to simply offer intercultural content; textbooks must be matched with the contexts in which they are used by teachers and students. Teachers with much intercultural experience can likely augment *any* textbook on their own; some teaching contexts are themselves highly intercultural and thus the selection of a textbook is less important. But other teachers need to assess the areas in which they are lacking or recognize the ways that their teaching context might raise barriers to intercultural understanding. Teachers can then come to a more informed and effective process of textbook selection.

799 Blakeslee, Ann M. "Bridging the Workplace and the Academy: Teaching Professional Genres Through Classroom-Workplace Collaborations." *Technical Communication Quarterly* 10.2 (Apr. 2001): 169–92. Print. Rpt. in Dubinsky [808].

Two case studies of classroom-workplace collaborations in which students solved workplace problems as part of an academic course requirement demonstrate how such collaborations help in the teaching of professional genres. Students in a 300-level class of undergraduates only and students in a 400-level class of both undergraduate and graduate students completed projects that were provided by professionals in industry or academia. The results suggest that classroom-workplace collaborations may have several benefits. The collaborations can prove valuable to the students because they expose them to workplace activities and cultures, introduce them to the genres associated with those activities and cultures, and provide occasion for reflection and application of students' classroom and theoretical knowledge.

800 Blakeslee, Ann M., and Rachel Spilka. "The State of Research in Technical Communication." *Technical Communication Quarterly* 13.1 (Jan. 2004): 73–92. Print.

Technical communication scholars and teachers must have a common understanding of the questions, methods, and directions needed for research in the field. Blakeslee and Spilka propose a specific agenda. In seeking quality of research, scholars need to be consistent and systematic in their approaches, focusing on common, agreed-upon questions for the field, in order to build a coherent and unified body of knowledge. Greater funding and support for research is needed, internally and externally. Research should be disseminated more widely, with the impact of research findings more effectively communicated. Students need more comprehensive training in research methods. Researchers need to be aware of the benefits and drawbacks of "borrowed" methodologies, and the pluralistic uses of research methods in general, even as they seek more collaboration and understanding across disciplines. Academic-practitioner relationships are of key importance to research in technical communication and should be carefully created and maintained. Academics need to interact and collaborate with practitioners and need to be able to show how their research benefits industry.

801 Blyler, Nancy Roundy, and Charlotte Thralls, eds. *Professional Communication: The Social Perspective*. Newbury Park: Sage, 1993. Print.

Fourteen essays examine the ways that the social paradigm in the study of writing and rhetoric can contribute to an understanding of professional communication. Essays include Charlotte Thralls and Nancy Roundy Blyler, "The Social Perspective and Professional Communication: Diversity and Directions in Research"; Bruce Herzberg, "Rhetoric Unbound: Discourse, Community, and Knowledge"; Ben Barton and Marthalee Barton, "Ideology and the Map: Toward a Postmodern Visual Design Practice"; Thomas Kent, "Formalism, Social Construction, and the Problem of Interpretive Authority"; Joseph Comprone, "Generic Constraints and Expressive Motives: Rhetorical Perspectives on Textual Dialogues"; James Porter, "The Role of Law, Policy, and Ethics in Corporate Composing: Toward a Practical Ethics for Professional Writing"; Janice Lauer and Patricia Sullivan, "Validity and Reliability as Social Constructions"; and Mary Lay, "Gender Studies: Implications for the Professional Communication Classroom." Winner of a 1993 NCTE Award in Technical and Scientific Communication.

See: Nancy Roundy Blyler, "Theory and Curriculum: Reexamining the Curricular Separation of Business and Technical Communication" [838].

802 Bridgeford, Tracy, Karla Saari Kitalong, and Dickie Selfe. *Innovative Approaches to Teaching Technical Communication*. Logan: Utah State UP, 2004. Print.

Approaches to teaching technical writing need to take into account how creative the field can be, despite the field's reputation for being bound to tradition and linked to a limited canon. Technical communication will be influenced by rapidly changing cultural and technological trends, and so innovative approaches are necessary. Understanding traditional forms and genres is only a beginning—new literacies will need to be developed. Inspiration and advancement in technical communication can be generated from diverse sources. This collection proposes new pedagogical theories, practices, and partnerships to equip technical communicators for changes in the workplace and for a changing world. The eighteen collected essays speak to teachers, offering innovative ideas for the classroom, but also for lifelong learning, suggesting ways that the classroom can engage other cultures, professional settings, and communities.

803 Brockmann, R. John, ed. *The Case Method in Technical Communication: Theory and Models*. St. Paul: Assoc. of Teachers of Technical Writing, 1984. Print.

The case method holds that writing is best learned by performing in situations that specify data, characters, politics, and a writer's role. This collection offers seven essays on using and generating cases, an annotated bibliography on the case method in communication, eight cases for writing, and two cases for graphics. Includes R. John Brockmann, "What Is a Case?"; Marcus Green, "How to Use Case Studies in the Classroom"; and Charles Sides, "Comparing the Case Approach to Five Traditional Approaches to Teaching Technical Communication."

See: Robert L. Brown Jr. and Carl G. Herndl, "An Ethnographic Study of Corporate Writing: Job Status as Reflected in Written Text" [839].

804 Bryan, John. "Seven Types of Distortion: A Taxonomy of Manipulative Techniques Used in Charts and Graphs." *Journal of Technical Writing and Communication* 25.2 (1995): 127–79. Print.

Whether distortions in presenting data in graphic form occur inadvertently, through guile, or because of software defaults, the increased use of graphing software requires communicators to be more vigilant about distortions. Seven types of distortion have been well documented: manipulation of scale ratios (extreme differences between x and y axes); manipulation of the second dimension (fat lines representing what should be one-dimensional lines); manipulation of the third dimension (drop shadows and perspectives that inaccurately suggest volume); color distortion (highlighting or diminishing particular data); manipulation of composition (using design, typography, orientation, or embellishment to distract or overinterpret); manipulation of symbolism (failing to distinguish comparative data or obscuring data with illustrations); and manipulation of affect (using emotionally charged illustrations).

805 Connors, Robert J. "The Rise of Technical Writing Instruction in America." *Journal of Technical Writing and Communication* 12.4 (1982): 329–52. Print. Rpt. in Dubinsky [808] and in Johnson-Eilola and Selber [813].

The need for technical writing instruction grew in the latter part of the nineteenth century in the United States as engineering education grew and classical education shrank. However, no courses in technical writing were offered before 1900, reflecting the hope that freshman composition would suffice. It did not, as complaints in professional journals about nearly illiterate engineers attest. The first technical writing textbook, in 1908, concerned usage for professionals. The 1911 textbook by

Samuel Chandler Earle is the first genuine attempt to address the needs of an advanced undergraduate technical writing course. It condemned the "two cultures" split, chastising English teachers for regarding engineers as philistines. Earle used the modes of discourse as his pedagogical model. By 1920, though, books using technical writing formats began to appear, along with a wave of books that attempted to humanize the engineering student by combining literature with writing instruction. World War II dramatically increased the need for technical writing instruction: technical writing became a distinct job description, and teaching technical writing began to have more professional status, a trend particularly strong since the 1970s, with the appearance of professional societies and journals.

806 Couture, Barbara. "Categorizing Professional Discourse: Engineering, Administrative, and Technical/Professional Writing." *Journal of Business and Technical Communication* 6.1 (Jan. 1992): 5–37. Print.

Because knowledge depends on interpretation that is constrained by communal values (see Winsor, "The Construction of Knowledge in Organizations: Asking the Right Questions about the *Challenger*" [830]), scholars of professional writing need to develop an understanding of how discourse is framed and interpreted in organizations. Rhetorical categories can help reveal both textual and contextual elements in interpretive frames. Such categories are not technical labels but indicators of situations, disciplines, and forms that operate in particular contexts. Three rhetorical categories that identify group values and their effect on interpretation appear to have theoretical and empirical validity. The first, engineering writing, responds to the professional values of scientific objectivity, professional judgment, and corporate interests. The second, administrative writing, reflects decision-making authority and promotes institutional identity. The third, technical/professional writing, aims to accommodate the audience by meeting professional readability standards. Defining the characteristics of these types more precisely can help describe writing in ways that are more telling and more usable for those who teach professional writing.

807 Draga, Sam, and Van Doss. "Cruel Pies: The Inhumanity of Technical Illustrations." *Technical Communication* 48.3 (Aug. 2001): 265–74. Print.

A review of research on the ethics of visual communication reveals that the definition of ethics is almost always associated with deception and distortion. While it is important to incorporate visuals with honesty and accuracy, technical communicators should also expand their understanding of the ethics of visual communication and develop techniques that bring humanity as well as honesty to technical illustrations. Too often, particularly in writing that reports human fatalities, visual images objectify and dehumanize people for purposes of statistical manipulation. However, using pictographs or superimposing bar graphs and line graphs on pictures or drawings of human subjects are two possible ways to humanize the visual display of information.

808 Dubinsky, James M. *Teaching Technical Communication: Critical Issues for the Classroom*. Boston: Bedford/St. Martin's, 2004. Print.

Teaching technical communication requires a broad extra-disciplinary understanding, as well as an understanding of key evolving issues in the discipline itself. This collection organizes disciplinary and interdisciplinary approaches, with an emphasis on the needs of students. Key historical and theoretical texts are combined with resources that can be used in the classroom. The collection contains thirty-one essays, organized under eight chapter themes, including historical texts such as a selection from Quintilian's *Institutio Oratorio*, as well as landmark essays and new approaches. Each chapter also includes an essay under the heading "Applied Theory" and a list of additional readings.

809 Harris, John S. *Teaching Technical Writing: A Pragmatic Approach*. St. Paul: Association of Teachers of Technical Writing, 1992. Print.

Beginning teachers of technical writing (and more experienced teachers looking for new ideas) can learn much from a book that not only presents materials and methods for teaching the course but also speaks frankly about the career path of such teachers in the academy. In twenty-one chapters, Harris defines technical writing, describes programs and textbooks, and tells how to work within an indifferent English department, design a course, teach special forms (proposals, correspondence, term papers, graphics), grade papers, and get promoted.

810 Hart-Davidson, William. "On Writing, Technical Communication, and Information Technology: The Core Competencies of Technical Communication." *Technical Communication* 48.2 (May 2001): 145–55. Print.

Writing is the core technology that all information technology systems seek to leverage; by extension, then, technical communication plays a central role in all information technology systems. In the development of information technology, technical communicators deal with two critical issues: identity (fixed or fluid) and strategy (situated or flexible). Technical communicators in both the workplace and the academy, however, can take on an even more pivotal role through the construction of theories about their work that expand the core expertise by raising new questions, researching new possibilities, and inventing new information technologies that build on their expertise and that help shape policy. By claiming and cultivating the conceptual spaces where identity and strategy are closely aligned, technical communicators can enter discourses in social, ethical, and political arenas.

See: Thomas N. Huckin, "Technical Writing and Community Service" [694].

811 Johnson, Robert R. *User-Centered Technology: A Rhetorical Theory for Computers and Other Mundane Artifacts*. Albany: State U of New York P, 1998. Print.

Modern technology is for the most part system- or artifact-centered. However, the end of technology should be refigured in terms of the user: the human who interacts with the technology. Based in rhetoric, the user-centered model focuses on the user's situation. User-centered theory classifies user knowledge in terms of practitioners, producers, and citizens. User as practitioner assumes that users are just that—mere users of tools that have already been designed and delivered; user as producer assumes that users not only employ the technological tools available to them, but also are capable of designing and maintaining them. User as citizen envisions users as contributing, responsible members of technological enterprises. The user as citizen produces and participates, rather than just consuming. In addition to user knowledge, human-technology interaction and technological determinism are also central to user-centered theory of technology.

812 Johnson-Eilola, Johndan. *Datacloud: Toward a New Theory of Online Work (New Dimensions in Computers and Composition)*. Cresskill: Hampton, 2005. Print.

Computers and networks have offered not a revolution, but rather a series of small shifts that have gradually changed our work and personal lives. These everyday changes also reshape how we communicate, not in a radical and monolithic manner, but subtly and continually. These changes can be seen as representing five specific "new" communicative strategies or needs: one, creativity should no longer be seen as the generation of "original" material, so the critical and synthetic work of gathering and rearranging existing material is paramount; two, users need to develop means of understanding and organizing *more* information than ever before; three, this information must be understood in its political and social context; four, new spaces need to be developed to allow users to engage in symbolic-analytic work *as* they sort and filter information; and five, the architecture for these new spaces needs to be attuned to contemporary life.

813 Johnson-Eilola, Johndan, and Stuart A. Selber. *Central Works in Technical Communication*. New York: Oxford UP, 2004. Print.

Technical communication should be seen as having a sophisticated body of research, concerned not only with the pragmatic "how-to" of technical communication, but also with conceptual, theoretical, and methodological issues. This collection offers a comprehensive and "coherent map" of technical communication scholarship. The thirty-two selections cover histories, rhetorical perspectives, philosophies and theories, ethical and power issues, research methods, workplace studies, online environments, and pedagogical directions. A set of "alternative contents" offers more than one hundred suggestions for further reading. The intended audience for this book includes teachers and practitioners, but the book is aimed primarily at advanced undergraduate and graduate students in the field, with a focus on the most relevant academic issues in technical communication.

814 Johnson-Eilola, Johndan, and Stuart A. Selber. "Policing Ourselves: Defining the Boundaries of Appropriate Discussion in Online Forums." *Computers and Composition* 13.3 (1996): 269–91. Print.

Computers and writing specialists need to consider the mechanisms of language and how discourses "write us." For example, as individuals operate in online forums, they internalize certain discourse laws and then "police" themselves and others. An analysis of one public, nonacademic listserv for technical writers, TECHWR-L, demonstrates the regulating mechanisms that function in online forums and the consequences of violating them. Common messages were strictly on-topic and followed accepted practices, for example, that participants should make their presence known. When threads developed that transgressed the boundaries of conventional discourse in technical communication—such as discussions of racism and sexism—subscribers posted complaints and commands to get back on topic or they enacted the silent treatment. The authors analyze the debate over appropriate topics and recommend that students learn to recognize discourse regulations.

815 Johnson-Eilola, Johndan, and Stuart A. Selber. "Sketching a Framework for Graduate Education in Technical Communication." *Technical Communication Quarterly* 10.4 (Fall 2001): 403–37. Print.

Graduate education in technical communication should offer an expansive view of the field. One way to achieve that view is through a three-dimensional framework that places the multiple and varied approaches to technical communication into one coherent structure. Rather than introducing students to the field of technical communication through an historical survey or through the conventional topics, this framework, geared toward a standard entry-level course in technical communication, organizes the field's modes of analysis (in this case, rhetorical, spatial, empirical, and critical modes) into three categories: thinking, doing, and teaching. Such an arrangement highlights and encompasses the diversity of the discipline and can also provide a space in which the discipline can grow. A sample syllabus is included.

816 Kynell-Hunt, Teresa, and Gerald J. Savage, eds. *Power and Legitimacy in Technical Communication, Vol. I: The Historical and Contemporary Struggle for Professional Status.* Amityville: Baywood, 2003. Print.

Technical communication lacks much of the status of other more mature professions. Few outside of the field understand it, and within the field, there is little consensus about what the discipline's identity, scope, and goals should be. This book focuses on how those in the field have struggled for legitimacy and negotiated for status and power, attempting to establish a "coherent body of disciplinary knowledge." The collected essays offer historical perspectives and also suggest strategies for professionalization and progress, with a focus on service, relationships with industries and academies, as well as pedagogical questions. Contents include Katherine T. Durack, "Instructions as 'Inventions': When the Patent Meets the Prose"; Teresa Kynell-Hunt, "Status and the Technical Communicator: Utilitarianism, Prestige, and the Role of Academia in Creating Our Professional Persona"; Dale L. Sullivan, Michael S. Martin, and Ember R. Anderson, "Moving from the Periphery: Conceptions of Ethos, Reputation, and Identity for the Technical Communicator"; and Brenton Faber and Johndan Johnson-Eilola, "Universities, Corporate Universities, and the New Professionals: Professionalism and the Knowledge Economy."

817 Longo, Bernadette. *Spurious Coin: A History of Science, Management, and Technical Writing.* Albany: State U of New York P, 2000. Print.

Within the framework of the historical tension between scientific knowledge-making and liberal arts knowledge-making, technical writing becomes both a genuine and a counterfeit form of currency of scientific knowledge. The scientific knowledge constructed and communicated by scientists and engineers is taken as true currency in a culture dominated by scientific culture, whereas the scientific knowledge made by technical writers with liberal arts backgrounds is considered spurious. The unscientific language practices that can, and do, make scientific knowledge must be transformed into science before they can become genuine currency of scientific knowledge. Intellectual practices spanning centuries of Western civilization, such as the use of clear, correct English; the need for maximum efficiency of production and operation; the need to contribute to the wealth of scientific knowledge aimed at bettering the human condition; the tension between the role of science and the role of art within a culture; and the urge to purify language and standardize practice, frame this cultural history of technical writing.

818 Markel, Mike. *Ethics in Technical Communication: A Critique and Synthesis.* Westport: Ablex, 2001. Print.

The relationship between ethics and technical communication should be considered a practical art rather than an abstract theory. Traditional ethical systems do not offer effective problem-solving techniques, but they do provide necessary insight into values that have long been a part of civilization. In developing new, practical approaches to ethics, the long heritage of philosophical ethics has to be considered. Likewise, business ethics should also be studied in order to understand the relationship between ethics and technical communication, because technical communicators typically face one of business ethics' most common conflicts—the conflict between an organization's utilitarian thinking and an individual's subjective, rights-based thinking. Overall, technical communicators wrestling with issues of truth telling, liability, multicultural communication, intellectual property, and codes of conduct will benefit from an approach to ethical decision making that involves clearheaded, practical thinking about rights, justice, utility, and care, in a free and open discourse.

See: Carolyn B. Matalene, ed., *Worlds of Writing: Teaching and Learning in Discourse Communities of Work* [852].

819 Miller, Carolyn R. "A Humanistic Rationale for Technical Writing." *CE* 40.6 (Feb. 1979): 610–17. Print. Rpt. in Dubinsky [808] and in Johnson-Eilola and Selber [813].

A pervasive positivist view of science is the source of the erroneous belief that technical writing is a skills course. Believing truth to be a function of perceiving material reality, positivists wish scientific and technical rhetoric to subdue language and transmit bare technical knowledge. Technical writing textbooks endorse this antirhetorical belief. The shortcomings of the positivist view are evident in the confused definitions of technical writing it produces ("clarity" neither defines nor characterizes technical writing), in its emphasis on form at the expense of invention, and in its tendency to analyze audience in terms of "levels" (which reduces to vocabulary choice). Yet scientists themselves no longer hold a positivist view but understand that knowledge is inseparable from the knower: communal discussion and argument determine knowledge. From this perspective, teaching technical writing is a form of enculturation, not a set of forms and techniques, but an understanding of how to participate in a community, a thoroughly humanistic endeavor.

820 Miller, Carolyn R. "What's Practical about Technical Writing?" *Technical Writing: Theory and Practice*. Ed. Bertie E. Fearing and W. Keats Sparrow. New York: MLA, 1989. 14–24. Print. Rpt. in Dubinsky [808].

Technical writing has long been regarded as practical in the "low" sense of being mundane and untheoretical. This view gives rise to a contradiction in technical writing instruction: that workplace writing is at once imperfect (requiring improvement through instruction) and authoritative (the goal of instruction). This contradiction mirrors the larger conflict between practical and humanistic studies in the recent history of education. Professional education tends to acquiesce in treating common industry or professional practice as useful and therefore good. There is a "high" sense of practicality, though, that can be applied to technical writing and other professional education. Aristotle characterizes rhetoric as *techne* or art, a middle term between theory and practice, "a productive state that is truly reasoned." To this should be added Aristotle's sense of phronesis or prudence: rhetoric in this sense is a form of conduct, like ethics, drawing upon observation of human affairs in order to take socially responsible action. Practical rhetoric of this sort must allow for criticism and judgment, and take responsibility not only for the corporation but for the larger community in which it operates.

821 Rude, Carolyn D. "Toward an Expanded Concept of Rhetorical Delivery: The Uses of Reports in Public Policy Debates." *Technical Communication Quarterly* 13.3 (Summer 2004): 271–88. Print.

Students in technical communication can be prepared to promote social action and encourage public debate. Students can be well-suited for professional jobs in which they also shape policy and opinion. These projects promoting social change may be seen as unlike many other professional communication projects because social change is a long-term process. Thus, studying these projects and processes might also allow for expanded notions of the rhetorical tasks involved in technical communication. For instance, delivery can be seen as more than just publication—delivery might encompass a "comprehensively defined" rhetorical situation with many interconnections and no one discrete end-point or product. Looking at one specific central text—the report—and examining one specific rhetorical situation, Rude develops some key objectives that might facilitate the teaching of technical communication as civic engagement: publication is a means to an end rather than an end; means of delivery can distort messages, but delivery can also be seen as the way good ideas reach people who can use them for public good; policy change is slow, so plans for dissemination and action must be seen as incremental and continual; the writer is not responsible for just a publication, but is instead connected to a web of delivery—a public with varied and ongoing uses for and interactions with the text.

822 Scott, J. Blake, Bernadette Longo, and Katherine V. Wills, eds. *Critical Power Tools: Technical Communication and Cultural Studies*. Albany: State U of New York P, 2007. Print.

Traditionally, technical communication has been seen to have a "largely uncritical, pragmatic orientation." Yet, technical communication has always been shaped by unequal power relations. Engaging the cross-fertilization of cultural studies and technical communication allows the authors in this collection to explicitly situate the field within social and cultural contexts and to reveal power dynamics that have been traditionally overlooked. The result is that the parameters of both technical communication and of cultural studies are stretched and realigned. The collection is divided into three sections: theory, research, and pedagogy. The collection features an introduction by the editors entitled, "Why Cultural Studies? Expanding Technical Communication's Critical Toolbox" as well as an afterword by Diana George. Contents include Myra G. Moses and Steven B. Katz, "The Phantom Machine: The Invisible Ideology of Email (A Cultural Critique)"; Bernadette Longo, "An Approach for Applying Cultural Studies Theory to Technical Writing Research"; Jeffrey T. Grabill, "The Study of Writing in the Social Factory: Methodology and Rhetorical Agency"; Michael J. Salvo, "Rhetoric as Productive Technology: Cultural Studies in/as Technical Communication Methodology"; J. Blake Scott, "Extending Service-Learning's Critical Reflection and Action: Contributions of Cultural Studies"; and Katherine V. Wills, "Designing Students: Teaching Technical Writing with Cultural Studies Approaches." Winner of a 2007 NCTE Award in Technical and Scientific Communication.

823 Selber, Stuart A., ed. *Computers and Technical Communication: Pedagogical and Programmatic Perspectives*. Greenwich: Ablex, 1997. Print.

Placing computers and computing activities within the cultural context of a technological society, seventeen essays examine the pedagogical and programmatic issues that face technical communication teachers and program directors. The essays, arranged in four sections, address challenges that must be met if humanistic instructional practices at both the undergraduate and graduate levels are a goal of technical communicators. Part I, Broadening Notions of Computer Literacy, focuses on the design and use of computer hardware and software in a variety of contexts, such as social, cultural, political, ethical, and legal. Part II, Exploring Pedagogical Frameworks for Computers and Technical Communication, considers the ways teachers and program directors might facilitate critical literacies suggested by Part I. Part III, Examining Computer-Supported Communication Facilities from Pedagogical Perspectives, calls attention to the complications and challenges in supporting the computing needs of technical communication programs. Part IV, Planning for Technological Changes in Technical Communication Programs, offers guidelines for long-term thinking about computers and technical communication in instructional and institutional contexts. Essays include Stuart A. Selber, "Hypertext Spheres of Influence in Technical Communication Instructional Contexts"; James E. Porter, "Legal Realities and Ethical Hyperrealities: A Critical Approach Toward Cyberwriting"; Johndan Johnson-Eilola, "Wild Technologies: Computer Use and Social Possibility"; Ann Hill Duin and Ray Archee, "Distance Learning Via the World Wide Web: Information, Engagement, and Community"; Brad Mehlenbacher, "Technologies and Tensions: Designing Online Environments for Teaching Technical Communication"; Richard J. Selfe and Cynthia L. Selfe, "Forces of Conservatism and Change in Computer-Supported Communication Facilities: Programmatic and Institutional Responses to Change"; Tharon Howard, "Designing Computer Classrooms for Technical Communication Programs"; Stephen A. Bernhardt and Carolyn S. Vickrey, "Supporting Faculty Development in Computers and Technical Communication"; and Pamela S. Ecker and Katherine Staples, "Collaborative Conflict and the Future: Academic-Industrial Alliances and Adaptations." Winner of a 1998 NCTE Award in Technical Communication.

824 Selfe, Cynthia L., ed. *Resources in Technical Communication: Outcomes and Approaches*. Amityville: Baywood, 2007. Print.

This very practical resource book offers seventeen chapters, each with a specific set of stated outcomes for teachers of introductory technical communication courses. The goal of the volume is to provide teachers with example texts and materials, assignments and sequences, and connections both to academic research and the perspectives of those in business and industry. For example, a chapter by Ann Wysocki on design has stated outcomes that include "students will be able to use different modalities rhetorically in developing communications." The outcomes are clearly foregrounded (they are even included in the table of contents); within each chapter, key sections are in bold and lists and recurrent headings help to organize information; appendices to each chapter include actual assignments aimed at a student audience, sample student work, and so on.

825 Simmons, W. Michele. *Participation and Power: Civic Discourse in Environmental Policy Decisions*. Albany: State U of New York P, 2007. Print.

Since the late 1960s, many environmental regulations have required public involvement and approval. The government has been required to communicate the risk involved in policy decisions. This communication offers important models for technical communicators to study, as such discourse often seems to "educate" and engage democracy, but more often encourages conformity and rarely engages the public effectively. It is necessary to understand the ways that risks are socially constructed, the ways that policies are discursively, technically constructed, and also the ways that institutional conditions can promote or prevent citizen participation in addressing these risks and reshaping policies. In many environmental policy documents, information is organized and presented inaccessibly, language is jargon-filled, and scientific knowledge remains unquestioned. Simmons advocates for a participatory framework in which citizens are empowered to contribute their own knowledge to the creation of such documents, so that they reflect the needs of communities, refuse to erase conflict, and are more user-friendly and accessible. To provide models for such engagement, Simmons details how she and her students have participated in community environmental projects.

826 Smith, Elizabeth O. "Strength in the Technical Communication Journals and Diversity in the Serials Cited." *Journal of Business and Technical Communication* 14.2 (Apr. 2000): 131–84. Print.

A citation analysis of the ninety-nine most frequently cited serials for technical communication scholars over a ten-year period demonstrates the strength of five technical communication journals: *IEEE Transactions on Professional Communication*, *Journal of Business and Technical Communication*, *Journal of Technical Writing and Communication*, *Technical Communication*, and *Technical Communication Quarterly*. Identifying the journal these serials call on for background and support also demonstrates the diversity of the technical communication discipline. Because of this diversity, technical communication scholars must be skilled in accessing and analyzing information from across the disciplines. The list of serials covered provides newcomers to technical communication with a good starting point for exploring the field, while experienced professionals may encounter new source materials.

827 Spilka, Rachel, ed. *Writing in the Workplace: New Research Perspectives*. Carbondale: Southern Illinois UP, 1993. Print.

Nineteen essays report on research in workplace communication based on the social-perspective model and examine implications of recent research for teaching and future research. Includes Barbara Couture and Jone Rymer, "Situational Exigence: Composing Processes on the Job by Writer's Role and Task Value"; Jamie MacKinnon, "Becoming a Rhetor: Developing Writing Ability in a Mature, Writing-Intensive Organization"; Judy Segal, "Writing and Medicine: Text and Context"; Jennie

Dautermann, "Negotiating Meaning in a Hospital Discourse Community"; Graham Smart, "Genre as Community Invention: A Central Bank's Response to Its Executives' Expectations as Readers"; Rachel Spilka, "Influencing Workplace Practice: A Challenge for Professional Writing Specialists in Academia"; and Stephen Doheny-Farina, "Research as Rhetoric: Confronting the Methodological and Ethical Problems of Research on Writing in Nonacademic Settings."

828 Spinuzzi, Clay. *Tracing Genres Through Organizations: A Sociocultural Approach to Information Design*. Cambridge: MIT P, 2003. Print.

Workers are not simply the victims of poor information design. Instead, they constantly adapt and innovate to support and streamline their work. This said, many communicative innovations in the workplace remain invisible. Information design is constantly revised in unofficial and unpredictable ways as individuals and groups of workers adapt tools and texts for their needs. "Genre tracing" offers a method and means to understand these innovations and offers to provide a genealogy of the ways workers adapt communicative activities and systems for unforeseen uses. Each genre can be seen as embedded in the unique culture of the workplace and as developing organically from this context. Spinuzzi utilizes four connected studies of Iowa traffic workers to trace genres used to understand a database of traffic accidents. He shows how existing information design helps and hinders workers and how ad hoc revisions allow for new insights. Finally, "genre tracing" is shown to be a useful method for analyzing technical writing, and Spinuzzi suggests that his methodology can also guide information design. He calls for decentralized design in which workers become codesigners of both the genres they use and the civic structures that support their innovative work.

829 Staples, Katherine, and Cezar Ornatowski. *Foundations for Teaching Technical Communication: Theory, Practice, and Program Design*. Greenwich: Ablex, 1997. Print.

This collection includes twenty-two new essays divided into four sections: Theoretical Foundations, Practical Foundations, Professional Roles for Technical Communicators, and Program Design. Each essay is concise and includes a thorough bibliography. Theory topics include an overview, by Mary Coney; organizational context, by Teresa Harrison and Susan Katz; rhetorical theory, by Ornatowski; social construction theory, by Mahalingam Subbiah; and cognitive psychology, by Janice Redish. Topics in the practical section include ethics, by Scott Sanders; gender, by Linda LaDuc; collaboration, by Rebecca Burnett, Christianna White, and Ann Hill Duin; new technology, by Henrietta Shirk; and media design, by Stuart Selber. In the professional roles section are essays on technical writing, by Roger Grice; technical editing, by Elizabeth Turpin and Judith Gunn Bronson; and visual communication, by Kenneth Rainey. Program design includes an overview by M. Jimmie Killingsworth; four-year programs, by Sam Geonetta; two-year programs, by Staples; certificate programs, by Sherry Burgus Little; service courses, by Nell Ann Pickett; research programs, by Billie Wahlstrom; and evaluating programs, by Meg Morgan.

830 Winsor, Dorothy. "The Construction of Knowledge in Organizations: Asking the Right Questions about the *Challenger*." *Journal of Business and Technical Communication* 4.2 (Sept. 1990): 7–20. Print.

Research on communication failures that led to the *Challenger* explosion asked why those who knew about the faulty O-rings failed to pass the information on to decision makers. This question betrays a simplistic notion of knowledge and a conduit model of communication. Knowledge is, in fact, socially conditioned and does not come about, as is usually imagined, by contemplating evidence. The engineers and managers of the *Challenger* project were using different ideas of what counted as evidence, influenced by factors other than evidence, chiefly by membership in task groups with particular views of the project. Knowledge is not certain. Thus, information—such as that the O-rings were faulty—cannot simply be passed on. Reception of a report does not signify reception of information because information does not convey its own interpretation. The questions to ask in this case concern the rhetorical power to affect communal knowledge, which is the crucial factor. See also Couture [806].

831 Winsor, Dorothy. "Engineering Writing/Writing Engineering." CCC 41.1 (Feb. 1990): 58–70. Print. Rpt. in Johnson-Eilola and Selber [813].

We accept the idea that knowledge is shaped by language, but engineers tend to see knowledge as coming from physical reality without textual mediation. Textbooks often reinforce the view of language as merely a means of transmitting information. A study of a veteran mechanical engineer's writing showed, though, that most source documents and his own writing were based on other documents rather than direct observation. Writing about a new engine, the engineer referred not to the engine but to documents reporting the results and interpretations of tests, to technical summaries, and to handouts used in oral reports. Moreover, many of the reports were written in such a way as to suggest that decisions were consistently made in an orderly way on the basis of prior information, rather than on hunches or instinct. These reports reflect the engineers as they imagine themselves to be. Engineering writing, like all writing, constructs the world that the writer can bear to inhabit.

832 Zachry, Mark, and Charlotte Thralls, eds. *Communicative Practices in Workplaces and the Professions: Cultural Perspectives on the Regulation of Discourse and Organizations*. Amityville: Baywood, 2007. Print.

Discourse is regulated in complex ways in workplaces and professions, and this regulation is not always imposed from above. People self-regulate and negotiate regulations collaboratively; regulation is contextual. Regulation and power do not flow unidirectionally. Thus, regulation must be studied from the perspectives of relationality, situatedness, and agency. Each of the contributors to this collection investigates discourse, power, and regulation from these expanded and critical perspectives. The collection includes Dorothy Winsor, "Using Texts to Manage Continuity and Change in an Activity System"; Clay Spinuzzi, "Who Killed Rex? Tracing a Message through Three Kinds of Networks"; Carl G. Herndl and Adela C. Licona, "Shifting Agency: Agency, *Kairos*, and the Possibilities of Social Action"; Dave Clark, "Rhetoric of Empowerment: Genre, Activity, and the Distribution of Capital"; Barbara Schneider, "Power as Interactional Accomplishment: An Ethnomethodological Perspective on the Regulation of Communicative Practice in Organizations"; David M. Boje, "The Antenarrative Turn in Narrative Studies"; and Robert P. Gephart Jr., "Hearing Discourse." Winner of a 2008 NCTE Award in Technical and Scientific Communication.

Business Communication

833 Alred, Gerald J. "'We Regret to Inform You': Toward a New Theory of Negative Messages." *Studies in Technical Communication: Selected Papers from the 1992 CCCC and NCTE Meetings*. Ed. Brenda R. Sims. CCCC Committee on Technical Communications. 17–36. Print.

Five factors determine how direct or indirect the communication of a negative message should be: (1) the reader's and writer's stakes in the message; (2) expectations of the discourse community or culture; (3) the ethos or value the writer wishes to project; (4) the writer's anticipation of the reader's response; and (5) the writer's and reader's personality characteristics. Standard advice to "buffer" negative messages is incorrect. Sometimes a buffered message will appear obtuse or insulting, especially to an American. Hence, the five factors should be consulted. However, many other cultures value indirectness, so American business students should learn indirect style options for use when cultural conditions demand it.

834 Bazerman, Charles, and James Paradis, eds. *Textual Dynamics of the Professions: Historical and Contemporary Studies of Writing in Professional Communities*. Madison: U of Wisconsin P, 1990. Print.

In the workplace, "textual dynamics are a central agency in the social construction of objects, concepts, and institutions." Fifteen essays examine the textual construction of professions, the dynamics of professional discourse communities, and the operational force of texts. Essays include Charles Bazerman, "How Natural Philosophers Can Cooperate: The Literary Technology of Coordinated Investigation in Joseph Priestley's History and Present State of Electricity (1767)"; Greg Myers, "Stories and Styles in Two Molecular Biology Review Articles"; James Zappen, "Scientific Rhetoric in the Nineteenth and Early Twentieth Centuries: Herbert Spencer, Thomas N. Huxley, and John Dewey"; Robert Schwegler and Linda Shamoon, "Meaning Attribution in Ambiguous Texts in Sociology"; Carl Herndl, Barbara Fennell, and Carolyn Miller,

"Understanding Failures in Organizational Discourse: The Accident at Three Mile Island and the Shuttle Challenger Disaster"; and Amy Devitt, "Intertextuality in Tax Accounting: Generic, Referential, and Functional."

835 Beard, John D., Jone Rymer, and David L. Williams. "An Assessment System for Collaborative Writing Groups: Theory and Empirical Evaluation." *Journal of Business and Technical Communication* 3.2 (Sept. 1989): 29–51. Print.

Group writing, ever important in business communication courses because of the prevalence of project teams in industry, is difficult to grade and often produces dissatisfaction among students and teachers. A system applying 50 percent of the grade to the final product (all group members get the same grade), 25 percent to oral interaction (an individual assessment), and 25 percent to the composing process (an individual assessment) proved to be highly satisfactory to students in this study. This system requires informal observation of group meetings, collecting all working papers, assigning a journal focused on interactions and composing behavior, and a peer evaluation form. Participants reported high motivation to contribute to the group, a positive sense of the learning experience, and a belief that the grades were fair.

836 Beason, Larry. "Ethos and Error: How Business People React to Errors." CCC 53.1 (Sept. 2001): 33–64. Print.

Nonacademic readers may not share the notion that errors in written texts are serious only if they impede effective communication. Error must be understood in terms of its impact on judgments made about writers who create errors; at the same time, errors must be defined not as the breaking of handbook rules but as mental events or consequences outside the text. Fourteen business people, identified through purposive sampling, responded to questionnaires designed to gauge error gravity, and follow-up semistructured interviews revealed that all subjects had concerns about the writer's image. While there are no quantitative formulas for anticipating reactions to errors, people's negative reactions to errors in business discourse seem to center on the writer's credibility and how it is jeopardized by errors. Image problems ranged from that of the hasty, careless writer to the faulty thinker, poor oral communicator, or a representative of the company who can be a liability.

837 Bird, Shelley. "Sensemaking and Identity: The Interconnection of Storytelling and Networking in a Women's Group of a Large Corporation." *Journal of Business Communication* 44.4 (Oct. 2007): 311–39. Print.

Even in corporate settings, storytelling is used to construct identity, to make sense of complex and changing situations, and to form networks. Storytelling has both instrumental and expressive benefits in the workplace. Utilizing action research, Bird constructs an ethnographic study of a women's resource network at a large Fortune 500 company, analyzing a variety of modes of communication. Bird finds that this support network had a positive effect on women's commitment to their organization, allowing them to negotiate identity and agency, navigate difficult workplace transitions, and form networks through collaborative storytelling. These networks benefited both the women and the corporation.

838 Blyler, Nancy Roundy. "Theory and Curriculum: Reexamining the Curricular Separation of Business and Technical Communication." *Journal of Business and Technical Communication* 7.2 (Apr. 1993): 218–45. Print.

Business and technical communication have conventionally been separated in academe, a separation supported by institutional practices and by a formalist rhetoric that posits business communication as chiefly persuasive and technical writing as chiefly informative. Social-epistemic rhetoric, which links language with knowledge and centers on the social context of discourse rather than taxonomies of finished products, posits that discourse does not reflect reality but presents visions of reality that have been accepted as true. Social-epistemic rhetoric treats both business and technical writing as thoroughly rhetorical, a view confirmed by studies of workplace writing. The curricular division has thus lost its rationale. Teaching that emphasizes the ways that social context influences content and form decisions is superior to labeling and dividing typical forms. Students are better served when they learn about the social construction of knowledge and the ways it illuminates the production and reception of workplace communication.

See: Nancy Roundy Blyler and Charlotte Thralls, eds., *Professional Communication: The Social Perspective* [801].

839 Brown, Robert L., Jr., and Carl G. Herndl. "An Ethnographic Study of Corporate Writing: Job Status as Reflected in Written Text." *Functional Approaches to Writing: Research Perspectives*. Ed. Barbara Couture. London: Pinter, 1986. 11–28. Print.

Despite convincing research, commonsense observation, and direct instruction, some professionals continue to use ineffective techniques such as excessive nominalization and long project narratives in their writing. These features appear to be signs of status and anxiety rather than decisions about effective writing. In one study, nominalization was greater for those whose job position had changed or seemed vulnerable. It was also greater in writing for the eyes of upper management and greater generally for those who worked in a corporation undergoing internal reorganization. Nominalization appears to be an attempt to be hypercorrect and to show sophistication. Inappropriate narration seems to come most from young technical professionals who are maintaining a distance from decision making (which depends on interpretation, not narration) and mirroring scientific method. These and perhaps other instances of less effective writing choices reflect social circumstances in the workplace. Stress tends to reduce fluency; nominalization and narration tend to preserve anonymity; hypercorrection reflects insecurity about status. These forces are more powerful than conscious knowledge about preferred writing conventions.

840 Cardon, Peter W. "A Critique of Hall's Contexting Model: A Meta-Analysis of Literature on Intercultural Business and Technical Communication." *Journal of Business and Technical Communication* 22.4 (Oct. 2008): 399–428. Print.

"Contexting" is a very popular but also unsubstantiated theory in business and technical communication. Edward Hall's theory of low- and high-context culture holds that some forms of communication are more direct than others, carrying less meaning that is coded or implicit. The theory has been used to suggest that some cultures communicate in a high-context manner and others in a low-context manner. An analysis of journal articles in business and technical communication on the subject of intercultural communication reveals how influential "contexting" has been in the field to explain communication across cultures. Yet this model has not been empirically validated. Cardon provides several recommendations for researchers who seek to address and apply contexting in business and technical communication, mapping some ways that Hall's theories might be further tested and validated.

841 Cross, Geoffrey A. *Forming the Collective Mind: A Contextual Exploration of Large-Scale Collaborative Writing in Industry*. Cresskill: Hampton, 2001. Print.

New trends have significantly changed the nature of writing in many industries. Specifically, management styles that value process and collaboration have replaced the traditional division of labor and the emphasis on individual tasks. While many researchers have attempted to understand the scenes and contexts of writing, and have extended this inquiry to the workplace, this ethnographic study examines a large-scale collaboration among more than one hundred people at a large corporation. Total Quality Management (TQM) is one notable managerial style that values teamwork and group decision making. In this study, TQM was used to frame a large-scale collaborative writing project. This led to innovative new approaches to invention, drafting, revision, and coordination, and, finally, the creation of a "collective mind." Such large-scale collaborative writing can be used not just as an instrument of TQM (or any other managerial style) and an extension of its values, but also as a means of changing an entire workplace culture. This study won the ABC Best Publication Award in 2002.

842 Cross, Geoffrey A. "The Interrelation of Genre, Context, and Process in the Collaborative Writing of Two Corporate Documents." *Writing in the Workplace: New Research Perspectives* [827]. Ed. Rachel Spilka. Carbondale: Southern Illinois UP, 1993. 141–52. Print.

To consider how textual features are produced in organizational cultures by collaborators, this ethnographic study describes the collaborative writing of an executive letter and planning report for a large insurance corporation. Bakhtinian theory generates a view of group writing based on the political situation and genre: group writing as cacophony, as monotone, and as symphony. In this study, generic and contextual differences helped create two very different collaborative processes: cacophony occurred in the letter-writing process because writers had different perceptions of the composite audience and of standard English. The subsequent report-writing process, however, was more monovocal as a result of a more stable corporate culture, a more multivocal genre, and postproduction rerouting. The interaction of genre and context caused a conflictive process with the letter and an accordant process with the report; genre and social forces must be considered together. More real-world studies of group writing of different genres need to be conducted to trace how generic conventions and social forces shape the group-writing process.

843 DeVoss, Dànielle Nicole, Julia Jasken, and Dawn Hayden. "Teaching Intracultural and Intercultural Communication: A Critique and Suggested Method." *Journal of Business and Technical Communication* 16.1 (Jan. 2002): 69–94. Print.

Today's students will certainly experience and interact with different cultures in substantial and evolving ways within their work and personal lives. Perhaps most notably, many students will eventually work overseas or in highly intercultural contexts in North America. The authors define "intercultural communication" as communication in which cultural differences are large enough to lead to dissimilar interpretations and expectations. If we don't explicitly teach intercultural communication, these misunderstandings will remain, and students will perpetuate them, as they also fail to connect in a global marketplace. The authors analyze textbooks to reveal the common starting points, and the lack of follow-through, in addressing intercultural issues in the field. The authors then offer ways to initiate discussion and design activities in the classroom—discussions and activities that might feel complex and uncomfortable to some students. This discomfort, however, might be seen as productive. For instance, students are asked to recognize the characteristics of their own cultures, their assumptions and stereotypes about other cultures, and then to see how discourse and design conventions are culturally embedded and prone to the same biases.

844 Geisler, Cheryl, et al. "IText: Future Directions for Research on the Relationship between Information Technology and Writing." *Journal of Business and Technical Communication* 15.3 (July 2001): 269–309. Print.

Information technology (IT) used in text-centered interactions appears to be altering the very character of texts and the interactions of those who use them. Research on ITexts (e-mail and the like) brings together and draws from a variety of research traditions that provide foundational understandings of ITexts: rhetorical theory, activity theory, literacy studies, genre theory, usability research, and workplace writing. Because specific issues arise when texts move from print to online, IT research must take into account, for example, the interplay of visual and verbal, credibility, or information overload. ITexts are bound to have an influence on the digital divide, organizational life, education, and everyday life. Building on skills and concepts derived from a rhetorical tradition that is design-oriented, research on IText must acknowledge the complexity of the meaning-making process, the historical forces that shape interactions with texts, and the powerful impact these new electronic environments are having on society.

845 Hagge, John. "The Process Religion and Business Communication." *Journal of Business Communication* 24.1 (Jan. 1987): 89–120. Print.

Process activists argue that rigorous empirical research supports their claim of the superiority of process over product. However, process research suffers from many flaws, such as the assumption of protocol reliability and the tiny number of cases studied. Moreover, some research confirms that writers may prefer linear to recursive processing. Process pedagogy is problematic, even vacuous, often amounting to nothing more than repackaging of standard procedures. Process advocates often use mystical language in their claims for the liberatory effects of the process method. This utopianism arises from misunderstandings of the difference between linguistic competence and performance and from an arguable assumption about the existence of prior mental processes. Aside from its questionable basis in theory, the process method is inappropriate for business writing, which depends upon textual predictability and context-linked effectiveness.

846 Henry, Jim. *Writing Workplace Cultures: An Archaeology of Professional Writing*. Carbondale: Southern Illinois UP, 2000. Print.

A sea change in theoretical movements and technologies have reshaped the very conceptualization of writing; given this shift, composition must attend to a growing class of professional writers by investigating subjectivity based on empirical findings in workplace cultures. Over a seven-year period, eighty-four writers enrolled in an MA program in professional writing and editing conducted ethnographic analyses of workplace cultures and served as research subjects for this study, based on Foucault's concept of archaeological work. Researchers in a Cultures of Professional Writing class conducted autoethnographic work and engaged in intersubjective research; the results help to bring together academic understandings of subjectivity and lived workplace realities for a greater understanding of subjective work identities. Construing work sites as fieldwork sites gives writers the opportunity to take stock of the organizational structures and processes of workplaces and empowers them as a professional class by helping them to understand cultural production via writing in organizational sites. Composition theory aimed at exploring agency should consider the many workplace subject positions constructed in specific organizational contexts and must revisit theories of authorship. Appendices include researchers' abstracts of workplace ethnographies.

847 Jameson, Daphne A. "Implication Versus Inference: Analyzing Writer and Reader Representations In Business Texts." *Business Communication Quarterly* 67.4 (Dec. 2004): 387–411. Print.

Reader-response theory offers unique insights into writer and reader representations in business texts. In business communication, the relationships and distinctions between implied readers and writers and inferred readers and writers are addressed rarely. Yet studying these concepts could help business communicators understand the "gulf" that often exists between what writers intend and what readers interpret. Borrowing ideas from literary theory, philosophy, and communication studies, teachers can reveal the ways writers represent themselves in texts (implied writer), how writers depict their readers and give them roles (implied reader), the ways that readers imagine being addressed by an author (inferred writer), and how readers perceive and enact the qualities and roles that have been given to them by authors (inferred reader). Jameson explores and illustrates these roles through analysis of letters written by the CEO of Citigroup, a workplace party memo, a corporate alumni letter, and a letter to a client about a delinquent account. Jameson then makes practical suggestions about how to teach implication and inference to students.

848 Jameson, Daphne A. "Telling the Investment Story: A Narrative Analysis of Shareholder Reports." *Journal of Business Communication* 37.1 (Jan. 2000): 7–38. Print.

When the situation is complex in terms of ambiguous content, technical subject matter, and challenging writing processes, analyzing such documents as narratives offers a better understanding of writers' options and the implications of their choices. Studies of shareholder reports have rarely drawn on narrative theory; however, two methodological approaches, reading them as narratives and analyzing them as written texts, led to complementary conclusions about a random sample of shareholder reports, including all verbal components but excluding numerical components. Three dimensions create the report's story: level of directness or indirectness, underlying fabula, and the theme. The mixed-return reports were less direct than the top-return reports, with statistically significant differences. The mixed-return reports also develop a variety of themes (e.g., blame) that defy simple categorization as direct or indirect; mixed-return reports encourage readers to participate in constructing the story, offer multiple narrators, embed a variety of subgenres, and develop a nonlinear narrative hyperstructure. Each narrative element has both verbal and visual manifestations that interact with one another. Winner of Outstanding Article for 2000 in *Journal of Business Communication.*

849 Jameson, Daphne A. "Using a Simulation to Teach Intercultural Communication in Business Communication Courses." *Bulletin of the Association for Business Communication* 56.1 (Mar. 1993): 3–11. Print.

It is nearly impossible to explain the enormous variety of cultural differences using real cultural information. Moreover, presenting cultural "differences" masks the fact that Western culture is also "different." Simulation games have, however, been successful in sensitizing people to the nature of cultural difference as well as providing concrete suggestions about successful interaction. In simulations, participants assume a role spelled out for them by instructions, and then interact in character. Debriefings following the games are reliably lively, revealing a vast range of cultural assumptions and ideas for improving intercultural relations. Jameson describes a successful simulation game in which participants learn to represent three invented cultures coming together in a business venture.

850 Kogen, Myra, ed. *Writing in the Business Professions*. Urbana: NCTE, 1989. Print.

Fourteen essays investigate professional and pedagogical concerns in the development of business communication as an academic discipline. Essays include Linda Flower, "Rhetorical Problem Solving: Cognition and Professional Writing"; Jack Selzer, "Arranging Business Prose"; Edward P. J. Corbett, "What Classical Rhetoric Has to Offer the Teacher of Business and Professional Writing"; Janice Redish, "Writing in Organizations"; George Gopen, "The State of Legal Writing: Res Ipsa Loquitur"; John DiGaetani, "Use of the Case Method in Teaching Business Communication"; David Lauerman, "Building Ethos: Field Research in a Business Communication Course"; C. H. Knoblauch, "The Teaching and Practice of 'Professional Writing'"; and John Brereton, "The Professional Writing Program and the English Department."

851 Locker, Kitty O. "Factors in Reader Responses to Negative Letters: Experimental Evidence for Changing What We Teach." *Journal of Business and Technical Communication* 13.1 (Jan. 1999): 5–48. Print.

Traditional textbook advice about writing negative messages—a set of six principles, including the use of a buffer—has been contradicted by empirical evidence and various points of critique. Two bodies of evidence suggest that it is time to change what we teach about the content and arrangement of negative messages: a summary of the scholarly debate over the past twenty years and studies conducted on negative messages in recent years. Most of the quantitative research on negative messages deals with content and arrangement, and the literature provides the most support for the principle "explain why you are refusing." This researcher tested with university students three of the traditional principles—use a buffer, place the reason before the refusal, and end on a positive note—with a credit refusal pretest design and a graduate school rejection experiment design. Pretests and experiments suggest that in negative letters, buffers do not matter, strong resale is counterproductive, and giving a brief reason before refusal makes people more likely to say the decision is fair. Also tested were the effects of gender and situational context, but results suggest that gender is not a factor in readers' responses to negative messages. Implications for writers of negative letters are outlined, along with implications for further research.

852 Matalene, Carolyn B., ed. *Worlds of Writing: Teaching and Learning in Discourse Communities of Work*. New York: Random, 1989. Print.

Adequate understanding of writing in the workplace cannot be provided by traditional academic analyses of texts and processes. The special concerns of collaborative writing, audience constraints, and the conventions of workplace writing must become part of the undergraduate writing curriculum. Twenty-three essays analyze discourse communities of work, including Kristin Woolever, "Coming to Terms with Different Standards for Excellence for Written Communication"; Stephen Doheny-Farina, "A Case Study of One Adult Writing in Academic and Nonacademic Discourse Communities"; Janette Lewis, "Adaptation: Business Writing as Catalyst in a Liberal Arts Curriculum"; Theresa Enos, "Rhetoric and the Discourse of Technology"; Nancy Wilds, "Writing in the Military: A Different Mission"; Janis Forman, "The Discourse Communities and Group Writing Practices of Management Students"; Carolyn Matalene, "A Writing Teacher in the Newsroom"; Aletha Hendrickson, "How to Appear Reliable without Being Liable: C.P.A. Writing in Its Rhetorical Context"; Philip Rubens, "Writing for an On-Line Age: The Influence of Electronic Text on Writing"; John Warnock, "To English Professors: On What to Do with a Lawyer"; and James Raymond, "Rhetoric and Bricolage: Theory and Its Limits in Legal and Other Sorts of Discourse."

853 Rogers, Priscilla S. "Analytic Measures for Evaluating Managerial Writing." *Journal of Business and Technical Communication* 8.4 (Oct. 1994): 380–407. Print.

Persuasiveness, not correctness, is the most desirable quality of good managerial writing. But persuasiveness is difficult to judge. Holistic evaluation—widely used for MBA writing assessment—does not provide a useful tool for identifying persuasiveness, and is not useful for teaching or research. Two other assessment tools are superior. One, the Analysis of Argument Measure, assesses writing in terms of Toulmin's argument attributes—claim, data, and warrant. Evaluators were able to reach a high degree of consistency in the tests of this measure. The other tool, the Persuasiveness Adaptiveness Measure, assesses writing in terms of achieving the desired reader response. Higher scores are awarded to writing that is clear about recommendations, deals with potential reader objections, demonstrates the desirability of the recommendation, and so on. Here, too, graders reached a high degree of consistency. While high scores on these two measures do not ensure success, the measures do identify important elements of persuasive writing and can sensitize writers to rhetorical considerations.

854 Rogers, Priscilla S., and Jone Rymer. "Analytical Tools to Facilitate Transitions into New Writing Contexts: A Communicative Perspective." *Journal of Business Communication* 38.2 (Apr. 2001): 112–50. Print.

How can we help writers move into new writing contexts? What writing skills carry over from context to context? A field study using essays from the Analytical Writing Assessment (AWA) of the GMAT (Graduate Management Admission Test) led to the development of a set of analytical tools for diagnosing students' potential problems in MBA writing assignments. MBA writing experts and students in two contrasting business schools participated in this exploratory field study, designed to explore how to use the AWA to help new graduate students identify deficiencies that might interfere with their development as effective MBA writers. The study identified and described traits for successful performance in MBA writing and developed them into analytical tools for use in consultations with students; these tools were subsequently tested for their appropriateness in bridging discourses.

855 Smart, Graham. "Storytelling in a Central Bank: The Role of Narrative in the Creation and Use of Specialized Economic Knowledge." *Journal of Business and Technical Communication* 13.3 (July 1999): 249–73. Print.

Narrative plays an important role in professional discourse and a central part in the analytic and policy work of Bank of Canada economists. Both genre theory and distributed cognition theory contribute to understanding the collaborative process of narrative construction. A view of genre that encompasses "an organization's drama of interaction" clarifies the nature of the collaboration through which an organizational narrative is constructed and used. Distributed cognition, an extension of activity theory, attends to the symbolic representations that groups employ for reasoning and for accomplishing work. One particular narrative—the monetary-policy story—operates as a vehicle of organizational thought, evolving across a number of written genres, and serves several purposes within the institution. Eventually the monetary-policy story, presented in one version of the White Book, is used by the bank's executives as a shared cognitive and rhetorical resource for conducting and communicating policy. A wide variety of qualitative data, collected over several years, traces how the monetary-policy story is constructed in three stages, over time and across a set of written genres, and how knowledge-making is constructed within a professional organization.

856 Spigelman, Candace, and Laurie Grobman. "Why We Chose Rhetoric: Necessity, Ethics, and the (Re)Making of a Professional Writing Program." *Journal of Business and Technical Communication* 20.1 (Jan. 2006): 48–64. Print.

Professional communication programs can and should teach more than just practical work-world skills—they should be placed within the liberal arts tradition, focus on rhetorical knowledge, and equip students to make ethical decisions. Further, programs must be flexible, responsive, and willing to engage ongoing tensions between the philosophical and practical, skills and theories, applications and ethics. The authors recount the struggle to create a program at their own institution as they make these arguments and recognize these debates.

See: Rachel Spilka, ed., *Writing in the Workplace: New Research Perspectives* [827].

857 Starke-Meyerring, Doreen. "Meeting the Challenges of Globalization: A Framework for Global Literacies in Professional Communication Programs." *Journal of Business and Technical Communication* 19.4 (Oct. 2005): 468–99. Print.

In the context of increased globalization, professional communications programs need to help students to develop new literacies by revising curriculum. Globalization has led to several interconnected trends: the transnationalization of business through digital networks, the blurring of boundaries, increased interaction between global and local discourses, as well as ongoing ideological contestation about the impact of globalization. Textbooks, courses, and programs need to respond to these changes and allow students to enter these new discourses. Students must be equipped to recognize, respect, and critically work across boundaries, borders, and contexts. Global partnership networks, while difficult to create and facilitate, would offer students opportunities to meet some of the challenges and changes of globalization, and participate in a new social, political, and communicative global order.

858 Suchan, Jim. "The Effect of High-Impact Writing on Decision Making within a Public Sector Bureaucracy." *Journal of Business Communication* 35.3 (July 1998): 299–328. Print.

Readers interpreting reports written in a high-impact style—theoretically more effective—did not make significantly better decisions than readers interpreting the same report written in a bureaucratic, low-impact style, one in keeping with the organization's norm. Organizational context factors—perceived work roles, job design, organizational structure, report genre expectations, and organizational language norms—were more important for readers' assessments of reports than high-impact style. Report Assessors at a medium-size federal government agency make decisions solely on the written reports of Information Gatherers. Seven report characteristics were revised to reflect high-impact writing; however, because they had developed a variety of creative means to sort and organize information, Report Assessors perceived the high-impact treatments as abnormal discourse. Both qualitative and statistical data were used to conclude that the theoretical frameworks and the assumptions that shape teaching in business and managerial writing need to be seriously reexamined.

859 Sullivan, Patricia, and Jennie Dautermann. *Electronic Literacies in the Workplace: Technologies of Writing*. Urbana: NCTE, 1996. Print.

Fourteen chapters in four sections address issues of written literacy and electronic literacy in workplace settings and the challenges to traditional views of writing. Chapters include the following: Jennie Dautermann, "Writing with Electronic Tools in Midwestern Businesses"; Brenda R. Sims, "Electronic Mail in Two Corporate Workplaces"; Johndan Johnson-Eilola and Stuart A. Selber, "After Automation: Hypertext and Corporate Structures"; Tharon W. Howard, "Who 'Owns' Electronic Texts?"; Craig J. Hansen, "Networking Technology in the Classroom: Whose Interests Are We Serving?"; Nancy Allen, "Gaining Electronic Literacy: Workplace Simulations in the Classroom"; Robert R. Johnson, "Tales from the Crossing: Professional Communication Internships in the Electronic Workplace"; Cynthia L. Selfe, "Theorizing E-Mail for the Practice, Instruction, and Study of Literacy"; and James E. Porter and Patricia Sullivan, "Working across Methodological Interfaces: The Study of Computers and Writing in the Workplace."

860 Tyler, Lisa. "Ecological Disaster and Rhetorical Response: Exxon's Communications in the Wake of the *Valdez* Spill." *Journal of Business and Technical Communication* 6.2 (Apr. 1992): 149–71. Print.

Following the *Valdez* spill, Exxon contributed to public perceptions of its corporate arrogance through eleven communication practices that damaged its credibility and antagonized the public. These include understating the likelihood of a spill and overstating the company's ability to respond; slow response by corporate leaders following the spill; refusing help by local residents; emphasizing its efforts rather than its accomplishments; excessive optimism; presenting itself as a victim; attempting to control information flow; and anger and rudeness. Exxon fell into a spiral of defensive communication, blaming others, attempting to maintain control, and generally being self-regarding. This is an excellent case for teaching about ethical business practices and crisis communication, for the implications—regarding promises, responsibilities, and post-crisis behavior—are exceptionally clear.

861 Varner, Iris, and Linda Beamer. *Intercultural Communication in the Workplace*. Boston: McGraw-Hill, 1995. Print.

Both domestic diversity and international commerce demand competence in intercultural communication. Culture is a learned, coherent view of the world that determines what is important, evaluates attitudes, and dictates behavior. High-context cultures rely on complex and implicit messages, value relationships, and avoid giving negative messages. Low-context cultures make messages explicit and value directness. Cultures differ in terms of their assumptions about the source of knowledge (e.g., from received wisdom or from experiment), about the value of doing versus being, about the centrality of the individual or the group, about privacy and authority. Students can learn to use basic differences, and categories of questions to ask. By knowing some of the basic differences among cultures and the implications of interpersonal, group, and written communication when applied to each, students can broaden their repertoire of behaviors and become successful at intercultural communication. Twelve chapters cover these topics plus nonverbal communication, information gathering and decision making, negotiation, legal concerns, and the impact of business structures on relationships.

862 Winsor, Dorothy. *Writing Power: Communication in an Engineering Center*. Albany: State U of New York P, 2003. Print.

Power, knowledge, and text are interconnected, even though their relationships are often transparent to us, largely because they hide "beneath the surface of everyday life" and even beneath the surface of workplace life. Yet it is important for rhetoricians and writing teachers to understand that texts are a "means to create and occupy positions of power." In many businesses, texts structure relationships; they may allow for power dynamics to be reinforced or provide opportunities for negotiation and knowledge-generation. Regardless, texts are part of the social fiber of any business. Text, knowledge, and power connect in rich and significant ways in the field of engineering. Disciplinary texts are often collaboratively written, tools and genres are diverse and specialized, organizational hierarchies are often complex, and one must use a wide range of rhetorical tactics to master and control one's own writing. Thus, by studying one specific engineering center, Winsor reveals how texts are used to build, maintain, and/or negotiate knowledge and power. A shifting focus, from managers to engineers to interns, allows for a view of the full cross-section of power relations. The use of vignettes between chapters also offers thick description of real writing contexts. ABC Outstanding Publication for 2004.

Composition Books from Bedford/St. Martin's

Below you'll find a list of Bedford/St. Martin's titles that are of interest to composition instructors. We publish a complete line of handbooks, rhetorics, readers, research guides, and professional resources. Please visit our Web site, **bedfordstmartins.com**, for full descriptions and ordering information, or contact your local sales representative.

Professional Resources

The Bedford/St. Martin's Series in Rhetoric and Composition

David Bartholomae, *Writing on the Margins: Essays on Composition and Teaching*, 2005

Paul Butler, *Style in Rhetoric and Composition: A Critical Sourcebook*, 2010

Ellen Cushman, Eugene R. Kintgen, Barry Kroll, and Mike Rose, *Literacy: A Critical Sourcebook*, 2001

Thomas Deans, Barbara Roswell, and Adrian J. Wurr, *Writing and Community Engagement: A Critical Sourcebook*, 2010

Lisa Ede, *On Writing Research: The Braddock Essays 1975–1998*, 1999

Lisa Ede and Andrea A. Lunsford, *Selected Essays of Robert J. Connors*, 2003

Carolyn Handa, *Visual Rhetoric in a Digital World: A Critical Sourcebook*, 2004

Brian Huot and Peggy O'Neill, *Assessing Writing: A Critical Sourcebook*, 2009

Gesa E. Kirsch, Faye Spencer Maor, Lance Massey, and Lee Nickoson-Massey, *Feminism and Composition: A Critical Sourcebook*, 2003

Cynthia Lewiecki-Wilson and Brenda Jo Brueggemann, *Disability and the Teaching of Writing: A Critical Sourcebook*, 2008

Andrea A. Lunsford and Lisa Ede, *Writing Together: Collaboration in Theory and Practice*, 2012

Paul Kei Matsuda, Michelle Cox, Jay Jordan, and Christina Ortmeier-Hooper, *Second-Language: Writing in the Composition Classroom: A Critical Sourcebook*, 2011

Duane Roen, *Views from the Center: The CCCC Chairs' Addresses, 1977–2005*, 2006

Mike Rose, *An Open Language: Selected Writing on Literacy, Learning, and Opportunity*, 2006

Michelle Sidler, Elizabeth Overman Smith, and Richard Morris, *Computers in the Composition Classroom: A Critical Sourcebook*, 2008

Terry Myers Zawacki and Paul M. Rogers, *Writing Across the Curriculum: A Critical Sourcebook*, 2012

Background Readings

Timothy Barnett, *Teaching Argument in the Composition Course: Background Readings*, 2002

Susan Naomi Bernstein, *Teaching Developmental Writing: Background Readings*, 3rd ed., 2007

James M. Dubinsky, *Teaching Technical Communication: Critical Issues for the Classroom*, 2004

T. R. Johnson, *Teaching Composition: Background Readings*, 3rd ed., 2008

Andrea A. Lunsford, *From Theory to Practice: A Selection of Essays*, 3rd ed., 2009

Venetria K. Patton, *American Literature: A Sourcebook for Teachers*, 2006

Norman A. Stahl and Hunter Boylan, *Teaching Developmental Reading: Historical, Theoretical, and Practical Background Readings*, 2003

Bibliographies

Gregory R. Glau and Chitralekha Duttagupta, *The Bedford Bibliography for Teachers of Basic Writing*, 3rd ed., 2010

Nedra Reynolds, Jay Dolmage, Patricia Bizzell, and Bruce Herzberg, *The Bedford Bibliography for Teachers of Writing*, 7th ed., 2012

Teaching Advice and Classroom Materials

Richard Bullock, *The St. Martin's Manual for Writing in the Disciplines*, 1994

Cheryl Glenn, Robert Connors, and Melissa Goldthwaite, *The St. Martin's Guide to Teaching Writing*, 6th ed., 2008

John Golden and Laura Lull, *Teaching Ideas: A Video Resource for AP English*, 2009

Katherine Gottschalk and Keith Hjortshoj, *The Elements of Teaching Writing: A Resource for Instructors in All Disciplines*, 2004

Beth Hedengren, *A TA's Guide to Teaching Writing in All Disciplines*, 2004

Christina Murphy and Steve Sherwood, *The St. Martin's Sourcebook for Writing Tutors*, 3rd ed., 2008

Nedra Reynolds and Rich Rice, *Portfolio Teaching: A Guide for Instructors*, 2nd ed., 2006

Leigh Ryan and Lisa Zimmerelli, *The Bedford Guide for Writing Tutors*, 5th ed., 2010

Marcy Carbajal Van Horn, *Teaching with Hacker Handbooks: Topics, Strategies, and Lesson Plans*, 2010

Edward M. White, *Assigning, Responding, Evaluating: A Writing Teacher's Guide*, 4th ed., 2007

Teaching Media

Adjunct Central, bedfordstmartins.com/adjunctcentral
Bits: Ideas for Teaching Composition, bedfordstmartins.com/bits
Just-in-Time Teaching Materials, bedfordstmartins.com/justintime
Todd Taylor, *Take 20: Teaching Writing*, bedfordstmartins.com/take20

Composition Texts

Handbooks

Diana Hacker and Nancy Sommers, *The Bedford Handbook*, 8th ed., 2010
Diana Hacker and Nancy Sommers, *A Pocket Style Manual*, 6th ed., 2012
Diana Hacker and Nancy Sommers, *Rules for Writers*, 7th ed., 2012
Diana Hacker and Nancy Sommers, *A Writer's Reference*, 7th ed., 2011
Diana Hacker and Nancy Sommers, *A Canadian Writer's Reference*, 5th ed., 2012
Diana Hacker, Stephen A. Bernhardt, and Nancy Sommers, *Writer's Help*, 2011 Web site, writershelp.com
Andrea A. Lunsford, *The St. Martin's Handbook*, 7th ed., 2011
Andrea A. Lunsford, *EasyWriter: A Pocket Guide*, 4th ed., 2010
Andrea A. Lunsford, *The Everyday Writer*, 4th ed., 2010

Rhetorics

Rise B. Axelrod and Charles R. Cooper, *Axelrod & Cooper's Concise Guide to Writing*, 5th ed., 2009
Rise B. Axelrod and Charles R. Cooper, *The St. Martin's Guide to Writing*, 9th ed., 2010
Nora Bacon, *The Well-Crafted Sentence: A Writer's Guide to Style*, 2009
Lisa Ede, *The Academic Writer: A Brief Guide*, 2nd ed., 2011
Stuart Greene and April Lidinsky, *From Inquiry to Academic Writing: A Practical Guide*, 2nd ed., 2011
X. J. Kennedy, Dorothy M. Kennedy, and Marcia F. Muth, *The Bedford Guide for College Writers with Reader, Research Manual, and Handbook*, 9th ed., 2011
X. J. Kennedy, Dorothy M. Kennedy, and Marcia F. Muth, *Writing and Revising: A Portable Guide*, 2010
Kathleen T. McWhorter, *Successful College Writing: Skills, Strategies, Learning Styles*, 4th ed., 2009
Lee Odell and Susan M. Katz, *Writing Now: Shaping Words and Images*, 2010
Mike Palmquist, *Joining the Conversation: Writing in College and Beyond*, 2010
John J. Ruszkiewicz and Jay Dolmage, *How to Write Anything: A Guide and Reference with Readings*, 2010

Research Guides

Diana Hacker and Barbara Fister, *Research and Documentation in the Electronic Age*, 5th ed., 2010

Marcia F. Muth, *Researching and Writing with 2009 MLA Update*, 2009

Mike Palmquist, *The Bedford Researcher with 2009 MLA and 2010 APA Updates*, 3rd ed., 2011

Brenda Spatt, *Writing from Sources: A Complete Guide to Working with Sources*, 8th ed., 2011

Bonnie Stone Sunstein and Elizabeth Chiseri-Strater, *FieldWorking: Reading and Writing Research*, 3rd ed., 2007

Research Media

Douglas Downs, *i-cite: visualizing sources*, 2006

Mike Palmquist, *The Bedford Bibliographer*, 2006

Margaret Price, *The St. Martin's Tutorial on Avoiding Plagiarism*, 2003

Composition Readers

Rhetorical Readers

Jane E. Aaron and Ellen Kuhl Repetto, *The Compact Reader: Short Essays by Method and Theme*, 9th ed., 2011

Rise B. Axelrod and Charles R. Cooper, *Reading Critically, Writing Well: A Reader and Guide*, 9th ed., 2011

Nancy R. Comley, David Hamilton, Carl H. Klaus, Robert Scholes, Nancy Sommers, and Jason Tougaw, *Fields of Reading: Motives for Writing*, 9th ed., 2010

Paul Eschholz and Alfred Rosa, *Subject and Strategy: A Writer's Reader*, 12th ed., 2011

Cheryl Glenn, *Making Sense: A Real-World Rhetorical Reader*, 3rd ed., 2010

X. J. Kennedy, Dorothy Kennedy, and Jane E. Aaron, *The Bedford Reader*, 11th ed., 2012

X. J. Kennedy, Dorothy Kennedy, and Jane E. Aaron, *The Brief Bedford Reader*, 11th ed., 2012

Laurie G. Kirszner and Stephen R. Mandell, *Patterns for College Writing: A Rhetorical Reader and Guide*, 11th ed., 2010

Kathleen T. McWhorter, *Seeing the Pattern: Readings for Successful Writing*, 2006

Alfred Rosa and Paul Eschholz, *Models for Writers: Short Essays for Composition*, 10th ed., 2010

Thematic Readers

Chris Anderson and Lex Runciman, *Open Questions: Reading for Critical Thinking and Writing*, 2005

Robert Atwan, *America Now: Short Readings from Recent Periodicals*, 9th ed., 2011

Robert Atwan, *Convergences: Themes, Texts, and Images for Composition*, 3rd ed., 2009

Lynn Z. Bloom and Louise Z. Smith, *The Arlington Reader: Contexts and Connections*, 3rd ed., 2011

Gary Colombo, Robert Cullen, and Bonnie Lisle, *Rereading America: Cultural Contexts for Critical Thinking and Writing*, 8th ed., 2010

Nancy R. Comley, David Hamilton, Carl H. Klaus, Robert Scholes, Nancy Sommers, and Jason Tougaw, *Fields of Reading: Motives for Writing*, 9th ed., 2010

Paul Eschholz, Alfred Rosa, and Virginia P. Clark, *Language Awareness: Readings for College Writers*, 10th ed., 2009

Stuart Greene and April Lidinsky, *From Inquiry to Academic Writing: A Text and Reader*, 2nd ed., 2012

Lee Jacobus, *A World of Ideas: Essential Readings for College Writers*, 8th ed., 2010

Anne Kress and Suellyn Winkle, *NextText: Making Connections Across and Beyond the Disciplines*, 2008

Catherine G. Latterell, *ReMix: Reading and Composing Culture*, 2nd ed., 2010

Andrea A. Lunsford and John J. Ruszkiewicz, *The Presence of Others: Voices and Images That Call for Response*, 5th ed., 2008

Sonia Maasik and Jack Solomon, *California Dreams and Realities: Readings for Critical Thinkers and Writers*, 3rd ed., 2005

Sonia Maasik and Jack Solomon, *Signs of Life in the USA: Readings on Popular Culture for Writers*, 6th ed., 2009

Donald McQuade and Christine McQuade, *Seeing & Writing*, 4th ed., 2010

James S. Miller, *Acting Out Culture*, 2nd ed., 2011

Joan Mims and Elizabeth Nollen, *Mirror on America: Short Essays and Images from Popular Culture*, 4th ed., 2009

Rolf Norgaard, *Composing Knowledge: Readings for College Writers*, 2007

Elizabeth Wardle and Douglas Downs, *Writing about Writing*, 2011

Cultural Studies Readers

Robert Atwan, *America Now: Short Readings from Recent Periodicals*, 9th ed., 2011

Robert Atwan, *Convergences: Themes, Texts, and Images for Composition*, 3rd ed., 2009

Barclay Barrios, *Emerging: Contemporary Readings for Writers*, 2010

David Bartholomae and Anthony Petrosky, *Reading the Lives of Others: A Sequence for Writers*, 1995

David Bartholomae and Anthony Petrosky, *Ways of Reading: An Anthology for Writers*, 9th ed., 2011

Gary Colombo, Robert Cullen, and Bonnie Lisle, *Rereading America: Cultural Contexts for Critical Thinking and Writing*, 8th ed., 2010

Paul Eschholz, Alfred Rosa, and Virginia P. Clark, *Language Awareness: Readings for College Writers*, 8th ed., 2000

Anne Kress and Suellyn Winkle, *NextText: Making Connections Across and Beyond the Disciplines*, 2008

Catherine G. Latterell, *ReMix: Reading and Composing Culture*, 2nd ed., 2010

Andrea A. Lunsford and John J. Ruszkiewicz, *The Presence of Others: Voices and Images That Call for Response*, 5th ed., 2008

Sonia Maasik and Jack Solomon, *California Dreams and Realities: Readings for Critical Thinkers and Writers*, 3rd ed., 2005

Sonia Maasik and Jack Solomon, *Signs of Life in the USA: Readings on Popular Culture for Writers*, 6th ed., 2009

Donald McQuade and Christine McQuade, *Seeing & Writing*, 4th ed., 2010

James S. Miller, *Acting Out Culture*, 2nd ed., 2011

Joan Mims and Elizabeth Nollen, *Mirror on America: Short Essays and Images from Popular Culture*, 4th ed., 2009

Short Essay Readers

Jane E. Aaron and Ellen Kuhl Repetto, *The Compact Reader: Short Essays by Method and Theme*, 9th ed., 2011

Robert Atwan, *America Now: Short Readings from Recent Periodicals*, 9th ed., 2011

Becky Bradway and Douglas Hesse, *Creating Nonfiction*, 2009

Joan Mims and Elizabeth Nollen, *Mirror on America: Short Essays and Images from Popular Culture*, 4th ed., 2009

Alfred Rosa and Paul Eschholz, *Models for Writers: Short Essays for Composition*, 10th ed., 2010

Argument/Critical Thinking Readers

Rise B. Axelrod and Charles R. Cooper, *Reading Critically, Writing Well: A Reader and Guide*, 9th ed., 2011

Sylvan Barnet and Hugo Bedau, *Contemporary and Classic Arguments: A Portable Anthology*, 2005

Sylvan Barnet and Hugo Bedau, *Critical Thinking, Reading, and Writing: A Brief Guide to Argument*, 7th ed., 2011

Sylvan Barnet and Hugo Bedau, *Current Issues and Enduring Questions: A Guide to Critical Thinking and Argument, with Readings*, 9th ed., 2011

Sylvan Barnet and Hugo Bedau, *From Critical Thinking to Argument: A Portable Guide*, 3rd ed., 2011

Laurie G. Kirszner and Stephen R. Mandell, *Practical Argument: A Text and Anthology*, 2011

Andrea A. Lunsford and John J. Ruszkiewicz, *Everything's an Argument with Readings*, 5th ed., 2010

Annette Rottenberg, *Elements of Argument: A Text and Reader with 2009 MLA and 2010 APA Updates*, 9th ed., 2011

Annette Rottenberg, *The Structure of Argument with 2009 MLA and 2010 APA Updates*, 6th ed., 2011

Alphabetical Readers

Barclay Barrios, *Emerging: Contemporary Readings for Writers*, 2010

David Bartholomae and Anthony Petrosky, *Ways of Reading: An Anthology for Writers*, 9th ed., 2011

David Bartholomae and Anthony Petrosky, *Ways of Reading Words and Images*, 2003

Samuel Cohen, *50 Essays: A Portable Anthology*, 3rd ed., 2011

Donald McQuade and Robert Atwan, *The Writer's Presence: A Pool of Essays*, 6th ed., 2009

Index of Authors Cited

Numbers refer to entries within the bibliography.

Hugh Blair 3
Campbell, Bain
331 -interviews-
Re-read comm coll writers-
focus upon part for region-

385
~~388~~
389
Revision 145